FRAGILE FORTUNES
THE ORIGINS OF A GREAT BRITISH
MERCHANT FAMILY

FRAGILE FORTUNES
THE ORIGINS OF A GREAT BRITISH
MERCHANT FAMILY

Elizabeth Neill

ryelands

Originally published by Halsgrove, 2008

Front cover: *The Canal Basin*, a print by J.W.M. Turner
reproduced by kind permission of Kevin White.
Cover design and typesetting by Heather Oliver

British Library Cataloguing-in-Publication Data
A CIP record for this title is available from the British Library

ISBN 978 1 906551 02 5

RYELANDS
Halsgrove House
Ryelands Industrial Estate
Bagley Road, Wellington, Somerset TA21 9PZ
Tel: 01823 653777   Fax: 01823 216796
email: sales@halsgrove.com
website: www.halsgrove.com

Printed in Great Britain by CPI Antony Rowe

For James and Joe

Gibbs.

CONTENTS

LIST OF ILLUSTRATIONS

PREFACE

Over twenty years ago, Elizabeth Mercy Gibbs, who lived in a cottage in Clyst St. George, lent me *The History of Antony and Dorothea Gibbs and of their contemporary relatives, including the History of the Origin & Early Years of the House of Antony Gibbs and Sons,* by John Arthur Gibbs, published in 1922. This was a fascinating account of a local family shaken by personal failure brought on by political and economic crises and war. Although I found the book absorbing, I always felt that as a family history, it was an incomplete and a somewhat eulogistic account of Antony Gibbs' life, though this perhaps was to be accepted given that it was through him that the present family is descended. He was clearly an affable and likeable man, but Gibbs' book was so obviously an attempt to play down his role in the ruination of his family, preferring to blame it on a natural *defect* in his character.

There was also very little information in Gibbs' book of the impact that Antony's bankruptcy had on other members of the family. What effect did it have on Vicary's early political career or on George, a West India merchant who acted as Antony's mentor and banker and who appears to have provided some stability in the family; or on his sisters who with no dowry had little chance of marriage? Although their Topsham cousins were mentioned in passing, I found it strange that there was so little information about Abraham, who was a successful merchant banker in Italy in the first decade of the nineteenth century. There were also the vague references to Edmund Granger and Samuel Banfill, Antony's partners in the Exeter firm. Gibbs' book tended to play down their contribution but after Antony's failure, the firm continued trading successfully for many years. It was reassuring to discover the true details of their business activities in the Devon Record Office, which put them in a very different light.

My interest in the family was reawakened several years later when I came across the records of Antony Gibbs & Sons in the Guildhall Library in London. Although listed as business records, they contained letters dating as far back as 1744 and provided a fascinating insight into the family and prompted my own research. This book, which has taken several years to complete, is a much broader account, which amongst other things redresses the balance.

In early documents relating to the Gibbs the name of both the Fenton and Clyst St. George families were spelt in a number of different ways including *Gib, Gibb, Gibbes, Gibbs,* and *Gybbs.* In the interests of consistency, with the exception of the introduction, I have used the modern spelling of *Gibbs* in the text. Similarly Pytte, their estate in Clyst St George, has been spelt in a number of ways including, *Pit, Pytt, Claypeight, Clay Pitt* and *Peight,* but I have used its modern spelling throughout. It should also be noted that *Clay Pitt* was not merely a house but an area of about nineteen acres consisting of gardens, orchards, meadows, and fields, as well as the house and outbuildings.

The history of the firm of Antony Gibbs & Sons is also well documented. In 1958, Wilfred Maude was commissioned to write *Merchant Bankers, A brief record of Antony Gibbs & Sons and its associated houses' business during 150 years, 1808-1958,* which was printed privately. More recently, the family has had a considerable amount of publicity with the sale of Tyntesfield near Bristol and with the publication of James Miller's *Fertile Fortune, The Story of Tynesfield.* My own book is about the origins of the Gibbs family, from their arrival in Clyst St. George in 1540, to the 1850s when their fortune was assured. Set against the political and economic context of the time, it traces the fortunes of two generations and describes how they used their extensive network of family and friends to support each other and expand their business activities.

Preface

I have spent many hours in the Guildhall Library reading original letters amongst the records of *Antony Gibbs & Sons* and piecing together the lives of George Abraham and his family. This was absorbing but it soon appeared that these records too had been 'sanitised' in earlier times to remove anything that showed Antony in a bad light. Abraham Gibbs of Palermo was also enigmatic. Reputed to have been one of the most influential men in Sicily, his life ended suddenly and tragically. After a number of enquiries, the Archivio di Stato in Palermo, knowing that with very little Italian I would never be able to use their archives effectively, put me in touch with Rosario Lentini, an economic historian who had been researching Abraham's life for many years.

In writing this book, with the exception of Gibbs' book and Lentini's research I have drawn as much as possible from original papers rather than published works. The main collection of Gibbs papers including those of the firm of Antony Gibbs & Sons are in the Guildhall Library and I am eternally grateful to the staff for their kindness and patience. My sincere thanks go also to the librarians and staff of many institutions for their support including the British Library, the Devon Record Office, the Devon and Exeter Institution, the West Country Studies Library, and the Archivio di Stati in Naples and Palermo. The staff in Palermo in particular must have been exasperated by my regular emails asking for more information, but they always responded promptly. My thanks to Madge Dresser of the University of the West of England for her advice and to Patricia Denny at the Society of Merchant Venturers in Bristol who made me very welcome and provided very substantial lunches; to Anne Webster of Venton Manor for letting me use her notes on the history of Fenton and its early occupants and to Helga Hughes of the Red House, Carolyn Cheffers-Heard of the Bridge Inn in Topsham and Kevin White; to Mary Greenacre of the National Trust for allowing me access to Tyntesfield to photograph the portraits, long before it was open to the public. I also acknowledge a deep debt of gratitude to Rosario Lentini for his enthusiasm about the project, which I value greatly. He generously made all his research available and read the draft chapters on Abraham Gibbs.

I am also indebted to various members of the family. To Polly Holmes à Court for the information and portrait of Charles à Court; to Lord Aldenham for allowing me into his home to photograph his ancestors; to Dr Denis Gibbs for his advice on Robert Remmett's career and to Christopher Gibbs for tracking down family portraits. Finally, my sincere thanks to Nicholas Gibbs who has been a staunch supporter throughout this project.

Friends and family have also lived with the Gibbs family for so long. Lynda Palmieri cheerfully translated many letters and papers. Richard Kellaway accompanied me on my first visit to Tyntesfield after a very eventful journey to take photographs – but that is another story! Heather Oliver has provided much help and advice and has undertaken the considerable task of typesetting the entire book. I gratefully acknowledge their help. I must also thank my husband David for his patience over the last few years. He improved the photographs, produced the maps and the pedigree and has painstakingly read each draft. It was his encouragement that kept me going and I think he now knows more about the Gibbs family than I do.

Pedigree of the Gibbs family of Clyst St George and Topsham

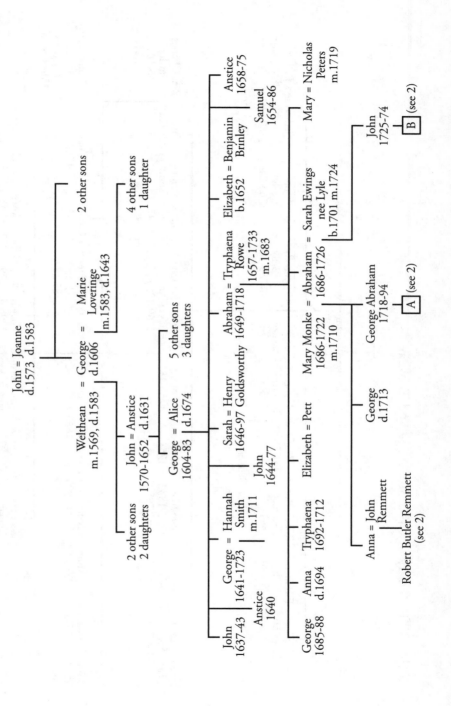

Pedigree of the Gibbs family of Clyst St George and Topsham

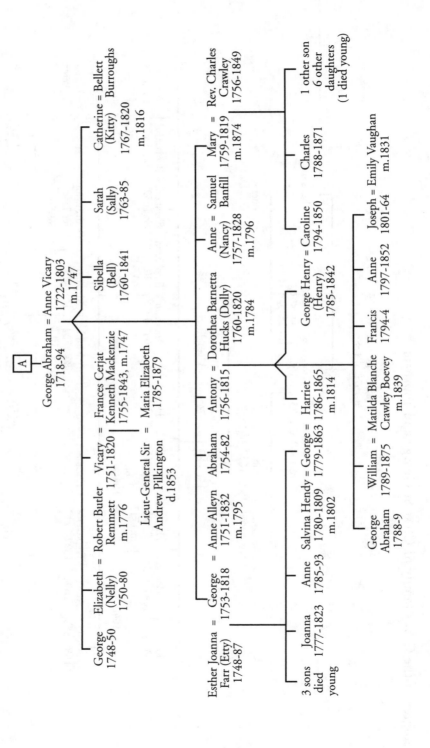

Pedigree of the Gibbs family of Clyst St George and Topsham

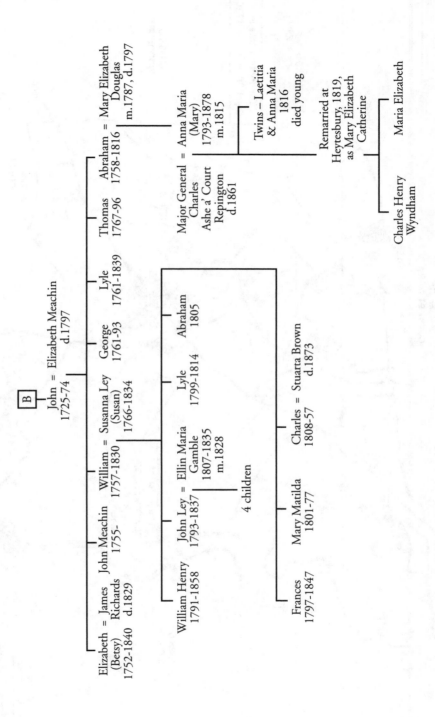

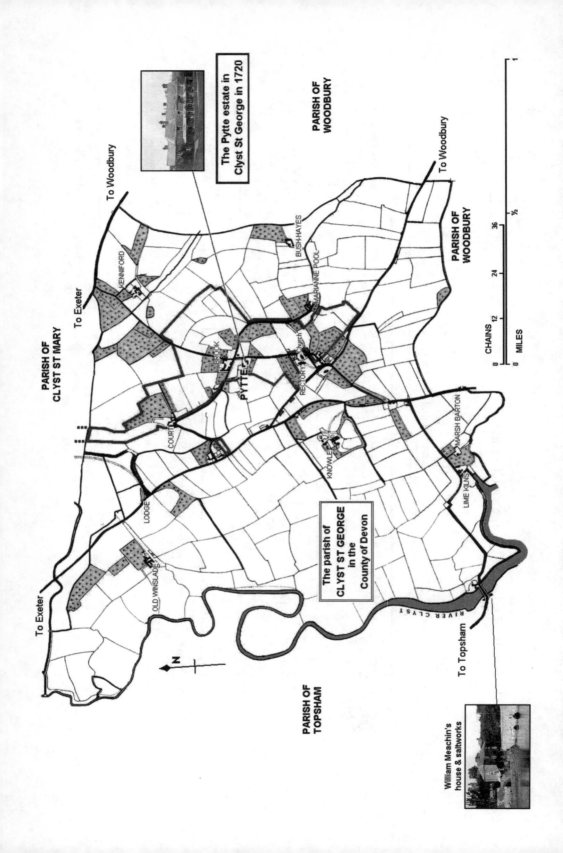

The Pytte estate in
Clyst St George in 1720

PARISH OF
WOODBURY

PARISH OF
WOODBURY

To Woodbury

To Woodbury

PARISH OF
CLYST ST MARY

To Exeter

To Exeter

KENNIFORD

BUSH-HAYES

MARIANNE POOL

BROOK

church

PYTTE

RECTORY

COURT

KNOWLE

LODGE

MARSH BARTON

LIME KILNS

OLD WINSLADE

The parish of
CLYST ST GEORGE
in the
County of Devon

RIVER CLYST

To Topsham

PARISH OF
TOPSHAM

N

William Meachin's
house & saltworks

CHAINS   0   12   24   36

MILES   0   ¼   ½   1

INTRODUCTION

The earliest records show that this line of the Gibbs family appeared in Fenton near Dartington in Devon in the fourteenth century. Fenton is derived from an old English name *fen tun* meaning *marshy farm*, but from the nineteenth century it has been known as Venton. It was first mentioned in 1242 and is thought to have been part of the Manor of Dartington. In the thirteenth century the Book of Fees indicates that a John de Fenton owned the estate. After 1386 the first William Gibb inherited Fenton from the de Fenton family and he and his wife Cecily were living there after 1392 either as leaseholders or freeholders.[1]

The original manor house was built in the fifteenth century and consisted of a rectangular courtyard with a great hall and a storage barn. In 1437, a chapel was licenced so that Thomas Gibbs (William's son) and his wife Margaret could hold services there. From the 1470s to the 1530s, three generations of the Gibbes [sic] family lived there, becoming infamous for their criminal activities. William and his son Thomas attacked and robbed neighbouring farms, stealing livestock and evicting tenants. In 1467 a John Gibbs (possibly William's brother) was an MP for Totnes, the same year that he was summoned for kidnapping William Strode, a minor and forcibly marrying him to his daughter Alice. For the next hundred years, John's son and grandsons kept a private army and embarked on a reign of terror in the area. On one occasion they attacked the village of Rattery, besieging the church and threatening to kill the rector who had claimed that William (John's grandson) owed £21 to the church, but believing that he was owed 63 shillings by the rector, William stole the collection box. The case was tried before the Bishop of Exeter and William was bound over for 100 marks. Incensed at the judgement, he carried off eleven ewes and their lambs belonging to the church and then returned with his son Thomas and a band of supporters determined to kill all those who had opposed him. One villager was assaulted with 'a sword and a buckler' and took refuge in the churchyard 'the same by the space of two hours' until the Gibbs gave up and left. The following Sunday, while the villagers were at prayer, William and Thomas returned 'to Rattery with staves and bucklers, bows and arrows, in the manner of a new insurrection with 23 and above and… there assembled them riotiously… to… great fear and dread' to take their revenge on those who had spoken out against them. For this and their many other crimes they were called to London to appear before the Court of Star Chamber on a number of occasions.[2]

In 1570, this line died out and Fenton passed by the marriage of William's daughter Silvester to Walter Wootton of Great Eaglebourne.[3] It was around this time that a sibling branch of the Fenton family arrived in the parish of Clyst St. George some four miles south east of Exeter and one and a half miles from the port of Topsham. The parish of Clyst St. George, also known as Clyst Wick, consists of 1001 acres of land and in the mid-seventeenth century had around one hundred and fifty inhabitants living in scattered farmsteads and cottages. It is the 'most southern of the six Clyst parishes in the valley of the small river Clist or Clyst, which falls into the Exe at Topsham',[4] and 'situated just above the influx of the river Clist into the Exe, and about 6 miles from the sea'.

The name Johannes Gybbe of Pytt first appears in a certificate of an assessment concerning a subsidy made to Henry VIII dated 10 December 1524. In the mid-sixteenth century, the Gibbs or Gybbe family were tenant farmers, renting a small farm in an area known as Cley Pitt (ClayPitt) or Pytt in Clyst St. George and a number of other fields in the neighbouring parishes of Clyst St. Mary and Woodbury. It seems that they prospered and on 1 May 1560, a John Gybbe purchased Pytt and other lands totalling around 100 acres from Thomas, Lord Wentworth for £110. In 1571, John's brother, the

Reverend William Gybbe, who was the local rector, left a number of small bequests to the '*poor mens box*' in the parishes of Clyst St. George, Clyst St. Mary and Sowton, and 10 shillings for '*ye reparacion and maintenance of Apsam Causey*', the path over the marshes to Topsham. John died in 1594 and was buried in the church at Clyst St George where a brass plaque on the floor of the nave read,

'THE BODY OF JOHN GIBBE INTOMBED HERE DOTH RESTE,
WHO DYING DID HIS SOULE TO HEAVEN ABOVE BEQUEST
HIS FAITH IN JESUS CHRIST MOST STEDFASTLY WAS SETT
INSURED HOPE THEREBY TO SATISFY HIS DEBTE.
A LIVELY THEAME TO TAKE ENSAMPLE BY,
CONTEMNINGE DEATH IN HOPE A SAINT TO DY.
OBIIT XXIII0 DIE DECEMBRIS ANNO 1594'[5]

On his death, the estate passed to his son William who in 1631, bequeathed the 'tenement and Garden called Claypitt or Peyght with 23 acres and the tenement of Court Place Farm' to his nephew and Executor John Baker. By 1652 Claypitt had passed to a George Gibbs, 'the yeoman brother and heir of John Gibbe deceased late son of John Gibbe of Pitt yeoman'. George was the grandson of the John Gybbe who had arrived in Clyst St. George a century before.[6]

CHAPTER 1

GEORGE AND ABRAHAM

George Gibbs was born at Pytte in 1604 and was baptised in Topsham on 3 November. After his marriage to Alice in around 1638, they lived at Clay Pitt about half a mile from Court Place Farm, which was still owned by John Baker a distant relative. Their marriage spanned over thirty-five years and ended with Alice's death in 1674. They had nine children of whom two, George junior, baptised in 1641, and Abraham baptised in 1649, are of importance to the continuing story of the Gibbs family of Clyst St. George.[1]

Throughout the commonwealth period, George and Alice were staunch members of the established church and after the Restoration rejected all forms of dissent. By 1652, he had inherited Pytte and as the family flourished, had acquired considerable influence in the village. In 1647, he became a collector of the Poor Rate, a churchwarden in 1652 and 1656 and an Overseer in 1660. He died in 1683 and bequeathed '*to the poor of the Parish 40s*' [shillings]. The rest of his estate was divided between his children and grandchildren.

'To George Gibbs his eldest son, the goods and household stuffs in his dwelling-house. To Samuel Gibbs his son, 20/-, and the land which he had purchased for him in Clyst St George to him and his heirs forever. To Sarah Goulsworthy, his daughter, £20. To Henry Goulsworthy, his grandson, 5/-. To Elizabeth Brinley, 20/-...To his son Abraham [of Topsham] all the residue of his goods.'[2]

1

His eldest surviving son George, then aged forty-two, inherited Pytte on his father's death, becoming head of this line of the Gibbs family. As his wealth increased, so did his status in the local community but like his father, George remained a yeoman farmer. During this period, many such men in rural England bordered on gentleman status and could be described as being 'half farmer and half gentleman', with their horses pulling the plough all week and being 'put into the coach' on Sunday. After his father's death, George extended his landholding by purchasing part of Ashmore Manor in the neighbouring parish of Clyst St. Mary.[3] A staunch Anglican, he erected a mural monument in memory of both his father and grandfather in the north aisle of the church at Clyst St. George. The monument was surmounted with the crest and arms of the Gibbs of Venton. Its stone pillars are supported on skulls, which are garlanded with laurels and a baroque cartouche with winged cherubs on the scrollwork. Beneath the monument was a tablet that read,

"In perpetuam rei memoriam"

> The first above mentioned G. Gibbs has purchased lands in the pish of Clist St. Mary, at ye value of three hundred and ten pounds for ye use and encouragement of day labourers…Such of them as constantly keep to their psh. Church and are known to be of sober conversation, and also for the erudition of one poor boy at Grammar school till well qualified for the University'. Laus Deo
> E.P.S. & V.C.[4]

During the commonwealth period, non-conformist beliefs had taken hold in Devon and became the official form of worship in many parish churches. Presbyterians, who represented the largest non-conformist group, rejected the organisation of the established church, in particular, the elevated role of bishops, resulting in many Anglican clergy being ejected from their parishes. The Restoration in 1660 saw the reinstatement of the Anglican clergy in Devon, and with the enactment of the Second Conventicle Act in 1670, and the withdrawal of the

Declaration of Indulgence in 1673, there followed a twenty-five year period of religious intolerance and persecution. In Exeter, religious differences became political differences. The local gentry voted Tory, while dissenters who formed an influential minority, tended to be involved in trade and commerce. As such, they were associated with persecution and religious toleration and were generally viewed as Whigs. After the Toleration Act, the Exeter Chamber adopted a more pragmatic approach. Although its members were predominantly Tory, it elected seven members, who were mainly merchants and tradesmen and for a short time both sides of the political and religious divide were represented.

In the years following the Restoration, a rift developed in the Gibbs family over their religious differences. George was a conformist but in 1675, his sister Elizabeth married Benjamine Brinley, a wealthy Exeter grocer and influential Presbyterian. Brinley was one of the original members of the Committee of Thirteen, elected by the Exeter Presbyterians to set up and administer a fund for the payment of ministers. Although a Presbyterian meeting had existed in Exeter since 1656, it was after 1689 that they built their Meeting House in the city. The original members of the committee were wealthy merchants and cloth manufacturers, who like Brinley, had been persecuted during the previous twenty-five years. Over the next forty years, Committee members came from a number of families who were to be linked to the Gibbs family through business, religion and marriage, including John Short, Samuel and Nicholas Munckley and Antony Vicary.

George's younger brother Abraham settled in the neighbouring parish of Topsham. Unlike his brother, Abraham had rejected the Established Church and after the death of his father in 1683, had married Tryphaena Rowe, the daughter of John Rowe of Shobrooke. The Rowe family has been described as being 'Presbyterian true blue', and it was Abraham and Tryphaena's marriage that changed the course of the Gibbs family history. They had six children, two sons and four daughters, in a marriage spanning thirty-five years.

The parish of Topsham, which included the hamlet of Weare, runs along the river Exe from the boundary with the parishes of Clyst St.

George and Clyst St. Mary as far as the barracks on the outskirts of Exeter. Topsham itself is now a picturesque town on the river Exe with its narrow streets and pretty houses, but for two centuries its port flourished and 'in the time of William III the number [of vessels] employed in the Newfoundland fishery exceeded that of any port in the kingdom, with the exception of London'[5]. In the mid-sixteenth century 'Apsam' was described as 'a pretty townlet on the shore, a 4 miles upper in the haven. Here is the great trade and road for ship that useth this haven: and [e]specialy for the ships and merchant men's goods of Excester'.[6]

The period between 1680 and 1730 was one of prosperity for Topsham. At the beginning of the eighteenth century, the town was little more than a village having grown around 'one long irregular street, running parallel to the shore'. In 1660, the population of the parish was around eleven hundred. In the late seventeenth century, Topsham was exporting large quantities of serge to Amsterdam and Rotterdam. Fishing was also an important industry as was shipbuilding, which had been established during the Elizabethan period and the port though small, handled the majority of Exeter's woollen trade to the rest of the world. The next forty years saw the rapid expansion of trade and shipbuilding.[7] This led to an increase in ancillary manufacturing trades, including nail, chain and rope making. The population rose steadily as artisans, tradesmen and labourers flocked into the town from the surrounding rural areas. In 1701, a customs census lists 134 men as 'seamen' and 111 as 'seafaring men'. Twenty years later it was noted that 'several artificers and tradesmen relating to the shipbuilding trade as anchorsmiths, shipsmiths and the like had presumed to erect shops, sheds or hovels' on the Strand.[8]

There was a long tradition of dissent in Topsham with flourishing Presbyterian and Quaker communities. Presbyterianism had taken hold there when the dissenting minister Amos Short preached there in 1645. Nine years later, in July 1654, such was their concern at the growth of non-conformity in Topsham that forty-six conformists petitioned the protector for assistance to maintain a minister. By 1672, a Presbyterian meeting had been established in the town.[9] Four years later, there were eighty Non-conformists, and by 1715, the numbers had grown to over six hundred supporters.[10]

After their marriage, Abraham and Tryphaena became part of this growing community of merchants, shipbuilders and mariners. Although he owned large tracts of land in the parish and was a merchant and trader, like his brother he too was described as a yeoman. He also owned a number of limekilns in the area known as Higher Limekiln Field at the top of Lime Street (renamed Shapter Street after 1725), which runs directly from the Strand.[11] As early as 1624, limestone had been landed at the quay and had long been burned in kilns in Topsham to produce manure for local farms, quicklime for mortar and for tanneries to remove hair from hides. The stone was brought to Topsham in 80-ton sloops from quarries in Berry Head and Babbacombe and culm from the quarries in Wales. Abraham prospered from the trade and in 1709 he built a substantial family house in Lime Street near his kilns and owned several small cottages and tenements there.[12]

The Exeter Chamber controlled all shipping in the river Exe down to the sea including the village and port of Topsham. All goods in or out of the port at Exeter had to be discharged at Topsham Quay and stored in public cellars and warehouses. Merchants paid for these services. Such was the level of trade that by 1711 a large number of private quays had been built along the banks of the Exe where non-dutieable goods were landed. Many local merchants used these to avoid paying the Quay and Town Dues imposed by the Exeter Chamber.[13] At the bottom of Lime Street was a slipway called Oak Slip and in 1710 Abraham and John Chapple, a merchant mariner and prominent Quaker, who also owned a number of kilns in the parish, were prosecuted by the Chamber for 'Landing or Shipping off' from 'several landing places and Gravel grounds' between 1706 and 1709 to avoid paying dues. The Chamber argued that all private ports and landing areas should be considered within the port of Topsham making all goods landed or laden liable for payment. Abraham and Chapple were ordered to repay the 'duty to the said Keymaster for the Voyage Landing or Shipping' of any 'oils ....Sydor [sic] Large Haulks and Small Haulks pebble Stones paving Stones pinboil Stones Mill Stones Lyme Stones and other tinmade goods & Merchandizes [sic] or of boards handpiles of firewood & some other Such like goods of Imported or Exported into or out of the said Port of Topsham', and to pay any outstanding dues 'Charged by Weight or Quantity & if by Quantity by what Quantity do such goods pay or are charged in spoil why and what is the said ffee toll or duty payable'.[14]

The first decade of the eighteenth century was a period of good harvests and relatively stable prices but in the harsh winter of 1715, many paupers 'perished through the severity of the season. Such was the concern at the plight of the poor, that a number of prominent ship-builders, merchants and mariners in Topsham, including Abraham and his son, also called Abraham, purchased several properties 'near the churchyard and the Keye', including the Lamb Inn as well as the Kings Head in Exeter, for the benefit of the poor. The charity was known as Shere's Gift. The rents and profits were to 'be employed for the good & pious uses' to provide relief to the deserving poor in the town and were not to be used to 'take away the Charity & Benevolence of the Said Parishioners of the Poor Inhabitants of the said Parish....by diminishing the monthly Rates & Collections but to the intent that the Rest of the Poor of the said Parish may be better provided for by augmenting their monthly contributions as their necessity shall require'.[15]

Meanwhile, Abraham's elder brother George continued to live at Clyst St. George, remaining unmarried for the next thirty-seven years. His dislike of all things Presbyterian made him determined that Abraham should not inherit Pytte for with no son of his own, his younger brother was his natural heir. For many years, George had tried to persuade him to conform but to no avail and Abraham remained staunchly Nonconformist. As the years went by, George continued to be thoroughly 'displeased with his Topsham family', more especially by the behaviour of his young nephew, also called Abraham.

In 1707 Abraham and Tryphaena's only surviving son, Abraham Jr, fell in love with Mary Monke, a distant relative and second daughter of Nehemiah and Mary Monke, a local family from Clyst St. George.[16] The romance was fraught with difficulty from the outset. Young Abraham rebelled against his pious puritan background with its daily round of bible reading, worship and prayer and Mary came from an Anglican family. Both sets of parents were opposed to the match as Abraham Jr and Mary were underage. In August, when they were both twenty, they eloped to Exeter determined to obtain a licence and to marry in the city. Their parents were furious and Abraham published a caveat which was distributed throughout the area:

> Let no licence of matrimony be granted to Abraham
> Gibbs Junior, of Topsham to intermarry with Mary
> Monke of ye same, spinster, before Abraham Gibbs
> of the same, father of the said Abraham, be first
> called, who hath entered this caveat.[17]

The young lovers were thwarted and forcibly brought home, but parental opposition did not dampen their ardour. A year later, in November 1708, just before Mary's twenty-first birthday, they unsuccessfully tried to elope again. It was not until 1711, when they were both aged twenty-four that they finally married on 7 March in the parish church in Topsham, not as Abraham had hoped in the Presbyterian meeting. Although disapproving of his nephew's behaviour, George was delighted that he had defied his parents had married in the local church. Abraham and Tryphaena only forgave him when a grandson was born and christened George in the Presbyterian meeting, but the child only survived a few months and was buried in Topsham on 9 December 1713. The following year Mary gave birth to a healthy daughter whom they called Anna.

Despite any hopes the Topsham family may have had of inheriting Pytte, George, now in his late sixties, decided to find himself a wife in the hope of producing an heir. With the help of his friend Francis Pease, the rector of Clyst St. George he soon found a young woman who was thought to be entirely suitable. Robert Smith from the nearby parish of Heavitree had a twenty-one year old daughter called Hannah. Although Smith was a prosperous merchant, he had nine children, many of them daughters, and could not afford to provide them all with suitable dowries. Despite this, Smith was concerned that he was marrying his daughter to a man so much older than herself, and so before the marriage took place negotiations began in earnest to reach an agreement that would satisfy all parties. A trust was set up to provide for Hannah's future and it was agreed that on her husband's death, she would continue to live at Pytte for her lifetime. George transferred Pytte and part of his estate into the trust and Smith did likewise from his estates in Heavitree. Although the two men shook hands on the deal, they decided that because of the difference in George and Hannah's ages, the contract would not endorsed until the marriage was consummated. He and his young bride were married on his seventieth birthday, the 14 December 1711, by Pease in the little church at Clyst St. George. After an agonising wait, the marriage settlement was signed – four days later. The three trustees, including Pease, were charged with managing the barns, houses, tenements, farms, fields and orchards, to maximise the income and 'pay and apply the yearly rents and any profits of the premises', estimated to be around 'eighty pounds and upwards', annually to Hannah during her 'natural life and for her child or children yet unborn'.[18] The following year, in gratitude for Pease's role in the marriage arrangements and 'in consideration of his zeal for the Church of England' George conveyed 17 acres of land called Leaches Field in Clyst St. George, for his future benefit.

George and Hannah's marriage was certainly not a union made in heaven, but merely one with the sole purpose of producing an heir but for the next eight years no child was born to them. Whether Hannah became pregnant and suffered a series of miscarriages during this time is not known. Still childless and with his brother dead, George clung to the hope that his nephew Abraham could be persuaded to accede to his wishes and to conform if he wished to inherit Pytte. His hopes were raised when in 1718 Mary gave birth to a son in Topsham, whom they called George Abraham. Whether his name was an attempt to reconcile the two brothers is unclear, but George's own happiness was complete in October 1719 when, at the age of seventy-eight, Hannah gave birth to a son, called George after his father. Their happiness was short-lived; the baby survived only a few months, dying the following March.

Meanwhile in Topsham, not long after the birth of his grandson, Abraham Gibbs Sr died at the age of sixty-nine to be buried on 28 August 1718. Although still described as a yeoman, he had prospered during his life and on his death left a considerable estate of land and property, including the house in Lime Street adjoining his lime kilns.[19] He left his 'dear and loveing wife Tryphaena Gibbs' two hundred pounds and an annual rent charge of twenty pounds 'free and clear of and from the Land Tax and all other Rates and Taxes burthens impositions and outgoings – payable out of the Rents and Profits of my Estate in Topsham'. Although he bequeathed the main house to his son, Tryphaena was allowed, 'the use of four rooms in my new Dwellinghouse in Topsham (that is to say the Parlor, Parlor Chamber, the Buttery and the little Chamber over the Buttery during her naturall [sic] life and the use of all such household Goods as she should happen to want. As also the Garden before the sd House to be wholly at her use during her naturall life....'. His daughters Elizabeth and Mary each received £250 with the bulk of his estate going to his son. Although Abraham Jr was now thirty-one and had been married to Mary for seven years, his father remained convinced that he would readily sacrifice his Presbyterian principles to inherit the estate at Clyst St George, and had appointed his brother-in law Benjamine Brinley and two other Presbyterian friends as executors.

At Pytte, now nearly eighty, George finally gave up all hope of producing an heir. For a man who had spent most of his life as a bachelor, there seemed no reason to remain married, so he and Hannah agreed to part. It was an amicable separation, provided for in their marriage settlement. Hannah gave up her right to Pytte and readily returned to her father's house. The trust set up at the time of their marriage was abolished and George agreed to pay her father an annuity for taking her back.[20] He continued to live at Pytte knowng that his nephew, Abraham of Topsham would, as his heir-in-law, expect to inherit his estate and become head of this line of the Gibbs family. However, George remained adamant that he should not do so unless he adhered to the tenets of the Established Church. Not long before his death, and no doubt encouraged by Pease, George included a codicil to his will stipulating that unless, 'Abraham Gibbs of Topsham' baptise and educate his children in the Anglican faith 'rather than continue to practice as dissenters' he and his heirs would not inherit Pytte. He named Pease his 'most affectionate friend and Minister', as his heir. If Abraham complied with his wishes then Pease should surrender his rights for a moderate sum. As Hannah was already provided for under a separate agreement, she was not a beneficiary. Not long after she returned to her father's house, she had met John Wilcocks, a widower whose wife had died a few months earlier. Wilcocks had a young son by his first marriage, and within weeks of her separation had begun calling on her, beginning a long courtship during which time they cohabited openly in her parents' home.

George died on 7 August 1723, aged eighty-two, to be buried two days later in the churchyard at Clyst St. George, bringing to an end this branch of the Gibbs family. A devoted Anglican, he had been a churchwarden for a number of years. Against the record of his burial in the parish registers is a note '*vir nulli pietate secundus*', a compliment extended to no one else in the registers. During his life, he was well-known for his piety and philanthropy towards the poor. On his death he made a number of bequests including, '24 loaves to be given to the poor of Clyst St. George and Clyst St. Mary three times a year' and 'every second year………6 hatts for 6 poor boys to be kept at reading school, and that they have a bible each at going off' and for '£4 for 4 years for one lad of the psh, going to University, provided all be children of such as are in constant communion with ye Church of England, and constant at ye parish Church'.[21]

He also left the Ashmore estate in Clyst St. Mary 'in trust for charitable uses'.[22] The charity known as Gibbs Gift, provided 4s payable quarterly by the tenant of Old Kiddecott, a tenement in Ashmore to be spent on bread for poor labourers.[23]

After his father's death, Abraham and Mary continued to live in the family house in Topsham with his mother and children. In August 1722, Mary suddenly died at the age of thirty-six. Although desolate at her loss, in such a close-knit community Abraham did not have to lookfar for a new wife. Towards the end of 1723, he married Sarah Ewings, the twenty-three year old widow of his friend Robert who was the son of the wealthy shipmaster John Ewings. The Gibbs and Ewings all knew each other well. A few months after her father's death, Abraham's sister Mary had married Nicholas Peters in Exeter Cathedral on 15 March 1719. A widower, prominent Presbyterian and local surgeon, his first wife had been John Ewings sister.

Abraham and Sarah had much in common. As a young woman, she too had rebelled against her parents to follow her heart. In 1719, at the age of eighteen, she and the twenty-four year old Robert Ewings had eloped to Exeter.[24] Unlike Abraham and Mary, they were successful in marrying and a little over a year later Sarah gave birth to a daughter. However, it was not to be a long marriage. Robert died shortly after the birth, leaving Sarah as a wealthy young widow. She also had a fortune of her own, being the heiress daughter of Robert Lyle, another prosperous merchant mariner and owner of the *Providence*.[25] The Lyles were prominent Anglicans and whether Abraham planned to comply at this time with the terms of his uncle's will is unclear but on 7 March 1724, he and Sarah married by special licence in Exeter Cathedral not the Presbyterian Meeting in Topsham. The following year Sarah gave birth to a son, called John.

Angered by the terms of his uncle's will, Abraham was determined to challenge Pease's occupation of Pytte in the courts. He accused Pease of taking advantage of his uncle's advanced age and frailty to persuade him to add the codicil to his will putting all his estates in trust for him `and had presented him 'who had not the same read over or was not acquainted with the meaning', with the new document for signature. He also accused Pease and his fellow trustees of deliberately misman-aging the estates 'to depreciate the value' so that he could claim it was impoverished and not pay Hannah her annuity. At the time of Hannah and George's separation, Pytte had been valued at around £200, enough to provide her with an income of £80 a year. Now it no longer generated sufficient profit and Pease's actions had the effect of devaluing his inheritance as his uncle's heir in law. Abraham also maintained that it was only the lands in Clyst St. Mary and Heavitree that had been included in the trust and not the Pytte estate in Clyst St. George. Pease quite naturally denied all the charges arguing that George had been 'displeased with the Topsham family for many years'. He had changed his will, not as Abraham alleged just before his death, but in 1718 after his great-nephew, George Abraham's birth. While the court accepted Pease's assurances, they looked into further into Abraham's claims and asked him to confirm whether he had complied with his uncle's request 'to frequent the Church of England' or not.

With his marriage to Sarah in Exeter Cathedral, it appears that Abraham had taken the first steps to comply with his uncle's wishes to gain his rightful inheritance. However, before probate was granted, he died suddenly at the age of forty, only three years after his uncle and the case was set aside. He was buried at Topsham on 20 September 1726. It would seem from the speed in which his own will was drawn up, that Abraham was aware that his end was near. It was written and signed on 16 September, a couple of days before his death. At the time, his daughter Anna was twelve years old, George Abraham eight, and their half-brother John was just over one year. With his father and grandfather dead, young George Abraham would normally have been his great-uncle's uncle's heir-in-law, but in the absence of a court ruling, Pease continued to occupy Pytte.

Whatever his intentions, Abraham took great care to ensure that the two children by his first marriage to Mary were provided for. Even at this time the Gibbs star was in the ascendant. The fortunes of the Topsham line of the family had greatly increased within two generations and, unlike his father, Abraham had acquired sufficient wealth and status to be listed as a 'Gentleman'. He had inherited estates in both Topsham and the nearby town of Crediton from his father, and his finances had significantly improved on his marriage to Sarah, even though at the time of his death her first husband's estate had not been settled.[26]

From the terms of his will, it appears that the Gibbs, Ewings and the Lyle families had come to an agreement on how the children from his two marriages would be provided for. While his mother lived, it seemed unlikely that his eldest son would ever gain his rightful inheritance, and so the bulk of Abraham's wealth was left in trust to George Abraham and Anna, his children by Mary. He bequeathed George Abraham £500 and £300 to Anna. Knowing that John would inherit his mother's estate, he received 'Twenty Guineas and no more'. Abraham's executors, John Ewings (Sarah's brother), and the Reverend Mr. Christopher Ewings, were 'requested of them to take all due care of my s^d. children and the Legacies to them respectively given to place out at interest for their best advantage and more liberall education as to them shall seem to require.[27] The residue of the estate went to his '…Beloved wife Sarah', and he conferred 'unto her such lands Tenements and other Effects of which she was possessed before my marriage with her' under the terms of their marriage contract.[28]

Abraham was not alone in challenging his uncle's will. Smith and Wilcox (Hannah's father and husband) also claimed that Pease had not honoured the separation agreement. When she and George had separated, he had agreed to pay Smith a lump sum of £10 to take her back into his home and an annual pension of £20 for the rest of his life. The contract also charged that the executors should 'pay and discharge the debts', incurred during the separation and provide Hannah with '£20 to be payed to her quarterly for her natural life'. As she had married Wilcox three months after George's death Pease refused to pay either her or Smith what they were due, claiming that her marriage had invalidated the agreement. In his deposition, Pease argued that Hannah had met Wilcox within weeks of returning to her father, and he had deliberately courted her to get his hands on her allowance. Instead of the promised £80 a year, Pease had offered an annual payment of £20 for sixty years, which he considered a generous compromise. After investigating all sides of the argument the court found for Smith and

Wilcox, declaring that it was 'well satisfied that the sd Jn Wilcox was not Imposed upon by reason 'of knowing of her allowance when their courtship began'.[29]

Meanwhile, after her husband's death, Tryphaena continued to live in the family house in Topsham. There is little doubt that throughout their life, like any grandmother, she had a considerable influence on her family and after her son's death continued to play an active part in the general upbringing and education of her grandchildren, especially George Abraham and Anna the children of Abraham's first marriage to Mary. Despite all the advantages that inheriting his great uncle's estate would have brought to her grandson, Tryphaena remained true to her religious principles. She refused to compromise her beliefs and both George Abraham and Anna were raised as Presbyterians attending the Topsham Meeting.

She died in 1733, 'of considerable advanced age', and like her son, left the bulk of her estate to her two elder grandchildren, no doubt secure in the knowledge that the Lyles would take provide for young John. She bequeathed 'her wrought iron plate to be divided between her three grandchildren, George Abraham, Anna, and John, the first and second to have £30 apiece and John £5'.[30]

CHAPTER 2

GEORGE ABRAHAM

After her husband's sudden death Sarah and her son John and step-children George Abraham and Anna, lived the tightly knit Presbyterian community in Topsham. In 1729, she married Robert Framington, a neighbour and local maltster, and although she moved out of the Gibbs family house, the two families remained close. Tryphaena lived there with her daughter Mary and her husband Nicholas Peters, who had returned to Topsham following Sarah's marriage. With the Gibbs, the Lyles, the Ewings and the Peters all in such close proximity they formed a very close and supportive extended family for Sarah and Robert, bound by family, marriage and religion.

Nicholas Peters was an apothecary and surgeon and was well respected amongst the medical fraternity of Exeter. He was a friend of Bartholomew Parr Snr, one of the first surgeons appointed to the Devon and Exeter Hospital. The Parr family had been long-standing friends of Abraham and Tryphaena, Parr's father having been the dissenting minister in Clyst St George and Rewe.[1] In 1730, Peters became a churchwarden in Topsham and three years later was appointed as 'Surgeon to the Workhouse' with responsibility for caring for the poor of the parish, a post he held until 1739.[2] Such was his standing in the community that he was a trustee to a number of charities for the benefit of Presbyterians. These included Greenfield's Gift, which was to provide for 'a minister of the Presbyterian meeting in the parish' and 'the education and instruction of so many and such poor children in the Presbyterian way, and in buying and providing for them the catechism,

15

called the Assembly's Catechism'[3]. In this environment, there is little doubt that the two elder Gibbs children, George Abraham and Anna both had a strict Presbyterian upbringing. Having such a distinguished uncle as Peters must have influenced George Abraham's childhood and his eventual choice of career in no small measure. Peters himself had a son by a previous marriage, another Nicholas, who was about the same age as George Abraham so the two boys grew up together.

Fate has a strange way of changing the fortunes of a family. Had George Abraham inherited Pytte on his great-uncle's death, his education would have prepared him for life as a member of the minor gentry. He would probably have attended a lesser public school, going on to Oxford or Cambridge before returning to Pytte to become a country squire. Instead, he spent his childhood under the influence of his extended family. He seems to have had a good education, most likely at one of the growing number of dissenting schools in Topsham, before going on to the Exeter Free Grammar School. Established by the Exeter Chamber before the interregnum, the grammar school, situated just outside the city walls near the East Gate, was originally intended for the sons of freemen. Based on the principles of hard work and godliness, by the early eighteenth century it was providing a complete education to the sons of Exeter's growing professional and middle class. Other pupils at the time were John Heath and Hugh Downham, later Dr Hugh Downham, and John Graves Simcoe, who was later to become the first Governor of Upper Canada (now Ontario) and founder of the city of Toronto. All of these men remained long-standing friends of George Abraham and his family.[4]

With no fortune to speak of, both George Abraham and Nicholas Peters Jnr were destined for the medical profession, a perfectly acceptable career for young men of their social standing in the early eighteenth century. It is not known where they received their training but it is likely that they were apprenticed to one of Peters many medical friends and would have studied anatomy and the techniques of surgery. George Abraham also appears to have been fluent in French and owned several publications published by the *Académie*

Royale de Chirurgie of Paris detailing the latest surgical procedures.[5] Despite the number of advances in medical thought at this time, real improvements in surgical technique were rare; diagnosis was a matter of deduction and, without anaesthetics, surgery had to be performed at lightning speed!

In 1740, when he had completed his apprenticeship as a surgeon, George Abraham, then in his mid-twenties, decided to resurrect the challenge to his great-uncle's will. On George Gibbs' death, Pease had moved into the house at Pytte and lived there until his own death in 1738, at which time the estate passed to his eldest son, also called Francis, who had lived there since. With each of the claims and counterclaims to his occupation between 1723 and 1740, both Pease and his son had relied on the various dispositions made and executed during George's lifetime, to justify their occupation. George Abraham based his appeal on the wording of his great-uncle's will, which stated that it was *only* the properties and lands in the parish of Clyst St. Mary that had been left in perpetuity to Pease. All the other land and properties (including those in Clyst St. George) were for Pease's *life only* and on his death should have reverted to George Abraham as his uncle's heir-at-law. There followed a lengthy dispute in the courts over the will, lasting until 1744, when both parties agreed that on payment of £300, Pease would terminate his tenancy of Pytte and give up all his claims to the farms and lands in the parish of Clyst St. George. He continued to occupy Ashmore Manor in Clyst St. Mary until 1749 in a house that became known as Peases, and more recently as Shepherds Farm.

At the age of twenty-six, George Abraham, the son of Abraham Gibbs of Topsham had finally achieved his ambition. Whether he had agreed to compromise his strict Presbyterian beliefs is unclear, but he was now a man of property and was determined to regain all his inheritance. In 1753, he purchased Court Place Farm for £630 and by 1761 had acquired the 100 acres that had formerly made up the Gibbs lands.[6]

During his minority, he had received a slender allowance from his father's estate. It was now time to find a wife; and he did not have to look far. Through the close-knit local dissenting congregation in Exeter, he met the eminently suitable Anne Vicary who had a fortune of £10,000.[7] She was the twenty-two year old daughter of Antony Vicary, 'a wealthy man, who kept a grocer's shop, in combination....with a linen draper's....', and whose wife Elizabeth was the daughter and heiress of Nicholas Munckley, another wealthy Exeter merchant.[8] Like his uncle Benjamin Brinley, both the Vicary and Munckley families were prominent Presbyterians and had served on the Presbyterian Committee of Thirteen in Exeter.

In 1744, George Abraham proposed. He was a man with little sense of humour, taking himself seriously at times to the point of pomposity. Although devoted to Anne he wanted her to appreciate how lucky she was to be chosen 'from the rest of her Sex as a suitable and deserving Woman for the Object of his Love'. What was perhaps as important was her sizeable dowry, essential for any young man at the beginning of his career![9] George Abraham himself was hardly handsome. A small man with a slight frame, he had bulging eyes, a long nose, and a full mouth with long thin straggly hair and a 'disagreeable hesitation' in his speech. Despite his appearance, Anne accepted his proposal.

The engagement was to last three years. Although now a man of substance, he chose not to give up his chosen profession for the life of a country gentleman. A trained surgeon, George Abraham decided to put off his marriage until he had established himself in his career. Whatever his aspirations and connections in the medical world, initially he had great difficulty in finding a position in Exeter and so he decided to move to Pytte and manage the estate until a vacancy arose at the hospital. He also planned to extend and improve the house for them to live in after their marriage, aware that he was marrying the daughter of a wealthy Exeter merchant and it had to be made worthy of her. As the work at Pytte progressed, he grew restless, for although he enjoyed country life, his strict upbringing had instilled in him a Presbyterian ethic and he became impatient to pursue his chosen profession.

The Devon and Exeter Hospital had opened in January 1743, one of the many provincial hospitals funded by public subscription in this period. At its opening the hospital had appointed its full complement of doctors, and it was to be four years before there was a vacancy. Where or whether George Abraham practiced as a surgeon during this period is unclear but it was not until the sudden death of John Patch in May 1746, that he was offered a probationary position at the hospital. For several months, he waited anxiously for news that it would be made permanent, but was not very hopeful. In July he wrote glumly to Anne that the Standing Committee were reviewing all appointments because the 'Question is come up again…to determine whether the number of Surgeons is to be reduced to three' or whether the number would be left 'where it is at present'. It was not surprising, he wrote, that the surgeons were 'for increasing their number, and consequently are making Friends in order to Push the Point'. Despite his concerns, he was delighted when he was offered a permanent post at the hospital. There surely had never been any doubt. One of the senior surgeons on the Committee was Thomas Glass, a great friend of George Abraham's uncle, Nicholas Peters. The Glass family, also dissenters, originated from Tiverton but the links between the two families went even further. Peters had translated Glass's literary work on fevers, which had first been published in Latin in 1742, into English.[10] In 1729, Thomas's younger brother Samuel, had been apprenticed to Peters, and so George Abraham and Samuel would have known each other very well and would have lived in the same house in Topsham during Samuel's apprenticeship.[11]

To Anne, like many women in the eighteenth century, her health was a constant cause of concern. Throughout their engagement, she suffered from a number of minor ailments, and spent the winters in Bath taking the waters while George Abraham remained in Exeter. He wrote to her every day while they were apart and there are continuous references to her health in their correspondence. On one occasion, when she caught a slight head cold and had taken to her bed, George Abraham was so worried that he wrote twice a day, begging her to promise that, at the 'Risque of injuring thy Health, which I fear is as dear to me, than it is to thy self, I have more Reason to give thee this Caution, because of the Situation you are in'. He went on, 'I hope you are not obliged to get out of Bed in the Night; if you are, I beg of thee…that for the future get the Chamber maid….to be in the Room, or some other person…. who can better endure such sort of Fatigue.'.

A few months after his appointment at the hospital was confirmed the date was finally set for their marriage. It soon became obvious that when they were married it would be impossible for them to live permanently at Pytte because of his commitments at the hospital. The wedding was planned for December 1747, and in the autumn, he began looking for a house in the city. Although George Abraham found a number that he considered suitable, nothing seemed to satisfy Anne. She found fault over the most trivial things. By mid-November, his patience had worn thin and he became increasingly exasperated and 'quite weary, my Dear Girl, of writing to thee about Houses'. With their marriage only weeks away, in desperation he took a lease on a house in Cathedral Close near the Bishop's Palace at eighteen guineas a year. The house was in 'a little square close by the old Episcopal Palace'. He wrote to Anne, 'You come through the outer door into a little square court which leads immediately into the house by a second door…'. The house was large having 13 rooms as well as garrets, a kitchen, offices, a brew house and garden as befitted an up-and-coming Exeter surgeon and his family. After their marriage, George Abraham planned to use Pytte as their country retreat near his childhood home of Topsham where his half-brother John lived with his family.

On the day before the wedding the marriage contract was signed. Anne's dowry was a considerable fortune for any young man. Aware of his personal and financial obligations, for his part, George Abraham put the premises 'called Pitt' and the 'closes of land with the appurts called Leaches land….and one close of land …called Bothays…and a Tenem^t called Court all with sd premises contained about 100 acres' in trust for his future wife.[12] The trustees were Anne's father, Antony Vicary, John Duntze a local merchant, and Henry Lloyd an Exeter Linen Draper. The following day he and Anne were married, not in the Presbyterian meeting as one might have expected but in St. Petrock's church only a few minutes walk from their home, but despite this, they continued to worship at the Mint Chapel.[13] Built in 1720, by a group of Presbyterians who had seceded from the James Meeting after a difference over the nature of the Trinity, the Mint was 'a plain and neat building; it is commonly called the Arian Meeting' but the congregation did 'not appear to follow to doctrine of Arius'. Despite the split amongst the Presbyterian community in Exeter, George Abraham and Anne remained true to their non-conformist beliefs for many years and only reverted to the Established Church when 'the minister and congregation of the Mint Meeting House in Exeter began to alloy their Presbyterianism with Arian doctrine.'

Anne's dowry much increased his income. To complete their happiness, the following year their first child was born; a son called George who was baptised at the Mint Meeting on 3 October 1748.[14] But their joy was short-lived when he died a few months later. This was the start of twenty years of childbearing for Anne, and despite earlier concerns about her health, she appears to have had had a robust constitution. A year later, a daughter, Elizabeth (Nelly), was born and from then on the children followed at regular intervals. In 1751 another son, Vicary, was followed by George, Abraham, Antony, Anne (Nancy), Mary, Sibella (Bell), Sarah (Sally), and Catherine (Kitty). All the children were named after members of the family, but only the girls were given nicknames. George Abraham took his responsibilities as a parent very seriously, and purchased a paper entitled *An Essay upon Nursing and the Management of Children from their Brith to Three Years of Age*, which was published in 1748 and covered all aspects of child-care.[15] Their marriage seems to have been a happy partnership that was to last nearly forty-seven years. During the early part, he was fully engaged as a surgeon at the Devon and Exeter Hospital, becoming a well-known and well-respected member of the local community.

Having received an education that enabled him to follow his chosen profession, George Abraham recognised its value for his own children, particularly his sons. He wanted their education to be linked to their future roles to enable them to make their own way in the world. In Exeter in the mid-eighteenth century, there was a growing recognition amongst 'respectable citizens' of the 'practical and social value of education' in a highly competitive world. To meet this growing need, a number of schools had sprung up in the city. As well as the grammar school, there were several private establishments where the curriculum was designed to meet the demands of the mercantile community. If a young man was to be successful in commerce, it was essential that he be able to have a depth of understanding of bookkeeping and accounts. Educating the boys locally had the added advantage that they would remain at home in their early years under the moral and religious supervision of the family, while having some contact with the sons of other local Exeter families. Like George Abraham, many of the friends his sons made during their early years at school remained so in later life, providing help and support within a much wider social and economic network.

Whatever plans George Abraham had for the future of his younger sons, Vicary was not destined for a life in commerce. As he would one day inherit Pytte, his father was determined that he should go to university to study law. Vicary was an exceptional student and obtained a Kings scholarship to Eton College. Given their religious beliefs, allowing their eldest son to go to Eton could not have been an easy decision for his parents, but they were not to be disappointed. In 1770, Vicary went up to Kings College Cambridge, the only one of George Abraham's sons to go to university. George Jr attended the Exeter Academy, a Presbyterian school that had been established in 1760. Other pupils there included his cousin Robert Remmett, as well the sons of many of George Abraham's friends including John Short, Bartholomew Parr and George Heath. Why young George should have been sent to the Academy is unclear for he was the only son to study there. Like Vicary, Antony and Abraham, were educated at the Grammar School, retaining an interest in the school for many years. In 1787, *Trewman's Exeter Flying Post* reported that Antony had become a 'promoter of a Society of past pupils of the Grammar School' and ten years later it was reported that Vicary was 'one of 4 stewards at the anniversary meeting of the Exeter Grammar School Society'.[16]

It was taken for granted that younger sons would either be apprenticed to learn a trade, or enter the church or the services, and it was essential that they made good marriages to increase their modest incomes. At this time overseas trade was 'so vastly great....no wonder that the gentlemen ... put their younger sons apprentices to tradesmen'. The Gibbs family was no exception. With Vicary on his way to a successful career in law, George Abraham took advantage of his large network of friends and family to secure the future of his younger sons. At this time, Exeter merchants were developing trade in the Mediterranean and many apprenticed their sons to merchant houses in Italy and Spain, where they could learn the business and the language. After leaving Exeter Academy in 1769, George, then aged sixteen, was apprenticed to a Bristol firm, owned by his mother's cousin, Samuel Munckley. In 1771, young Abraham was sent to Genoa, to a merchant house owned by George Abraham's old school friend John Short. Three years later, his youngest son Antony was apprenticed to Nicholas Brooke, a wealthy merchant who had established 'a very considerable trade' in Spain. Brooke was a man of considerable influence in Exeter being one of eight aldermen in the Chamber. George Abraham was determined that his sons, would grow up with a sense of values for 'the first principle [sic] object of my wishes is not that which goes under the name of success in the world. My greatest ambition is to see you all virtuous and worthy men'.

However, he continually worried about Antony's attitude to work. A likeable young man, Antony had inherited his father's stammer and had been spoilt from childhood. He had a tendency to embark on sudden and violent passions with little regard for their practicality. Although affable and enthusiastic about everything he did, his casual attitude was a concern to his father who considered it a worrying 'defect in his character', which was likely to cause him problems in later life. It was a relief therefore to learn that Antony had settled in Spain and was working hard. His 'heart seems to be much in his business, and his time is filled up from morning to night', and that 'one hour of every day is taken up in learning Spanish'. George Abraham was also determined that his five daughters should receive a good education though it is unlikely that they had the same schooling as their brothers. Although there were a number of girls' schools in Exeter, they were probably educated at home and were taught the traditional subjects necessary to run a genteel middle-class household. Later, they may have attended either Mrs Braddock's School near the Cathedral or Mrs Webber's Boarding and Day School for Young Ladies, where they would have been taught English Grammar, French, music, drawing and embroidery. The curriculum would also have included theology, and with particular attention being paid to arithmetic, an essential subject for young women at that time, so that they could deal with household accounts.[17]

George Abraham had other interests outside medicine. The period 1760 to 1778 was to be one of peace and prosperity for the Exeter serge trade with around 3,000,000lb being exported most years into the growing continental markets.[18] He had always remained close to John, who no doubt influenced by his uncle Daniel Ewings, went to sea, becoming a master mariner trading mainly in Newfoundland and the Mediterranean.[19] In 1761, the two brothers decided to go into business together and planned to purchase a new ship. To finance his share of the vessel, in December 1761, George Abraham mortgaged Pytte for £1000 to Sir Richard Warwick Bamfylde of Poltimore at three per cent interest.[20] Three years later, he and John established the firm of George Gibbs & Co having purchased a 140-ton brigantine, the *Ceres*, which had been built in Boston, Lincolnshire the previous year. They each owned a half share in the vessel, which was registered with Lloyds of London to sail on the Cowes to Holland and the Mediterranean routes. Such was the success of the venture, that two years later, in March 1763, George Abraham had repaid the loan to Bamfylde in full with interest and regained Pytte. For several years, he and John enjoyed the profits from what appears to have been a successful business venture. Trading enterprises were usually family concerns during this period. With John and his nephew Jack sailing in the in the Mediterranean and his own sons George and Abraham

24

settled in Bristol and Genoa, George Abraham believed that the Exeter firm of George Gibbs & Co was well-placed to develop trade throughout the Baltic and the Mediterranean through this web of family and business contacts.

In 1774, tragedy struck. In January, John had been in Hamburg planning a second trip in the *Ceres* later that year from Leghorn (Livorna) to 'Cephalonia for corn'. In mid-August, George Abraham received a letter from Jack telling him that his father had died. John had travelled to Leghorn to pick up his cargo but his departure had been delayed because 'his freighter has failed him a little'. When the *Ceres* had eventually set sail in mid-July, John had been fit and well but two days later had suddenly been taken ill, and on 'the passage from thence to the next port on 20th July the melancholy scene closed'. George Abraham was shocked at the news, for despite the difference in their ages, they had always been very close. He was worried to learn from Jack that his own son Abraham, who was still in Genoa had been greatly affected by his uncle's death, having spent 'so much time with him in a foreign country'. After completing his apprenticeship, Abraham had remained in Italy and was working as George Gibbs & Co's agent there developing the Italian side of the business. Although he had no other details, George Abraham believed that John's illness must have been due 'to a latent fever or at least a fever [which] must have come on very soon'.

On John's death, George Abraham became guardian to his brother's children. Although he admired his sister-in-law and thought her 'a very prudent and economical woman', who 'will take care that nothing is mis-spent or wasted' he despaired that she 'is utterly unused to business; that sought [sic] of attention therefore, which the boys will be continually wanting....cannot be expected from her'. He wrote to George Jr in Bristol, 'You know the mutual affection in which [he and I] lived so many years and the connection of interest there is between us...Now, I have [his] seven children added to [my] ten, for I must and will be a father to them as far as my ability reaches'. With Jack on the *Ceres*, his younger brother William decided to follow his brother to sea. George Abraham used his Exeter contacts to apprentice John's third son, Lyle, then aged about sixteen, to an English merchant house owned by his old friend John Heath. John's three younger boys, Abraham, George and Thomas remained at home in Topsham with their mother Elizabeth.

As the business with the *Ceres* had been successful, George Abraham and his sister-in-law decided to keep the vessel and for the next few years, they saw their profits increase from trading in the Mediterranean and on the transatlantic routes to Newfoundland and the North American plantations. On Elizabeth's death in 1778, she left her share of the *Ceres* to be divided between her children and appointed her two elder sons Jack and William as executors with George Abraham.

Meanwhile, having completed his apprenticeship, Antony returned to Exeter in 1778. Now twenty-two and fluent in Spanish, he was full of enthusiasm about the potential trade that could be developed with the Iberian Peninsula. His brother Abraham, who had spent nine years in Genoa, had also returned after the death of his uncle. The two brothers joined their father and cousins in the firm of George Gibbs & Co. By 1780, the business had expanded and the partners purchased the *Charles of Exeter*, a 40- ton single masted rigger and George Abraham was also part owner of the 35-ton *Fly of Exeter* with Nicholas Brooke Antony's former master. When Spain joined the American War of Independence as France's ally all trade with that country ceased and ships bound for Spain and Italy were particularly vunerable to attacks from enemy privateers. In December 1780, England was at war with Holland and no vessels cleared Exeter for Dutch ports for a year.[21] On 20 December and 2 January 1781, the Admiralty issued letters of marque authorising the *Charles* and the *Fly* to be armed for self - defence and to capture Dutch enemy merchant ships. The *Charles* carried '4 guns of 4 pounds' and '30 men or war' and the *Fly*, '2 guns of 4 pounds' and '21 men of war'. There is no record of them capturing anything.[22] It appears that later that year the firm no longer owned the *Charles of Exeter* and George Abraham had sold his interest in the *Fly*, and used the profit to set Abraham and Antony in business as cloth merchants working with their cousins exporting cloth to Spain and Italy. Two years later, with their uncle's agreement Jack and William decided to sell the *Ceres*, bringing to an end a venture that had yielded a considerable profit for many years.

With his sons settled in their professions, George Abraham continued to live at Palace Gate when on duty at the hospital, but he and Anne spent as much time as possible at Pytte with their four younger daughters, Nancy, Kitty, Sally and Bell. Two years earlier, in 1776, their eldest daughter Elizabeth (known affectionately as Nelly), had married her cousin, Robert Remmett in Exeter Cathedral. Robert, the son of George Abraham's sister Anna and her husband John Remmett, a clothier from Crediton, had attended the Exeter Academy with George and had then gone on to Edinburgh to study medicine, matriculating in 1772. In December of that year, he was admitted as a member of the Royal Medical Society of Edinburgh. In 1774, he wrote a *Dissertatio medica inauguralis de Opii in morbis inflammatoriis*, which was favourably reviewed in Medical and Philosophical Commentaries.[23] In 1795, the Remmetts settled in Plymouth where Robert started in practice and three sons were born in quick succession. In July 1779, while George Abraham and Anne were visiting them after the birth of their third son, the combined French and Spanish fleet, comprising some 66 ships, entered the channel and was met by the English fleet. Plymouth, which was full of French, Spanish and American prisoners, was thrown into disarray for fear of invasion and the west of England rallied to its defence. Using glasses, from the shore George Abraham could see the '... unequal combat of the *Ardent* with several of the enemy's ships....'. Fearful of an invasion he wanted the Remmetts to return with him and Anne to Exeter, but Nelly who had not recovered from the birth was too ill to be moved. Much to his relief, the threat of attack subsided and the enemy fleet withdrew.[24]

A few weeks later on 25 September, Nelly died and was buried in the north aisle of St. Andrew's Church in Plymouth. George Abraham and Anne were very distressed at the death of their beloved elder daughter, but their relationship with Robert was such that they found considerable consolation in being able to make regular visits to Plymouth to visit their grandsons. Seven years after Nelly's death Robert remarried, and he and his new wife remained on intimate terms with the Gibbs family. In 1794, he and Dr Samuel Fuge, another local physician, founded the Plymouth Medical Society and Remmett became its president. Later that year his second wife died and four years later with the establishment of the Plymouth Dispensary, Remmett was nominated physician extraordinary.[25] His sons were educated at Eton but only one, another Robert, survived to adulthood, the other two dying whilst at school. Remmett continued to act as the Gibbs family physician, and was called to offer a second opinion and minister to them in emergencies, treating them for many years.[26]

With his increasing wealth, George Abraham became well respected in and around Exeter and took an active interest in local politics. In October 1745, he had enrolled in an association of Exeter men in support of the King against the Young Pretender. By 1775, the party labels of Whig and Tory that had been attached to religious differences had disappeared. That year the first shots were fired at Lexington near Boston between troops and American colonists. A Tory, George Abraham was one of the signatories to 'an address of the High Sheriff, Gentlemen, Clergy, and freeholders of the County of Devon' which was presented to the King, assuring him of their loyalty and deploring 'the conduct of your American subjects, following the burning of the revenue cutter, the *Gasparee* by a mob.'[27] Among his special friends were Edward Addicot, John Mallett, Colonel Simcoe, and William Pitfield whom George Abraham described as '…my dearest and best friend'. When the Devon & Exeter Hospital had been established in 1743, Pitfield was one of four apothecaries who volunteered their services until a permanent apothecary was appointed. He continued in this capacity until his retirement by which time he had '….done the Hospital good service in looking after the drug supply' for some thirty-six years. Pitfield had also been the President and Vice President of the Court of Governors. When George Abraham drew up his will, Pitfield was named as an executor, but he died in 1775, several years before his friend. He left the hospital a legacy of £200 in the form of a Deed Poll on the Exeter Turnpike with the interest '….to be annually applied to the use of the Hospital until the Governors in the General Court (the President and Treasurer being present) shall think it expedient to sell them for the purpose of fitting up and preparing an apartment for Insane persons supposed to be curable'[28] The original benefaction was intended to provide a lunatic ward at the Devon and Exeter Hospital to treat middle class and professional persons who were not dependent on the poor rates.[29]

Another of George Abraham's close friends was Dr Hugh Downham whom he had known since their school days at the Exeter Grammar School. Downham went on to Balliol College Oxford and was ordained in 1763 in Exeter Cathedral. A friend of Thomas Glass, he too went on to study medicine at Edinburgh, returning to Exeter in 1770, later being appointed as a physician at the Devon and Exeter Hospital. Downham was also a poet and wrote a number of sonnets dedicated to his friends. In his *Poems to Thespia*, a series of love poems for his wife which were first published in 1781, he dedicated a sonnet to George Abraham:

> Much valued Gibbs (though thou didst not pay
> Devotion to the Muse) in early youth
> The same sensations which create my lay
> Haply inspired; which still approved by Truth,
> By Virtue, Nature, thy maturer breast
> Adorn, where every thought humane is placed
> But in a Friend, Husband, Father, most confest.
> With thy attention shall these lines be graced?
> Wilt thou the paths of Youth and Love retread?
> While their delightful scenes again appear,
> Thou, and the softer partner of thy bed?
> And surely never purer steps were there
> Yea, tread again their paths, their scenes review,
> And, from yourselves, pronounce them painted true.[30]

Eventually, George Abraham became the chief surgeon at the hospital and in 1778 was appointed as Steward on the management committee. He remained there until his retirement in December 1780, aged sixty-three, having been a surgeon for some thirty-four years. At the meeting of the committee on 18 January 1781, it was agreed 'That a letter be written to Mr Gibbs ackno-wledging and returning the thanks of this Committee for his long and assiduous services to this Hospital, and the strict attention to the patients under his care'.[31] The committee proposed that he be elected as a standing member by virtue of '... having been 34 Years a Surgeon of this Hospital, lately resigned, and ....now discontinued the Practice of Surgery....in Consideration of his long and eminent Services to this Charity and the Hospital Patients in his Care....'.[32] At the same meeting his long-standing friend and mentor, Thomas Glass as appointed to the committee. Both appointments were confirmed at the meeting of the general Court of Governors on 30 January 1781.

After his retirement, George Abraham remained in good health, continuing to take an active interest in public affairs as well as in his children and grandchildren. Although he had never wanted to play the part of the local squire, on his retirement he immersed himself in country life and began to take a more active role in managing the estate. The *Trewman's Exeter Flying Post* of 2 October 1788 included 'George Gibbs, Esq.,' in a list of flax growers who were entitled to a bounty from the Government having grown 53 stone of flax on the Parkhayes Estate in Clyst St. George'.[33] He and Anne began to spend more time at Pytte with their younger children as he looked forward to a peaceful and long retirement.

CHAPTER 3

HUMILIATION AND RUIN

Any thought that George Abraham might have had that his retirement would be peaceful was soon forgotten. Having been persuaded some years before by his sons, Abraham and Antony, to invest in their textile business in Exeter, he continued to take an active interest in the firm though he appears to have been blinded to his sons' lack of experience. Antony had always freely admitted that he was 'not naturally fond of business', preferring the country life, and both he and Abraham lived at Clyst St. George with their parents. Vicary and George were frequent visitors with their families to Pytte, but their attitude to work was very different from their younger brothers.

The next decade was to be one of changing fortune for the Gibbs family. It was a great shock in 1782 when Abraham became ill with a fever from which he never recovered. He had been courting a young woman, Dorothea Barnetta Hucks affectionately known as Dolly, the youngest daughter of Yorkshire wine merchant William Hucks, whose family had made their fortune in brewing and owned estates in Hertfordshire and Oxfordshire.[34] Originally from Knaresborough, Dolly was an attractive young woman and both Vicary and Abraham were captivated by her. In 1774, her sister Eleanor had married Henry Townley-Ward, a London solicitor and a friend of Vicary.[35] George Abraham and Anne considered Dolly a 'very pleasant & agreeable woman' and had high hopes that she and Abraham might marry. In the spring of 1782, Dolly went to stay with the Gibbs family at Pytte. Eleanor was delighted and wrote, 'I see by yours the Gibbs family

31

continue their friendship and attention to you; God reward them for it'. Within weeks, she and Abraham were engaged, much to Vicary's chagrin, but in the spring of 1782, Abraham became seriously ill and died a few days later. He was only twenty-eight years old.

Dolly began to make plans to return to Knaresborough. George Abraham and Anne who had become very fond of her, persuaded her to remain in Devon, knowing that Vicary too adored her. However, her father suddenly became seriously ill and in June, she was called back to Yorkshire where he died two weeks later. Shocked by this double tragedy, she was persuaded to go back to Devon to stay at Pytte. She had not long returned when the news reached her that her brother William, who had gone to Messina for his health, had died of consumption. Eleanor, grateful for the support Dolly was receiving from the Gibbs family wrote that it was fortunate 'that she is with such friends who make it their whole study to entertain her' and she thought them 'sincere well-wishers and best friends'.

On Dolly's return to Pytte, Antony was her greatest comfort and when he proposed a few months later, his parents were delighted that she accepted. His father was reassured that Antony, who had been running the firm of Gibbs Brothers Cloth Merchants since his brother's death, decided to delay his marriage until the business was on a more secure footing. Living as he was at Clyst St George, George Abraham was more concerned with managing his estate, having little exposure to the problems that Exeter woollen merchants were experiencing during the American Wars of Independence and Antony's sanguine attitude gave him confidence that all was well. If George Abraham had any misgivings, he was no doubt relieved at the resurgence in Exeter's woollen export trade after peace was declared in 1783. While Antony travelled in Europe, generating business, Dolly lived at Pytte and was treated like a daughter during their engagement.

The following year George Abraham and Anne had much to occupy their time as three of their children married. On 12 April, the family gathered in Devon for Mary's wedding to the Reverend Charles Crawley in Exeter Cathedral. Charles, the younger brother of Sir Thomas

Crawley-Boevey of Flaxley Abbey in the Forest of Dean in Gloucester-shire, was a penniless curate in a neighbouring parish. For the first few years of their marriage, the young couple lived at Pytte and much to the delight of George Abraham and Anne, their first three children, Anne, Mary and Charles, were born there. In June, Vicary married Frances Cerjat Kenneth MacKenzie, the daughter of Major William MacKenzie who brought with her a sizeable dowry. Her brother Francis was later to become Lord Seaforth.

A few weeks after Vicary's marriage, their youngest daughter Sarah, a consumptive who had been in poor health for some years, became critically ill. Adored by Antony, he nursed her himself for several weeks as she seemed to recover. In October, the family gathered at Pytte for Antony and Dolly's marriage, but her condition suddenly deteriorated and they considered postponing the wedding. Sarah persuaded them to go ahead which they did. A few days after Christmas, her condition became critical. She died a few weeks later to be buried in the church-yard at Clyst St. George.

After their marriage, Antony and Dolly lived in his parents' house at Palace Gate near the 'Town Walls'. He had been looking for a suitable house for more than a year, and like his father before him, had found nothing to suit both Dolly and himself. Rather than see their marriage delayed any longer, George Abraham offered him their house in Exeter until something suitable became available. Ideally, Antony wanted a house similar to Pytte, which was big enough for a family, and from where he could run his business. It was in May 1785 with Dolly's first child due in August he found a small estate, Exwick Barton with around 100 acres, in the hamlet of Exwick, a mile from Exeter on the banks of the river Exe, which included a large family house and was only a few minutes walk from an empty mill. He had also found a partner who was prepared to invest £10,000 into a new business but only if Antony could match his investment. Unable to do so, once again he approached his father. Still flushed with the success of his previous mercantile ventures, George Abraham agreed to put £10,000 into the firm, but he could not afford the additional £3000 for the estate. Over the last few years, he had invested considerable sums in his sons' business ventures that had drained his resources. He had also provided Mary with a dowry, and still had three unmarried daughters living at home. To everyone's relief, Vicary came to the rescue, his income having been boosted by a substantial fortune from his own marriage. He purchased Exwick Barton and agreed to lease it to Antony.

Within weeks, George Abraham had signed a ten-year partnership agreement with Antony and his new partner, Edmund Granger, to establish a firm trading as woollen manufacturers and merchants. The business was called Gibbs & Granger. For the next two years, all seemed well. Antony was busy renovating the mill and regularly reported that the business was flourishing. He and Dolly now had two children and were living in Exwick House. Mary and Charles Crawley were still living at Pytte with their growing family, and George Abraham and Anne spent many happy times visiting their children and grandchildren in Plymouth, Bristol and Exwick.

Contrary to Antony's assurances all was not well. In January 1787, the family was shocked at the publication in *Trewman's Exeter Flying Post* of an anonymous letter threatening him over his unpaid debts. Although George Abraham had made a substantial investment in the firm, he was yet to receive any dividends, and naively believed Antony's confident assertion that it was still early days, as the mill was not yet working to full capacity. He had no idea that his son was on the verge of bankruptcy.

But tragedy was never far away. In October, George's wife Etty died suddenly. She and George had been married for eleven years and had three children. Despite his worries, George Abraham and Anne travelled to Bristol for the funeral, which took place a few days later. He also continued to take an active interest in his late brother John's children, who were now all settled, but his niece Betsy, now in her mid-thirties was still unmarried and he remained her guardian. She was still living in the family house in Topsham that had been built by her great grandfather, but with no fortune of her own, had yet to find a husband. In order to provide her with an income, George Abraham persuaded her brothers to put the extensive number of properties left to them by their parents into a trust managed by him and Antony. With the income from the trust and her share of the profits from the sale of the *Ceres*, Betsy would be provided for in the future.

His concerns for Betsy were well founded. In the summer of 1788, George Abraham learned that she had fallen madly in love with a dashing young American several years her junior. Knowing that George had had extensive interests in the Caribbean and American plantations before the war, he wrote to ask him to check out the young man's credentials. 'You will have heard from Bell', he wrote 'of EG's new acquaintance. We thought it nothing more than a flirtation, but I understand from EG who is keen that the Gentleman had made a formal proposal, & desiring an interview with me...it is no easy matter for a young woman, in your cousin's situation, to make up her mind on the side of reason, when it is combated by intuition'. As the American claimed to have extensive estates in South Carolina, George Abraham asked George to look into his background for, 'your connections with Sth C were so considerable before the war with America, that I think the matter may be settled by some considerable witness in Bristol'. Within weeks, George confirmed that the American was a fraudster and swindler. When George Abraham told Betsy she was devastated and, after many tears, reluctantly agreed to end the engagement.

That Christmas the family gathered at Exwick for their traditional celebrations. In the New Year, Betsy and her brother William, who had returned from the Caribbean, came to stay for a few days. This gave the two men a chance to discuss her future. George Abraham was worried that now his niece was financially independent she was prey to any admirer with an eye to her modest fortune. Despite her mature age, it was obvious that she needed protecting from herself. William agreed with his uncle; with Dolly's third confinement only a few weeks away it was resolved that Betsy should move into Exwick House as Dolly's companion.

Towards the end of June, as the second anniversary of their business partnership drew near, the family learnt the true extent of Antony's financial difficulties and that he was planning to return to Spain to collect monies owed to him and to drum up new business. He left Exeter at the beginning of August and it was anticipated that he would be away for about five months. It was only when George Abraham learned from Granger that the banks had stopped all lines of credit, that he had any idea of the seriousness of the situation. As both he and Granger believed these were only short-term problems, they tried to raise more capital to keep the firm going until Antony's return. When Granger proposed a new ten-year agreement, in order to match his new investment, George Abraham turned to Vicary and Kenny to borrow £1500 from their marriage settlement. They readily agreed, but the trustees insisted on some guarantees and George Abraham had no option but to use Pytte as security.[36] In Antony's absence, Vicary agreed to underwrite his brother's share. He reluctantly transferred Exwick Barton, which included Exwick House that he had purchased two years before for £3000, to the business and it became part of the joint stock of the firm.[37] Despite his misgivings, he had no alternative but to agree that at the end of the partnership agreement Exwick Barton would be divided amongst the partners according to their shareholding.

In September, the situation was so dire that the partners were forced look for more capital to keep the business afloat. They approached Gerrard Duccarell, a wealthy Exmouth merchant who agreed to loan them £5000 for a six-month term at a prohibitive rate of interest. The partners were 'jointly & severally bound unto the said Gerrard Gustavus Duccarell in the penal Sum of Ten thousand Pounds of Lawful Money of Great Britain conditioned for the Payment of the Sum of Five thousand Pounds'[38]. George Abraham was completely bewildered. He had no idea that the firm was in such financial trouble but was suddenly aware that he could be liable for their combined debts.

Despite their worries, he and Anne continued to help their young daughter-in-law through this difficult period. Not long after her husband's departure, Dolly had suffered a miscarriage. Alone in Exwick House, she became very depressed as increasing numbers of local trades-men refused her credit. In order to take her mind off her worries, George Abraham suggested that she take the children to Bristol for a short stay. Having heard of her safe arrival, he tried to encourage her, writing 'George gives us a high econium of your magnanimity. This new trait of your character might never have been brought to light if it had not been for the present occasion and I think, my dear, you may count the credit you have done yourself as some recompense for your husband's company'.

It was a difficult Christmas as the family gathered at Pytte waiting anxiously for word from Spain. In the midst of all their worries, there was some good news from Bristol. In mid-January, they heard that Samuel Munckley had offered George a partnership in the firm. George Abraham wrote to congratulate his son. 'We wish you all manner of success from your new engagement which, I trust, will prove very much to your satisfaction' adding that despite their present situation, 'it is a very kind mark of Mr. Munckley's goodwill'. With Vicary now acting as Recorder on the Western Circuit, in contrast to their worries over Antony, George Abraham and Anne were very proud of their two elder sons' success.

A few weeks later tragedy struck the family again. At the beginning of March, while on a visit to the Townley-Wards with the children, Dolly's one-year old son, called George Abraham after his grandfather, suddenly became ill and died. He was buried in Layton in Essex.[39] For Dolly, the loss of her little son caused her much greater distress than she could ever have imagined. On her return to Exeter a few days after the funeral, the family were relieved that she seemed to be bearing up for the sake of the other children and she kept herself busy responding to letters of condolence from friends and family, knowing that Antony was expected in home at the end of the April. When she learned that he was to remain in Spain for several more months, she once again became very depressed. Worried at her mental state, her father-in-law arranged for her to see a physician who prescribed laudnam to relieve her symptoms.

Despite the fact that the previous year had seen a number of business failures in Exeter, and the impending threat to his own position, George Abraham remained confident that his son would sort things out. A few weeks before, he had written to George with the news of a recent failure that had caused shockwaves throughout the city. The well-known and long established firm of Cuiller & Sons had gone down with over £20,000 of debts, having always been considered one of the most successful businesses in Exeter. He took some satisfaction that the general feeling in the city was that the economic climate was not the cause. Fellow tuckers, he wrote, believed that it was old man Cuiller's profligate sons who were guilty, 'especially the oldest one', who a few months before had married 'an innocent young woman of twenty & of a small fortune'.

Antony's repeated assurances that he was achieving some success in Spain gave them some confidence, but by mid May, the truth was finally dawning on George Abraham that he and his family were ruined. The loan to Duccarell remained unpaid and the banks and other creditors were starting bankruptcy proceedings against him. As a trader, the law allowed him to escape prison by declaring himself bankrupt, rather than becoming an insolvent debtor, which could mean indefinite imprisonment.[40] At the end of June, a Commission of Bankruptcy was appointed to deal with his affairs and to see if he could legally discharge his debts. Fortunately, it comprised his old friends Dr Hugh Downham, John Jeffrey Short, and John Coddrington, a surgeon apothecary at the hospital. They were sympathetic for his plight knowing that he was an old man and an innocent victim in the family's ruin.

The truth could not be hidden. On 16 July 1789, two notices were published in the *Exeter Trewman's Flying Post*, one referring to George Abraham and the other to Antony. The first read:

> 'All persons having any demands on MR. GEORGE
> ABRAHAM GIBBS of the City of Exeter, Merchant,
> are desired to send the Particulars thereof to Dr. Hugh
> Downham, John Jeffrey Short, Esq., and Mr. John
> Coddrington, all of Exeter, or one of them; and all
> Persons indebted to the said GEORGE ABRAHAM
> GIBBS, are thereby required to pay their respective

Debts to the said Messrs Downham, Short and
Coddrington, who are legally authorised to receive
the same, or to one of them otherwise they will be
prosecuted without further NOTICE'.[41]

The family was devastated and humiliated. George Abraham had
invested all his savings into Antony's business ventures, naively confident of success. It soon became clear that it was going to take the
commissioners several months to finalise his affairs and negotiate with
creditors, but early estimates indicated that their combined debts were
well in excess of £22,000, about £800,000 in modern terms.

As news of their failure spread amongst the tuckers and woollen merchants in Exeter many, knowing Antony as they did, were not surprised.
For months, it had been the gossip in the coffee shops and drawing
rooms throughout the city. Now bankrupt, George Abraham withdrew
from public life, retreating to Clyst St George with his family. Since
his retirement, he had been regularly attending the quarterly meetings
of the General Court of Governors and had continued to make an
annual subscription to the hospital charity. Although blameless in his
ruin, he felt obliged to tender his resignation. He remained at Pytte
while the commissioners began to sort out his affairs.

Hearing of his father's plight, George dropped everything and
travelled from Bristol. Aided by Vicary and his brother-in-law Charles
Crawley he began working with Granger and Samuel Banfill, an em-
ployee and old friend of Antony's, to unravel the accounts. Everyone
was anxious to keep the firm going until Antony returned, in case he
had managed to raise sufficient funds to pay off their debts. As partners
in the business, Granger and Banfill, like George Abraham and Antony,
now jointly owned a significant share of the firm's assets, including
Exwick Barton. Granger offered to turn them over to the administrators
if they would agree to authorise the banks to release sufficient funds to
pay off Duccarell. They agreed, anxious to prevent the business going
into liquidation until Antony's return, and Granger paid Duccarell
£1000 on account.[42] Vicary and George persuaded the commissioners

that as their father was an old man with considerable assets everything should be done to 'prevent the Expense and trouble of putting the said Commission into Execution'. It was agreed that if he would 'convey, assign and make over all his real and Personal Estate and Effects whatsoever', including his beloved Pytte, and his share of the 'very considerable Stock in Trade and Sundry Debts' of the firm to them, his creditors would release him from all his debts.[43]

Eventually at the end of July, Antony arrived home. After meetings with his family and commissioners, it was agreed that he should continue trading until he had discharged his debts. He planned to return to Spain to establish an agency business importing British textiles into the Iberian Peninsula, and Granger offered to pay off his creditors if Antony agreed to act as the Exeter firm's agent on the understanding that any commission earned was to be offset against his debts. Although his parents were distressed that they might not see their son and his family for many years, they knew he had no alternative. They were deeply saddened when, two weeks later, Antony took his family to Topsham and boarded a vessel bound for La Corunna. Following their departure a letter arrived for George Abraham, which read:

> 'I cannot my dear Sir, go away without saying noth-
> ing to you, tho' I have no excuse to make for my
> conduct. I most sincerely hope that what has now
> passed, tho it may make some people think it im-
> possible I should feel towards you and my dearest
> mother, the affection that I ought... I have deceived
> no one more than myself and it has been fom too
> anxious a desire to keep from my friends what
> I know would distress them, that I have brought
> upon them and myself ten times more than was
> necessary or possible, if I had concealed nothing...
> and whatever be the term of my life the whole of my
> debts are paid...'.

Distressed at his son's letter, he and Anne wondered whether they would ever see Antony again. They gratefully accepted an invitation from Charles to go to Northamptonshire with their daughters for the summer while the commissioners unravelled the firm's financial records. The Crawleys had left Clyst St George the previous year, moving to Stowe Nine Churches in Northamptonshire after Charles had inherited a living and a legacy from his uncle, a Dr. John Lloyd. A few days later George Abraham and his family travelled to Stowe where they were to spend several months.

The commissioners estimated that George Abraham's debts amounted to £15,000 but the value of his share of the business had halved and was now worth around £5861. As Granger wished to keep the firm going at all costs, the commissioners agreed that he could buy his partner's share, and once the debt was repaid, it would revert to Antony. This effectively reduced George Abraham's debts to around £9000. As news of the full extent of his problems spread, immediate family members including his daughters, Nancy, Kitty and Bell, and his sons-in-law Charles Crawley and Robert Remmett sent what they could afford. Edward Addicot and William Pittfield, his old colleagues at the hospital, and a number of grateful patients rallied round with loans. With his niece's and nephews' agreement, he conveyed all the properties that he had held in the trust fund for them since 1786, to be sold. Betsy, William, Abraham and young Thomas willingly agreed to forego their inheritance to help their uncle. However, as the months went by only £6100 was raised, and it became inevitable that he would have to give up his beloved Pytte to meet the shortfall. On 23 June 1790 in an agreement between the commissioners, George Abraham, Vicary and Kenny and the trustees of their marriage contract (to which George Abraham still owed £1500), and Charles Crawley, it was agreed that Pytte and all the lands in Clyst St. George should be sold 'by public sale or private contract'. On 17 September 1790, the following advertisement appeared in The *New Exeter Journal,*

To be sold – The Fee Simple and Inheritance of the
FOLLOWING LANDS

Lot 1. All the CAPITAL MESSUAGE, FARM AND
LANDS called PEYTT, LEACHES LAND,
COURT PLACE and PASKEY HOUSE, situate in
the parish of Clyst St George in the County of
Devon Consisting of a convenient Dwelling-House,
Courtlage, Garden, Stable, Coach House, and
Outbuildings, detached from the Farm House;
and about five Acres of Pasture-Ground, late in the
possession of Mr. George Abraham Gibbs – and of
a good Farm-House and all necessary Outhouses;
and about 90 Acres of Land, in the Occupation of
Robert Nex, at the yearly Rent of £105 15s – also
those Two Cottages at Clyst St George aforesaid,
one of them lett to James Rutter, as Tenant at Will
at the yearly Rent of £.1 17s. And the other leased,
for Three lives to Antony Nex, and of the yearly
Value of about 5£.

Lot 2. All that Overland, Tenement, situate in Clyst St
Mary, in the County of Devon; consisting of about
15 Acres of Land, in the Occupation of William
Matthews, as Tenant at Will, at the yearly Rent of
15£.[44]

The auction took place on 9 October 1789 at the Globe Tavern in
Exeter. A reserve of £3500 was put on the whole estate, but the highest
bid was only £2,600, which all the parties refused to countenance, so
it remained unsold.

Whilst George Abraham and his family were at Stowe, a letter
arrived from Antony telling them that he and Dolly had arrived safely
at La Corunna. His son's letter was full of hope and optimism for the
future, lifting his father's spirits. A few days after the failed auction,

they set out on the coach to Devon. Although his affairs remained unsettled, he had recovered from the shock of the last few months sufficiently to be able to face his friends and wider family. He and Anne were extremely grateful to their daughter and son-in-law for their kindness and understanding at such a difficult time. Arriving back in Exeter in mid-October, now supported by Vicary, he and Anne moved back into their house in Palace Gate. He wrote to thank Charles, 'with Whom we have spent the summer in so much comfort that we can never forget your kind and effectionate [sic] attention which so greatly contributed to promote it'. Ruined and homeless, the family moved into their old house in Palace Gate, completely dependent on Vicary and George for financial support. With no hope of a dowry, it seemed that Nancy, Bell and Kitty would have to give up all hope of marriage.

On his return, George Abraham was dismayed to find that Samuel Banfill, now in partnership with Granger was living in Exwick House. Within days, Banfill offered Nancy, who was then aged thirty-nine, the position of housekeeper. George Abraham felt bitter that she should be reduced to this, believing Banfill was taking advantage of Antony's misfortune. Nancy was much more pragmatic and graciously accepted the position. Within days, she had moved into Exwick, leaving her younger sisters, Bell and Kitty at home with their parents. Although there seemed little chance of them finding husbands, George Abraham retained hopes for Bell. Some years previously, it was thought that she and her cousin, Lyle, John's son, had 'an understanding'. Lyle, having been apprenticed some years before in Genoa, was expected to return to England within the next few years. However, that was not to be and Bell waited in vain. With the onset of war in 1796, Lyle chose to remain in Italy and Bell accepted she would never marry. Kitty on the other hand, was twenty-two at the time of her parents financial ruin and resented her reduced circumstances. After Sarah's death some years before, she was the youngest child, becoming spoilt and rebellious. As Nancy noted some years later, throughout her life Kitty 'showed the greatest dislike of her father and mother which must have been born with her'.

In November, the mail brought a long letter from Antony with the news that he and his family were living in Madrid. Although worried to learn that his son had 'been obliged….to take up of Granger and Banfill Three hundred pounds besides the £150 I had of George', he was relieved that Antony was confident that he had already taken steps to establish his agency business. 'I have every reason', he wrote, 'to think that next year my gains will be more considerable & you may depend on my remitting you something to account of the immense sum I owe you before the end of the next year'[45]. Although delighted at the news, George Abraham warned that Antony should be cautious in all his dealings as he was not in the position 'to make any doubtful and hazardous speculations, however tempting they may appear'.

The family looked forward to Antony's letters. In mid-June, they received word that Dolly had given birth a few weeks before to a son whom they called William. It had been a difficult pregnancy and birth and she was taking a long time to recover. Antony also told of some difficulties they were having with Betsy, stating that he was arranging for her to return to England in July. Angry at his niece's attitude, George Abraham replied that he believed 'EG's behaviour' towards his family stemmed from resentment after he had insisted she end her engagement. She 'hardly seemed obliged by the trouble I took to extract her from the mortifying situation into which she had brought herself'. He vowed never to help her again. 'She is old enough to manage herself' he wrote, 'and if not, I am certainly much too old to manage her'. The best thing she could do on her return to England was to 'fix herself upon some good lady who wants a companion to fetch and carry for her, to which Betsy's talents are admirably adapted'.

It was a great relief, when towards the end of July, a letter dated 24 June arrived telling them that 'Dolly recovers strength, tho' slowly & in such very hot weather as we have here, it was not expected that she should recover fast'. Antony wrote that on returning home after a long spell travelling around Spain, he found that Betsy and Dolly were barely speaking to each other. George Abraham was furious. For him, family loyalty always came first. He resolved that on her return to Exeter he would have nothing more to do with her.

Despite his anger, he was pleased that Antony had secured a contract with a Manchester firm. With war on the horizon, both he and Anne had been concerned for his safety, but Antony assured them that he thought that it would only last a short time. He confidently estimated that his earnings over the next twelve months should exceed £900; he expected to achieve over £20,000 of business yielding a £500 profit, but added the caveat that if there was a prolonged war in Europe, he 'could not bear the expense of it' and his income 'must necessarily be very much reduced'. Antony was still very worried about Dolly's health; she still found the heat very difficult, but if things went to plan and trade continued at the present level for the next twelve months, he should be able to bring his family back to England.

As 1790 dawned, the threat of bankruptcy was still hanging over the family. The estate in Clyst St. George was still unsold but George and Vicary had managed to persuade the administrators to give them more time to see if they could raise the funds to cover their father's debts. In March, Charles Crawley offered to buy the estate and two months later purchased it by private treaty. It is not clear whether Crawley really wanted Pytte or whether he bought it out of affection for his wife and her family. Mary loved the old house where she had spent her child-hood, and where she and Charles had spent the first few years of their marriage. Although now settled in Stowe it is unclear whether they ever planned to return to Devon. They had many happy memories of Pytte; their first three children had been born there and they wanted Mary's parents to use it as their country house. George Abraham was overwhelmed at his son-in-law's generosity. He wrote 'Our thoughts & feelings are the same with yours & we find ourselves equally inca-pable of expressing them'. After the sale, a letter arrived from Charles telling him that the family could use the house whenever they wished. George Abraham told George, 'I have received a very kind letter from Mr Crawley in which he expresses his consideration for us in the purchase of the estate…and that any place that is the habitation of his family would be agreeable to us. Antony too was delighted that Pytte was to remain in the Gibbs family. The guilt that he felt at his parents' plight was profound, and now the Crawleys owned the estate it would continue to '… contribute to the comfort of many branches of the family'. Although now living in Palace Gate supported by Vicary, George Abraham and Anne could now visit Pytte with their daughters whenever they wished and for the next few years, they continued to live quietly, visiting family in Bristol, Plymouth, Stowe and London.

* * * *

Although the proceeds from the sale of Pytte were insufficient to cover all their debts, Antony remained optimistic about his prospects in Spain, confident that they would quickly be discharged. George Abraham was more cautious knowing that his son's natural optimism often blinded him to reality. In May, he wrote urging Antony to consult George before taking any unnecessary risks. It was several weeks before he received a reply, which made him feel very guilty. 'I am sensible', Antony wrote, 'that it would be to me the greatest possible advantage and comfort if I could adopt those parts of his [George's] character and conduct in which no one is more convinced than myself that I have been deficient or knows more fatal consequences of that deficiency'. He knew that he could never attain 'the same excellence in those points which George possesses'. George Abraham, anxious to reassure his youngest son that he was not comparing the two brothers, replied on the 29 July that 'George is a great example and I know nowhere a better character than his. But you will consider that he began it right and had the advantage of an excellent master, and has been in the practice of regularity these 20 years'. He understood that 'two men may have equal merit in this respect and yet not be exact copies of each other. I believe one of the best general rules is to cultivate the habit in all transactions of life, little as well as great, for there is such a mutual connection and dependence in human actions that you can hardly do anything well or ill habitually which does not in some way lead to doing others after the same manner'.

For the next twelve months, as civil unrest worsened in France, the family waited anxiously for news. To their relief in the autumn they learned that Antony had decided to bring his family back to England the following spring. After Christmas, they received word that as Dolly could not face the sea passage, they were planning to travel overland across France. In May 1792, they heard that they were due to leave Madrid in early June, and if all went to plan, would arrive in July. Mary had invited her parents to spend the summer at Stowe, and it was agreed that Antony and Dolly would meet them there on their return to England. At the beginning of June, George Abraham and Anne left Exeter but were forced to break their journey in Bristol. The last few years had taken their toll and he had become very frail. Now nearing seventy, he found the journey too arduous, arriving in Bristol completely exhausted. Dismayed that he might not be able to go on to Stowe, George Abraham tried to write to Antony, but was too weak to hold a pen.

Some weeks later they received word that Antony's departure had been further delayed. Dolly had been unwell and William had contracted smallpox. He had been so ill that they thought they would lose him, but had now recovered and had 'entirely lost the fever as well as the ague'. Dolly too was now much better 'having received considerable benefit from a course of opium prescribed by a young physician who had studied at Edinburgh'; they were leaving Madrid within the week. By the beginning of July, George Abraham had recovered his strength sufficiently to write to allay Antony's concerns about his health. 'At seventy years of age' he wrote, he was grateful that he had 'very few of the infirmities which generally accompany that time of life. But I must have been unreasonable and childish to the last degree to have expected any long continuance of health, my constitution being naturally far from strong.....I am free from any painful distemper and, I thank God, the complaints in my stomach are ...much less...than they were...'.

George Abraham and Anne remained in Bristol for several weeks until he felt strong enough to go on to Stowe, but they were to be disappointed again. While there, another letter arrived from Cadiz with the news that Antony had been forced to delay his departure again because he had managed to secure a 7-year Government contract worth £150 a year. 'If I lose it now', he wrote, 'I shall never have a chance of getting it again or at least until seven years are over'. At the end of August, they were overjoyed to hear that Antony and Dolly had arrived safely in England with their children and were staying with the Townley-Wards for a few days. George Abraham immediately put pen to paper to let Antony know that their plans were '...subject to the main object of spending as much time with you as we can during your short residence in England...'. He and Anne travelled to Stowe to await their arrival. Antony and Dolly finally arrived there in September. Although the Crawleys would have liked them to stay for several weeks, after a few days Antony was impatient to get back to Devon. He could ill-afford to remain in England a day longer than necessary for as soon as his family was settled, he was bent on returning to Madrid. The two families set off together on the long journey to Devon, but as George Abraham was soon exhausted, he and Anne decided to rest at Redland while Antony and Dolly continued on to Exeter.

There, George Abraham took to his bed, and it was several days before he felt well enough to sit in a chair. As the date for Antony's departure drew near, he became agitated that he was too weak to write, so he asked George to send him a note explaining why, after a lifetime of daily correspondence between them, he was unable to write. Antony, who had been increasingly concerned at not hearing from his father, suggested that either Kitty or Bell could 'be your clerks'. George Abraham knew that once he had returned to Spain, he would probably never see him again. There was no doubt that Antony was closer to his father than his elder brothers, and despite his failings George Abraham was determined to absolve him from all blame for the family's ruin. As he was due to leave on 30 October, George Abraham summoned all his strength to put pen to paper knowing it might be his last opportunity and he 'was not able to express from the weakness and pain that I feel in writing'. He wrote,

'I have felt myself so dissatisfied with the kind of letter which you have received from me, and I cannot help saying however unnecessary you may think it, that my mind was not so full of the idea of your doing justice to them as to exclude consideration of another and tenderer nature. We have always felt what is dear to your excellent wife and your dear little children and I think that making a decent and comfortable provision for them ought to go hand in hand with any other object that you may have in view. The prospect too of an exemption for yourself from the drudgery you have endured (and must still endure), which you shall be in circumstances to take and regulate situations in your own country and be able to chase your own company. These things, if it please God to give you health and success, some of your family may live to see realized; for your dear mother and myself, it is enough that we are happy in the idea and probability of them. So now I shall conclude my supplement, with the most affectionate wishes for your good voyages and all other Good things, in which your dearest mother and all here wish.

My dearest Ant^{ny}

Your most affec^t father

   GAG

The following week George Abraham had recovered sufficiently and, determined to see Antony before he left, decided to make the arduous coach journey to Exeter, arriving there the day before his departure. The following morning they said their sad farewells, but despite Antony's assurances that he would be back in the spring, both men must have feared that this would be their final farewell.

His son was to return sooner than anyone imagined. The following

March, news reached Exeter that Antony had been involved in a serious accident and was critically ill. He had been traveling in a postilion with his friend John Head, when the horses bolted, throwing him under the wheel of the carriage. He had severe head injuries and his right arm had been crushed. Had it not been for Head's prompt action, Antony would not have survived. The family waited anxiously for news, but it was to be several months before he was well enough to return to England. Arriving in Exeter at the end of August, they were shocked by his appearance. Although his facial scars had healed, he looked gaunt and had still not regained the use of his arm.

By 1793, George Abraham's health was failing fast. In October, Head, who had returned to England, came to Exeter to see Antony, staying at Exwick House where he dined with the Banfills and the Grangers. In gratitude for his prompt action in saving Antony's life, the Gibbs invited him to dinner at Palace Gate with Mrs Hucks and her two sons John and Joseph, but when Head arrived, George Abraham was too ill to make an appearance.

By the spring of 1794, Antony was making plans to return to the Iberian Peninsula. Although George Abraham admired his determination to make amends, it was with a heavy heart that in early August he said goodbye once again. Within days, his health deteriorated and he took to his bed, but never recovered. He died three months later on 10 November 1794 at the age of seventy-six. Two days later, the *Trewman's Exeter Flying Post* reported that 'Sunday last died in an advanced age, at his house in this city, Mr. Gibbs, formerly a respected surgeon of this city, but who for some years past retired from the business.'[46] The following week, on a cold November day, the family gathered at Clyst St. George and George Abraham was buried in the little churchyard only half a mile from Pytte. After the funeral, Vicary, who had been unable to attend, suggested that a memorial stained glass window was put in the church; the tablet underneath read:

> To His Honour to whom be Glory forever. This
> window is dedicated in memory of George Abraham

Gibbs of Pytt, [sic] who was buried near this place,
November 17, 1794[47]

After her husband's death, Anne continued to live at Palace Gate with Kitty and Bell, completely dependent on Vicary for support. It gave her great joy when two years later Nancy, who had been Banfill's housekeeper at Exwick House for some years, married her employer in Exeter Cathedral. Although Kitty continued to be very bitter at her situation, Anne's life was relatively peaceful. For the next few years, much of her time was spent visiting her children and grandchildren and with Antony now living permanently abroad, she and Dolly remained very close.

As the century drew to a close Anne's strength began to fail, and for the next three years she was nursed by Bell and a very resentful Kitty. She died on 11th August 1803 and was buried near her husband in the churchyard at Clyst St. George.

CHAPTER 4

VICARY

Vicary, George Abraham's first surviving son was born in October 1751 and baptised at the Mint Meeting the following month.[1] He attended the Exeter Grammar School and such was his ability that in 1764 he became a Kings Scholar at Eton College. Although proud of their eldest son, his parents must have given serious consideration as to whether Vicary should go away to school where he would no longer be under their strict Presbyterian supervision. Despite his obvious ability, George Abraham remained unconvinced that public school was the right place because his son would 'in his life be exposed to a variety of temptations' and such places were 'not conducive to good manners'.

Vicary left Eton in 1771, going on to Kings College, Cambridge where he became a Craven Scholar. In 1774, a year before matriculation, he was elected a fellow of the university. A notable classisist, he excelled at both Eton and Cambridge, and at the latter had 'greatly distinguished himself as a Greek scholar', graduating with a BA in 1776 and an MA in 1778. Vicary remained a fellow until his marriage. He had always planned to enter the legal profession and in 1769, before going on to university, had enrolled as a student at Lincoln's Inn. After completing his pupilage, he practiced for ten years as a special pleader drawing up pleadings and attending to judges in chambers. Called to the Bar in February 1783, Vicary joined the western circuit and before long had 'an extensive connection of clients, and was soon looked upon in the profession as one of the soundest lawyers and most useful junior of the day'[2].

Despite his ability and unquestionable intelligence, coming as he did from a relatively modest background and with no fortune, he had few of the prerequisites for success. Nor did his appearance help; a small man of around '5 feet 4 inches in height, and of meager frame', he had a 'shrill, sharp, and unmusical' voice.[3] Although devoted to his family and with an 'undergrowth of kindly feelings'[4], his public persona was rigid and discourteous, later earning him the name of 'Sir Vinegar Gibbs' through the 'acidity of his temper and the sourness of his language, which spared neither litigants, barristers nor criminals'.

During his time at Eton, Vicary formed 'friendships with several noble and eminent men that lasted till the end of his life'. One of his favourite relaxations was the theatre where he had 'an extensive familiarity with almost every line of Shakespeare'.[5] In his social life he 'shone, and they who partook of it were loud in their declaration of the charms he imported to it. A lifelong Tory, Vicary's friends from 'both sides of politics bear witness to his virtues, his high religious feelings, his honourable principles, his goodness of heart, and the kindness of his disposition, notwithstanding occasional irritabilities of temper'.[6]

Vicary, like the rest of his family was enchanted by Dolly. Her elder sister Eleanor had married his friend Henry Townley-Ward. Despite his hopes of something more, Dolly was more attracted to his younger brother Abraham. In 1792, she was staying at Clyst St George when suddenly Abraham became seriously ill and died a few days later. Dolly was devastated but for Vicary who had long admired her, it was an opportunity to make his feelings known. In June, after what he thought was a decent period of mourning, with the support of his family he wrote to Dolly to let her know of his feelings. 'Nanny [his oldest sister Elizabeth] and you and Mary [his youngest sister] are the most dearest persons in the world to me....you know how much we are interested for you'. However, before she could respond her father became seriously ill and she hastened to Yorkshire with no time to consider his offer. After her father's death, Dolly returned to Devon and stayed with his parents at Pytte.

Whether she took Vicary's intentions seriously or whether there was any formal attachment between them is unclear, but in January 1783, he learned that she and Antony were engaged. Vicary, who was living in London at the time, was very dejected to hear the news and wrote to her, 'I shall leave you to collect my opinion from my behaviour', adding 'only that this circumstance, though it cannot add to my regard for you, will I hope afford me now frequent opportunities of showing it'. Not one to allow this to cause a rift in the family he accepted the situation, continuing to concentrate on his career and being called to the bar the following month. It was a great relief to Antony when she and Vicary were 'sociable again as usual' for 'after you he has my first claim to friendship; you may suppose how anxious I must be for you to remain always on the best of terms together'.

The following year, on 8 July 1784, he married Frances Cerjat, the daughter of Major William Mackenzie in London. Frances (known affectionately as Kenny) was from a well-connected family. Her brother was a friend of George, and was later to become Lord Seaforth and Governor of Barbados. On his marriage, Vicary was required to surrender his fellowship, but for a man with no family pedigree or fortune there were other advantages, namely a sizeable dowry, Kenny having been left £2000 by her late brother Frederick Mackenzie Humberstone. On their engagement, the legacy was put in trust and it was agreed that after their marriage £500 was to be paid to Vicary and the remaining £1500 was to be invested 'in such landed or other security as s^d Vicary Gibbs and his wife' should agree.[7] A year after his marriage a daughter, Maria Elizabeth was born to them. She was to be their only child.

Aware of his good fortune and the gratitude he owed his parents, Vicary was always willing to use his influence to help his family. Antony, who was now married, had recently gone into business with his father and Edmund Granger, and had leased a mill in Exwick. Unable to raise the funds to buy the adjoining house, Antony approached Vicary for a £3000 loan, which was refused. Instead, Vicary agreed to raise a mortgage on his marriage settlement and he purchased the estate outright. On 5 August, he bought by 'Bargain and Sale' the freehold estate of Exwick Barton for £3000 and put it in trust for Antony on a long lease. He considered it a good investment. Not only did the 'barton' have a substantial family house for his brother's growing family, but there were also a number of cottages and small farms on the estate, whose rents yielded a good income.

Vicary's activities on the western circuit enabled him to visit his family when he appeared at the assizes in Exeter, held at the guildhall and session-house twice a year. With his ability, 'superior knowledge, [and] the fame which preceded him', he soon proved himself as a circuit judge and in Westminster Hall. He and Kenny visited Exeter every summer for at least two months staying either with his parents at Clyst St. George or at Exwick House. Despite his growing fame, he was keen to retain his links with the south-west and continued to support a number of local charities and institutions, including a subscription to the Devon and Exeter Hospital and attending the anniversary dinners for past pupils of the grammar school.[8]

It was with some consternation in January 1787, when he first learned of Antony's business difficulties. The Exeter firm was in dire financial straits and needed an injection of capital to keep it afloat. As neither his brother nor his father had any further funds to invest, Vicary reluctantly agreed to transfer Exwick Barton to the firm's assets to prevent it from sliding into bankruptcy. In a deed dated 8 August 1787, he transferred his 'properties in Exwick purchased in Trust' for Antony to the firm of Gibbs Granger & Banfill so that it 'be considered as part of the joint stock & at the end or other determination of the said Copartnership be divided and possessed accordingly' by the four partners of the Exeter firm.[9]

For the next year, he continued to be very worried that his family might face bankruptcy. There was the added anxiety at the impact this would have on his career. A few weeks after Antony's departure for Spain in August 1788 to generate new business, his father confided in him that he and Granger had been forced to take out a large loan to keep the firm going. Despite any misgivings Vicary may have had, the news from Spain continued to be optimistic and like the rest of the family, he could do little but wait. Some weeks later, his father asked if he could use Pytte as security and borrow £1500 from his marriage settlement and despite any reservations he and Kenny had, they agreed.[10] In spite of Vicary's fears, it was a great shock the following July to hear that bankruptcy proceedings had been instigated against his father and brother. Worried at the effect that financial ruin would have on their parents, he and George began to work with the appointed commissioners to try to untangle their father's affairs.

On Antony's return from Spain in July 1789, it was agreed that the only course open for him was to return there with his family to establish an agency business and work to discharge his debts. As his father been forced to turn all his assets over to the commissioners and was now homeless, with his lucrative work on the western circuit Vicary was in a position to support them financially. He moved his parents and sisters back into their house in Palace Gate where he paid the rent and gave them a small allowance to live on.

A few weeks later, he was incensed to learn that Samuel Banfill had taken advantage of his family's misfortune and moved into Exwick House. Banfill had been taken on as a penniless clerk and although Vicary believed he was an able man, he thought that he was 'not of an amiable disposition', and had never warmed to him, finding him somewhat pompous and uncompromising. 'Self-conceit and obstinacy will always be in his way' Vicary wrote of him and at times his 'affectation and tiffiness are worse than ever'. It was the final straw when Banfill offered Nancy a job as housekeeper and he strongly advised her to refuse the position. Despite his objections, he was forced to concede that with Nancy working at living at Exwick House, the costs of supporting his family were significantly reduced.

It was to be many months before the commissioners had finally sorted out his father's finances. Meanwhile, Vicary and George set about contacting friends and family to try to raise sufficient money to avert financial ruin. Despite their generosity, there was a significant shortfall and it was soon obvious that Pytte would have to be sold to try to cover his father's debts. As Vicary was the eldest son, the commissioners gave him the first option to purchase Pytte, as it was his rightful inheritance. Initially he considered buying it to keep it in the family and 'to accelerate the winding-up of my father's affairs', but having spent £3000 two years before on Exwick Barton, had not sufficient funds to pay the market price. Nevertheless, he made a low offer that was not accepted and Pytte was put up for auction in October 1789 with a reserve of £3500, but only £2600 was bid and it was not sold.

The following spring, Crawley expressed an interest in buying Pytte, but before making a firm offer, asked Vicary if wanted to take up his option again. Although he had made the offer the previous year to keep Pytte in the family, Vicary had no real wish to return to Devon, seeing his future in London. He and Kenny had also recently purchased an estate at Hayes Common in Kent.[11] On 2 April 1790, he wrote to Crawley that he was 'obliged to you for leaving me the option of purchasing my father's Estate at George's Clyst...the trustees may finally resolve to dispose of it, but I had determined not to go beyond the sum I bid for it in the first instance'. Knowing that his parents' affairs would be concluded if the estate were sold, he was naturally anxious to help Crawley raise the money. He told him that 'if the trustees lower their price I understand they will offer it to me before any other person by which means I may assist you, if you wish to be the Puchaser at such reduced price. In that case part of the money settled on your wife and children, say £2000 may be advanced to the Trustees of your Marriage Settlement on a mortgage of the Estate'. Vicary offered to raise the balance on a mortgage. Later that month, Crawley reached an agreement with the commissioners to purchase Pytte by private treaty for £3250. This still left the £1500 that George Abraham had borrowed two years before still owing to Vicary and Kenny's marriage settlement. After discussions with the trustees and the commissioners dealing with his father's affairs, they reached a compromise to the satisfaction of all parties. The outstanding £1500 should, 'remain & continue on the security of the same premises with the collateral security of the Bond of the s^d Charles Crawley which he had accordingly executed & that the other lands comprised in the s^d recited Mortgage should be exonerated from the Bond'[12]. As Crawley did not have sufficient funds to repay the £1500 to the trust after purchasing Pytte, the commissioners agreed that it could 'remain due on the s^d security ' and 'should be considered as part paym^t of the s^d purchase money of £3250'. Crawley undertook to repay Vicary within two years and the commissioners accepted that the £3250 paid for the house included the outstanding £1500.

With his father's affairs now concluded, Vicary could concentrate on his career. In 1793, he returned to Exeter to defend the Rev. William Winterbotham, who was accused of using seditious language in two sermons in Plymouth. In the first, on the double anniversary of the gunpowder plot, Winterbotham had applauded the French Revolution and criticised the abuses in British monarchy. This aroused so much local antagonism that he was prosecuted and brought to Exeter for a two-day trial the following July. *Woolmer's Exeter and Plymouth Gazette* reported that 'Mr Gibbs pleaded very ably for the defendant and several persons from Plymouth and Dock endeavoured to confute the accusations brought against him'.[13] Despite Vicary's efforts, Winterbotham was found guilty on both counts and sentenced to two years imprisonment with a £100 fine for each sermon.

The following February, Vicary was appointed as Recorder in Bristol with an honorarium of fifty guineas a year and there he continued to instill terror into all who appeared before him. One unfortunate declared that 'Gibbs nose would remove iron-moulds from linen'.[14] Another contemporary wrote of him, that despite being '… a skilful special pleader and an acute and learned lawyer……he is wholly destitute of humour and possessed of so caustic and bitter a manner…. Confident of his own legal strength he was equally uncivil and outspoken to his own clients' and although he was 'somewhat narrow minded and impatient on the Bench…. was a thoroughly conscientious judge….'.[15]

Vicary's loss of the Winterbotham case seems to have done his career little harm. There had previously been calls for parliamentary reform but the French Revolution gave the movement renewed impetus. Initially Pitt's government considered the revolution a domestic issue, that would have little impact at home, but as news of the events in France swept Britain, there were fears that revolution would spread across the channel. Parliamentary reform groups sprang up all over the country causing government concern at the influence of French revolutionaries. On 1 February 1793, France declared war on Britain. In May, the House of Commons passed Pitt's bill to suspend Habeas Corpus and issued a proclamation against seditious writings. Later that year twelve supporters of parliamentary reform were imprisoned, to be tried for high treason as the government attempted to revive the principles of constructive treason. Among those arrested were the celebrated philogist John Horne Tooke, John Thewall, and Thomas Hardy a shoemaker and Secretary of the London Corresponding Society. Although he had lost the Winterbotham case, Vicary's performance had so impressed Tooke that he recommended him as junior counsel to Erskine who was acting for them.[16] Hardy was acquitted but the government was determined to indict Tooke and Thewall. The trial lasted for six days but the prosecution failed to procure a conviction, the jury taking only eight minutes to settle their verdict. The three were acquitted without any evidence being offered against them, it was thought mainly by Erskine's eloquence and Vicary's summation of the evidence. That too proved to be a dramatic occurrence. As Vicary rose to address the jury on Hardy's behalf he appeared overcome at the occasion, and 'fainted away'.[17] It was reported that 'After he had somewhat recovered himself, he turned about suddenly, and bursting into tears, assured the jury that it was his anxiety for the miserable man at the bar, his own consciousness of his inability to do him justice in his defence that he wished, that had overpowered him.'[18] Despite his emotional outburst, such was his performance that at the end of the trial, the losing prosecutor, the Attorney General Sir John Scott, passed him a note complimenting him on his knowledge and ability. 'I say from my heart', he wrote, 'that you did yourself great credit as a good man, and great credit as an excellent citizen, not sacrificing any valuable public principle; I say from my judgment that no lawyer ever did himself more credit or his client more service; so help me God!'[19]

After the trials, public gratitude for the services that Erskine and Vicary had rendered to the cause of constitutional liberty was manifested in a number of ways. As they were traveling home 'on the last night of the trials,' Erskine's 'horses were taken from his chariot, amidst bonfires and blazing flambeaux', and he 'was drawn home by the huzzaing populace to his house in Serjeant's Inn'. With Vicary at his side, he addressed the crowd from a window. 'Injured innocence still obtains protection from a British jury; and I am sure, in the honest effusions of your hearts, you will retire in peace, and Bless God'.[20] Coins and commemorative medals were struck in their honour, including one with the conjoined heads of Erskine and Vicary with, on the obverse side, the wording 'PATRIOTS WHO FOR SACRED FREEDOM STOOD'. For his part in the trials, Vicary received the thanks of the Friends of the People, but despite his success, he remained disconsolate. His father, who had been ill for some time, had died during the trial and he had been unable to return to Exeter to attend the funeral.

His spirits were lifted the following February when he was offered a parliamentary seat at the Duke of Marlborough's borough of Woodstock. Although flattered he declined, writing 'I am satisfied it would be impudent in me, in the present state of my business at the Bar, to embarrass myself from any association from it. I must therefore beg leave to decline the proposal'.[21] The following month he became Kings Counsel at the age of thirty-two.

Vicary was well aware of his growing fame and was now enjoying a lucrative practice on the circuit. Despite this, he did not forget his roots or the debt that he owed his family and he and Kenny spent several weeks each summer in Exeter and Exwick visiting his mother and sisters who were dependant upon him for all their needs. Two years after his father's death, he was annoyed to learn that Banfill and Nancy were to marry. Although feeling that she was marrying beneath her, he had to admit that Banfill had been far more successful in running the mill at Exwick than Antony could ever have been. Despite this, he still disapproved of the match, but for Nancy's sake, he and Kenny wrote warmly offering their congratulations and good wishes. 'They have both very good sense, and very good nature', he noted, 'though Nancy's understanding, from her having mixed with better and more various company, is more corrected and set off to better advantage than his'.

Vicary also remained close to his brother George and they met regularly while he was in Bristol. They also had a number of mutual friends including Lord Seaforth, the Governor of Barbados. Vicary continued to support Antony in a number of ways, especially after his accident in Spain in 1793. Aware of his own good fortune he generously provided financial assistance until his brother had recovered sufficiently to return to the Iberian Peninsula and used his influence to further Antony's business. After his return to Portugal, Vicary approached Lord St. Helens for a letter of recommendation for him to present to the consulate in Lisbon. St. Helens was a friend and distant relative by marriage to George, and had been appointed envoy at the British embassy in Madrid and had met Antony on a number of occasions. Vicary was delighted to report that he 'speaks in the highest terms of Antony and says all the people in the country respect and esteem him and his family in the greatest degree'.[22] Most importantly he saw it as his duty to shoulder the burden of maintaining his family, believing that 'these are times when we who can get money ought to assist our friends whose exertions are shut up by them and I can well afford [this] out of the profits of the circuit'.

Despite having turned down Pitt's offer of a seat in government a few months before, in November 1795 his career took on a political dimension, when through his friendship with judge James Mansfield, he was appointed solicitor general to the Prince of Wales, a post he held for five years before becoming attorney general in July 1800.[23] It was four years later, in February 1804 that the king used his influence to secure Vicary's appointment as chief justice of Chester, a position that was held with a seat in parliament. The Prince of Wales apparently commented on his appointment that 'he had forced Gibbs upon the indecision of the chancellor; that he was determined to bring him forward, because he was no party man, that he knew one or two factious men had been at him but they had not succeeded'.[24] In politics Vicary, a zealous Tory, was returned for Totnes two months after Pitt's return to power in May 1804. The following year he was knighted on 20 February.

CHAPTER 5

GEORGE

At the age of twelve, young George left the Grammar School and went on to the Exeter Academy.[1] This, the second non-conformist academy in Exeter, had opened in 1760 under Micaijah Towgood, one of the ministers at the St. George's Meeting. Its aim was to train young men 'for the ministry and other learned professions as well as for commercial life'. However, in its twelve-year span, only four of its forty-eight students went on to the ministry, most going into commerce.[2]

George was the only one of George Abraham's sons to receive a Presbyterian education. During his four years at the Academy, he would have studied biblical interpretation and Greek literature under Towgood, together with divinity, mathematics, bookkeeping, science, and all aspects of commerce. Leaving the Academy in 1769, at the age of sixteen he was destined for a future in trade. His father apprenticed him to a Bristol merchant house owned by Samuel Munckley who had been born in Exeter.

Samuel was the second son of Nicholas Munckley, a tucker and dissenting minister whose wife Elizabeth was the aunt of George Abraham's wife.[3] In 1738, Nicholas Munckley had died suddenly of 'a violent fever' leaving two young sons, Nicholas Jr. and Samuel. His widow married John Duntze, a Lutheran immigrant from Germany who had settled in the city, becoming a wealthy clothier. Duntze, who also had two sons by a previous marriage, took on the responsibility for bringing up Samuel and his elder brother Nicholas, proving to be a good father to his stepsons. Nicholas had inherited a considerable fortune and gone on to study medicine, eventually becoming physician to Guys Hospital in London. Young Samuel had no inheritance and in 1738, at the age of fourteen, was apprenticed to Richard Farr Jr. who, with his father and uncle, owned a rope-making firm in Bristol. The Farr's were a well-known Bristol family, having made their fortune in the African trade. They also had a number of business interests including a shipyard and dock at Bristol.[4] Richard Farr Jr. was a member of the Society of Merchant Venturers and in 1763 had been the mayor of the city. John Duntze provided the £300 bond money at the commencement of Samuel's apprenticeship.[5]

Having completed his apprenticeship in 1746, Munckley joined one of the largest firms of sugar merchants in Bristol. The colonial trade from the West Indies and the North American plantations had been growing rapidly since the sixteenth century, and such was his success that within a few years, he had purchased the *Culloden*, which traded in Africa and the American plantations and owned shares in a number of vessels including the *Nancy*, which sailed on the Bristol-Hamburg routes.[6] Although he invested in at least one slaving venture, it appears that this was his only direct involvement in the trade, and by the mid-1760s, Munckley was acting as broker for the planters in the West Indies.[7] Ten years later, he owned the *True Briton*, the *Clifton*, the *Snow Hope* and the *Blaize Castle*, all sailing between Bristol, Jamaica, and the American plantations, as well as trading directly with Ireland and Europe. His vessels left Bristol for the West Indies laden with a variety of goods for the colonies ranging from clothing, pots and pans and furniture to building materials and other essential items for the development of the plantations. Return cargoes consisted mainly of sugar and to a lesser extent, rum, cotton, ginger, tobacco, and rice, which were landed and warehoused, to be re-exported to the Continent. Other imports included butter and oats from Ireland, hemp, brandy and iron ore from northern Europe and the Baltic, and wines from the Mediterranean were shipped via Hamburg to Bristol for export to the colonies.

In 1768, Munckley became Master of the Society of Merchant

Venturers and when George began his apprenticeship the following year, he had significant business interests in the plantation trade in the Caribbean and the American mainland. He was living at 53 Queen Square 'whose most prominent residents were connected in a dense web of business and kinship interests either to the African trade or, increasingly as the century wore on, to the trade in slave-produced commodities'.[8]

It was in 1770 that Munckley's wealth received a greater boost when his brother Nicholas died leaving him the bulk of his fortune.[9] This inheritance enabled him to expand his business interests. He invested in the John Freeman and Copper Company, making copper wire and brassware for the African trade, pans for sugar making and copper nails and sheets for sheathing ships to protect them from the West African teredo worm.[10] Later that year, he went into partnership with fellow merchants Thomas Harford and Henry Bright in the Harford Bank, one of the first banks in Bristol, which was used by the majority of merchants involved in the African and West India trades. By that time, the African trade was already in decline, due in part to the American War of Independence. Four years later, Munckley resigned from the Harford Bank and the following year, became a partner in the Whitson Court Sugar House in Bristol, enabling him to further maximise his profits from the sugar trade.[11] He also acted as a broker for the other sugar merchants and the West Indies plantocracy. A member of the wealthy mercantile elite, Munckley was much-respected in the city. A staunch Presbyterian and a Whig, he was known as 'the 'Chancellor,' by his business associates and was consulted 'on almost all occasions as an arbitrator in disputes, being possessed of sound, unbiased judgement'.[12]

* * * *

George became part of this world when he arrived in Bristol in 1769 to start his seven-year apprenticeship. His father paid a £400 bond 'with the apprentice', who lived in Munckley's house in Queen Square.

Initially George appears to have been homesick. Life in Bristol was very different from that in Exeter, but when he voiced his feelings, he got short shrift from his father who lost no time in reminding him of his obligations, for

'…under the care of so virtuous and worthy a man as your master… his behaviour to you is so little like that of a …master that you will hardly know what it is to be an apprentice, unless which God forbid, your abuse of his indulgence should oblige him to alter it. But we promise ourselves a very different effect of your present happy situation, and that you will be induced to make every return of obedience and gratitude in your power by studiously attending to your master's inclinations, and pursuing every step which you have reason to think agreeable to him without waiting for his express directions. This is the kind of service the most liberal and pleasing to perform, as well as the most agreeable to receive – proceeding from a principle of duty and affection, however labourous [sic] it may be, it can never be irksome. Duty and interest rightly understood must be the same in all cases. But in the case of Master and Apprentice, they are so closely united that the apprentice… plainly sacrifices his own interests and must be a fool not to do so…The mind of a young person cannot be more profitably employed in resolving the principles of right action – such particularly are gratitude and affection for your master which have a strong influence in engaging the heart on the side of virtue. …[and George should not] …suffer this or any other visit to interfere with business or Mr. Munckley's inclinations to which you will always have to conform… .'.

Eventually George settled down to his new life. Living and working with Munckley was an education in itself and he soon grew to respect his mercantile ability. Despite this, there was continual pressure from his father to work hard and behave with integrity and honesty. George was expected to write to his parents every day giving a full account of his activities and he received a reply by return. Along with words of encouragement, in George Abraham's letters was the ever-present threat of criticism for failure. Even George's letters to his brothers and sisters were corrected. In one letter there were, 'two or three little faults ...one is that you make your sentences too long which necessarily introduces some degree of obscurity and you add to this fault by wrong punctuation'. In another, he was rebuked because 'in the 35 lines in your letter to Antony there is but one full stop'. George seems to have accepted his father's authority without question and quickly began to learn the business. Having him in the firm was an advantage for Munckley, who was able to further develop his network of family, relations and friends to expand his trade in the Mediterranean. George's younger brother, Abraham was in Genoa, and his uncle John was trading on the *Ceres* on the Baltic routes into Italy and Greece. In order to deal with the growing business, George was tasked with learning Italian.

In the year after completing his apprenticeship in 1776 at the age of twenty-two, he became a member of the Society of Merchant Venturers of Bristol, and was appointed to the Standing Committee, becoming junior warden the following year.[13] He remained with the firm which was renamed Samuel Munckley & Co and was situated in Princess Street (or Prince's Street as it was known) near the quay; the other associates in the business were the brothers James and Thomas Richards and Richard Twine, who were all experienced merchant mariners. Munckley had employed both Richards' brothers on the West India routes for some years. Twine had been master of the *Fox*, which in 1757 had been used as an emigrant and convict ship sailing between Bristol and Maryland. Ten years later, he captained the 120-ton *Greyhound*, an African slaver, which on one voyage carried 410 slaves to the West Indies, Munckley had invested in the voyage, which carried a return cargo of sugar and ginger from Barbados to Bristol.[14] By the time George joined the firm the Africa Trade had begun to decline, but its business was dependent on slave-produced commodities.[15]

In Bristol as in Exeter, ties of apprenticeship, religion and marriage were common for it was essential that younger sons make good marriages to boost their often-modest incomes. George, like Munckley was a committed Presbyterian, worshipping at the Lewins Mead Meeting in the city. The Meeting, which had been built in the 1690s, was also attended by many of the wealthy members of the local community, including slavers, bankers, ship owners and merchants who dominated the African and West Indies trade and who were linked by family and kinship. Amongst its worshippers were many of Munckley's friends and business associates including the Richards brothers, the sons of the Reverend William Richards, the Farrs and the Bright families.

There, George met Esther (known affectionately as Etty), the heiress daughter of Richard Farr Jr. George was twenty-three and Etty, seven years older. Her father was a wealthy and established merchant with long-standing slaving connections. The Farr family lived in a fine house in Prince's Street where their neighbours were also heavily involved in the African trade. Perhaps the most important consideration for George was that Etty had a substantial dowry, which would improve his prosperity and their marriage was invaluable in establishing him in business in Bristol's genteel society. Whether he truly loved her is unclear, but she possessed all the qualities that would make her an ideal wife. When he proposed she accepted and they married not long after he had completed his apprenticeship. The following September, Etty gave birth to a daughter, whom they called Joanna and who was followed a year later by a son, called George. However, the new baby, never strong, only survived a few months. Within a short time, Etty was pregnant again and on 27 December 1779, bore a second son who was again named George. Now with a growing family, George and Etty moved to a larger house in the more salubrious Orchard Street, a few minutes from his compting house in Lodge Street.

Whether it was due to his Presbyterian education is unclear, but George was the only member of the Gibbs family to retain his non-conformist beliefs for most of his life. On Sundays, he took his family to Lewins Mead where their friends assembled for the morning service and where they sat together for bible reading in the afternoon. In 1777, he was appointed as an assistant to the treasurer and he played an active role at the Meeting, both as a Deacon and as a member of the treasury committee, becoming treasurer two years later. It is likely that both Joanna and George Jr. were educated at Stokes Croft School, which had been founded in 1722 by the Meeting. Initially the school took up to thirty boys, from eight to fourteen years, and provided them with an all-round education, opening its doors to girls some years later. All prospective students were required to pass a preliminary examination before they could be admitted with preference given to the children of families who worshipped at Lewins Mead.[16]

George's marriage cemented his links with the Farr family and the dense web of kinship and business interests that existed amongst the African and West India merchants in Bristol. Both Richard Farr Jr and his father were active in the African trade, having invested in fifty-seven slave voyages between them.[17] Henry Bright, Munckley's friend and fellow partner in the Harford Bank, had spent several years in the West Indies, working with Richard Meyler who owned extensive sugar plantations in Jamaica, and had married Meyler's daughter Anne.[18] The Bright family too had long held considerable power and influence in Bristol. Henry was sheriff and later mayor of the city. Although successful, the firm of Munckley & Co was relatively small compared to those owned by the Brights and the Farrs,

Of all George's friends, Richard Bright stood out. He was the only son of Henry Bright, who like George had attended a dissenting school, the Warrington Academy. On his return to Bristol, he had joined the family firm. George first met Richard at Lewins Mead and the two became lifelong friends. With the death of his father in 1777, Richard, then aged twenty-three, inherited the family fortune, which consisted of properties worth around £30,000 and his father's personal estate of

£40,000. On Bright's marriage in 1784, he and his bride set up home at the family house at Ham Green just outside Bristol. Two years later their first child, called Henry after his grandfather, was born, followed at regular intervals by other children. The Gibbs and Brights lived only a short distance from one another and George and Etty were regular lvisitors to Ham Green, where the children played happily in the extensive gardens.[19]

By 1775 and for the next ten years sugar remained the mainstay of Munckley's business despite the onset of the American War of Independence. With annual imports of sugar in the region of 14,000 hogsheads, Bristol had been specialising in the refining of raw sugar dating back to 1760, with around twenty sugar refineries in the city. Munckley's investment in the Whitson Court Sugar House provided an important impetus to the firm. Although not one of the largest of Bristol's sugar merchants, between 1770 and 1780, Munckley & Co imported 2447 hogsheads of sugar, mainly from Jamaica and Barbados. The firm acted also as commission agent for the planters both in the plantations and the Amercian colonies, receiving the standard 2½ per cent commission once the sugar was processed and sold.[20] During the eighteenth century, many merchants dealing in sugar also had a share-holding in the plantations, and George, through his links with the Bright family invested in their Jamaican estates.

As well as owning their own ships, the firm also consigned smaller cargoes on a number of vessels to offset the high risks involved in the trade. Thus, the costs, risks and profits of each voyage were spread according to the individual shareholding, with the senior partner holding the largest share.[21] By 1776, the *Blaize Castle* and the *Hope* had been sold and the firm purchased a new ship, the snow *Fanny*. Munckley, George, James and Thomas Richards and Richard Twine jointly owned the vessel, with the shares divided between them according to their investment. The business was renamed Munckley Gibbs & Richards although at this time neither George or the Richards' brothers were partners.

Although the *Fanny* was primarily a Jamaicaman, its first voyage was to St. Petersburg but from 1777, it made eleven consecutive annual voyages to the West Indies. For the first seven, Munckley invested fifty per cent in the costs of the voyage, with the other partners each investing one-eighth, which was all they could afford. The average duration of a direct round trip to the Caribbean was little over eight months although not all of that time was spent at sea. Crossing the Atlantic took around six weeks, with the rest of the time being spent in port trading and re-provisioning for the return trip. The risks to any voyage did not just include the weather, piracy, accidents, shipwreck, disease, mutiny, or war; should the vessel arrive in port after the failure of a sugar crop she 'might be forced to sell her cargo at a loss or be obliged to return to England in ballast', resulting in considerable loss for the owners.

Thomas Richards captained the vessel for all but one of the *Fanny's* trips to the West Indies and his role was crucial to their success or failure.[22] Although many larger merchant houses had agents in foreign ports during this period, smaller firms like Munckley Gibbs & Richards were reliant on merchant mariners and the consignment trade. If their trading ventures with the *Fanny* were to be profitable, it was essential to have an experienced captain whom they could trust and who was 'well acquainted with market conditions'.

On the *Fanny's* first voyage, 'a pretty considerable Cargo amounting to £2296.10 without insurance' was consigned to Richards to 'dispose of for our best advantage'. He was instructed to 'advise us [Munckley Gibbs & Richards] frequently of your proceedings, particularly by the Pacquettes as they come round quick in winter time sending your letters....to Messrs Bright & Duncombe in Kingston who will forward them to us'. The cargoes shipped on outward journeys consisted of a wide range of merchandise for the plantations, including negro clothing, shoes, cloth, glassware, brass, white lead, coal and bricks, as well foodstuffs including flour, oats, butter pork, beef, and salt. On one occasion, the cargo included sixty barrels of pilchards, sent at the '*risque of the owners*'.

Despite national celebrations to mark Admiral Rodney's victory off

Cape St. Vincent in January 1780, great divisions in the country over the political uncertainties of the American Revolution resulted in waves of unrest and riots particularly in the north of England. The previous year there had been a nationwide petition against ministerial corruption and inefficiency as all sections of the opposition united against the Prime Minister, Lord North, to attack the iniquities of George III's government. As the war, begun in 1776, dragged on at sea, the British navy was stretched fighting both the French and Spanish fleets, which had joined in support of the American colonists. This led to the closure of the Spanish and Dutch ports to British shipping whilst the Italian market was at risk from privateers. The Royal Navy was called in to protect the merchant fleet and blockade enemy ports. On the *Fanny's* second voyage in 1778, Richards had to sail to Cork to join a convoy to cross the Atlantic. On arrival in Barbados, after delivering his cargo, he was instructed to load the return cargo and wait in port for the convoy.

From the first three voyages, the partners saw their profits increase, but as the war dragged on, they inevitably began to decline. In 1781, a hurricane caused havoc in the Caribbean resulting in the failure of the sugar crop. As the demand for sugar increased at home, so the price rose sharply. By October, prices ranged from 58/- to 66/- per hundredweight, but the duty had risen to 11/9d per hundredweight, reducing the profits on imports.[23] With the threat of attack from French and Spanish ships in the Caribbean, return voyages from the West Indies were often delayed as vessels waited for a convoy. Arriving back in Bristol much later in the year often resulted in increased freight charges and insurance costs. Exposure to more extreme weather conditions led to a number of ships being lost. This and the loss of the colonies had a major impact on both the West Indian and African trade. The latter was 'virtually suspended' resulting in severe financial difficulties and a number of business failures in Bristol, including George's father-in-law Richard Farr, who was ruined.

After the restoration of peace in 1783, Britain recovered her colonies in the Caribbean. Although Bristol ships resumed their voyages to West Africa and the American mainland, the slave and sugar trades never reached their pre-war levels. The high price of sugar led to a reduction in consumption, and with a good crop the following year, prices continued to decline. Information reached Munckley Gibbs & Richards that there was a severe shortage of wine in the West Indies. As no Bristol ships 'ever touch at Madeira', planters were obtaining supplies from London merchants. For George, this was an opportunity worth investigating. In January of that year, the *Fanny* left Bristol for her annual voyage across the Atlantic with instructions to sail to Madeira and purchase a consignment of wine, before proceeding to Barbados. There, after loading a large cargo of sugar, he was to sail to Jamaica. However, after the vessel had sailed for Ireland, word had reached Bristol that the Barbadian sugar crop had failed. On arrival there, Richards heard 'bad accounts from Jamaica of the Hurricane having… done considerable damage' to the crop. He sent word to Bristol and waited for further instructions, which arrived several weeks later. He was to remain there to see 'if there should be any Dutch prizes or French carried into Barbados laden with sugar, coffee or cotton etc'. If so he could 'lay out the proceeds of the owners Goods and even extend it a Thousand Pounds which you may draw for, in such articles …as you think can be purchased the most reasonable – the prices are left to your discretion to go a little higher than the limits you have from Mr. M.'.

By 1785, such was the decline in the demand for colonial produce that the price of landed sugar reached the all-time low of 43/- per hundredweight. A number of refineries in Bristol were forced to close, and Munckley gave up his partnership in the Whitson Court Sugar House. Despite these difficulties, colonial produce continued to dominate their business. In such a difficult period, it became clear to the partners that they should have a representative in Caribbean rather than depending on a third party factor. Later that year Samuel Richards, Thomas's younger brother, was sent to Barbados as the firm's agent. A trusted relative, they knew he could be relied on to provide information on commodities and prices to enable the partners to 'dispose of' cargoes 'for our advantage'.

As they had made a considerable profit on the wine on the previous trip, it was decided that the *Fanny* should to make another stop at Madeira on its next voyage. In December 1783, it set out to Barbados, with Richard Twine Jr. on board. Thomas Richards' instructions included a 'list of the Cargo on board your Ship, [valued at £918.18.8d], also an invoice of Sundry articles [valued at £646.8.3d] consigned lyourself and brother SR which they will be pleased to dispose of where they judge most for our advantage'. Twine was instructed to look at the local markets and identify which commodities to purchase, with the caveat that he be 'governed by what the other Ships get to the West India Islands'. The trip was successful and made an overall profit of £1033. The following year Twine moved to Madeira as the firm's agent and arrangements were made with the naval convoys for the *Fanny* to make a regular stop there on her annual voyage to the West Indies.

This was to be Richards last voyage on the Fanny. On arrival in Barbados, he decided to remain there with his brother, dying of yellow fever three years later. After his death, his wife, who had been left behind in England, sold his share in the the vessel to George and her brother-in-law James, thus increasing their holding to three-sixteenth shares each.[24] The *Fanny* made two more trips to the Caribbean, and two years later, at the end of its 12th voyage, the shareholders decided it should be sold. The adverse effect of the American revolutionary war in the Caribbean was beginning to be felt. The loss of the rum trade to North America and the increase in import duty on sugar to pay the escalating costs of the British Government all had an impact on profits and many British sugar refiners began looking for other sources of supply. The profits from each voyage had been steadily falling for several years, the condition of the vessel had deteriorated, and a considerable amount needed to be spent on refurbishing her for another voyage. In 1790, the it was sold to the Bristol slaver, James Rogers, for £900 with the proceeds divided between the partners according to their shareholding.[25]

In contrast with the success of his business career, the 1780s proved to be a difficult decade for George and his family. In January 1781, Etty, then thirty-nine, was pregnant again. In April, she gave birth to another son, whom they called Richard after his maternal grandfather. Their happiness was short-lived. The infant was a sickly baby surviving only a few months. At the time of his death, Etty was already pregnant again, her fourth pregnancy in four years. In December, she gave birth to another son, but he too only lived a few hours. It was indeed a sad Christmas for the family. George was also worried that his father had invested so much into his brothers' firm, believing that they were both too inexperienced to manage a business. After Abraham's death, he began to have real fears about Antony's ability to run the Exeter firm on his own, considering that he was over confident and sanguine about his own ability. When Antony became engaged he hoped that marriage would have a stabilising influence on him.

Yet again, 1784, was to be a year tinged with sorrow. In June, Etty was was pregnant again. Five months later, they travelled to Devon for Antony and Dolly's wedding, staying at the house at Clyst St. George, where he was very alarmed to find his sister Sarah so ill. Whilst there, George had a chance to discuss Antony's plans for the future. His brother was set on finding a home large enough for his family and where he could establish a mill for the manufacture of woollen cloth. Against any misgivings he may have had over Antony's timing, especially with the general decline in the woollen trade, George, was relieved that he had found a wealthy partner in Edmund Granger to finance the project.

Three months after Sarah's death in January 1785, Etty gave birth to a healthy daughter, whom they called Anne after her grandmother. But two years on tragedy struck again. On 29 October 1787, at the age of thirty-nine, Etty suddenly died. Whether this was due to another pregnancy is unclear for in the eighteenth century one in ten women died in or within the first month of giving birth. She was buried a few days later at St. Nicholas Church in Bristol. She and George had been married for eleven years, and at the time of their mother's death, Joanna was twelve, George Jr ten, and Anne two and a half years old. It had not been long since George had moved his family to a more salubrious residence in the fashionable suburb of Stoke Bishop, not far

1.Copy of a portrait of George Abraham by Prince Hoare

2. Abraham and Tryphaena's house in Shapter Street, Topsham

3. George Abraham as a child. Artist unknown

4. Pytte House, Clyst St George circa 1900

5. The original monument erected in the church at Clyst St George by George Gibbs of Pytte to his father which was partially destroyed when the church was bombed in 1940.

6. The Devon & Exeter Hospital, circa 1752

7. The Rt. Hon. Vicary Gibbs (1751-1820)

8. Antony's brother Abraham who died in 1782

10. A caricature of Dr Robert Remmett

9. Anne Gibbs, née Vicary

11. Mary Gibbs (later Crawley)

12. Antony Gibbs, circa 1784

13. Dorothea Barnetta Gibbs née Hucks, circa 1784

14. Exwick House where Antony and Dorothea lived from 1785–1789

15. The County Steam Laundry formerly Exwick Mill (Lower Mill) where Antony, Edmund Granger and Samuel Banfill established their woollen mill

16. Part of one of the mill's water wheels awaiting demolition

17. The Hermitage at Exwick where Samuel Banfill lived after the mill was sold until his death in 1842

18. Samuel Munckley

19. Nicholas Munckley, physician of Guy's Hospital

20. Dr Robert Remmett, cousin and family physician; founder of the Plymouth Medical Society

21. Antony Gibbs by Edward Paltry, R.B.A. after a half length drawing by John Downham

from Clifton, which had become Bristol's most popular suburb where many of the wealthy mercantile elite now lived.[26] He was now a widower of thirty-four, with three young children and he welcomed his sister Bell's offer to move in with him to manage the house and the family. Four months later, in January 1788, although still submerged in grief, he accepted the appointment on to the Standing Committee of the Society of Merchant Venturers, for a two-year term in preparation to becoming Master.

Despite his own difficulties, George continued helping his less fortunate relatives in a number of ways. In the autumn of 1788, he heard from Bell that his cousin Betsy had become captivated by a young American, called Bremat, who claimed to be the 'nephew of Mr Laurents, who is or was, president of the American Congress' with 'great landed property in Carolina'. In November, he was surprised to receive a letter from his father asking him to check out the young man's credentials. Over the last few years, George had made many contacts both in the West Indies and in North America, and knew Laurens, a wealthy planter and slaver from South Carolina, who was now living in Bristol having taken a house in Queen Square, near Munckley. Within a short time, he had established that the young American was a swindler. He heard that Betsy had reluctantly agreed to end the engagement, and was relieved when her brother, William, who was about to start working for the Bristol firm as a merchant mariner on the West Indies routes, decided to go to Topsham to help her decide on her future.

Although busy with his family, his business activities and his work for the Society of Merchant Venturers, George was stunned when, in August 1788, Antony stopped at Bristol on his way to Dover, to tell him he was leaving for an extended trip to Europe to collect monies owed to the Exeter firm. It was only then that George learned the true extent of his brother's financial problems and that he and his father were on the verge of bankruptcy. There was little he could do and like the rest of the family, would have to wait for Antony's return.

Against the downward trend in the African and West India trade, the Bristol firm's business continued to expand and George's wealth and status increased amongst the local mercantile elite. Towards the end of 1788, Munckley, aged sixty-five began to make plans to retire and decided to reorganise the business, making both George and James Richards' partners in the firm. It was some weeks later that he learned that bankruptcy proceedings had been instigated against his father and, with Munckley's blessing, immediately left for Exeter. There he found that his family was ruined. With Vicary's help, his parents and sisters were moved back into Palace Gate and George returned to Bristol knowing that nothing more could be achieved until Antony's return.

In May, news reached him that Antony had landed in Dover and on his way back to Exeter, broke his journey to discuss the situation with George, who was appalled to learn the full extent of his brother's indebtedness. Nevertheless, he was persuaded that as there was considerable business to be had in the Iberian Peninsula, Antony had no alternative but to return there to establish an agency business and George generously offered him £150 towards his expenses. There, Antony would act as the Bristol firm's agent on the usual commission.

George was very worried that the shock and humiliation of financial ruin had seriously affected his father's health. Knowing how distressing it was for his parents to remain in Exeter, it was a relief when Mary invited them to Stowe, leaving him and Vicary to work with the administrators to try to reach an agreement over their father's affairs. It was some weeks later that the commissioners agreed to drop bankruptcy proceedings against their father and to give them time to try to raise sufficient funds to cover the debts. George and Vicary turned to friends and family for help but despite all their efforts were unable to raise the required amount and it was soon evident that their father's assets would have to be sold. It was a great relief when Samuel Banfill and Edmund Granger offered to buy both George Abraham's and Antony's share of the Exwick firm to reduce their liabilities.

George was a pragmatic man and hoped to turn Antony's failure to his advantage. The wartime slump was affecting the profits of the West India merchants with their dependence on colonial produce, and as the abolitionist movement gathered momentum, many looked to expand into new markets. This and the decline in the African trade led to a spate of financial difficulties, further exacerbated by the fear that Dolbein's bill to regulate the conditions of slaves and reduce numbers on voyages would threaten the prosperity of the city. The American War heralded a decline in the reliance on ships' captains as more and more commission agents became based in foreign ports. Munckley Gibbs & Richards now had Samuel Richards in the Caribbean and Antony in Spain.[27] This gave the firm a real opportunity to re-export colonial goods to the region and develop the import trade with the Iberian Peninsula. Mediterranean produce, including fruit, olive oil and wine, was in great demand and was shipped through Munckley Gibbs & Richards for distribution throughout the hinterland. Antony's departure to Spain created new opportunities for the firm. By managing his financial affairs, George was in an ideal position manage his business and to curb his brother's tendency to embark on any over-optimistic schemes.

* * * *

By the late 1780s, Bristolians appear to have adopted a pragmatic attitude towards the slave trade. Although 'every body [sic] seems to execrate it,..no one thought of its abolition…',[28] it was judged that the 'evil must be tolerated in order to sustain a general prosperity…'.[29] The campaign for abolition had begun in 1780, with William Wilberforce's attempts to introduce a Bill in Parliament. Six years later, Thomas Clarkson published '*An essay on the slavery and commerce of the human species*', which had an immediate impact on public opinion. The following year the Society for the Abolition of the Slave Trade was founded, but progress was slow until 1788 when calls for abolition gained momentum. On 28 January, Bristol became the first city outside London to set up an abolitionist committee to petition Parliament in support Wilberforce's campaign and the Bill. This support came mainly from the Quaker, Baptist and dissenting congregations. A leading abolitionist was John Estlin, the minister at Lewins Mead. Although most of his congregation consisted of wealthy African and West India merchants, planters and Merchant Venturers, all anti-abolitionists, it did not appear to cause either him or them any difficulties.

As a response to the formation of the Bristol abolitionist group, the West India interest in the city became more vigorous and organised in its opposition. At the Society of Merchant Venturers general meeting in March 1788, it was agreed that the privy council be petitioned in support of the trade on the grounds that any regulation would not only damage the sugar trade but would inevitably lead to a rebellion amongst the slaves. 'When it shall be known in our Colonies' and 'excite such a Spirit of Mutiny as given your petitioners the most serious Concern for their Safety and that of the free inhabitants'. They requested that Government forces be sent to Jamaica to quell any uprising should the Bill become law. A small sub-committee was formed to prepare further petitions against abolition for Parliament. George, a staunch anti-abolitionist and on the Society's Standing Committee, played an active role in the proceedings. Despite the efforts of the West India lobby, in response to the growing concern about the conditions in the 'Middle Passage', in July as parliament was about to go into its summer recess, William Dolbein unexpectedly introduced his bill to regulate the number of slaves that could be transported on slave ships. The West India interest claimed that this would threaten the profitability of the trade, but despite vigourous opposition, the Dolbein Act became law.

The following year saw the beginning of a nationally orchestrated campaign against abolition by the West India and African interest that had very real anxieties on the effect that it would have on their businesses. Sugar was the most important import into Britain in the eighteenth century and they argued that slavery was a political and economic necessity for the nation, for the 'Trade to Africa not only constitutes in itself a considerable part of the British Commerce, but that it is of essential consequence to the West Indies colonies'.[30] After a meeting of all interested parties in London in March 1789, a petition was drawn up against abolition. On 3 April, the Bristol Society of

Merchant Venturers learned that the House of Commons planned to go into committee in three weeks to consider the total abolition of the slave trade. Ten days later, a meeting was convened at Merchants Hall in Bristol for 'the Planters, Merchants manufacturers and others, in this City' who were concerned with the British West India Islands and the Trade to Africa' to support the London cause. Sixty-five people attended the meeting including ten Africa merchants, thirty-four manufacturers and shipowners, and twenty-one West India merchants and planters. The latter group included George and Richard and Lowbridge Bright. Over 1000 copies of the London petition were printed for distribution throughout the city. It was resolved that a committee of no less than forty seven members be appointed to co-ordinate the pro-slavery response and to prepare future petitions opposing abolition. The meeting requested the support of the Society of Merchant Venturers and proposed that it should use its 'Corporate capacity to unite with this Meeting, and to grant the Use of their Hall and direct attendance of their Clerk at their several Committees'. It was also agreed that the committee would 'cooperate with the Committee of the Merchants Hall and with the London committee, in such Measures as shall be deemed most effectual to resist the Abolition of a Trade which the Welfare of the West India Islands and the Commerce and revenue of the Kingdom so essentially depend'.[31]

Over the next few weeks, the Society of Merchant Venturers organised a number of petitions, arguing that the African trade was crucial to the wealth and prosperity of the city and accounted for more than three-fifths of the its trade. Abolition would result in financial ruin and was 'rash and ruinous' for the people of Bristol with the closure of sugar refineries putting thousands of labourers out of work. In order to prevent this, merchants asked for compensation if the slave trade were to be abolished. The following January, George was elected master of the Society of Merchant Venturers to lead the anti-abolition campaign. On 12 May, as Wilberforce made his first anti-slavery speech to parliament, six Bristol petitions were presented from the different factions.[32] The West India interest stated that as the African and

Caribbean trade accounted for three-fifths of Bristol's total trade, abolition would bring decline and ruin to thousands. The Select Committee, which began to hear evidence on 29 January 1791, took several months to sift through all the arguments thus thwarting the abolitionist attempts to secure a speedy end to the trade. In the event, Wilberforce's bill was easily defeated by 163 votes to 88.

By 1790, Bristol's dominance of the slave trade had passed to Liverpool. Many attributed this to a change of attitude by Bristolians to whom slavery was becoming repugnant at a time when many in England were valuing the idea of liberty and the rights of man. 'The Ardor for the Trade to Africa for men and women, our fellow creatures and equals, is much abated among the humane and benevolent merchants of Bristol', believing that 'the people of Liverpool in their indiscriminate rage for Commerce and for getting money at all events have nearly engrossed this Trade, incredibly exceed London and Bristol in it, employ many thousands of tons of shipping for the purpose of buying and enslaving God's rational creatures, and are the venders (horresco referens) of the souls and bodies of men and women! To almost all the West Indian Islands !!!'.[33] By 1787, 'there were but 30 ships employed in this melancholy traffic' and as the number of clearances from Bristol to the Caribbean declined, with Antony as its agent in Malaga, Munckley Gibbs & Richards increased its trade with Europe and the firm was able to ride the difficulties.

As the West India interest in Bristol greeted the defeat of Wilberforce's Abolition Bill with relief, abolitionists continued to hold public meetings in the city, mounting an effective press campaign. While many merchants tried to distance themselves from any involvement in the African trade, they still enjoyed the profits from colonial produce. In April, a group of female abolitionists known as the 'anti-saccharites', organised a national boycott of slave-produced sugar.[34] Even though they were ridiculed in the press, the boycott had a significant impact on the sugar interest in the city. Fortunately, for George, its impact was short-lived but two years later, a slave revolt in St. Domingue resulted in severe disruption to sugar supplies. As

Wilberforce's campaign intensified, later that year the House of Commons voted in favour of abolition but after intense lobbying the bill was defeated by the House of Lords, many of whose members themselves had significant interests in the West Indies. Instead, the Commons accepted Dundas's amendment proposing the abolition of the slave trade to the British West Indies to come into effect in 1796.

In 1790, while master of the Society of Merchant Venturers, George had been invited, on Munckley's resignation, to become a member of the New West India Association, which had been formed eight years earlier by a number of prominent Bristolians to protect their interests against the effects of the abolitionist movement.[35] Its twelve founder members included Richard and Lowbridge Bright and Munckley was its first president. It was a very select group: one resolution passed at its inaugural meeting on January 28th 1782, was that 'no Stranger whatever shall at any time be invited as a Guest unless by a Card from the Society and with the approval of the President'.[36] New members were accepted only upon the death or resignation of members. Although originally formed to defend their collective interests, the West India Association's activities were largely confined to their own commercial interests and it acted as a pressure group, petitioning both Parliament and the Admiralty on a variety of issues, including the regulation of customs duties and the provision of convoys to protect the merchant fleet on trans-Atlantic voyages. Its members met monthly at the Bush Tavern in Bristol where, judging from the minutes, there was often more spent on claret than business done!

* * * *

Financial ruin had taken its toll on the family. When his parents visited him in the summer of 1790, he was shocked at his father's appearance. Now over seventy, George Abraham had suffered a number of minor illnesses, and barely had the strength to get out of bed. George hastily wrote to Antony telling of their father's condition, and was relieved to learn that his brother was planning to return to England with his family the following year. Meanwhile, he continued to devote a considerable amount of time to their affairs in Devon.

Within a few weeks of Antony arriving in Spain, reports reached Bristol of problems between Dolly and Betsy. It was some months later that he heard that his cousin was returning to England and that his father was refusing to have anything to do with her. George was much more realistic. He had always been fond of his high-spirited cousin and would not see her made homeless because of his brother's folly. He was also grateful for the contribution that she and her brothers had made to help his father, and her brother William was now working for the Bristol firm. It was now three years since Etty's death and Bell was anxious to return to Exeter and so he offered Betsy a temporary home until she found a suitable alternative. Arriving in Bristol in July 1790, she quickly settled in and took over the management of the house. After William's marriage to Susanna (Susan) Ley, they too came to live with George. He had offered William the shorter safer crossings to the Mediterranean and in the early days of their marriage, Susan accompanied her husband on his voyages. Between expeditions, the couple returned to George's house and lived there with Betsy, George and his children.

In the summer of 1792, George heard that Antony was expected back in England within weeks. After a short stay with the Crawleys, he and Dolly, accompanied by his parents, broke their journey at Bristol for a brief visit on their way back to Exeter. It was no surprise to learn that he planned to return to Spain as soon as Dolly and the children were settled. Now based in Malaga, Antony was in partnership with a Spanish associate, concentrating on exporting a wide range of Spanish produce, mainly fruit, wine and oils to Britain. With William now sailing between Bristol and Italy, the Bristol firm was developing trading links with his cousin Lyle, who was based in Genoa. From Italy came a variety of Mediterranean produce, including wines and fish, mainly pilchards and sardines. In this way, through their family links the brothers and cousins traded together for their mutual benefit.

The following March George received an urgent letter from his father begging him to come immediately. Antony had suffered a serious accident and a distraught Dolly was threatening to go to Spain to be at his side. With war against France imminent and afraid for her safety, George knew it was unsafe for her to go. He travelled to Exeter with his children where a distressed Dolly begged him to find her a passage on the next available ship. Entreating her to remain calm, he persuaded her to wait for more news. A few days later, a letter arrived from William Branscombe, with the news that Antony had regained consciousness and had been taken to a friend's house to recover.

While they anxiously waited for further news, tragedy struck George's family once again. His beloved little daughter Anne, who was only eight years old, suddenly became ill with a fever and died, to be buried in Clyst St George a few days later. Despite his grief, George remained with his parents for several weeks until they knew that Antony was out of danger. Once they heard that he was well on the road to recovery, George took Joanna and George Jr back to Bristol. There, to his surprise, Betsy announced that she had become engaged to his friend and partner James Richards. On her return to England, George Abraham had cynically remarked that 'first object will be...to fix herself upon some good lady who wants a companion to fetch and carry for her, to which Betsy's talents are admirably adapted'. As the weeks became months she had not attempted to find a suitable position and there is little doubt that she enjoyed the comforts in George's house. Richards was a wealthy widower with no children and unknown to everyone and been calling on Betsy for several months. Their engagement came as a relief to the family as her future was now secured. To provide her with a small dowry, George agreed with Antony that her loan, made to his father ten years before, should be repaid on her marriage. Betsy and Richards were married in April 1794 and moved to his house in the village of Abbots Leigh, just outside Bristol, where a number of wealthy West Indies merchants and bankers had purchased country estates.

George continued to provide work for her brother William after his marriage to Susan Ley, but as the political situation worsened, it was considered too dangerous for her to sail with her husband. While he was at sea, Susan and the children continued to live in George's house. Joanna and George Jr were thrilled. They adored her and got on famously with their younger cousins. At one point, the house in Orchard Street was so full of his cousins and their children that it might well have provided the impetus for Betsy's marriage.

CHAPTER 6

ANTONY

The export trade from Exeter to the southern European ports flourished during the latter half of the eighteenth century. The trade with Italy was dominated by two main groups of ports, from Genoa to Leghorn and from Naples to Salerno and Messina.[37] George Abraham, like many of his Exeter friends, was involved in the export of woollen cloth to Italy and Spain in partnership with his half-brother John, who had spent much of his life as a merchant mariner trading in the Mediterranean. In 1774, his youngest son Antony was apprenticed to Nicholas Brooke, an Exeter merchant whose business had been built exporting Devon woollen cloth to Spain. Antony's attitude to work had always worried his parents, but he appeared to settle into his new life and 'as 'Mr Brooke is extending his Spanish branch' was tasked with learning Spanish'. During the next few years, Antony was to become fluent in the language.

Returning to England in 1778 at the age of twenty-two Antony joined George Gibbs & Co, and the following year, his older brother Abraham, who had completed his apprenticeship in Italy, returned to Exeter after the death of their uncle John and he too joined the firm. With the uncertainties of the woollen industry, Abraham and Antony, like many of their contemporaries, diversified into other areas including insuring cargoes for other merchants. With war imminent, knowing how inexperienced his sons were and the high risks involved in insurance, their father was cautious about this shift, writing to Antony in 1779 that 'If anything very eligible should be offered in the way of insurance you may take a moderate sum. If such risks should be proposed as we would rather be without, you may use my absence as a pretence for shirking them.'

Both Abraham and Antony quickly established themselves amongst the woollen merchants in Exeter, becoming members of The Company of Weavers, Fullers, and Shearmen. Antony was elected assistant warden in September 1778, and Abraham warden two years later. In 1781, the brothers, financed by their father established their own business, trading under the name of Gibbs Brothers Cloth Makers, and operating out of a warehouse in Exwick, on the west side of the river Exe. Initially the new business appeared to flourish. Two years later, Antony became Master of the Guild and Company, and the following year was appointed by his fellow merchants on to the committee to investigate the illegal export of wool, which had been causing increasing concern amongst merchants in both Bristol and Exeter. In 1782, the *Trewman's Exeter Flying Post* reported that in a public meeting held at the Exeter Guildhall on 14 May, 'Mr Anthony [sic] Gibbs' was one of 26 appointed to consider a letter from Lord Shelburne, Secretary of State, suggesting the raising a local corps for national defence.[38] Two years later, the paper reported that Antony was one of the 27, appointed at a meeting of woollen merchants and manufacturers in the Guildhall on 17 February 1786, to deal with the illicit exportation of wool.

It was not long before their lack of experience became evident. Antony was an impulsive young man. He saw the immense profits that the established Exeter merchants were making from the woollen trade. Swept along by the euphoria of increased demand, he and Abraham sought to make the most of every business opportunity, allowing themselves to be tempted into overtrading, and offering extended credit to customers with little regard to margins. It appears that their father was underwriting the business as early as 1782, and creditors were sending Gibbs Brothers' bills directly to him for payment; it was not long before the firm had run into serious cash flow problems. While they looked urgently for other sources of credit, they tried to keep the true extent of their problems from their father.

At this time, both Antony and Abraham were living at Clyst St George with their family. Antony always loved Pytte and, as a child, he and his brothers and sisters had looked forward to the times when they escaped the city to enjoy the country. Having spent a happy childhood there, he disliked city life, acknowledging that he was 'not naturally fond of businesses', preferring country pursuits. Riding was one of the country pleasures he enjoyed and every day he rode into Exeter on horseback to the warehouse.

It was at this time that Abraham first met Dorothea Barnetta Hucks. Dolly, as she was affectionately known, first became acquainted with the Gibbs family when she moved into Exeter in 1780 with her brother William who had suffered from consumption for some years. Her sister Harriet had died of the disease the year before and it was feared that Dolly too had succumbed and had been treated by Sir George Baker.[39] It was not long after her arrival in Exeter that she first became met Abraham who was immediately entranced with her. His affection was returned; within a few months, they were engaged.[40] After his sudden death in 1782, Dolly was devastated and 'felt his death very much'. As she prepared to return to Knaresborough, in June she received word that her father had been taken ill and she immediately went back to Yorkshire to be with him. Some weeks after his death, Dolly returned to Pytte. She soon had other admirers including Vicary and Antony but in the weeks that followed it was Antony who proved to be her greatest comfort. More likeable and good-natured than Vicary he had soon won her heart and within a few months, it became obvious to all that they were in love. When he proposed in January 1783, she gladly accepted.

Knowing that Dolly had no dowry to speak of and believing that Antony would never be in a position to support a family, her mother opposed to the match, still hoping that she would marry Vicary. Mrs Hucks wrote to Eleanor that although she had become very fond of Antony she was convinced 'of the impossibility of [him] keeping a family in the genteel way which I am sure with his generous spirit he would like to do'. Although the Gibbs family were 'people for whom

I have the greatest regard and who merit from me every act of friendship if in my power, not only on your account, but also on that of your poor dear brother's', she believed that her son-in-law 'Mr Ward would put a negative on the match from the face of affairs'. However, Mrs Hucks was soon resigned that nothing she said would change her daughter's mind. She wrote to Dolly, 'I leave you mistress of yourself; you are not a child – your future happiness with him must entirely depend on his success in business and his life; if you dare run the risqué, it is yourself which must abide by it'. How true her words would prove to be.

Widowed and alone in Knaresborough, Mrs Hucks decided to take a house in Exmouth until her daughter's wedding. Originally, Antony and Dolly had planned to marry in October, but aware that his father had financed his business, and in view of the uncertainties in the woollen trade, Antony proposed that they should delay their marriage until the firm was on a more secure footing. 'My Dearest Dolly', he wrote a month after their betrothal, 'I am engaged in a kind of work that is the most villainous drudgery if compared to the pleasure of writing to you'. He continued, 'you told me last night you could not better conceal your affection from me never attempt, my dear life, to conceal, what it gives me so much pleasure to know'. Theirs was to be a long engagement and during that time they wrote to each other daily when apart, a habit that continued for much of their married life. Despite their later difficulties, this was an indication of the affection and trust they held for each other. In their letters, they not only exchanged sentiments of love but also all the family gossip. During their engagement, Dolly, fearful that she too would succumb to the 'family disease', spent the winters in Wells or Bath taking the waters and many of Antony's letters show great concern for her health.

Between 1778 and 1783, the Exeter wool trade had seen a change of direction. During the American War of Independence, Spanish markets closed when it entered the war. Exeter merchants experienced 'the very great difficulties which within these few years have been thrown upon our trade with Spain'[41]. The Italian trade also declined in value and

Holland, which stayed neutral until 1780, remained an important entrepôt for British goods, distributing them to other European markets. Once Britain entered the war, the Dutch ports were closed and trade to Hamburg also declined. This was offset by a rapid expansion in the Flemish market as neutral Ostend replaced Holland as the entrepôt to the European markets.

With the Treaty of Versailles in 1783, the world was at peace again and the immediate post-war period was one of moderate prosperity. Many of Exeter's mercantile elite, having foreseen the changing economic climate, had already diversified into new markets. Those who in previous decades had made their fortune in the woollen industry had turned to banking to hedge against the instability of the trade. Familiar with handling credit whilst trading overseas, they became engaged in financing the various stages of the production of cloth. This period also saw the establishment of several new banks in Exeter, founded on capital generated by the woollen trade. Wealthy cloth merchants like John Duntze, John Baring, Samuel Milford and the Kennaways established banks in the city. Duntze (Munckley's stepfather), with his son and two other partners had founded the Exeter Bank as early as 1769. The following year, Baring in partnership with his son and Charles Collyns founded the Devonshire Bank and, in 1786, Samuel Milford, who made his fortune in the export trade to Italy, opened the Exeter City Bank. This move from mercantile enterprise to banking in the latter half of the eighteenth century was not just confined to Exeter. In Bristol, Henry Bright and Samuel Munckley had also branched into pure finance with the establishment of the Harford Bank.

The collapse of the Spanish market had led to financial ruin for many merchants in both England and Europe. After Versailles, it was to be several years before Spain resumed its place as the leading market for the Exeter woollen trade, despite an early resurgence in 1783. With little regard to the situation in Europe, Antony, with his typical sanguine attitude continued to trade, offering extended credit to his Spanish customers at a level made precarious by the changing political and economic conditions. Since his brother's death, the firm had continued to trade under the name of Gibbs Brothers Cloth Merchants although he was now running the business with some help from his father. Unlike George, with little formal training in commerce, Antony was soon in trouble. One of his major failings was his dislike of paperwork; he rarely kept accounts, and having no idea of the true state of his business continued to overstretch himself. Later that year, Samuel Banfill, the son of a family friend from Topsham joined the firm as his clerk.

With the cessation of hostilities, in February 1783, Antony sent Banfill to Spain to drum up some business with customers and his old business contacts.[42] Originally, Banfill was to be away for about nine months. As things were so uncertain, Antony persuaded Dolly to put off their wedding 'beyond the period already fixed' until his clerk's return or until such time 'of my having saved a thousand pounds'. Both were disappointed at the delay but Antony, conscious that his father had sunk a considerable amount of money into the firm, was adamant. He wrote to Dolly, that as 'a great deal of the money which we have in the business is borrowed of my father, and in case any accident should happen to him would in all probability be called in. This would create the necessity our lessening the business to such a degree as very considerably to diminish the profit; therefore, before my expenses are increased the capital in the business should be increased'.

In June, Antony received a letter from Banfill telling him that all 'goes on well' and he hoped 'to secure a great benefit from his travels'. He remained confident that Banfill will '…certainly be home within six weeks, and I am sure nothing will prevent our marriage immediately after his return'. Despite his optimism, Antony was having serious cash flow problems and had confided in Dolly about the 'low state' of his finances. One of his customers, a Thomas Binford, whose business had failed a few weeks before, suddenly died owing him over one thousand pounds. In despair, Antony thought he would get nothing until the estate was settled. It was a great relief a few months later to receive six hundred pounds from Edmund Granger, one of the executors of the Binford estate. Granger, of Rougement Castle and an old friend from

house

the Exeter Grammar School, was a wealthy wine merchant having married 'a very agreeable young lady with a genteel fortune' in 1777. He had a number of other business interests owning extensive properties in and around Exeter, was a partner in the Exeter Woollen Drapery Company, and had invested in plantations in South Carolina and Jamaica. He was also part-owner of a number of ships sailing from Exeter to the Caribbean, importing sugar from the West Indies through the Bristol firm of Munckley Smith & Co and exporting Italian and Portuguese wines to the American plantations and Caribbean. Each year he went on what he called his 'Adventure' visiting business contacts in Oporto, Jamaica or the Carolinas to generate new business. Such was his wealth that he was always willing to invest in new ventures.[43]

As 1784 dawned, Antony heard that Banfill expected to be back in May. Full of optimism, he decided that the time was right for him and Dolly to marry. She was becoming increasingly impatient by the delay and spent more and more time with friends in Wells and London. The planned wedding in October, would give Antony time to look for a suitable house. Although he was still living at Pytte, he had other plans for the business once he and Dolly were married.

During this period, a number of Exeter merchants including John Baring, John Duntze and Abraham Kennaway had purchased small estates on the outskirts of the city and had built workshops and workers tenements adjoining their homes so that they could supervise the various stages of the manufacturing process. Like Duntze, Baring was a German Lutheran immigrant, who had made his fortune in the cloth trade. He had purchased Larkbear House, situated 'on the north side of Holloway Street' as a family residence in 1737, and established a woollen manufactory on the site.[44] Antony longed to emulate him. Premises like Larkbear House with its 'large press-shops, packing rooms, linhays, tenter-grounds, and all conveniences on the demesne for finishing woollen cloths' were ideal where 'great mercantile concerns have been carried on there for more than a century'.[45] He enthusiastically wrote to Dolly that 'Mr. Baring, Mr Cuiller and Mr Kennaway[46] have all of them press shops in the courts in which their houses stand',

and he wished after their marriage to 'take a house with offices under the same roof...' and transfer the business there. In practice, this was not to prove easy. Antony had great difficulty in finding something that would suit both their needs, for Dolly also wanted to live outside the city. In 1784, the firm of Gibbs Brothers was still operating from its warehouse. Despite his financial difficulties, he dreamt of owning a small estate that included a family house near a mill where he could establish a small factory.

Antony also a great admirer of Baring, taking an active role in his electoral campaigns and in the 1784 election was appointed to the committee 'to serve Mr Baring'. It was an exciting campaign. The Exeter Chamber supported Baring and Buller in the election, but Bamfylde, a Foxite Whig, through his landed background had a more traditionalist appeal and secured the anti-establishment support in the city. Once his own election was secure, Baring wanted to throw his support behind Buller, but Antony and George Hirtzol, another member on the committee, persuaded him not to do so. Baring remained neutral with Antony and Hirtzol casting their remaining votes for Bamfylde. Buller was out of the contest, losing by more than sixty votes. Baring and Bamfylde were returned with the former winning by more than 150 votes.

In May, with Banfill's return imminent, Antony at last found what he thought was the ideal residence and wrote to Dolly that it 'was without doubt the best in Exeter'. The rooms are 'high, bright, extremely pleasant...' with a 'hall and parlour, a little parlour, storerooms and kitchen 'which is very good but not very large...'. Also included ...are buildings for the conveniences of the business....all under the ground floor are offices, cellars and laundry....in the cellar are pipes through which any quantity of water may be conveyed into the house...'. On the second floor there was a drawing room and three bedrooms '...with a floor above only for servants'. But when Dolly learned it was being sold because the owner's wife 'did not like the house because of the smoke from the press shop', she refused to consider it. Antony was desperate and it was a great relief when his parents offered to 'give up their house [in Exeter] 'til we can get one for ourselves' and move permanently to Pytte. Unable to find a suitable house that they could afford, he and Dolly decided to take up his parents' offer and although neither thought this was the ideal solution they agreed that it would be better than waiting another year before getting married.

There was great excitement as their marriage drew near, but this was tempered at the end of August when his sister Sally, who had suffered from consumption for some years, became critically ill. Antony was devastated. He and Sally had always been very close and, forgetting his own business worries, he nursed her day and night, in the hope that she would recover, even discussing postponing his wedding again. Dolly was full of admiration and love. Mrs Hucks wrote of him, 'It is impossible not to love him for his attention to his sisters; a good son and brother must, I think make a good husband'. Despite Sally's ill health, they decided to go ahead with the wedding.

But Antony had other worries. Banfill's return did not herald the hoped-for good news. Despite the increase in woollen exports to Spain a number of their customers were experiencing severe financial difficulties having not recovered from the economic impact of the war. As the firm's cash flow problems worsened, banks and suppliers refused to advance it any more credit. While he devotedly nursed his beloved Sally, the Devonshire Bank had refused to honour a bill for £1416. Unable to ask his father for any further financial help, he turned to Granger who agreed to advance him £20 to tide him over and keep his creditors at bay. In spite of his financial concerns, he and Dolly were married on 3 October 1784 at the church at Littleham, just outside Exmouth. After their marriage, they moved into his parents' house on the 'Town Walls'.

Despite their happiness, it was to be a sad Christmas. As the family gathered at Pytte for the festivities, Sarah's condition worsened and she died early in the New Year. On a cold January day, they all walked the two hundred yards behind the cortège to the little churchyard in Clyst St. George where she was buried. Their sadness was eased when, a few weeks later, Dolly announced she was pregnant. Antony was thrilled.

It made him more determined than ever to find a home of their own but now he was married he knew that he had to face up to his growing financial problems.

By May, unable to obtain further credit Antony once again looked to Granger for help. Some debts had remained unpaid for over two years. Granger agreed to settle the Gibbs Brothers Cloth Merchants account with the Devon Bank amounting to £1400 at five per cent interest.[47] Antony continued borrowing money from him on a regular basis to pay off his creditors and by August owed Granger a further £2250. He also needed additional funds to maintain his wife and sustain his lifestyle. Despite his growing indebtedness, he had not lost sight of his dream to have a home where he could develop a factory for the production of woollen cloth and was looking for something similar to Pytte, a substantial house with a small estate. In May, he found what he thought would be an ideal home in the hilly hamlet of Exwick, a short distance from his warehouse. Known as Exwick Barton the estate consisted of around 100 acres with large house known as Exwick Manor House that had been owned by the late Thomas Binford. The particular advantage of Exwick House was that it only a few minutes from an empty mill, which Antony planned to lease from its owner, local landowner James Buller (who had lost the election the previous year).

Dolly was delighted; she loved Exwick House. Overlooking the river Exe, it was a substantial property with beautiful gardens and extensive views towards the city. On the ground floor, there was a large airy dining room, a laboratory, breakfast room as well as two kitchens and the servants' hall. Upstairs were a drawing room and library, as well 'Four best Bed Chambers…. Two adjoining Dressings Rooms…. a Gentleman's Dressing Room…. and Four other Bed Rooms…'. Outside there was a walled kitchen garden of about one acre, an orchard, servants' quarters, coach house and stables.[48] The whole estate consisted of the 'Mansion House, ffarm house [sic], Dwelling house, Cottages, Gardens, Orchards, fields Closes of Lands & heredi-taments'.[49] As the houses and cottages were all let, Antony believed that

2065m/T2/9

he could combine his ambitions, of being both a member of the local gentry and a successful entrepreneur.

Many of his creditors were demanding payment and he continued to borrow from Granger at an alarming rate as all other sources of credit were closed to him. Undaunted, he proceeded with his plans to buy Exwick Barton and take on the lease for the mill, one of three in Exwick, known as Higher Fulling Mill and situated on a long leat from the river Exe.[50] There had been mills on this site since mediaeval times. The premises comprised of a 'Fulling Mill, Mill house with Appurtenances with such share or part of the Mill Stream'. Antony planned to use it for fulling cloth, and to build dye and washing houses, workshops, rack fields, and spinning shops and also dreamt of building cottages for his workers. It was estimated that the new firm needed capital of twenty-five thousand pounds. Antony approached Granger and his father to see if they would be prepared to invest in the venture. Granger agreed to put £10,000 into a new business if George Abraham would match it and offered to lend Antony a further £5000 for his share. Confident that was a good investment, his father also readily agreed.

On August 1st 1785, having purchased the remaining sixty years of the lease of the mill, the three partners, Granger, George Abraham and Antony signed a ten-year partnership agreement to 31 October 1795, to trade as woollen manufacturers and merchants from Higher Fulling Mill in Exwick. The outstanding £4268 in Antony's loan account was transferred into the new business. Although the new firm was called Gibbs Granger & Banfill, Samuel Banfill was not a partner.

With Dolly's confinement only weeks away, she and Antony were still living in his parents' house in Palace Gate. Raising the £3000 needed to purchase the freehold of Exwick Barton was not easy. With all his resources committed to the new business, George Abraham was unable to provide any further funds. Knowing Vicary's situation had improved since his marriage, Antony approached him for help. Rather than giving his brother a loan, Vicary decided to purchase the freehold of the estate as an investment. Within days of the contract being signed,

Antony and Dolly moved into Exwick House. Three weeks later, on 25 August, she gave birth to a healthy son whom they called George Henry (known as Henry throughout his life). During the customary four-week lying in period, she was expected to remain in bed with the windows closed and a fire burning while she recovered from the birth. Dolly would have none of it. Instead, she entertained a continual stream of visitors who came to admire little Henry. Four weeks later, her 'convalescence' over, he was christened on 24 September, in the parish church in Exwick. — *no parish church at this time*

Antony was determined that his family should want for nothing. He continued to borrow from Granger as he and Dolly furnished their house and entertained numerous guests. His parents, thrilled by their new grandson, were frequent visitors, as was Mrs Hucks, who had moved into Exeter to be near her daughter. Dolly's brother John was a regular caller, having found employment as a mariner on the *Dilligence*, a passenger ship that ran three times a week between Exmouth and Exeter. John was particularly fond of little Henry and regularly popped in to see them when in the city. As Mrs Hucks wrote to Eleanor, 'John is not a little proud of his Nephew'.

As the mill needed enlarging and refurbishing, Antony continued to use his existing premises until the work was completed. Initially the new firm appears to have shown promise for this was a period of moderate prosperity for Exeter's woollen trade. While he and Banfill concentrated on cloth production and sales, Granger managed their accounts and collected outstanding debts. Unlike Antony, Granger only allowed their customers sixty days credit, before charging them a high rate of interest. However, despite his enthusiasm for the new project, Antony still had a large number of personal debts dating back several years, and the banks continued to refuse him further credit, as did local traders and shopkeepers. In the thirteen months between June 1786 and July 1787, unknown to his family he had borrowed nearly £900 from Granger against his personal loan account in the firm.

Work to extend the mill began in the summer of 1786. By the end of August, thirty-one elm trees had been felled to clear the site; three

Which mill?

loads of stones and 3450 bricks had been delivered. Workshops, spinning shops and dyehouses were constructed so that the various processes in the manufacture of cloth could be carried on under one roof. The building works took several months and then the factory and mill were fitted out with spinning machines, looms and other equipment. The initial works were completed in the spring.[51] The partners had high hopes that once the factory was in full production, they would be able to recoup their investment within a few months.

Funded by Granger, Antony continued trading while developing the mill at Exwick. All outstanding bills were put through his account with the new firm. He seems to have been unaware of the true extent of his indebtedness to Granger and that both he and his father were also liable for the arrears run up by the firm of Gibbs Brothers Cloth Merchants, between 1780 and 1786. Despite the rumours that now freely circulated amongst the merchants at Tuckers Hall, George Abraham too seems to have had no idea about the parlous state of his son's finances. Nearing seventy, he and Anne spent most of their time either at Clyst St. George or visiting Bristol or Stowe, while Antony and Dolly tried to maintain their normal lifestyle, determined to preserve appearances. In October 1786, their second child, a daughter called Harriet, was born and that Christmas, as they continued to entertain their friends and family at Exwick, Antony seemed as confident as ever about the future, determined that no one should know the true extent of his financial difficulties.

To his dismay, in the new year his problems were made very public. On 25 January, *Trewman's Exeter Flying Post* published an anonymous letter from a long-standing creditor, which threatened to burn down his premises. It read:

> January 12, 1787
> Mr Antony Gibbs, I have took this opportunity
> in sending thes few lines as a friendly Caution
> concerning many Destervervence that have hapned
> Times past you Damnation Black Skandalous Dog

now to be very Pecuhlor I cant stop about it to your very great surprise you shall find your little Pile of Buildings one morning all in flams and not only your Buildings but you will find the Racks cut from end to end you Damnation Black Dog. Excuse the writing.[52]

Although addressed to Antony and relating to his personal debts, it reflected badly on the firm. The partners immediately published a response offering £1000 reward for any information on the author. Whether they discovered the source of the letter is unclear. In the event, the premises appear to have survived the threat, but Antony's financial problems had now been made public. Granger and Banfill were concerned at the adverse effect this would have on the business. With the mill at Exwick nearing completion, in order to reduce his outgoings, Antony decided to let the warehouse previously used by Gibbs Brothers Cloth Merchants to concentrate his efforts at Exwick. On 11 March, he put an advertisement in the *Trewman's Exeter Flying Post*, which read, 'A mill at Exwick, near Exeter, in the possession of Messrs Gibbs and Co, to be Lett, at Midsummer next. Enquire of Mr Joseph Elliott, Exeter.'.[53] However, in such difficult times, the mill remained empty. Despite this setback, Antony remained convinced that his financial difficulties were only temporary.

Granger was no fool. Although now related to the Gibbs family through his sister's marriage to the Boevey-Crawley family, he was determined to protect his investment.[54] As news of Antony's financial difficulties became the talk of the coffee shops, Granger grew increasingly worried that the firm was showing no sign of making a profit. With the works now complete, the firm needed another injection of capital to keep it afloat until the mill was working to full capacity. As the second anniversary of their partnership approached, Granger proposed a new agreement to reflect their new business enterprise. As their original shares had almost halved in value, it was agreed that the capital in the business be increased to £26,000 'for their principal or

Joint Stock in Money together with what they have already invested in the business'. Banfill was also to become a partner. As neither Antony nor his father had any further funds to invest, they asked Vicary to release Exwick Barton to fund their share. Concerned that his family were on the verge of bankruptcy Vicary had no option but to agree. In an agreement dated 8 August 1787, all his 'properties in Exwick purchased in Trust' for Antony, were transferred to ownership of the Exeter firm 'as part of the joint stock & at the end or other determination of the said Copartnership be divided and possessed accordingly' by the partners.[55]

Satisfied that his investment was secured, on 28 August Granger signed a new ten-year contact with George Abraham, Antony and Banfill to form a new joint stock company called Gibbs Granger & Banfill. They became 'co partners & joint traders in the Business of a merchant and in the Buying Fulling Racking dressing finishing selling bartering and transporting and importing all such Woollen Goods and other Goods Wares and Merchandises and Things'. Of the £26,000 capital Granger contributed £12,000, George Abraham £10,000, and Antony and Banfill £2000 each. The new firm was to operate solely from the mill at Exwick. All premises and stock still held by Antony and Banfill from the firm of Gibbs Brothers, 'belonging to them as co-partners were to be Sold and disposed of for the most money…and the money shall be considered as part of the Joint Stock of the said parties'. Under the new arrangement, perhaps surprisingly, Antony was responsible for keeping the day-to-day accounts, something he disliked intensely, while Granger continued to maintain the firm's cashbooks and ledgers. The new firm was not liable for the personal or other business debts incurred by the partners before the new agreement. It was also agreed that Antony could continue to live in Exwick House and keep it 'for his own and separate use' at a yearly rent of £25 and was to pay for the 'House and Window Tax and to keep the Glass of the windows in Repair', and all other rates and taxes.[56]

Despite Antony and Banfill's efforts, by the end of December the firm's losses continued to increase, mainly because so much of their time had been spent overseeing the work at the mill. As 1788 dawned, Antony knew he was on the verge of bankruptcy. Throughout the previous year, he had continued to draw on his loan account from Granger at 5 per cent interest. His old debts were still outstanding and his creditors were now impatient for payment, while repeated requests failed to yield any funds from his Spanish customers.

That Christmas, as Dolly's third confinement drew near, Antony's family and his cousin Betsy came to stay for a few days, possibly oblivious to his financial difficulties. They all enjoyed the festivities and it appeared to them that Antony and Dolly had not a care in the world. The only thing to mar their enjoyment was Betsy's unhappiness after she had reluctantly ended her engagement to a young American who had been found to be a swindler. After Christmas, Betsy came to live at Exwick House to help Dolly with her growing family. At the end of January, another son was born, whom they named George Abraham after his grandfather.

When Granger proposed that the firm should buy the remaining sixty years lease of the mill the partners readily agreed. For the last two years, it had been renting the premses on a short-term lease but having invested so much capital in the building, it seemed a good idea to purchase the remaining lease to protect their investment. In an indenture dated 8th February 1788, Granger and Antony each paid £126 for the residue of the original ninety-nine year lease for the 'fulling mill and mill house with appurtenances, the dwelling house and stream of water'.[57]

By the end of July, Antony had borrowed a further £600 from his loan account. Nor was the firm yet showing a profit. The building work had taken considerably longer to complete and was more expensive than expected and the mill was still not operating to full capacity. As his shareholding had reduced in value since August 1785, so his loan account had increased and by 1787, Antony's debts to the firm exceeded Granger's share of the business. From his former activities with the firm of Gibbs Brothers Cloth Merchants, a number of his customers in Europe still owed him considerable sums of money, and he was still, after four years, unable to pay his suppliers. The banks were now urgently pressing him to settle his accounts. Desperate to escape his creditors, Antony decided that there was no alternative but to go to Spain to collect what was owing to him and try to generate more business. Dolly was devastated and begged him not to go, but he was adamant knowing he had no alternative. Although she knew things were very difficult, it is probable that she had no idea of the depths of their financial problems. After many tears, she reluctantly agreed and on 3 August 1788, Antony and Banfill left Exeter to travel to Dover where he planned to seek a passage to France.

Banfill accompanied him as far as Honiton. There they visited his old friend John Simcoe and it is likely that they discussed his situation. Before continuing his journey, Antony gave Banfill a letter for Dolly urging her to be strong at such a difficult time. He wrote, 'the sacrifice we must now make must....be to our advantage in the end....and will produce a profit for the business then we shall have the satisfaction of having done our best'. He begged her not to be too depressed or upset for' if you let the servants perceive that you are more agitated than might be expected, it will encourage report that I am gone on account of circumstances, which the Tuckers in Exeter are I find, still attempting to make people believe'. With promises to write every day, Antony set off for London while Banfill returned to Exwick to run the firm in his absence.

Shortly after Antony's departure, both Granger and Banfill decided they had no alternative but to mortgage both the house and lands in Exwick Barton and the mill and factory to raise money to keep the business going until his return and, despite his reservations George Abraham had no option but to agree. They approached an Exmouth merchant, Gerrard Duccarell, who agreed to lend them £5,000 on a £10,000 mortgage for six months. Should either of the partners, or all of them 'not pay the said Sum of Five thousand Pounds and the Interest thereof or any part thereof....the said Gerrard Gustavus Duccarell...would take over the property'.[58] Although unhappy at the terms, it gave the partners a few months breathing space until Antony's anticipated return after Christmas.

Meanwhile, after leaving Honiton, Antony had broken his journey at Bristol where he unburdened his problems to George who could do little to help except to offer to look after his family while he was away. Before leaving he wrote another note of encouragement to Dolly urging her to stand firm for 'What is an absence of four or five months and upon such an errand when compared to what we see other people may say....stifle your feelings....you know my dear Dolly why I did not mention my intention of going abroad to you sooner, and I hope what I hid from motives of affection, has not been taken in the opposite light... .'. After arriving in London Antony stayed a few days with the Townley-Wards before proceeding on to Dover, where he waited for a vessel to take him across the Channel.

* * * *

Landing in Calais on 11 August, Antony travelled overland to Amiens and then on to Paris where he hoped 'to settle some old accounts to our satisfaction... .'. In the event, he did not manage to generate any business there, complaining that he was in 'France at a shocking time for business... .'. From Paris he made his way to Orleans but was so plagued by the fleas that 'you never saw such a miserable figure as I am made by the bugs which torment me in this place....and there is not business so I shall let them drink no more of my blood... .'. He left Orleans on 30 August travelling to Tours and on to Limoges, Lyons and Toulouse. In Limoges, he found one or two merchants interested in importing woollen cloth and planned to return there on his return from Spain noting that '...this place seems to be of more consequence than all France... .'. At Lyons he had ....one of the most disagreeable disputes to settle ' but succeeded in doing a considerable amount of new business. He then boarded a boat and travelled down the Rhone to Toulouse where he met with '...a parcel of rascals whom I cannot oblige to pay what they owe...'. A few days later Antony arrived in Bayonne where the '... whole country is in a bustle here on account of the mutiny of the parliament... .' There he found a letter from Dolly telling him that she was pregnant again, was very depressed suffering from severe morning sickness. She complained that she was getting much fatter with this pregnancy than before and with no money was having to let out her old clothes and asked if she could buy a ticket for the Exeter lottery. Although Antony was not a gambler and disapproved of the lottery considering it 'a bad practice for poor people', he agreed that in their present situation he was 'inclined to take a chance myself' and told her that if she should win 'the £20,000 in the lottery, you shall soon see me as fat as yourself'.

By the end of October, Antony had reached Pamplona where he found a note from Dolly telling him she had suffered a miscarriage and begging him to return home. Although saddened by the news and worried about her health, he replied, 'Would it not be an egregious folly [by returning sooner] to suffer the comfort which I promise myself on my return to be broken in upon by consideration of my not having completed the business which I am come to transact & to which I make such heavy sacrifices'. A few days later he arrived in Bilboa, where he found the economic situation much more difficult than he had imagined. H wrote to her that 'there have been many failures in this country….but [fortunately] we are concerned in none nor have anything to do with those who are expected to fail; but this is much more than our neighbours [in Exeter] can say…'.

After her husband's departure, Dolly took the children to stay for a few days with George and Etty and then went on to Hayes to visit Vicary and Kenny. While there she became aware of how lenient they were with their daughter, and wrote to Antony asking whether they should be less strict with their own children. In his reply he noted that she had 'remarked a good deal on Vicary & Kenny's manner of bringing up their children & you will probably have compared their manner in this respect with ours & that of Charles & Mary'. He suggested that she try to learn from them, recognising that 'impatience has been a great fault in my temper, and in the management of children nothing can be worse than this', adding 'I think you will find that George's method with his children approaches more to perfection than either of the others'.

Antony remained in Bilboa until Christmas then made his way to Madrid, arriving there in January 1789. It seemed as if his luck had changed. Within a few weeks, he was writing enthusiastically that 'as the business gathers upon me so fast' he was unable to return to England and would remain in Madrid for an extra month. Yet again, his natural optimism clouded his judgement. By April as the promised business failed to materialise, he wrote despondently that he would be returning to Exeter for there is 'little business here....despite all my labours'. Despite the uncertainty that he must have felt about his own future, when a letter arrived from his father with the news that George had been offered a partnership in the Bristol firm, he immediately congratulated his brother noting that 'in the midst of our poverty we shall....have the satisfaction that some of our nearest friends and relations get rich around us'. Though to Dolly he wrote 'that.... without those riches we are as happy as they.'.

Although he had originally planned to sail to England, in the event he decided to travel overland through France. Whether he was merely putting off the inevitable is unclear as he made his way back to Calais, calling in at Bayonne, Toulouse and Lyon. Waiting for him there was a letter from Dolly with the news that their beloved son, George Abraham had died a few weeks before on 3 March. She was grief-stricken and again remonstrated with him for delaying his return. Despite this, he would not accept any censure for his prolonged absence. On 2 April, he replied, 'No one knows how much I suffer from having been obliged to delay so long & if I were in decent circumstances I would not have submitted to it, but I have imposed it as a religious duty on myself and a religious duty on my family'. Nevertheless, he was anxious to get home to her, and made his way north through France as quickly as possible. Again, despite promises from a number of merchant houses in the larger towns, the situation in France was so uncertain, that he had been unable to generate any new business. As he travelled north, he wrote despondently on 17 April, telling her that he would be home in July but despite all his efforts, they were ruined. Even in the face of disaster, he managed to add 'let us thank God, my Dearest Dolly, for the blessings we have left and submit with resignation to the misfortune that has befallen us'.

Meanwhile in England, Granger and Banfill had spent many anxious months hoping that the mail would bring some good news. The day of reckoning with Duccarell had passed but when Granger heard that Antony was due in July, he managed to persuade him that they would be able to repay the loan on his return. In May, Granger was not surprised to learn that bankruptcy proceedings had begun against both Antony and his father and commissioners had been appointed to look into their affairs. Knowing that that he was likely to lose everything if Duccarell was not paid something on account, he approached the commissioners asking them to 'advance him the sum of £3000' and offered 'to convey to them....all the Messuage tenements and lands', in Exwick Barton that were held by the partnership, and also 'such sum of Money as on the balance of such Accounts be due and owing [to the business] from the said George Abraham Gibbs and Antony Gibbs...with lawful Interest'.[59] The commissioners, anxious to keep the business going until Antony returned, agreed and at the beginning of July, authorised the Devonshire Bank to lend Granger £3000, subject to the proviso that the premises could be redeemed on repayment of the loan.[60] This gave Granger some extra time and on 14 July, he paid Duccarell £1000 of 'the principal sum of £5000'.

When Dolly received her husband's letter some weeks later she was beside herself. Until then, all the news from him had been so optimistic. For nearly a year, she had supported him and had managed to conceal the reality of their financial situation from her friends and family. Now there was nothing left. Not only had Antony lost all the monies settled on her on her marriage but also everything he had borrowed from his father. Distraught, she confided in her mother, telling her to prepare for the worst. Despite her daughter's confidence, Mrs Hucks immediately wrote to Eleanor to warn her of the impending disaster, but the bad news had already reached the metropolis. Eleanor's reply dated 10 June confirmed 'what I heard a month ago....poor

Antony's mind will now be more at rest and he entirely knows what he has to trust to and is now a new man…'.

Antony reached Paris on 5 July 1789 as the first convocation of the Estates General for over one hundred years was being held in the city, and from there made his way to Calais to seek a passage to Dover, arriving back in England later that month. Even then, he had begun to devise a plan for his future. His only prospect of rebuilding his life was to return to Spain and establish an agency business. He knew the country and spoke the language. All he needed were one or two contracts while he got himself started. Knowing that all was lost and he would be declared bankrupt once he returned to Devon, he decided to visit one of his existing customers in Norwich before returning to Exeter. There, he negotiated a three year contract to act as their commission agent on a retainer of £150 a year with a 2 per cent commission, instead of the normal 2½, on orders over £8000.

On his way back to Exeter, he called in to see George in Bristol. Knowing that he was responsible for his father's ruin, Antony was determined to make amends and rebuild the family's fortunes. He told George of his plans and offered to act as Munckley Gibbs & Richards' agent in the Iberian Peninsula, confident that such an arrangement would be to their mutual advantage. Knowing how impulsive his brother could be in his business dealings, initially George was sceptical, believing that it was Antony's sanguine attitude that had led to his failure. His natural optimism was a quality his father had always considered a fundamental defect in his character and even as a child had the 'old habits of pushing hope and expectation as far and perhaps further than you ought in reason to do'. Eventually he was persuaded and agreed that Antony had no alternative but to return to Spain with his family while he and Vicary sorted out the financial chaos that he was to leave behind. George, aware of his brother's dislike of paperwork, insisted that he keep control of Antony's accounts and manage his debts and he generously lent him £150 towards his expenses.

Antony arrived back in Devon at the end of July, only to find that in his absence, several firms in the city were in serious financial difficulties and there had been a number of recent failures. He was shaken to find that bankruptcy proceedings had already been instigated against both him and his father and commissioners had been appointed to deal with their affairs. On 16 July 1789, an advertisement had appeared in *Trewman's Exeter Flying Post* requesting that,

> 'All persons having any demands on MR. ANTONY GIBBS of the City of Exeter, Merchant, are desired to send the Particulars thereof to Richard Collyns and John Waymouth, both of Exeter, or one of them; and all Persons indebted to the said ANTONY GIBBS, are thereby required to pay their respective Debts to the said Messrs Collyns and Waymouth, who are legally authorised to receive the same, or to one of them otherwise they will be prosecuted without further NOTICE'.[61]

Antony went straight to see Granger and Banfill who told him of their discussions with his commissioners. It was to be many months before the extent of his debts was known, but he knew that 'he was considerably indebted to the said Partnership of Granger Gibbs & Banfill above what his share in the business would amount to & that by the Terms of the said Articles of Co partnership'. An initial examination of the ledgers indicated that that he owed around £18,000, (around £720,000 in today's money). As Antony was legally allowed to try to discharge his debts by a distribution of his assets, Waymouth & Collyns agreed that he could continue trading until they were paid off. On 31 July, he 'conveyed and assigned among other lands all of his share and Interest in the premises' in Exwick to the commissioners 'upon trust to be sold for the benefit of his Creditors'. As the firm owned the freehold of Exwick Barton and had purchased the remainder of the lease on the mill, the Commissioners agreed that 'All the Hereditaments and Premises belonging to the said partners should be sold and the produce thus applied to the partnership Debts'.

It was agreed that on his return to Spain, Antony would act as the Exeter firm's agent for the next ten years, the length of their partnership agreement, and all his commission would be used to repay his debts. Granger wanted to keep the firm going at all costs for if it was liquidated he knew he would lose everything. He was worried that if the premises, stock and other assets were sold, and 'all the debts due to the Partnership including the Capital' which he had invested in the firm, paid out, 'there would be nothing left to divide amongst the Partners' and there would not be sufficient to pay off their combined debts. He persuaded Banfill that the best way forward was for the firm to take on George Abraham and Antony's debts and convert them to a loan. They applied to the commissioners requesting that 'all the right estate & interest of sd Anthony Gibbs [sic] of and in/among other lands/ the Premises aforesaid' could be conveyed to them.[62] Although the commissioners agreed in principle, nothing would be done until the final accounts had been settled.

On 12 August, Antony and Dolly packed all they could carry and prepared to leave Exeter. Although his parents knew of their plans, they had no idea when they were actually leaving. Antony hoped they could slip away, but Dolly, who was still mourning her dead son, refused to leave without saying goodbye to her mother. Mrs Hucks was beside herself, not knowing when she would see her daughter and grandchildren again. She gave Dolly a present of £50 to help them with their expenses. Two weeks later Antony and his family left Exwick, accompanied by Betsy, Dolly's maidservant and a nurse to help with the children. William Branscombe the young son of a family friend who had been working for Antony for some years also went with them. As the Paris crowd stormed the Bastille, they boarded a boat at Topsham quay bound for La Corunna.

CHAPTER 7

EXWICK AND MADRID

It took many months for Collyns and Waymouth to gather sufficient information about Antony's affairs to agree to Granger's request not to liquidate the firm. In the meantime, he and Banfill set about re-organising the business. The value of the premises had increased considerably, but not enough to offset the trading losses of the previous two years and meanwhile the loan from Duccarell remained unpaid. It was estimated that Granger's original £12,000 investment was now only worth a little over £7569 and Banfill's £2000 only £1089. With Antony gone and George Abraham ruined, the two remaining partners decided to wind up the firm of Gibbs Granger & Banfill and transfer the loan accounts to a new company that was restyled Granger & Banfill.[1]

Granger was not a vindictive man. He had known the Gibbs family for many years and sympathised with George Abraham's plight. As both he and Antony were signatories to the lease for the mill, after Antony's departure, he proposed that it be assigned to Banfill and himself and that they buy out their former partners. George Abraham's share of the business was valued around £5861 and Antony's at £1472, making a total of £7333.[2] The commissioners agreed on condition that this sum was directly paid to them. Granger concurred, offering to purchase George Abraham's shares including his share of Exwick House, on his own account while the new firm paid for Antony's, on the understanding that it should be treated as a loan. Before he left, it was agreed that any commission that Antony earned would be set against his outstanding account. Aware that he needed some capital to establish his business, Granger and Banfill each gave him with a small loan, and as a sign of their goodwill gave Antony until 31 August 1797, the end of their original partnership agreement, to repay all his debts to them.[3]

After his departure, the commissioners asked Banfill to arrange for the contents of Exwick House to be sold at auction. Mrs Hucks, who was anxious to purchase a number of her daughter's possessions, gave him a list of furniture and other items that she wished to buy. Too distressed to attend the auction herself, she was furious, a few days later to learn that he had bought most of her daughter's furniture for himself. Indignantly she wrote to Dolly, who by that time had arrived in Spain, '…Mr B has bought a greater Number of things I'm told amongst the rest yours, and the White bed with most of the furniture in the Room. I had liked to have had very little and hardly yet know what is Bought for me'. However, in the event, Banfill did not let her down, and she acquired nearly all the items she wanted.

Nevertheless, it soon became clear why Banfill had purchased so much. As Granger had no use for Exwick House, he agreed that his new partner, who now owned one-third of the firm, should live there. A few days after the auction, Banfill moved into the mansion and furnished it with his friend's former possessions. Exwick House was a large family residence, far too big for a young bachelor. He soon realised that he needed a housekeeper and offered Nancy the position. Both George and Vicary thought it demeaning that their sister should be reduced to this, urging her to refuse. Nancy was more realistic. Now aged thirty-three with no fortune of her own and with her father ruined, her family was completely dependent on Vicary for support. She was an educated woman and several years older than her employer and as his housekeeper, would have a permanent home and some independence. Her duties included managing the house and servants and keeping the household accounts. Whether Banfill thought that Nancy had also acquired Antony's *defect* is unclear but in the early days, she was extremely irritated that he insisted on her justifying all expenditure and checking the accounts each evening. It was many months before Banfill had the confidence to trust in her ability.

When the commissioners had finally calculated their combined debts, Antony's were over £18,000 and George Abraham's were in the region of £12,000. All too aware that he was responsible for his family's ruin, Antony agreed that he should shoulder the combined burden. A number of friends and family had generously lent money to try to avoid bankruptcy, but the total raised was only £11,680. Such was the feeling amongst his old friends that one, John Graves Simcoe wrote, if '...he had not family he would be glad to lend [more than]....£1000', but in the event seems managed to lend him over £1900.[4]

Once the accounts were finalized, the commissioners acceded to Granger's proposal that the house and mill be transferred to him and Banfill. In a deed dated 16 and 17 September 1790, 'Richard Collyns and John Waymouth as Trustees....released and assigned unto Edmund Granger & Samuel Banfill....all the Share Right & Interest of the sd [sic] Anthony [sic] of and in/among other lands/the premises aforesaid...' in Exwick Barton.[5] As Antony was still a signatory on the original lease for the mill, any increase in the value of the premises was to be offset against the loan when the business or the property was eventually sold.

* * * *

Antony and Dolly arrived at La Corunna at the end of August 1789. The Bay of Biscay had proved exceptionally rough for the time of year and Dolly was continually ill with a 'a violent disorder of her bowels' which 'with [her] other complaints were very alarming'. Betsy too was very ill and spent much of the voyage confined to her cabin with severe headaches and sickness. They were forced to delay their departure for Madrid until they had both recovered sufficiently to travel. While there, a letter arrived from Dolly's mother. Still very distressed at their leaving, Mrs Hucks wrote, 'I think I never loved your Husband so little....as at the moment he told me you were to leave this House so early in the morning'. Dolly was touched that her mother had bought her favourite possessions at the Exwick House sale and was saving them for her return, but was puzzled as to why Banfill bought most of their furniture. She was also very concerned to learn that her brother John was now experiencing financial difficulties having run up considerable debts. Her mother seemed resigned to the fact that if she refused to settle them he too would be ruined.

By the end of September, they were living in Madrid, having taken some cheap lodgings for a month at five shillings a day, until they could find a house in a better part of the city. On 2 November, Antony wrote to his father to assure him that he had every confidence in the future. 'I have not only, my Dearest Sir, the strongest inclination that I verily believe that I shall have it in my power to convince all those who have behaved kindly to me, that I am not so unworthy of their regard as I know some people have represented me....Believe me, My Dearest Sir, it is not in my nature to disappoint those friends'. He reported that they had taken a furnished house in Madrid for 'only £55 a year' and that it was much cheaper to live in Spain than in England. They were very short of money and so to establish his business he had been 'obliged....to take up of Granger and Banfill three hundred pounds besides the £150 pounds I had from George [and] I have had some flattering proposals from several people of consequence here, to establish a warehouse of goods in general in the woollen line'.

As soon as he had arrived, Antony had begun working as a travelling agent for a number of English merchant houses including Munckley Gibbs & Richards and Granger & Banfill, although any commission earned through the Exeter firm was to be offset against his debts. He was determined to succeed and as soon as his business showed a profit, planned to repay the outstanding loans from his family. Full of confidence, he wrote, 'on the 9th of the month G & B will send me £100 on account of services and I shall remit them on that day £70 besides. This will reduce my debt to them of something less that half a years salary....and I shall be out of their debt the 9th May. I shall remit George fifty pounds the 9th of February and the balance the 9th August, which will be the end of my first years business'. With his salary and commission, he anticipated 'clearing £700 in the first year', and was convinced that he would be able to repay Banfill, Mrs Hucks and his brother George before too long.

Antony's letter showed clearly that he had lost little of his misplaced optimism. Easily impressed by promises of others, he told his father that, after only a few weeks in Spain he had identified a number of new opportunities and planned to undercut existing agents on both commission and price, to establish his business. He was also considering 'doing something on commission in the line of Muslins and Irish Linens'. As an afterthought, he also asked his father to send out a butter churn so that Dolly could try to make some butter. 'We pay 2d a pound for stinking Dutch butter & for the best fresh butter 3/6 a pound' he wrote 'but this we have not tasted'.

Once the family was settled, Antony left Madrid to travel throughout the country to drum up business. For the next year, he was away for periods of up to six weeks at a time, only returning for a few days between trips. Dolly, unable to afford to pay for help in the house, became very despondent as her pregnancy progressed. She wrote to her mother at the beginning of December, 'I cannot tell you how uncomfortable I am without him, understanding very little of the language and being in a strange place among a very disagreeable set of people which all Spaniards are you will not wonder at me feeling as I do'. She continued, 'my time was never so much employed as it is now, for you know…we have only nurse and Allice [sic] and that we wash small things and iron everything at home, and I never put out the least thing to make or mend. Allice and I are the only workers at the needle for six people and other things that are always to do in a family'. She also mentioned that she was having difficulties with Betsy, who had kept to her room, refusing to help with the children. Betsy, she wrote, is 'disappointed with our manner of living' and that she had no opportunity to meet 'nice people' and grumbled continually about their situation. The heat, she claimed, gave her a constant headache. Betsy refused to learn Spanish, even though Dolly had offered to pay for lessons, which she could ill-afford and felt that her cousin could at least have made an effort to learn the language for 'she has nothing else to do'.

For Antony, business considerations were paramount, allowing little time for frivolity or for his family. With few social contacts, Dolly's energies were confined to running the home and looking after her children. Although she had little time to learn the language herself, she was determined that the children should learn Spanish, and somehow found the money from her housekeeping even though they cost 'more than I am able to afford'. She was overjoyed when the butter churn arrived from Exeter and could begin to make butter. Although she found a number of other basic items were more expensive, they found it much cheaper to live there than England and could do so 'more decently and comfortably'.

It was to be a very bleak Christmas far from friends and family, made more uncomfortable by Betsy's attitude. As Antony was due to leave on another extended period after Christmas, he tried to speak to his cousin, but this only appears to have made matters worse causing Dolly to complain that after his departure Betsy had become even more uncooperative. On his return in mid-February, the women were barely speaking to one another. With Dolly's confinement due in May, Antony promised his cousin that if she would remain until after the birth, he would try to find her a passage back to England and he left high hopes that the situation was now settled.

It was not to be. On his return at the end of April, he found the tension between them worse and was forced to concede that Betsy now 'loves Dolly now as much as my mother loves dogs!' He implored his cousin to make allowances for his wife's ill temper, who at eight months pregnant was finding it very difficult to cope in the heat. Three weeks later, on 22 May, Dolly delivered another son, who was called William. It had been a long labour and a difficult birth and whilst the new baby was large and healthy, his mother was confined to bed for several weeks.

Knowing how anxious his parents were for news, Antony wrote to them every week. In a letter dated 16 June, he reported that 'BG has been of little use and much mischief from the disappointment [his bankruptcy]'. 'As to her sincerity of character', he wrote, 'more than from the loss of any usefulness that she might have been of. I have had two very severe conversations with B & her own account is I think as much against her as any I can give. She says plainly that her friendship for Dolly is much lapsed'. He went on, 'The cause, the want of attention to her in the ship (you know she was ill herself and had the children to care for), the want of attention to her at Corunna, particularly Santiago and lastly a total alteration, she pretends, in Dolly's temper and disposition, which she says are become intolerable.' Although they both knew of Betsy's reputation for being very difficult Dolly 'never wd believe it', and it was a relief that she was returning to England in the next few weeks.

His anger was, however, tempered with realism. He recognised that Dolly had to accept some share of the blame. 'We must ...do Betsy the justice to allow that her health has been very indifferent at times & I can not be surprised at her wanting to be home'. Since William's birth she had 'been a little more desirous to please', but things had come to a head when Dolly discovered that she had written to some mutual friends 'that there has been nothing wanting [here] to make her comfortable, but what she ought to have brought with her'. He wrote, 'I don't think B has written since Dolly's confinement to a single friend of hers or ours – she is certainly not much interested herself and thinks the same possibly of other people'. Since William's birth, Betsy 'had for some little time been more attentive & I think she goes on improving' but despite her attempts two women rarely spoke to each other. In July, Antony put Betsy on a boat for Dover accompanied 'by a Gentleman from Birmingham'. Well aware of his father's reaction to the news, Antony begged him not to mention the events in Spain on her return, for 'Unless B begins to talk improperly at home, I hope no notice will be taken of what has happened'.

A week after his cousin's departure, an angry letter arrived from his father. 'EG's behaviour' George Abraham wrote, 'must have been a trouble & disappointment...that she should have failed in the offices of humanity' and he would never forgive her. When she heard this, Dolly began to feel very guilty, writing immediately to her mother-in-law, asking that they show no bitterness to Betsy, who was now penniless, homeless and alone. She begged her mother-in-law to treat Betsy with kindness. However, George Abraham was adamant, forgetting the cause of his niece's present situation. George was much more understanding, well aware of the debt of gratitude that his father and brother owed their Topsham cousin, and he offered her a home with him in Bristol until she found something more permanent.

The last few months had been a period of great uncertainly for Antony and Dolly, but without Betsy, life became more settled. He had made a number of connections with both English and local Spanish merchants, but now war seemed imminent after the seizure of British ships by the Spanish at Nookta Sound off Vancouver. Militarily weak, Spain hoped that its ally France would support its claim for a monopoly of trade but was to be disappointed, being forced to accede to British demands. Both countries tried to settle their territorial differences and on 28 October 1790, the Nookta Bay Agreement was signed in Madrid. The chief negotiators for the British were Antony's friend Antony Merry, the *Chargé d'affairs pro tem*,[6] and the British Ambassador, Alleyne Fitzherbert, who was a friend of his brother George.[7]

Humiliated, the Spanish government introduced a number of retaliatory measures against the British, the most important of which to Antony, was the prohibition of cheap muslins imports from England, to come into effect after sixty days. When the prohibition was announced in March 1791, he was in Lisbon and had met Lewis Stephens who owned the firm Lewis Stephens & Co. Stephens had around £50,000 of muslin in stock, which he offered Antony the chance of selling in Spain on commission before the prohibition came into effect. Delighted at such an unexpected opportunity, Antony decided to undercut his fellow agents on price and take a reduction in commission, confident that within the next two months he could gain orders for it in the region of £20,000 from Andalusia alone, to yield an income of between £500-£600. He hurredly returned to Madrid, and after successfully obtaining a number of large orders, returned to Lisbon and shipped the consignments to Cadiz and Seville. George had advised him not to reduce both the price and his commission, but Antony had stubbornly gone his own way with the result that even though his commission on the muslins was over £1000, once his expenses were taken into account, he barely broke even.

Despite his efforts to make amends for his past actions, Antony knew that his father blamed himself for the 'defect' in his character leading him to have unrealistic expectations. Afraid that it would be passed on to the children George Abraham had suggested that Dolly 'should apply to their children's training the lesson of his experience and of his liability to fail in steady application'. Writing to Dolly, Antony reported that 'this disposition in me was discovered early by my father, but his constant occupations prevented him paying that regular attention to it, which was required, and my mother…has not a grain of it in her disposition'. He bore no resentment towards his father for this apparent neglect adding that his parents, 'were both so thoroughly satisfied at discovering in me such strong traits of sensibility and good humour that they never suspected that anything essentially wrong could come from so good a stock, and thence paid less attention to this fatal defect in my disposition'.

For Antony, this was only the beginning. Europe was in turmoil again which led to a sharp decline in his business. His debts remained in the region of £20,000 but he was convinced that if the hostilities only lasted a few months, he could ride out the economic difficulties, although he was realistic enough to recognise that if the war was prolonged, he '…could not bear the expense of it as my income must necessarily be much reduced…'. Within months of arriving in Spain, he had begun to feel more confident for his future. Now well established he had made a significant number of contacts across the country, but his family's health continued to cause him great concern. Henry had been 'attacked twice by something like jaundice', and although Dolly was now fully recovered from William's birth, she still found the heat very grueling during the summer months. The older children quickly became proficient in the language. As Dolly told Bell, 'Henry and Harriet like much more to speak English than Spanish; they are quiet and shy as ever before strangers, and Henry is as stiff as a quaker when he has any compliments to make; he can talk Spanish as quick as English to Harriet ....and with great propriety and good pronunciation and reads it better than English for when he is reading to me he Spanishises all his words'.

As early as June 1790, Antony was forced to admit that Spain was no place for his family. He wrote to his father that he planned to return to England the following year, which 'will be on the whole more comfortable for Dolly to remain there with the children'. It would also provide him with an opportunity to visit a number of merchant houses to discuss future business with them. One of his largest clients was a Rochdale firm that dealt mainly in muslins. He believed that if he could sustain the present level of business, within the next few months he would have sufficient funds to move his family back to Devon. Although his business seems to have prospered, any plans of returning to England had to be abandoned. Young William had been very poorly, and he had been forced to dismiss his clerk for stealing £50 from him. He also felt that that William Branscombe was too inexperienced to leave in charge of the firm in his absence. Instead in July, he took a house with a large garden in La Granja in the Serra de Guadarrama and Dolly and the children spent the summer there, returning to Madrid in October. There she found that Antony, who was about to leave for Barcelona, had been unwell in her absence and had suffered from fainting fits, from which he now appeared to have completely recovered.

After he had left, Dolly's brother John, now aged twenty, arrived for an extended visit. Having bought himself out of his regiment, he had purchased a farm in Ireland but that too had failed. He had run up considerable debts and was a constant drain on his mother who was also supporting her youngest son Joseph at Eton. Mrs Hucks may have secretly hoped that Antony would take him into the business, something he resisted. Knowing that he was in no position to lecture his young brother-in-law, he wrote to Dolly from Barcelona that 'you can let him see the sense you have of his past conduct and how distressed you are on his account and on your mother's. It may be of service to him perhaps to consider the miserable slavish life which I submit to lead for the sake of being able to retrieve my lost time...'; he suggested that John be tasked with learning Spanish. On his return to Madrid in November, he found that his brother-in-law had settled into his new task with enthusiasm, and was 'attentive to me...but totally averse to any advice from his mother, me, or anyone else, alive to the foibles of all others, and unconscious to his own deficiencies'.

By the beginning of 1792, as his situation improved, Antony hoped to leave Spain later that year. Dolly was pregnant again and dreaded another summer in Madrid but in February, while he was in Seville she miscarriaged. When he arrived home two months later, she was still unwell. Knowing that he could delay their return to England no longer, he wrote to his father on 14 May that they would be setting out for England at the beginning of June and hoped to be in Stowe by 20 July. He could not resist adding that 'George will have the satisfaction from the favourable state of my books, & I must be content to wait for a few months the encashment of what is due to me'. He also warned that he would not be able to repay any of their debts. Most of his money was still tied up in stock; there was over £700 in Seville alone, which would 'not be free until the end of this year, besides four hundred pounds in the muslins'.

As the family prepared to leave Madrid, the mail brought a letter from Bell with the news that their father was unwell and asking for him. Antony replied by return that once again they had been forced to delay their departure. Dolly was still too ill to travel and William had suddenly developed a fever, which was diagnosed as smallpox, becoming so unwell that they thought they were going to lose him. After several anxious days, he began to recover, although the signs of his illness would remain with him for the rest of his life. By the end of June Dolly seemed much better 'having received considerable benefit from a course of opium prescribed by a young physician who had studied at Edinburgh', and William too was now fully recovered having 'now lost the fever as well as ague'.

They planned to travel overland to England but before leaving

Antony decided to make another quick visit to Seville and Malaga. There a letter arrived from Dolly. She was was pregnant again and complained that she had not heard from him since his departure. Irritated, Antony replied that she had no right to protest 'on my not writing you long letters when God knows that I am half plagued to death by constant and disagreeable occupations, which leave one little rest night or day'. From Malaga, he travelled to Cadiz to wait for news of a government contract that could be worth £150 a year for seven years. On 22 July, he wrote that he would be stay there until he knew about the contract for 'if I lose it now, I shall never have a chance of getting it again, at least until seven years are over'.

Returning to Madrid a few days later, he was shocked at Dolly's appearance. In constant pain and discomfort, she was suffering from severe morning sickness and was taking laudanum with increasing dependence.[8] Antony lost no time in completing the packing and within a few days, accompanied by their friend, Jacques Courant, the family began the long journey across France to Dover. Progress was slowed by Dolly's pregnancy and when they arrived at Bayonne, she was so unwell that they very nearly abandoned their plans of travelling overland and 'engaged with a Captain to give him £100 to go with his vessel to Topsham'. They arrived in Paris on 11 August the day after the Paris mob had attacked the Tuileries Palace where Louis XIV had been forced to take refuge and was now under virtual house arrest.

With Paris in turmoil, they were delayed for several days waiting for travel permits. Antony wrote to his father 'By the revolution of the 10th the government of this country is now in the hands of a few members of the national assembly who have the confidence of the Paris people'. A few weeks later, the old order issued the Declaration of Brunswick pledging to reduce Paris to rubble if Louis was harmed. With the enemy at the gates, there was an atmosphere of crisis in the city, exacerbated by a shortage of sugar and a decline in the assignat, the revolutionary paper money, which had first been introduced in 1789. As they left Paris at the end of August the mob stormed the Tuileries, massacred the 600 Swiss Guards who defended the palace, and incarcerated Louis

XIV and Marie Antoinette. When Antony and his family arrived in London in September, France declared itself a republic.

* * * *

After resting in London for a few days with the Wards, they travelled to Stowe to stay with Mary and Charles. Antony's parents had arrived there the week before for the family reunion. Overjoyed to see them again, his father was determined that his plans were entirely '...subject to the main object of spending as much time as we can with you during your short residence in England'. Once rested, they all began the long journey back to Devon, stopping for a couple of days at George's house in Bristol. Exhausted, George Abraham wanted to rest there and so Antony and Dolly continued by coach with the children to Exeter.

There they moved in with Mrs Hucks, who was living in a small house not far from the centre of the city. She was delighted to see her daughter and grandchildren, especially young William. Antony was convinced that Dolly's health would now improve and hoped she would reduce her dependence on laudanum. If she had wished that he would remain long in Exeter with her, she was to be disappointed. As soon as his family was settled in, he determined to return to the Iberian Peninsula. Within a few days, he left for Norwich, going on from there to London, Rochdale and Manchester, visiting existing customers and seeking new business. Calling in to see George once again on his way back to Exeter the two men agreed to work together importing Mediterranean produce which was in short supply in England.

On his return, he enrolled Henry into the Charles Lloyd School and had a number of meetings with Granger and Banfill. On 29 October, he wrote to his father who was still in Bristol that he 'had a satisfactory conversation with G&B in the most flattering manner to me. They expressed their sense of constant exertion in favour of their House'. Still worried about his father's health, he was concerned to hear from George a few days before he was due to leave that George Abraham wanted to write to him but was too weak to do so.

Antony was due to depart on 3 November. The day before he left he received a barely legible letter written two days earlier in his father's shaky hand that affected him greatly. Not knowing whether he would ever see Antony again, George Abraham was determined that his son should know he was forgiven him for his past actions. Throughout his life George Abraham had rarely shown his children any affection, bombarding them daily with letters of advice and admonishment; they had never questioned his authority. Although he had never been rebuked for ruining the family, this was the first letter that Antony had ever received from him acknowledging his efforts to restore the family honour.

The following day Antony set out for Falmouth to seek a passage to Lisbon promising to write every day. While there, knowing of Dolly's uncertainties at how she would face their friends, he wrote 'Don't you think for a moment of the neglect you will experience from most of my former friends in Exeter, but behave my Dearest love, on all occasions in a manner suitable.' After he left, Eleanor invited her to bring the children for a short visit to London. On the way, Dolly stopped in Bristol, and anxious repair the rift between them, invited Betsy to join her. Antony had warned her that 'There has been so much malice in Miss G towards our family, that I should not be surprised at her being apparently civil merely for the purpose of seeking occasion to mortify'. Despite this, both women enjoyed the visit but Dolly still found it difficult to forgive her for the disparaging references she continued to make about her life with them in Spain.

* * * *

On arriving in Lisbon, Antony made his way overland to Madrid. In mid-December a letter arrived from Dolly asking if they could afford to find a house as she was finding it very cramped living with her mother. Antony refused, not only because of the cost but he did not wish his family to become too settled in England. 'There is no idea of our taking up anything like a settlement at Exeter', he wrote by return, 'for if it were not for my dearest father I would have you leave the place at once tho' we were to spend £200 a year more in London'. He went on 'The pleasing side of the question is first of all the enjoyment and comfort of my father which not only reflects back on ourselves during the short remainder of his life but will be the greatest source of comfort to us after his death. For me it will soften the poignancy of that remorse which will have an end only with my own'. On his father's death, notwithstanding Dolly's previous unhappiness Antony was determined to bring his family out to Spain so they could be together again.

By 1793, he had been there long enough to know a great many people, both British and Spanish and was generally well respected by them. He continued to act as agent for an increasing number of British merchants and that year went into partnership with a Spanish friend, Juan Pomar, in a firm called Juan Pomar Gibbs y Cia, based in Malaga. The firm was concerned with exporting local produce into Bristol through Munckley Gibbs & Richards. Everything seemed to be going well, and he was optimistic that he could ride out the dislocation of trade that war would inevitably bring. However, his plans were short-lived. In February, while returning to Madrid from Seville with his friend John Head (later Sir John Head), he was involved in a serious accident. The postillion in which they were travelling crashed and the horses had bolted. Antony leapt out of the carriage. His arm was crushed and he suffered severe skull and facial injuries. His forehead and nose were 'laid open to the skull'. As the accident had occurred at night in a remote spot some distance from the nearest village, he was left bleeding by the side of the road while Head went for help and was later taken unconscious to the local village. Too ill return to Seville and not expected to survive, a courier was sent to Cadiz for Jacques Courant. A week later he had recovered sufficiently to be moved to Xeres where he was '...bled six times in the course of 48 hours...'. When Antony was sufficiently recovered, he was taken to Courant's house in Cadiz where he was to remain for some months.[9]

Distances made communication slow and it was several weeks before Dolly received news of the accident. Distraught, she wanted to leave immediately for Cadiz but the family was opposed to her

travelling alone through war-torn France. George came from Bristol
with his children to try to persuade her to wait for further news, but
a few days after his arrival, his youngest daughter Anne became ill
and died just before her ninth birthday. Despite their grief, George and
his two elder children, Joanna and George Jr remained in Devon with
his family until they heard that Antony was out of danger.

When news reached Antony of Dolly's plans, he was adamant that
she should remain in England. Worried that she would throw caution
to the wind to be at his side, he promised to write to her every day with
news of his condition. His recovery, however, remained slow. Although
his facial injuries healed quickly, he was still unable to use his right arm
three months after the accident. As this was his writing hand
Branscombe had to pen all his letters. In May he wrote to her, 'It is
mortifying, by every post to tell you that I am better and not be able
to write to you, but I get on but slowly and have my right arm so much
affected that God only knows how long it may last....'. Instead of
calming her, the fact that Branscombe continued to write on Antony's
behalf alarmed her even more and she was convinced that his condition
was still critical. She became even more resolute to travel to him,
causing Antony to be so concerned that, at the beginning of July despite
his difficulties, he managed to write to her himself using his left hand.

Cadiz 2nd July 1793

My Dearest Dolly,
I take the pen from William to write you, my dear-
est love, one line, and as it were by stealth. I have rec^d
thy last letter of the 6th June and tho' I should be the
happiest person in the world to see thee, am sorry to
observe thy determination of coming out by Lisbon,
for the heat of this country, at this time will never do
for thy constitution. I am obliged to write this very
fast and it is therefore worse than usual.

Thine evermost affec^t
Ant^y Gibbs

By mid-July, against his doctors' advice, Antony announced that he was well enough to return to Seville and resume his business activities, but they managed to pursuade him that he would only regain the use of his right arm if he returned to England for an extended period of convalescence. Reluctantly, he took their advice and three weeks later sailed from Cadiz arriving in Falmouth at the end of August where an anxious Dolly was waiting for him. She was shocked at his appearance, but once home he continued to make good progress. At the end of September, when John Head visited him he noted in his diary: 'On 29th September, went in the evening to Exwick to Mr. Banfill's to see Mr. and Mrs Gibbs who were there. Saw Mr. Gibbs who was wonderfully recovered & Mrs Gibbs a delightfully pretty woman. Also saw Miss Nancy Gibbs there – supped and walked home'.[10]

During the winter of 1793, they entertained a continual stream of visitors anxious to see how he was progressing. Vicary and Kenny arrived from London with their daughter and George brought his family from Bristol. If Dolly had expected her husband to be content to remain at home until he had fully recovered she was to be disappointed. Still without the full use of his right arm, he began making plans to return to the Iberian Peninsula. Even had he wished to remain in England he simply could not afford to do so under the conditions of his bankruptcy as he was bound to repay the balance on his loan account to Granger & Banfill by 1796, the end of their original ten-year agreement, and he still owed large sums to his friends and relatives. Money was a perennial worry and without earning any commission, he was unable to support his family.

Antony was also very anxious for Dolly. Now pregnant again, she constantly complained of headaches and stomach cramps and once again was taking increasing amounts of laudanum to relieve the pain. Worried that the habit was fast becoming a serious problem, he sought medical advice and she reluctantly agreed to try to reduce her dependence on the drug for the sake of their unborn child. She was still very unhappy living with her mother, complaining that it was too cramped for her and the children. William was now four years old and a boisterous child. With Henry now at school he was being particularly difficult.

In the face of this, at the beginning of April 1794 Antony set off on a tour of the northern cities, promising to be home for her confinement. Taking the chaise from Exeter to Bristol via Taunton, he planned to go to Bath with George to visit a number of potential clients. Concerned about Dolly's health, before he left Bristol he wrote, 'I observe what you say about being off the opium still. I hope you will remember what an Object it is with your Friends that you should diminish as much as possible the Quantity you take...and leave it off by degrees'. Knowing how difficult William was being he added 'Tell Wm that as soon as he can read the Bible well he is to go to school with Henry'.

From Bath, he went alone to Worcester and then to Rochdale, Manchester, Liverpool, Leeds and Halifax, and finally to Scotland. The trip was a great success and on his return had secured a number of contracts to import British woollens and linens into Spain and Portugal and export Iberian fruits, olives and wines into England. He arrived back in Exeter at the end of June just in time for Dolly's confinement. On 6 July, she gave birth to another son, whom they called Francis. Although desperately worried about his father's health Antony could not afford to remain in England longer than was necessary. At the end of August, when Dolly had recovered sufficiently to be released from her lying in, he made his way to Plymouth, to seek a passage to Lisbon, planning to travel overland to Malaga. George had agreed to act in loco parentis and to look after all his family's needs but, anxious to put Dolly's mind at rest, on his arrival in Malaga, he wrote 'you will receive your Supplies from George & I have today remitted him £250 for that purpose'.

For the next few weeks, he travelled to a number of Spanish cities, returning to Malaga at the end of December. There, he found a letter from Dolly, dated 11 November telling him that his father had died the previous day. He was grief stricken. For most of his life, he had written to his father every day and he anxiously asked by return 'were any of my Letters received before my Father's death'...how heartily do I wish myself in England'. Despite his grief, Antony knew this was impossible as he was 'preparing to set off for Madrid where I have old debts to recover'.

By the end of 1794, now based in Malaga, he was acting for a growing number of textile manufacturers. Although most of his money was tied up in stock, he regularly remitted funds against his loan account with Granger & Banfill. In February, he had written to Dolly telling her that he had sent £1000 to George with instructions that £200 be given to his mother and £30 to each of his sisters, 'which I hope they will consider as it is intended by no means as a Present, but as a sort of Pledge from me that I consider myself a much larger sum in their Debt'. He went on 'You will conclude from this remittance that my affairs go on much better than expected'. Antony was confident that if he could sustain this level of profit for the next fifteen years, he would be able to pay off all his debts. He would be returning to Exeter in the spring and he wanted her and the children to go back with him in the autumn. In the meantime, she must not worry about money. 'I have as my Banker, George', he wrote, 'so rich you must now draw smartly from him; & you can never tell me you have any Qualms about it knowing this as your Ladyship must, that he always paid ye greatest kindness & Goodwill, when far from having a farthing of mine in his Hands, I was many hundred Pounds in his Debt'.

Meanwhile in Exeter, at the beginning of April, little Francis suddenly developed a fever from which he never recovered. He was six months old and his mother was devastated at his death. Although saddened by the news, Antony's attitude was stoical. He continued working, arriving back home in mid-summer as planned. Although he had intended returning to Malaga in the autumn with Dolly and the children, with war imminent, he decided that they should remain in England for another year. As they were still living with Mrs Hucks, he reluctantly agreed they would look for a larger house. Dolly was anxious to move to Exwick to be near Nancy and Samuel. They had been great source of support to her and the two women had become great friends. Antony, grateful his sister's help, agreed and at Granger's suggestion, took a lease on a small house called Lower Cleave (Cleve), a few minutes walk from Exwick House. Within days they had moved into their new home.

He also had further discussions with George about repaying his father's debts. For Antony, the priority had been to pay off his outstanding loan account to Granger & Banfill, and on his return, having remitted another £200 to them had finally cleared his debts with the firm. This left well over £18,000 still owing plus what he now owed Vicary for maintaining his parents and sisters, as well as his own family. Worried about his growing indebtedness to his brother, he asked George to raise the subject with him. It was a great relief when George told him that 'respecting the effect which his [Vicary's] late advancement of rank in his profession has had on his business, with which he expresses himself well satisfied'. Vicary had agreed with Antony that he should repay his mother and sisters before his other creditors and was prepared to 'to postpone...his claim for the expenses of the family subsequent to my Father's misfortunes'. As Vicary was en-route to Exeter with his family for the summer, George suggested that the finer details could 'be discussed at a future date & in the meantime don't think about it too much'.

Just before Antony was due to leave for Falmouth, a letter had arrived from George concerning the effect the political situation could have on his business plans, in particular on the Malaga firm of Juan Pomar Gibbs y Cia. If Spain joined the war as France's ally, it 'will be an obstacle in the way of taking up ships for that country' and would affect his brother's ability to support his family and discharge his debts. As usual, Antony remained confident. On his return to the Iberian Peninsula, he planned to open an office in Lisbon. Over the last few years, he had made a number of contacts amongst the thriving British merchant community there, including Charles Lyne and his wife and his old friend Lewis Stephens, who had recently established a glass-making factory outside the Portuguese capital.[11] He was convinced that Stephens would offer him something in Lisbon. George was not impressed, advising him not to base his hopes on casual promises. The only way to succeed in business was through sheer hard work. On 7 October he wrote, 'I hope my dear Anty that the course you are in will lead you in time, tho' it may be thro' a good deal of labour to the acquisition of what will render you & your Family comfortable & happy…I think really that the connections you have formed in Spain afford a good prospect'.

The war-time delays as ships had to wait for escorting convoys proved to be a real problem for Antony as the majority of Spanish cargoes were perishable fruits and other foodstuffs. On his return to Malaga, he learned that Pomar had exported a large consignment of raisins to Bristol for the Christmas market. The fruit had arrived after Christmas and the merchant had refused to take delivery and so George offered to store the consignment in his warehouse until he could find a buyer. A month later, the mail ship brought news from Bristol that the raisins remained unsold, due to a drop in demand for what was considered a luxury item. 'The very extravagant price of all necessities of life & especially of flour,' George wrote, 'together with the resolution entered into very generally not to consume it in any of the luxuries of the table such as pastry for puddings etc. have had a great effect in reducing the consumption of raisins'. He saw no immediate 'prospect of any further business' in Spanish produce. Clearly worried at how war would affect Antony's trade, he added 'Any hopes for peace are now less favourable than for some time past', and advised that 'as the present prospects for the….business are unfavourable, your exertions should be directed to objects of profit which present themselves in other branches of your business' which though might be less profitable, would in the long term 'be more beneficial'.

As had now become the pattern in his life, Antony spent several weeks in England each summer, returning to the Iberian Peninsula at the end of September. In 1795, as he was making plans to return to Exeter, the mail brought a letter from Banfill with some good news. Despite the decline in the Devon wool trade, the firm had had its best year ever and had recently secured an order to supply £20,000 of flannel to Spain and Italy. He also told Antony of his engagement to

Nancy. Antony was delighted for despite his own misfortune, he and Banfill had remained good friends throughout, and he sent his sister £100 as a wedding present.

In the same mail was a letter from George who was not so pleased at his sister's news. Surely, he wrote, Nancy 'must be aware of all his [Banfill's] perculiarities, which indeed she acknowledges, at the same time as she expresses herself with the greatest confidence that it is not in the power of them to disturb her happiness'. Their marriage was 'an event which I by no means expected but which I most earnestly hope will conduce much to the happiness of the parties principally concerned and to the comfort of all our Family'. George added that 'the profits of Granger & Banfill are in a great measure owing to your instrumentality by the exertions you have made for them in Spain'. Antony would hear none of it. 'Never did Banfill do a thing which raised him so high in my opinion', he wrote, 'nor do I know a person in the world so calculated as my dear Nancy to improve his disposition, which I always thought good at bottom'. He added 'we shall enjoy again the dear little comforts of Exwick by seeing them in ye hands of so dear a friend'.

With the withdrawal of the British Fleet from the Mediterranean and the start of Napoleon's Italian campaign in 1796, many British merchants began buying Spanish produce speculatively as fears swept Britain that Spain would once again join the war as France's ally. In July, Antony received an order from a Bristol merchant for 20 tons of 'good quality Spanish cork' and as much Malaga oil as he could supply. For 'The circumstances of the French taking possession of Leghorn will I am persuaded advance the price of Gallipoli oil in this country'. When he arrived back in Lisbon on 4 October after spending the summer in Exeter, he purchased the cargo as directed, planning to send it on the *Nancy*, which he had chartered in Gibraltar. Despite his efforts, Antony was unable to ship the cargo as many owners refused to allow their vessels to sail in case they were captured or destroyed by the French.

A few weeks after Antony's departure, Dolly knew she was again pregnant once again. From the outset she suffered continual morning sickness and severe headaches, which no medicine seemed to cure. She had also caught a slight cold, which had developed into a severe cough and she had begun spitting blood, becoming worried that she too was developing what she always called her 'family disease'. Then William suddenly contracted measles and was poorly for several weeks. She asked Nancy if Harriet could stay at Exwick House, but unexpectedly her sister-in-law refused, seeming almost unfriendly. Lonely, depressed and unable to cope, she wrote an letter ill-tempered to Antony complaining about Nancy's unhelpfulness and that she had no money to buy the children any new winter clothes.

Her letter awaited him on his return to Lisbon the following month. Irritated that she should grumble about such trivia, he replied that she must never write in that way to him again. He also dismissed her concerns over Nancy. 'Whilst such Trifles are capable of arresting thy attention,' he wrote, 'there is nothing of real Consequence that needs give thee Uneasiness – when any Friend of mine, who I know from his general conduct really loves and esteems me, happens to say or do any Thing which looks the other way'. He also reminded her that until his business in Lisbon was well established, she should try to be a frugal as possible, or they might have to give up Lower Cleave and find a cheaper house in Dawlish. Although she could not afford new clothes for the children, he added that that he had recently bought himself two winter coats for he had no intention of 'remaining in this dirty Place this winter without half coats'. The letter infuriated her and she angrily protested about his threats to move and his extravagance. By the time an ill-tempered reply arrived from Spain some weeks later her anger had subsided

The next mail ship brought a letter from George written on 2 November, which filled him with guilt. Although delighted that Antony was 'reaping such considerable profits during your necessary detention at Lisbon' he told him that the Exeter firm was experiencing severe financial difficulties. 'The Spanish war must be felt very severely at Exeter & you do well to take measures for satisfying your debt there'. It then dawned on Antony why the relationship between his wife and sister had become so tense. While he enthused about how well he was doing, Nancy and Banfill's personal loans remained unpaid. He immediately wrote to George asking him to settle some of his bills with the Exeter firm and, filled with remorse by his impatience with Dolly, wrote telling her that she must not to take his remarks about 'Mrs Banfill's coolness and about taking lodgings in Dawlish on Account of the Expenses' too seriously. As George had also let slip that 'a certain lady is breeding again', he guaranteed to be home in time for her confinement.

When Spain entered the war as an ally of France, her trade to the South American markets was cut off by the British naval blockade. This resulted in a number of business failures including one of the largest firms in Cadiz, with debts of over one million dollars. In turn, this affected a number of smaller concerns in that country. With the embargo on Spanish ships and fear of attack by the French fleet, it became increasingly difficult for Antony to continue exporting Spanish produce to England. Likewise, it had a catastrophic impact in England, especially on the Devon wool trade, which saw four of its principal markets now closed. Banfill, who had recently returned to Exeter from Spain, was very worried that the embargo on British goods would be disastrous to his business. As some of his goods remained trapped in Lisbon he wrote to Antony asking that 'should a war take place with Spain and Portugal remain neuter, could English goods be transmitted to Spain through Portugal & how? Perhaps [disguised] as German or French manufactures'. Antony thought it a wonderful idea and he and Pomar immediately began making plans to smuggle goods into neutral Portugal for the English market and George agreed that they could be channelled through the Bristol firm. The next few months were a period of frenzied activity as rumours abounded that Spain was planning to invade Portugal. In January 1797, Antony was forced to closed his office in Lisbon and return to England.

CHAPTER 8

EXWICK AND THE IBERIAN PENINSULA

Despite the problems experienced by many local merchants, the Exeter firm flourished in the early 1790s. With Antony as its agent, Granger & Banfill was able to maintain its level of exports for the next two years despite the downturn in the Spanish market due to the imposition of heavy tariffs. The factory expanded and became one of the most successful in Exeter. Even faced with Antony's problems, Banfill remained a loyal friend and the two men corresponded regularly, exchanging news and gossip about trade and family matters. Nancy had quickly settled into her new role at Exwick House, acting as Banfill's host when he entertained the local gentry. She was also a great favourite amongst her nieces and nephews. The Crawley children were regular visitors and Joanna and George Jr spent many happy summers at Exwick after the death of their mother.

With the outbreak of war between France and Austria-Prussia in 1792, Banfill was afraid that if Britain joined the hostilities, it would have an adverse effect on his business for although the firm was now making a considerable profit, £4000 was still owed to Duccarell. To raise the capital to settle it Granger suggested they sell part of Exwick Barton to his brother-in-law, the Reverend Duke Yonge who was keen to purchase the estate. As all four partners were jointly and severally liable for the debt, they readily agreed. On 29 September 1792, Yonge paid Duccarell the outstanding £4000 and the firm paid the £890 interest. As Granger and Banfill had already repaid £1000 two years before it was agreed that the estate should be divided according to their holding, with Yonge owning four-fifths and Granger and Banfill one-fifth between them, the latter comprising Exwick House and twenty-three acres of land.[1]

When Antony brought his family back to Exeter in 1792, he convinced his former partners that, even if Britain entered the war exports of woollen cloth to Spain would not be affected. He now had many Spanish contacts and would be able to bypass any blockade. Over the past two years, he had succeeded in generating a considerable amount of business and had re-paid a large part of his outstanding loan account to the firm. Banfill and Granger were persuaded to employ him as their agent on the usual commission basis, and when he returned to Spain in mid-November he had signed a three-year contract, which all parties hoped would be to their mutual advantage.

It was not to be. In 1793, France invaded Flanders and Britain was at war again. In February, fearful at the loss of the European markets, Exeter's business community had opposed the renewal of the charter of the East India Company, and campaigned for the establishment of free trade to the Far East. Any hope that the firm would ride out the wartime dislocation to their Mediterranean trade was soon dashed; as war was declared, news reached Exeter of Antony's accident outside Madrid.

By the time a frail Antony arrived home at the end of August, Exeter was in the grip of war-time patriotic fervour, as its inhabitants raised funds for a volunteer force to fight off the enemy across the channel. The city had become a garrison town with officers needing accommodation, transportation and victualling. Military expenditure fuelled a boom that masked the decline of local trade and industry, particularly the wool trade. Exeter's exports to Spain had fallen to third place behind Italy and Holland, at 1525 bales of wool fewer than ten years before. As the French invaded Holland in 1794, British Orders in Council restricted trade to that country. The Dutch retaliated by prohibiting commerce with Britain. The resulting collapse of the overseas cloth market had a dramatic effect on the local economy.[2] As Exeter's citizens enjoyed the colour and pageant of the military, the effects of wartime inflation had begun to be felt. In 1794, as many merchants struggled with the loss of their overseas markets, six woollen manufacturing businesses were advertised for sale in the *Trewman's Exeter Flying Post*.[3]

With their traditional markets closed, the Exeter firm made strenuous efforts to increase exports to neutral Portugal and Italy. The following year it was trading with Antony's cousins Lyle and Abraham Gibbs. Lyle was employed in the Genoa office of the Exeter-based company, Heath & Co and Abraham was with a merchant house in Naples. 1795 was to prove more successful 'than any preceding year' for the firm. That year, Banfill's importance and influence in Exeter's mercantile community was reflected when he and two other merchants, John Cresswell and John Churchill, were appointed as managers in rotation of the Associated Shippers to Genoa and Leghorn. Such was his standing in the local community that the following January he received a letter from Mr. Claude Scott, the government's agent for the supply of corn. Scott asked that he inform the Exeter corn factors and merchants that 'the Emperor was disposed to permit the exportation of wheat to this country from Galicia by way of the Vistula' at the direction of the Privy Council.[4]

Amidst a growing number of business failures Banfill continued to develop the mill and the surrounding buildings. By the end of 1795, the Exwick site included '...spinning machines, workshops, dye-houses, tenter grounds, etc; also dwelling houses for the manufactur-ers...' They employed a large number of people which '...greatly increased the number of inhabitants' in Exwick.[5] The firm was at the forefront in the development of a 'proto-factory' in Exeter, part of the evolution from the workshop to the later factories of the industrial revolution. When their ten-year agreement ended in December 1795, he and Granger were confident enough in the future to continue their partnership for another seven years. Banfill had not only turned the business round to make a profit, but now was a man with estimated wealth of £4000. As his reputation grew, even Antony was forced to concede that 'Banfill conducts the business better than could be expected' but could not avoid adding that 'self conceit and obstinacy will always be in his way... .'.

Despite the uncertainties of the war, having made a modest fortune Banfill, now thirty-two proposed to Nancy. Only a few months off her fortieth birthday, she had been working as his unpaid housekeeper for more than six years. Although flattered by his proposal, Nancy was cautious about losing her independence. Before giving him an answer, she wrote to George asking him to 'come down to Exeter & by an inspection of his books, satisfy myself of the reality of the acct [sic] he has given of his circumstances'. She was annoyed when he refused because he felt that to do so would be interpreted as questioning Banfill's integrity. George told her that if she wanted to marry him she should take him on trust. The following month Banfill wrote to Antony that 'Mrs G [Dolly] I believe had hinted to you another concern in which I am more interested. Unless you are in England soon you may find at Exwick, Miss Gibbs under another name.'. The family had mixed feelings about the marriage. Antony was delighted but Vicary and George were less enthusiastic.

On 19 April 1796, Banfill and Nancy were married in Exeter Cathedral. A small wedding, it was attended by her mother and sisters, Kitty and Bell, Dolly and the children, and a few close friends. Their honeymoon was spent in Weymouth. On their return to Exwick House, Nancy, now the mistress of the house lost no time in making a number of changes as she and her new husband began to entertain their friends and the local gentry often on a lavish scale. Anxious to share her good fortune, she remained very close to her mother and sisters. Since her father's death, her mother had been spending more and more time at Exwick. Now too old to have children of her own, Nancy adored all her nieces and nephews, who continued to be regular visitors. She was especially fond of Dolly's eldest children, Henry and Harriet, who spent long periods at Exwick House, particularly during their mother's bouts of ill health.

A few weeks later, the Crawley family came to Devon for a few days staying at Clyst St. George and visiting Exwick on a number of occasions. They also called in to see Dolly who was confined to the house due to her advancing pregnancy. Whilst there, one of the children caught whooping cough, which quickly spread to all the younger members of the family, forcing Mary and Charles to extend their visit until they were fully recovered. They were still there in June when Antony returned for Dolly's confinement. It was an ideal opportunity to discuss the future of Pytte. Crawley admitted that he had only purchased it in 1790 for his father-in-law's sake, but as he and Mary were now settled at Stowe, they rarely used the house. As their father had died two years before, Crawley suggested it was now time to sell it. Although sad that the family's links with Clyst St. George were to be finally severed, they reluctantly agreed that Charles begin to make the necessary arrangements.

As Dolly and the children were still living with Mrs Hucks, one of Antony's first priorities before returning to the Iberian Peninsula in September was to move them into Lower Cleave, a larger house about half a mile from Exwick House. Despite their closeness, within months Dolly noticed that her relationship with Nancy seemed strained. When George brought his new wife Anne, and the children to Exeter in September for a visit, he too was conscious of the tension. Banfill confided in him that within months of his marriage the firm began experiencing financial difficulties. With the start of Napoleon's Italian campaign in 1796 and the withdrawal of the British fleet from the Mediterranean the Italian markets were cut off; the Exeter woollen trade had collapsed and a number of long established merchants and manufacturers were on the verge of financial ruin.

Although in the last year Granger & Banfill had seen a marked increase in trade with Portugal through their agent in Lisbon, with their traditional markets now gone, Banfill was pinning his hopes on Antony increasing trade further in the Iberian Peninsula. Until then, this was not just a difficult period for the business but also for them personally. In 1789, Nancy had readily given £150 to her father's administrators and Banfill had lent Antony a little over £1400 from the firm. Now they were struggling to make ends meet while his brother-in-law smugly boasted about his success in Spain. He and Nancy felt resentful, for although Antony had repaid part of his outstanding loan account, he had always put other family members before them. It came as welcome news some weeks later when, on George's advice, Antony remitted £100 to his account with the firm.

Despite this, Nancy remained generous and goodhearted, often being called upon to help her sister-in-law with the children. Antony had only been gone a few weeks when Dolly confided that she was pregnant again. This was to be a difficult pregnancy and Henry, Harriet and William spent a lot of time at Exwick House. On 22 December, Nancy wrote to her brother thanking him for the £100. Aware of his concerns about his family she told him that all was well in Exeter. Young Henry had fully recovered from the measles and 'Your wife is going to London' with the children to stay with Eleanor for Christmas. Nancy wryly commented that it was better for her to go now 'than a few months hence....for I assure you she begins to look a little Graceful already'. She had also received a letter from Mary telling her that 'Mr Crawley is in treaty with Mr Cotsford for the sale of the Estate at Clyst'. She hoped it would be sold soon and believed it was right for 'Mr Crawley to sell it, now that he comes into Devonshire so seldom'. It was difficult to manage an estate from a distance unless 'you have a Steward'.[6]

In 1795, the Exeter firm secured a £20,000 order for flannel for Spain and Italy. With war imminent, many ship-owners refused to sail, fearing attack by the enemy. Fortunately, after the onset of hostilities, Granger & Banfill succeeded in shipping the Italian part of cargo to Leghorn before the port fell to the French, but the Spanish cargo, valued at around £10,000, was trapped in France for some weeks, before being shipped to Lisbon on a neutral ship via Gibraltar. When Spain joined the war as France's ally, the firm's Portuguese agent refused to transport the flannel into Spain fearing it would be confiscated and it remained in Portugal. Antony had offered to try to sell the cargo for them but in January 1797, he was forced to close his office in Lisbon and return to England.

Arriving in Exeter in March, Antony was greeted with the news that Eleanor and Henry Townley-Ward had given Dolly a bond of £1400 to provide her and the children with some security. George had suggested that she 'seek Vicary's advice as to the legal construction of it' to ensure that she 'devise her interest in it after her death'. A condition of the gift was that it could not be used to fund Antony's business activities or to repay his debts. It was to be invested for Dolly so that she could live off the interest.

Even so, the next few months were to be a very difficult period for Antony, not only because of the delay in getting his money into England, but also because of the effect that war-time inflation had on the fluctuating exchange rate. Although his commission had been substantial during his last few months in Portugal, he lost a considerable sum on converting to sterling. He wrote to George explaining that while he waited for his funds to be transferred he was unable to pay his bills to the Bristol firm. His brother was sympathetic replying 'it is a sad thing that you should pay so dear by the curse of the Exchequer for getting your money home, but I am persuaded that it is well worth that sacrifice in order to have it in this country'. He promised Antony extended credit and offered to try 'to persuade the banks to do the same'

In May, Dolly gave birth to a baby girl whom they called Anne after her grandmother. This time it was an easy birth, but as soon as she had recovered, Antony was ready to leave again. His original ten-year agreement with Granger & Banfill expired at the end of July, and he remitted £159.1.7d against his long-standing account with the firm. This left only £250 still owing, which Granger agreed to write off as a bad debt. After lengthy negotiations, he and Banfill signed a new contract with Antony at a 4% commission. It was agreed that as soon as peace was signed he would leave immediately for Cadiz, where he planned to open an office.

Despite his optimism, the war dragged on and for the next eighteen months Antony was forced to remain in Exeter 'cut off ...from the Peninsula'. During this time, unable to earn a living the family was dependent on his brothers for support. In September Vicary sent him £100 with note that read, 'These are times when we who can get money ought to assist our friends....and I can well afford [this] out of the profits of the circuit'. By February 1798, such were his financial diffi-

culties that Antony seriously considered moving his family from Lower
Cleave to cheaper lodgings in Budleigh Salterton. He wrote telling
George of his plight and received £100 by return with a note telling
him that he was now in a position to provide for his needs and in not
to ask Vicary for financial assistance in future. 'I trust I need not say
a word to convince you, my dear Anty', George wrote, 'how cheerfully
I shall continue to supply your wants'.

Throughout 1797, all European trade from Exeter was virtually
suspended and Granger & Banfill's cargo of flannel remained unsold
in Portugal. With the traditional European markets closed and the
collapse of the overseas woollen trade, the firm was forced to broaden
its horizons, seeking new markets in the East, the Caribbean and the
former American colonies. That year, only six vessels cleared Exeter
carrying woollens, with three bound for Hamburg, two for 'Greetzyhl'
(Holland), and one for Lisbon.[7] For the last two hundred years, the
average value of annual exports from Exeter to the European markets
had been around £300,000, while sales to London and the East India
Company accounted for a similar sum.[8] By the turn of the century, the
traditional class of woollen merchant had disappeared in Exeter, and was
replaced by a '....a new class of industrialists – manufacturers and
cloth finishers...', who were mainly concerned with shipping cloth
to London for the East India Company.[9] While Granger & Banfill
continued to export serges that way, little attempt was made by other
merchants to break through the French blockade, and it is estimated
they lost £100,000 in business with the capture of Leghorn.[10] With
Britain and Spain at war, the embargo on Spanish vessels also resulted
in a number of spectacular business failures in Spain. One well-known
Cadiz firm went down with debts of over 'a million of dollars' with
resounding impact throughout the business community there.

The following July, Banfill sailed to Lisbon, planning to cross the
border into Spain to see if he could sell his flannel. Two months later,
Antony left for Falmouth, but his ship was delayed for two weeks by
light winds, and he did not arrive in Lisbon until mid-October. There
the two men travelled around Portugal visiting a number of merchant

houses. Confident that they had secured a number of large orders, Banfill arranged for his embargoed goods to be smuggled into Spain through Antony's Spanish contacts. It was to prove a profitable arrangement, enabling the Exeter firm to ship large quantities of serge and flannel cloth through Portugal into Spain over the winter months. Banfill returned to England but Antony decided to remain in Lisbon despite fears that Portugal was about to be invaded. At the end of October, he was delighted to report that he had earned over £2000 in commission. But this too had its problems. There followed a lengthy dispute between the two men over whether part of the commission on these sales should be paid to Antony or their existing agent in Lisbon. The dispute was eventually resolved when Banfill agreed that as many of his outstanding debts were paid off, Antony would be the Exeter firm's official agent in the Iberian Peninsula on a three-year contract with a retainer plus commission. As news of an impending peace was reported in the newspapers, he made immediate preparations to return to Spain to open an office in Cadiz.

On 3 October, as news of Nelson's victory of the Nile reached Exeter, the city was gripped with patriotic fervour, its inhabitants went wild with joy. Houses were decorated and wine flowed in the Guildhall. A fund was started to support the widows and orphans of those killed or injured in the fleet. While naval victories provided a welcome opportunity for celebrations and Exonians enjoyed the pageantry and ceremony of the increasing number of military occasions, these were offset by rising prices, hunger and business failures. Their financial difficulties forgotten, Edmund Granger and Samuel Banfill joined their employees in the joyous celebrations that swept the city.

Towards the end of March 1799, new orders tailed off and Antony was forced to warehouse a considerable amount of stock for the Exeter firm. He was alarmed to learn from George some weeks later that Banfill was considering adding an interest charge to their costs because of the delays in selling their goods; an action that he felt would be very unfair, believing that they had pushed shipments 'far beyond what you recommended'. Despite this, Antony remained confident. While the number of bankruptcies amongst his English friends increased, he continued to build his business and was now acting for several well-established German and Swiss firms. For the next year, despite the British blockade of the Dutch ports and the Anglo-Russian invasion of north Holland resulting in a number of bankruptcies there, his business continued to grow and his only real worry was that the problems in Holland might have an adverse effect on exchange rates.

In England, hopes for peace faded as French troops massed across the channel. Fears of invasion swept through the southwest and Exeter's first volunteer force was formed to defend the city. The following year there were four companies of volunteers, each under the command of members of the gentry or the mercantile elite and financed by public subscription. However, against the background of the naval victories and patriotic volunteering, there was considerable hardship in Exeter and the surrounding area. The winter of 1799 was especially cold with heavy snow and sharp frosts. Disruption to transport resulted in a sharp rise in food prices, leading to acute distress for the labouring poor, particularly those workers in the declining cloth industry. While wages remained at between 1s to 1s 2d per day, the price of potatoes rose to 2d per peck. Local magistrates firmly rejected calls to increase wages, but such was the distress throughout the county, that at the Easter Quarter Sessions, magistrates directed that a circular relating to the '*Act for making the better provision for the maintenance of the Poor and for diminishing the Consumption of Bread Corn...*', be circulated to all parishes.[11] The following winter saw no improvement and at a public meeting held in the Guildhall in April 1801, over £2000 was raised to purchase food for distribution to the poor.

By 1800, Exeter was becoming a commercial and industrial backwater compared with London and Liverpool. Many of the great names, such as the Barings and the Duntzes had already forsaken the city for the metropolis. As the war with France dragged on, smaller merchants, many of whom had insufficient capital to invest or diversify into new markets, were bankrupted or became cloth finishers selling into the limited but secure market offered by the East India Company. Granger & Banfill was not so dependent on the East India Company. It was able to maintain its contacts with its continental markets by switching much of its trade through Antony in Lisbon, which continued to develop as a neutral entrepôt. That year only nine thousand serges were shipped abroad from Exeter, the majority to Portugal by the Exeter firm to be smuggled into Spain.

At Exwick, the Banfills had other worries. Joanna, George's twenty-three year old daughter had come to Exeter for a short holiday in the summer of 1799, following her father's second marriage, but had become so unwell that he had agreed that she could remain at Exwick House. She had now been there for several months and refused to return to Bristol. As fears of invasion swept Exeter, George urgently requested that Nancy send her back so that she could be evacuated to the country with the rest of the family, but Joanna claimed she was still too ill to travel. Dolly too needed Nancy's help. With Antony now based permanently in Lisbon, she continued to be very depressed and young Henry, William and Harriet spent much of the time at Exwick House with Joanna. That Christmas, Anne Gibbs, who was now well into her seventies, caught a severe cold. As her condition deteriorated rapidly, Nancy, afraid that her mother would not recover, sent for George who came immediately and stayed until his mother recovered. Joanna's health too had improved and she agreed to go back to Bristol in the spring.

* * * *

Antony finally returned to in Exeter in July having been separated from his family for nearly twenty months. He had written to Dolly nearly every day though whether he had been faithful for all that time is unclear. There is no doubt that although he had missed his family, he enjoyed the freedom and independence that living in a foreign city allowed. Like most eighteenth century men, he no doubt had a pragmatic attitude to fidelity and could satisfy his other desires elsewhere. For Dolly, being alone in England was not easy. Her brother Joseph, who had been suffering from consumption for many years, was now living with her mother. In April, his condition had suddenly deteriorated and his college had sent him to Devon in 'an advanced stage' of the disease. In June, Mrs Hucks took him to Wells to take the waters, but with little hope of him recovering, they returned to Exeter to await the inevitable. Dolly too was unwell. Her doctors had diagnosed the headaches that she had been suffering from for many years as migraine.

Knowing that his future lay in the Iberian Peninsula and visits to England would be less frequent in the future, Antony decided that he would take his family back to Lisbon with him in the autumn. His friend, Charles Lyne, who had lived in Portugal for several years, had moved back to London earlier that year and had offered them his house in Lisbon. When George heard the news, he could not believe his younger brother's good fortune. He wrote, 'in the course of some years in which you have experienced much hardships and many untoward accidents and some severe trials, you have had, my dear Antony…not only the good fortune but the merit of acquiring several sincere friends from whose regard and attachment to you must derive great comfort as well as advantage'.

Three months later tragedy struck. As they made their final preparations to leave, Dolly collapsed with what was diagnosed as a 'severe stroke'. Wanting a second opinion, they sent to Plymouth for Robert Remmett who confirmed the diagnosis. Her headaches, which had been diagnosed as migraine, were thought to have been the cause. Though they had appeared worse with each pregnancy, Antony had been unsympathetic, believing them to be a symptom of female neurotic illness linked to bouts of depression. Despite the seriousness of Dolly's condition, Remmett was confident that given time she would make a significant recovery. She was confined to bed, and Antony devotedly nursed her day and night, fearful that she would have another stroke. It was several weeks before she was allowed to sit in a chair.

As Dolly's strength improved, Antony continued to make plans to take her and the children to Lisbon. At the beginning of December, her doctors reluctantly agreed that she was fit enough to travel and would benefit from living in a warmer climate. In the event, the plan was confounded. Yellow fever was rife in Cadiz and it was feared that it would spread to across the border. Napoleon had recently invaded Spain and as rumours spread that he was planning to invade Portugal, thirteen hundred British troops were landed there. Antony decided that spending a long cold winter in Exeter would now be safer than Portugal. Meanwhile Dolly, at the age of forty-two, suspected she was pregnant again and refused to make the arduous sea journey. She was also reluctant to leave her mother and her brother, whose condition was now critical.

With his family now remaining in Exeter, Antony needed to reduce his expenditure because he could not afford to maintain two homes. Over the last few months, he had earned nothing and estimated that in the past year his expenses had risen to £600 'over £100 more than had ever been spent before'. Both Henry and William were attending Charles Lloyd's School in Exeter, which was also very expensive. As Henry was now fifteen, Antony decided to take him to Lisbon, where he would teach him the business and supervise the rest of his education. William was to board at Blundells School in Tiverton. Dolly was devastated at the thought of losing both her sons but her protests went unheeded. With only Harriet and Anne at home with their mother, Antony decided that Lower Cleave was far too big for them and looked for something smaller nearer Mrs Hucks. He found a house needing some renovation on St David's Hill in the city, just over a mile from Exwick. Not only would it be cheaper to run, he thought it would be easier for her to manage. While it was being renovated, he rented a small terraced house for 4 guineas a month from Mr. Cutliffe, Dolly's doctor.

On 2 February 1801, Dolly recorded in her journal, 'My dear Antony and Henry set off for Falmouth in the Evening. Mr and Mrs Banfill dined here'.[12] They were delayed in Falmouth, and a week later sailed for Lisbon on the King George packet in a convoy, arriving there two weeks later. It was to be an exciting voyage for young Henry. Off the Bay of Biscay, Spanish privateers attacked the convoy, and he and his father 'were put under arms and took our place on deck'. When they arrived in the Portuguese capital, Henry wrote to tell his mother of their safe arrival. He enthusiastically described their exploits, thrilled that they 'had an opportunity of seeing how they prepare for action without having the danger, for the Spanish soon made off'.

It was some weeks later that a letter arrived from George who had been anxiously waiting for news of their safe arrival, 'especially after the arrival of the Walsingham Packett [sic] without any account of the King George. We are truly thankful for your safety both from the dangers of the sea and of the enemy and feel most happy that having been preserved from both you are again on terra firma'. He also hoped that 'Henry is well pleased with his new situation and doubt not that he will expect himself to give you all the assistance in his power, & that he will conduct himself so as to give you satisfaction in all respects'.

Although no longer neighbours, Nancy continued to help her sister-in-law as much as possible. Once again, Dolly was suffering with severe morning sickness and severe headaches. At forty-two years old, worn out by pregancy and ill health, she had borne six children in seventeen years, and a number of miscarriages. Originally, she hoped to move to St David's Hill at the end of March, but a week before the impending move, news reached her that William had been ill for a fortnight with a severe fever, and the school was sending him home. Worried that he might be contagious, Dolly sent little Anne to Exwick House 'to be out of way of William's fever'. A few days later, leaving him with her mother, she took the chaise to Exwick where she found 'my dear Anne ill in bed' and stayed overnight to nurse her. The next morning her mother sent word that William was worse, and she rushed home to be with him while Anne remained at Exwick nursed by Nancy for several weeks. Once both children were fully recovered, an exhausted Dolly found she could not afford to pay the doctor's bill. Beside herself with worry, she appealed to Eleanor and

George for help and it was a great relief when her sister responded with £50 and George with £20 towards their medical expenses.

Despite Antony's promises to be home for her confinement Dolly was to be disappointed yet again. In March, he had written that he had secured a large order, and would probably not be home for several months. He was remaining in Lisbon because 'my friends in general and particularly those in Rochdale have entrusted so many thousand pounds [of goods] to my hands'. On 12 April, George had written that he was delighted that Henry liked being with his father and added, 'He [Henry] has a disposition & an understanding that will lead him to be well satisfied with the station that is thought fittest for him' and that he 'will conduct himself in it with credit'. Worried about Dolly he urged Antony against 'indulging in any speculations concerning the particular time' (of her confinement) because she was finding this pregnancy so distressing, but the letter took several weeks to arrive.

The strain of trying to cope alone continued to take its toll on Dolly's health. After William returned to school, she undertook the move to St. David's Hill, seven months pregnant and still not fully recovered from her stroke. Within days, she suddenly began to experience severe stomach cramps. Noting in her journal on 31 May, 'very poorly and in danger of Miscarrying' she sent for Nancy. It proved to be a false alarm and for the next month, she spent long periods resting in bed. On 27 June, she 'put all my baby things in order'. Three weeks later, on 22 July, she wrote, 'very ill all day, went to bed at 6 o'clock got up again at ten, sent for Nurse and Mr. Cutliffe. Had a terrible time, woke in pain, Anne sent to Exwick'. It was to be a long labour. The following day Dolly wrote 'went to bed at two, slept all morning… woke at four my little boy was born at five'. She named the new baby Joseph after her brother.

After such a difficult birth, Dolly offered no resistence to being confined in bed. As she showed little sign of regaining her health, a worried Harriet sent for her uncle, Robert Remmett. On 31 July, Dolly wrote 'Dr. Remmett called and ordered me to take bark' which 'vomited and purged' her. Too weak to stand, she remained in bed for another week. On 8 August, she managed to walk 'between Harriet and the Nurse as far as the door' and a week later 'as far as the drying room'. Over the next fortnight, she continued to improve slowly and by the time Antony arrived home at the end of the month, was almost fully recovered. Impatient to return to Portugal, he only stayed for three weeks until Joseph's christening. It must have been a great relief for Dolly that this visit was not followed by another pregnancy.

On his return to Cadiz, Antony was bombarded with letters of complaint about the house in St. David's Hill. On three floors, Dolly found it difficult to manage with a new baby and was worried that it 'had a noxious damp smell'. The servants had all left after becoming ill with a putrid fever except for Molly, her maidservant. Anxious in case the children also became ill, Dolly spent as much time as possible away from the house visiting family and friends in London and Bristol. Exasperated by her complaints, but at the same time concerned for his family's health, he reluctantly agreed that she could look for a new house. Some weeks later she wrote that she had settled on a farm near Duryards, on the outskirts of Exeter at £120 a year 'which could be reduced to £50 by letting some of the land and selling the cider', but because of the delay in getting a response from Antony, the farm was let. Anxious that such opportunities should not be missed in the future, he agreed to send Henry home in the spring to help her.

Another source of comfort to Dolly were her friends. She was especially close to Susan Gibbs, the wife of Antony's cousin William who lived in a small house in Topsham once owned by their grandfather. Susan's husband, who was employed by Munckley Gibbs & Richards, was away for several months each year. In February 1803, Dolly became very worried about Susan. Three months before, her youngest son Lyle had been nearly 'scalded to death' and was still 'so bad that the poor fellow cannot stand alone yet & his mother was almost worn out by the constant attentions upon him'. Dolly invited her to bring her mother and children to stay with her in Exeter and told Antony that she was getting his 'stinking house ready for company....as Mrs W Gibbs, Mrs Ley & 3 of Mrs G's children are coming to stay for a fortnight'. While there, Susan confided in Dolly that William had left on Christmas Day to sail to Italy and she had not heard from him since. Now desperately short of money, she asked if Antony was in a position to repay part of the loan made to her husband some fourteen years before. Dolly, who would have been in a similar situation had it not been for the generosity of her family, immediately agreed to write and ask Antony. The visit was a great success, and Susan enjoyed her stay 'despite her anxiety about her little boy, and not yet having heard from her Husband makes her dreadfully nervous'.

Henry's passage to England was particularly rough as he spent several weeks at sea, finally arriving in England on 2 April. He had spent over thirty-six hours on board a merchantman with only bread and water to sustain him. Rather than disembarking in London and travelling overland to Exeter, he met up with a fishing vessel in the Channel whose master agreed to take him round the coast to Torbay. He went on to Topsham where he found his mother, sisters and younger brother, Joseph. Dolly who had been plagued by a racking cough, had taken lodgings in Topsham for 'a few weeks.... For the sake of the air and to wash my dear Joseph's face & back & sides in salt water'. A frail baby, he suffered badly from eczema, which he found very distressing. At the end of April, they all returned to Exeter and went to Exwick House to visit the Banfills. There, Dolly found a letter from Antony telling her that she could spend up to £2000 on a suitable house for the family. She and Henry looked at a number in the Exeter area but found nothing appropriate. In June, after Henry had returned to Spain, she left the younger children at Exwick and 'came down again on account of my health to Topsham'. While there, she looked at a number of houses but decided to wait for Antony's return later that year.

Sympathetic to Susan's plight, Antony agreed to settle her husband's debt on his return to England. He wrote to George telling him of his intention and that he had told Dolly to look for a new house. Surprisingly, George was unsympathetic to Susan's plight. 'I perfectly agree in the propriety of your paying Wm Gibbs the amt of my Father's debt to him as you propose [as] I think there is a perculiar claim to your consideration of him in the first place,' he wrote, 'but it will be quite time enough to do this when you return, & indeed he will probably not be in this country before that time'. He also advised Antony not to overstretch himself financially and increase 'the expenses of your Family in Exeter' because of 'the precarious state of public affairs' and the likelihood of '...further hostilities with France', which could result in an adverse movement in the exchange rate.

Aware that it would not be long before Spain entered the war as France's ally, Antony knew he had to take advantage of any opportunities 'if only for the boys who are to follow me in the business' as 'fortune is doing something for us now, and if we neglect her favours we ought to be always poor...'. During the next three months, amidst frenzied activity, he saw a rapid increase in sales, 'and though we should have ten years' war I have realized [sic] enough for us to breathe on during that time, and have laid the grounds besides for a noble establishment for our boys, who must take their sisters into partnership...'. In March alone, he remitted £13,500 in sales, but was to be disappointed. With war imminent, once again the fluctuating exchange rate was to erode his profits, which were far less than he had anticipated. In order to beat the embargo on British property, before leaving for England, he nominally transferred £20,000 of his stock to Spanish firms owned by his trusted friends for the duration of the hostilities.

Returning to Exeter that summer, he set about helping Dolly find a new house. Knowing they both hated the smell and dirt of the city, they looked at a number in Topsham and the suburbs, eventually settling on Cowley Cottage, a small property with some land, situated only a mile from Exwick near the bridge over the river Exe.[13] But before they could sign the lease, Antony's mother, who was now over eighty, became seriously ill and all thoughts of moving were temporarily shelved. She continued to deteriorate, dying on 16 August and being buried two days later. The following week, as soon as the lease was signed, Antony moved his family into Cowley Cottage. Dolly was determined to have her cows and chickens and the following year persuaded him to rent a small farm adjoining the cottage for £20 a year.

There she kept two horses, a cow and other livestock. With his wife and children settled, Antony decided to take young William, aged twelve, back with him to Spain. Despite Dolly's pleas, he was removed from Blundell's School, and in October, Antony, Henry and William left Exeter for Southampton for a passage to Honfleur. From there, they travelled overland through France to Cadiz, taking a month to complete the journey. For the next few years, Dolly lived in her cottage with Harriet, Anne and little Joseph, while Antony spent the winter and spring in Spain and Portugal, returning to Exeter for a month in August at the end of the trading season.

Following Nelson's attack on the Danish Fleet in 1801, the British Government had maintained tight pressure on any country that traded with France. It remained hostile to any non-monarchial French Government fearful that republicanism would spread across the channel. For all but fourteen months during that period, the Royal Navy maintained a tight blockade on the ports of Europe. This provided Antony with many opportunities and in 1802, he and Henry moved to Cadiz to open an office, successfully developing business partnerships both there and in Malaga over the next three years.

The brief respite following the Peace of Amiens was greeted with much rejoicing in Exeter. In May 1802, the formal proclamation was marked with traditional processions and great ceremony. At the Exeter Guildhall, Archdeacon Moore gave an address to the king on the blessings of peace as the militia and volunteers were promptly disbanded.[14] Two months later, in the July general election, John Baring retired and Edmund Granger unsuccessfully stood as a Tory against the Whig candidates, James Buller and Sir Charles Bamfylde. The Exeter Chamber gave their support to Buller who was given 'their votes and Interest', and he and Bamfylde were duly elected.[15]

The following year Britain was again on the verge of war with France. The renewal of hostilities and the massing of troops across the channel raised fears that Napoleon was preparing an invasion. After a meeting of the local nobility and gentry at Rougement Castle in May, Granger began to make plans to raise a corps of Exeter City Volunteers to protect the city against invasion.[16] In July, the Government had passed the 'Amended Act for the Defence and Security of the Realm', which required every parish to return a list of the names of all males aged between 17-55 years so that they could be enlisted into the militia. The following month Granger produced his plans for six companies of volunteers, each consisting of sixty men, and each with its own lieutenant colonel, and officers. He raised six hundred men to serve in the Western Military District, because 'the peculiar Situation of Men of Property, Tradesmen and other Respectable Persons renders it expedient that a volunteer corps, of limited service should be raised in the city…' against the 'haughty tyrant, the modern Attila' to protect the West Country against Napoleon's massed armies across the channel.[17] Both Antony and Henry managed to avoid being conscripted into the Militia. Antony, who was forty-eight, was considered 'too infirm' for service, due to his accident several years before, while seventeen year-old Henry escaped conscription because he 'Leaves England soon'.[18] Despite the threat of invasion, day-to-day life went on as usual. Church bells were rung across the city as news of naval victories reached Exeter. Even after the resumption of hostilities, traditional social activities, including the assizes ball and the Haldon races, continued to be well attended by the local nobility and gentry, and there was little concern for the general decline in industry.

In August 1804, the Devon woollen cloth industry had all but disappeared but this did not stop Granger and Banfill signing a new seven-year partnership agreement. The value of Granger's share of the business had fallen to £16311 and Banfill's stood at £4752, but the former agreed to continue financing the firm, providing at least £10,000 capital but 'no more than £20,000'. Banfill's investment was to be 'not less than £3,000, not more than £10,000'. Although a considerable amount of their trade was by then with the East India Company, they had continued to retain their contacts in the Iberian Peninsula through Antony.

The following spring young William came home to Devon, leaving Henry in Spain with his father. After visiting his uncle in Bristol, he went to Topsham where he stayed with Susan and his cousins for several days, before arriving at Cowley Cottage at the end of May 'with two Gibbs with him'. Later that summer, Antony and Henry returned to Exeter and the family spent a few happy weeks visiting friends, entertaining family and enjoying the theatre in Exeter. During August, George and Anne came to stay at Exwick House and Remmett came from Plymouth to see them. Since the death of his second wife in 1794, he had continued to be on very friendly terms with his former in-laws.[19] Despite the threat of a resumption of hostilities, Antony and William left for Falmouth in the middle of August, with Henry following a week later. Four weeks after their departure, Dolly miscarried.

* * * *

With war imminent, Antony returned to Lisbon with Henry and William the following April leaving his clerk William Branscome and his apprentice, Banfill's nephew William Mardon to manage what was left of the business in Cadiz. He little realised that it would be four years before he could return to Spain. In Lisbon they stayed with the Lewis Stephens who had a house there. On his arrival Antony wrote to Vicary giving his an account of 'the state of the Fleets' and telling him that he was 'much mortified at having the whole (of his business) so entirely destroyed in the way we have seen. The reduction of my capital has been bad enough, but the destruction of my establishment goes further' and 'shall now be looking for some other Line [sic] in which to employ our Industry'. Although despondent, he assured Vicary that he was not yet 'I thank God, reduced so low as you saw me 5 or 6 years since, nor ever shall again I hope, though if fortune should continue to prosecute me, there is no saying what humiliating circumstances I may still be reserved.

He also wrote to George giving him a full account of his financial affairs. Having left £20,000 of stock in Cadiz and Seville, he was still confident that he would be able to dispose of it if war could be avoided. He told George that several of his Spanish associates had suggested that he open an office in London but he was aware that his 'Capital would be too small for this, and my informations are, I fear, too limited'. In order to cut his expenditure he was sending Henry and William back to England on the next packet. Knowing that his income would be severely reduced for the foreseeable future, he wrote to Dolly on 27 April, suggesting that she sell the horses and cut back on the number of servants. He also asked her to ensure that the boys 'should make the best possible use of their time' in England and asked that she arrange for Henry to have French lessons.

On 18 May 1805, Britain and Spain were at war again and as expected, an embargo was placed on all English property leaving the goods of many British merchants stranded in Spain. Antony was confident that he would have no difficulty in disposing of his stock held by his Spanish friends, but the previous year had seen a bad harvest, and this and the economic dislocation caused by war, resulted in a sharp decline in demand, forcing him to look at other markets. Knowing that only Spanish ships could enter Iberian ports, he conceived the idea of exporting his goods to the Spanish colonies in South America. With Britain commanding the high seas and blockading hostile ports, he came up with a highly speculative scheme to charter a Spanish ship under a British license to transport his stranded goods through the Cadiz office. He wrote to Vicary with the details of his plan and his brother agreed to arrange interviews for him with the Board of Trade.

In mid-June Henry and William arrived in England and travelled to Bristol where William was to join his uncle's firm as a clerk. The following month, Antony sailed for London on what proved to be quite an eventful journey. As Mrs Hucks recorded in her diary:

> 1 September. Heard this evening that Mr. Gibbs was taken by a Spanish privateer.

> 2 September. I have experienced the most joyful surprise: when I thought him at Vigo he was retaken

> by an English ship before the enemy could reach it
> and arrived from Falmouth this afternoon 15 hours
> after we had this dreadful intelligence.[20]

On his arrival in Exeter, he was annoyed to find that Dolly and the children were on a short holiday at Dawlish where he went to see them briefly before going on to London. There, Vicary had arranged for him to meet with the Duke of Montrose, the President of the Board of Trade, who seemed enthusiastic about the plan. But Antony soon realised that the wheels of government turned slowly and he was to remain in London for several weeks. It was not long before he developed a liking for the social whirl of the metropolis. Although used to being entertained at the British embassies in Lisbon and Cadiz, Vicary, who had recently been knighted, mixed in a different social circle. On 18 October, he wrote to Dolly that he had met the Duke of Montrose at the Treasury the previous day. 'Tomorrow and again on Monday I am to have a particular Conference of a domestic kind with many of my good Friends of the Privy Council, and I find my Taste for this sort of Society is hourly increasing. Now to bring me back all at once to the Pigs and Poultry of a Devonshire Cottage will require no small Degree of Attention'.

The following week he was making almost daily visits to the Treasury in the hope that they had reached a decision. Several weeks later, having had a number of meetings with the Privy Council, he was still waiting for a response. By that time, the glamour of city life had worn thin. In November he wrote to Dolly that he was 'sadly tired of this London life' and anxious to return to Lisbon. While the capital rejoiced at the British victory at Cadiz, the 'Death of our great hero [Nelson] puts a stop to it', and hoped that in time she would be grateful to him for all his efforts. 'We should consider ourselves fortunate if in this melancholy Time for Business I should be put in a Way of doing something for my Family, which, if we look to the Merchants of Exeter, very few can do at present.' He went on 'we have great Comforts my dear Dolly, of another sort, tho' we can't boast much in the Way of Riches

– let me only ask thee what all the Riches in the world would be worth if we had reason to be ashamed of the Conduct of our Children'.

At the end of November, Antony learned that he had been granted his license and immediately sailed for Lisbon. There he chartered *La Hermosa Mexicana*, a brig of 420 tons 'burthen' to transport his stranded goods to South America on a round trip to Lima and London. He instructed his Spanish holder to prepare a shipment of textiles as the outgoing cargo for Lima, (at that time called the City of Kings). The vessel would bring Peruvian produce on the return trip. However, things did not go to plan and because of a number of delays, the license expired. Henry, still in Cadiz, travelled back to Lisbon with a band of smugglers and then on to London where, through the auspices of Lord Auckland, succeeded in getting the license extended. He returned with due haste to Lisbon and on 15 December, *La Hermosa Mexicana* finally sailed, arriving in Lima the following April. With the break up of his Spanish business, Antony had originally intended to establish a new banking house in London with the profits of the Lima trip. In the event, because of a number of delays, it took several years for the transactions to be completed and the venture failed to produce much of a return.

* * * *

Meanwhile in Exwick, with the resumption of hostilities, Banfill found that a considerable amount of the stock that had been shipped to Antony in Lisbon to sell on his behalf remained unsold in Portugal. So concerned were he and Granger that in their new ten-year partnership agreement, signed on 7 May 1804, they included a new clause to ensure that the 'unresolved Debts and Sums of Money due to the Partnership which were and are still embargoed and detained in the Spanish Dominions by order of the Government of Spain' were accounted for as part of Antony's debts. Both agreed that each would keep 'lists of accounts and balances due to them from 'any person or persons resident within the Spanish Dominions or goods or property embargoed there', and that the surviving partner could 'deduct & with-old' out of his share 'the proportion or sum of money appearing to be payable'.[21] Despite the gloomy outlook, they were both confident that the business would survive any downturn in trade.

For the next two years, the firm continued to expand its factory and develop the site. A contemporary writer described Exwick, as a hamlet that 'took its rise from the fulling and grist mills, long established here; a leat being cut from the river [Exe] below Cowley bridge, they are constantly supplied with a stream of water. In this hamlet Edmund Granger and Samuel Banfill, Esqs, have established a large woollen manufactuary, and erected spinning machines, workshops, dyehouses, tenter grounds etc. Also dwelling houses for the manufacturers, an establishment which has greatly increased the number of inhabitants.[22] The buildings, and the organisation of the factory in Exwick, were modelled on Arkwright's northern cotton mills. Banfill had copied his techniques, applying them to worsted spinning, and applied the factory system to the mill at Exwick. Using the latest technology, he managed to establish order in the workplace for the growing number of workers employed at the mill, and the firm continued to make a profit, albeit not at the level of thirty years before.

As the war dragged on, the Exwick firm's financial difficulties were not helped by an ongoing dispute between Banfill and Antony over the cargo of flannel exported to Spain some years before. It hinged on whether the profit should be offset against Antony's long-standing debt to the firm, or whether it should be used to paying off his other creditors. Antony argued that as these were goods that he had *bought* before the war but which had not been shipped to Spain until much later, they should not be included as part of his debt. Both Granger and Banfill believed that he should, as his personal debts to them were still around £5000. George offered to arbitrate along with another Bristol merchant. Although they were supposed to be impartial, perhaps inevitably, with his brother leading the investigation, the dispute was settled in Antony's favour. Granger reluctantly accepted the decision, Banfill did not, and this resulted in tension between the two families. Dolly was very upset that her friendship with Nancy should be strained in this way, and Antony acknowledged that until his debts to the firm were repaid the relationship between the two families would always be difficult.

Between 1805 and 1808, the political climate continued to deteriorate as France increased her involvement in the Iberian Peninsula and attempted to reduce British influence in Portugal, which had long been an ally of Great Britain. During that time, Antony made a number of visits to London with Henry, and he continued to expand his business interests there. In 1807, the French army with the acquiescence of Charles V crossed Spain and invaded Portugal. The Portuguese Royal family fled to Brazil and in December, the French occupied Lisbon forcing Antony to close his office and return to London. With his knowledge of the Peninsula and fluency with the language, the British Government offered him an appointment as one of four Commissioners dealing with Portuguese property that had been sent to England during the war. The post was admirably suited to his abilities. It entailed residence in London and included a small remuneration to cover his expenses, but more importantly, it brought him in close contact with the mercantile community in the metropolis. It was this, and the closure of his Spanish office that persuaded him that his family's future was in London. Leaving Henry in Lisbon, Antony took up his post as Commissioner in January 1807 and William, who had been working at George's firm in Bristol, moved to the capital to act as clerk to both the Commission and to his father.

CHAPTER 9

THE TOPSHAM FAMILY

While George Abraham, having lost all claims to his inheritance, was destined for a career as a surgeon, his sister Susanna (known as Anna), and his half-brother John by his father's second marriage to Sarah Lyle, had very different futures. Anna married John Remmett, a clothier from Crediton. They had one son, Robert Butler Remmett who, like his uncle went into the medical profession.[1] Whereas George Abraham and Anna had been christened in the Presbyterian meetinghouse, their half-brother John was baptised in Topsham church. It is not known where John was educated but, under the influence of his grand-father John Ewings and uncle Daniel Ewings, who were both successful merchant mariners, he went to sea and eventually he too became a master mariner.

In 1751, John married Elizabeth Meachin, daughter of William and Elizabeth Meachin whose father and grandfather had been salt traders and refiners in Topsham and Seaton in Devon for at least two generations. Her grandfather, also called John, and his wife had leased the salt works in Seaton from Sir John Trevelyn before moving to Topsham with their family. There, the Meachins' operated their salt business from 'a plot with a dwelling house (lately burnt down)' in what was known as Topsham Bridge Close 'on the east of the highway that leads to and fro Topsham Bridge'[2] at an annual peppercorn rent of two shillings and sixpence. This was in consideration '…of the improvement….' That they undertook to make and '…. to build at his own cost within a year a convenient dwelling house on the premises…'.[3] They erected their new house and salt refinery opposite the public house that later became known as the Bridge Inn. Twenty-five years later, their son William continued the family business having made a good marriage in 1723. His bride was the daughter of Sir Thomas Bury of Northam and she brought with her a considerable dowry. William owned a boat known locally as the *Water Tin Quart* or the *Tankard.* To collect salt for boiling, he floated the Tankard down to Exmouth Bar on the high tide, where it was pumped full of water; and then brought back on the tide to his refinery on the banks of the river Clyst near Topsham Bridge where the water was emptied in a 'chauldron and granulated by fire'.[4] Their success had enabled the Meachin family to amass a substantial fortune.

Elizabeth Meachin was a severe woman and although some years older than John, it was considered a suitable match. The marriage certainly improved his financial status, for she had inherited the bulk of her grandfather's estate. At the time of his death in 1749, old John Meachin had prospered, acquiring a considerable amount of property including two saltworks in Exeter as well as houses and lands in Dorset, Venn Ottery and Topsham.[5] After their marriage, John Gibbs and his bride moved into the family house in Shapter Street, built by his grand-father Abraham forty years before. The following year Elizabeth gave birth to their first child, a daughter called Elizabeth after her mother and grandmother but who was always known as Betsy. Three years later, their first son, whom they called John Meachin (Jack), was born.[6] Over the next eleven years, another five sons followed at regular intervals, William (1757), Abraham (1758), twins George and Lyle (1761) and Thomas (1767). John sailed in the Newfoundland fishing industry and like many mariners in the trade spent many months each year away at sea. The industry was based around St. John's and Conception Bay. British goods were exported to Newfoundland and cod was imported for the European markets of Spain and Italy. Like many wives of merchant mariners of the time, it is likely that in the early years of their marriage, Elizabeth accompanied her husband on his voyages to Newfoundland and back to the Mediterranean. It appears from the registers that their first three children had been born abroad, being later baptised after the family returned to England.

John Gibbs became a successful merchant mariner. In 1764, he and his half-brother George Abraham established the firm of George Gibbs & Co and and jointly purchased the *Ceres*, a 140-ton brig that had been built the previous year; they each owned a half share of the vessel. It was registered with Lloyds of London to sail on the Cowes to Holland routes. To fund his share of the vessel, in an agreement dated 19 September 1764, John and Elizabeth leased part of her grandfather's inheritance. This included 'all that plot & building thereon erected with the courtlage & Garden belonging & all that messuage courtlage & garden in Topsham, in a close called Topsham Bridge Close bounded with the sea on the east, the highway that leads to & from Topsham Bridge on the south & the…plot of ground on the west and lands…on the north.[7] For the next ten years, John was rarely at home, spending long periods sailing between Newfoundland, Hamburg and the Mediterranean, particularly Italy, as a reference to 'Uncle John's business in Italy' in the family letters indicates. Because of the success of their trading venture in Italy George Abraham apprenticed his own son Abraham to a firm in Genoa so that he could work more closely with his uncle as his agent. John's eldest son, Jack, became a mariner and joined his father on board the *Ceres*. They appear to have been very profitable, trading cod and other commodities in the Mediterranean for a number of merchant houses including Heath & Co, an Exeter firm owned by George Abraham's friend John Heath, and Munckley & Co of Bristol.

The extended network of family and friends enabled John to supply his family with European delicacies. In November 1773, he received a letter from George Abraham asking him to purchase some Spanish honey from Alicante, requesting that it be '*shipped on board the Ceres for Hamburg*', where Munckley & Co.'s agent would arrange for it to be sent direct to Bristol rather than have John bring it to England on the longer route via London. The following January, John wrote from Hamburg that he was planning another trip later in the year from

Leghorn to 'Cephalonia for corn' for Munckley & Co and would purchase the honey and have it sent to Nice where he would collect it on his return. As the '*Ceres* must go from Hamburg to London', he wrote, 'he [Munckley] may order the packet to Bristol', where it could be sent on to Anne in Exeter. This was John's second voyage on this route. The first had been very successful and he had made 'freight about £250 in 50 days'. It seems that this second trip was doomed from the outset. John's departure was delayed because 'his freighter has failed him a little'; the *Ceres* was finally ready to sail at the end of May. Six weeks later, a letter arrived in Exeter from Jack telling the family that his father had died two days after they had sailed and had been buried at sea. John had suddenly developed a fever and on 'the passage from thence to the next port on 20th July the melancholy scene closed'. Jack, who was on board with his father at the time of his death, took command of the vessel and sailed on to Cephalonia to complete the trip. His cousin, Abraham (George Abraham's son), who was in Genoa having just completed his apprenticeship was very fond of his uncle and he too was very upset by his death having spent 'so much time with him in a foreign country'.

Despite having spent much of his life away from his family, John and Elizabeth had remained devoted to one another. Fifty-one at the time of his death, he left all his 'Goods and Chattels' and his 'half part' of the Brigantine *Ceres* to his wife as well as 'my Candles and ffurniture all my household Goods of every kind and Quality and everything that I may be possessed of at the time of my death'. He instructed her to 'apply the same towards the Maintenance and Education of our Children and divide the same amongst them in just and proper manner'.[8] At the time of his death, their childrens' ages ranged from Betsy who was twenty-three to Thomas, who was just seven.

For many years, the same affection had not existed between Elizabeth and her daughter Betsy. With her husband away for long periods throughout their marriage, Elizabeth had found it difficult to manage with six children. Betsy adored her father and resented having to care for her younger brothers. In 1768, a few months after Thomas's birth, when she was just sixteen she had fallen madly in love with young Nicholas Peters, son their family friend who was an apothecary in Topsham like his father and grandfather. Betsy, an attractive high-spirited young woman was flattered by his attentions and thrilled when he sought her mother's permission to 'humbly address himself' to her. With her husband away for much of her marriage, Elizabeth, supported by George Abraham who was acting as her childrens guardian in John's absence, refused to countenance Nicholas's advances. Although only a few years older than Betsy, Peters already had a bad reputation with women and her mother was determined that she should be not linked with him in any way. Advised by George Abraham who claimed to have 'heard but a very poor account of the Gentleman' in the coffee shops in Exeter, she forbade her daughter to see him again. Betsy was inconsolable and threatened to elope, but her mother would not be persuaded.[9]

Within a few months, Betsy's romantic adventures once again caused concern. This time she became attracted to a soldier in the Welsh Militia, stationed in Topsham Barracks. One night, whilst drunk he made an, 'indecent proposal to her by letter'. When her mother discovered it she was furious and, unable to handle her rebellious daughter, decided that Betsy should be removed from temptation to preserve her reputation. George Abraham suggested that she be sent to live with his cousin Joan who had married Dr Thomas Morgan, a Welsh dissenting minister, and was living in Liskeard, so Betsy was packed off to live with them.[10] There, in an atmosphere of strict moral and religious pressure, it was hoped that her rebelliousness would be curbed. Surprisingly, Betsy was very happy living with the Morgans. She got on well with her aunt, and loved her young cousin Johnny, but she missed her brothers and longed to return to her family.

When he heard of John's death George Abraham assembled his brother's family at Pytte to break the news. Betsy was grief-stricken, begging her mother to allow her to return to Topsham, but she refused. Betsy's cousins were appalled by their aunt's intransigence. A letter written the following month by Nancy to her brother George vividly described the scene and portrays the animosity that existed between mother and daughter. Betsy, she wrote,

'was at George's Clyst when she received the melancholy news of her poor Father's death, and in the fullness of her heart, she clasped my Mother [Anne] round the neck, and said you are now my dearest madam, my best friend. This is a dreadful thing for a person to say who has a Mother but I believe it is strictly true, nor would she poor soul have said it at any other time. But I am not surprised at her throwing open her heart when she was in such great distress.... The loss of such an excellent Father, and I'm sorry to say her dearest and best friend, is greater than I can describe or anyone feel that has not unfortunately experienced it...Betsy was exceedingly unwilling to leave her Mother at this time, but she insisted upon it. It may seem very strange to you, but I really feel she is happy without her daughter as with her. I hope this melancholy event will soften her heart and be the means of her treating B [Betsy] with more tenderness, indeed I think she deserves it, perhaps her behaviour in some respects may have been impro-per, but I sincerely believe she is a very good tempered Girl, and I will answer for it has a great deal of sensibility.'. Rejected by her mother at such a sad time, Betsy tearfully said goodbye to her brothers and cousins, who were all deeply moved by her situation. The parting with Betsy Gibbs yesterday affects me so much. Poor Betsy's situation is truly deplorable. I can assure you my heart Bleeds for her, to say nothing of her circumstances. Mrs Morgan is so obliging as to take her to Liskeard, where I believe she will stay for some months. I hope to God the change of scene will contribute to restore to her, her peace of mind, which has been long lost'.

Jack was absent from Pytte, having remained in the Mediterranean to continue the voyage. When the younger boys heard of their father's death, they 'were all exceedingly affected'. It 'made such an impression on Abraham, 'as we were afraid would not have been easily removed, such a fixt melancholy I never saw in a childs face before. I think he [now] seems to begin to enjoy himself a little, and I hope will soon get the better of it. They all seem to be very well disposed boys, and I don't doubt of my Father being able to put them in some reputable way of getting their living, but what will become of poor Betsy I know not what until her brothers are well settled. I am afraid there will be but a very small income left; we have only to hope that something unforeseen may happen, to make her happier than we are at present have any reason to expect'.

After John's death, his widow remained in Topsham with her younger sons, whilst Betsy continued to be banned from the family home. Elizabeth was a capable woman, long used to coping with her large family, but on his death, her brother-in-law George Abraham formally took on the role of guardian to his brother's children. There was also their business connection. John and George Abraham had been partners in the firm of George Gibbs & Co for many years. In his will, John bequeathed his share of the *Ceres* to Elizabeth and George Abraham was keen that the business should continue. He also began to make plans for his nephews' future. Jack was nineteen when his father died and had been sailing with him for several years. Despite this, his uncle thought him too young to take command of the *Ceres* and he employed William Kingston, an experienced mariner to sail with Jack. The Lloyds Register of Shipping shows that Kingston captained the vessel for the next two years.

John's second son William, then aged seventeen, joined Jack on the *Ceres* and sixteen year-old Abraham was to sent to Leghorn to join his cousin Abraham (George Abraham's son), with instructions that he be put 'in the hands of his master, who is one of the most considerable merchants in the place'. He was apprenticed to a Henry Betts, one of a growing number of English merchants who had significant business interests throughout Italy. The three younger boys, Lyle, George and Thomas remained at home with their mother. In 1777, George Abraham arranged for Lyle to go to the Genoese office of Heath & Co, owned by his friend John Heath and George joined the army.

The following year, Jack aged twenty-four, took over as Master of the *Ceres* trading for the next two years on the transatlantic routes to Newfoundland and the North American plantations. The American Wars of Independence had cut the traditional trading routes with America and the barring of American ships supplying the British West Indies with fish provided an impetus for British shipping, particularly from the west-country ports. During this period Exeter became one of the three main ports of the Newfoundland fishing industry. Vessels from Topsham carried large cargoes of salt, provisions and manufactures as well large numbers of bye-boatmen as passengers. The long distance transatlantic voyages took several months to complete with vessels usually making only one voyage each year.[11] In 1779, while Jack was on his second voyage to Newfoundland, his mother died and Betsy returned to Topsham to care for Thomas who was still at home.

Elizabeth Gibbs had appointed her brother-in-law, George Abraham, and her two eldest sons Jack and William as her executors, and in her will had acted in accordance with with her late husband's wishes to divide her estate between all their children 'in a just and proper manner'. Despite her past difficulties with Betsy, she made sure her daughter was properly provided for, particularly as the burden of looking after Thomas would fall on her. She left her 'Dwelling House in Topsham' in trust for Betsy and Thomas but with the rider that when sold all her goods and chattels were to be divided between all her children.

If her executors decided to keep the *Ceres*, her half share would be divided into six equal parts. Jack and William, who were aged twenty-five and twenty-two respectively, should each have one sixth 'for their equal use and benefit'. They were instructed to 'layout and employ and improve the remaining four parts' for the 'equal benefit of my four younger sons' in trust until they reached the age of twenty-one. Betsy was to receive fifteen pounds a year from the 'ffreight or other profits and produce'. Should they decide to sell the vessel they should 'sell and dispose thereof either publicly or privately' to obtain the ' best price and Most Monies'. Once sold, both Betsy and William were to receive £100 from the profits, and another £100 was to be invested and retained in trust for young Thomas until he reached his majority. The residue or any 'surplus or overplus of money' was to be invested for 'my said two sons Abraham Gibbs and George Gibbs equally share and share alike….and to employ and improve the same at interest for their equal benefit'. Her executors could use the monies 'in the placing of them or any or either of them abroad to any Trade profession of Business as they shall think fit'. Even in death, Elizabeth had her favourites amongst her sons and poor Lyle was left nothing.

Jack too was to receive nothing if the *Ceres* was sold. Elizabeth considered that her eldest son was already well provided for. On her death 'as my customary son and the customary heir of my late deceased husband John', he would inherit all the Gibbs family estates. These included a considerable amount of land and property in Devon, as well as a small estate in the manor of Royke Regis and Elwell in Dorset, and a house with six aces in the parish of Wyck near Weymouth. She also owned a number of tenements in St Olave's parish in Exeter, several properties in Topsham including a house with 'three gardens, four orchards, and fifty acres of land and twenty acres of meadows, thirty acres pasture and common pasture in Venn Ottery and Topsham', all of which she had inherited from her grandfather.[12] There were a further twenty-seven acres of fields in Topsham, near the Bridge and salt works, which had been owned by her parents and which yielded a considerable income.

As the *Ceres* was in good condition, it was decided to keep the vessel and it continued operating for the next five years sailing under the name of George Gibbs & Co. Although Jack did not captain the vessel again, the venture certainly seems to have been profitable for several years. However, by 1783, the Lloyds lists indicate that the condition of the *Ceres* had deteriorated considerably and rather than refurbishing it for the transatlantic routes, it was decided to switch to the coastwise trade. Since the mid-eighteenth century, there had been a rapid increase in this trade to and from Exeter, due in part to the increase in population, which stimulated demand for a growing number of foodstuffs, manufactures and raw materials. Although this continued to be a profitable enterprise, two years later, Jack and William decided to sell the boat and go their separate ways. As specified in their mother's will, the proceeds were used to settle the younger boys in their chosen trade or profession.

Jack and William were to remain at sea as merchant mariners and Thomas who was described as a mariner,was in Nova Scotia in 1786, employed as the Exeter firm's agent.[14] Two years later, he joined the Royal Navy. Lyle and Abraham were settled in Italy. George who had joined the army, was to die unmarried in Jamaica in 1793 in a shooting accident, supposedly shot in the mouth by a cannon, which he thought not to have been loaded. This left Betsy, who was then aged thirty-four and still unmarried, living alone in the family house in Topsham. With her brothers now living abroad, there was no one to manage the family estates. George Abraham suggested that all their properties in Devon and Dorset be put into trust to provide them all with an income and it was agreed that he and Antony be appointed as trustees to manage them on their behalf.

As they had no reason to distrust their uncle, Jack and his brothers and sister agreed to his proposal to give up their individual rights to their parents' estate and put them in trust. The agreement stated that, after the deduction of administration costs the income from the properties would be re-invested. They each received an initial sum of twenty shillings and the trustees undertook in future to, 'pay and apply the overflow Money equally' to them. However, the trust deed agreement included a clause that was to prove crucial in the future. It allowed the trustees to sell or dispose of all the properties 'for such price or prices as can be gotten for the same…without or even against the further consent' of their cousins.[15]

Nothing more is known about Jack. Whether he remained at sea, joined the navy or returned to Nova Scotia is not clear. He did not marry and although the exact date of his death is unknown, it is recorded as being around 1788. It is presumed that he died and was buried at sea.[16] William too remained at sea, returning to England in 1790, to find his uncle and cousin bankrupt and his inheritance sold to pay their debts. Thomas later served as a second lieutenant on HMS Minotaur under Admiral McBride. He died in Jamaica of yellow fever in 1796, at the age of twenty-nine.

* * * *

Betsy longed to marry and have a family of her own. With her share from the sale of the *Ceres*, she now had some financial independence. In the summer of 1788, she met a young American several years her junior who was visiting Topsham. His name was Bremen. He was both charming and attractive, claiming to have extensive plantations in South Carolina. With the start of the American war he had fled to England leaving all his property, which he hoped to reclaim once the conflict was over. He also appeared to have good connections, alleging to be the nephew of the President of the American Congress who was at that time making a visit to Bristol. From the moment they met, Betsy was captivated by his southern charm. Despite her lack of experience with men, her uncle and cousins were not overly concerned thinking 'it nothing more than a flirtation'. However, within weeks she was hopelessly in love and when he proposed she joyfully accepted.

George Abraham believeing that Betsy had been 'thoroughly taken in', asked George to check out his story as his 'connections with S^th Carolina were so considerable before the war with America'. Although sympathetic to his niece's wishes, he refused to consent to the match until he had heard from George for 'it is no easy matter for a young woman, in Your Cousin's situation, to make up her mind on the side of reason, when it is combated by intuition'. Within a few days, George Abraham received word that all Bremen's claims were false. There were no estates in South Carolina and he was not related to the President whose name was Bremer not Bremen.

Betsy was heartbroken, and tearfully agreed to end the engagement. Some weeks later, a parcel for her from Naples was delivered to Exwick House where it remained for several days. Eventually it was sent on to Betsy in Topsham, who thought it was a present from her brother Abraham. When she opened it, she discovered it was from her former suitor and contained a 'nitting box from Spa' and a three-page love letter. Eager to rekindle their affair, Bremen had sent it via Abraham's office in Naples, hoping that her uncle would not suspect the identity of the sender. Anyone but love-struck Betsy would have returned the package immediately but when she read the letter all her doubts about him evaporated. The family was horrified when she joyfully told them that she and Bremen were to resume their engagement. Her uncle begged her to see reason and return the letter and the present. With so much family pressure, and after many tears Betsy reluctantly bowed to their wishes and agreed. On 8 December 1788, George Abraham wrote:

> Sir,
> I am desired by my cousin to acquaint you that she thinks it is improper to keep up any longer an intercourse, which she has many and very sufficient reasons, to be convinced, can only end in disappointment. I ought to add that she has come to the knowledge of more reasons since you left the neighbourhood. Any further explanation, as it would be unpleasant, so it seems unnecessary, unless it be your own desire, in which case I shall not decline it.
>
> You will receive by the Bath coach the inclose [sic] parcel which appears to have been sent by you many days ago, but did not come to my cousin's hands till last night, to whose house at Exwick it was carried, and left there, as I said, till yesterday... .'.

Despite her disappointment, Betsy put on a brave face. Her cousins, aware of her unhappiness treated her with considerable kindness. They also knew that in her desperation to marry she could well be prey to other unscrupulous suitors. A few days before Christmas, her brother William, who had returned to England after Jack's death, came to visit her for a few days. He was about to start working for the Bristol firm of Munckley Gibbs & Richards on the West Indies routes and had heard about Betsy's 'near miss'. He was worried about his sister and wanted to see her settled before he left England again. They spent Christmas together in Topsham before going to Exwick House for a few days in the New Year, and where George Abraham and Anne were staying. Betsy was shocked to learn that Bremen, after a whirl-wind romance, had married an heiress from Sidmouth while still pressing his suit with her. Bitter and humiliated she tried to put on a brave face and seemed relieved to have 'escaped from this profligate villain', but 'there is no knowing what is in the heart'. Poor Betsy; this was not the first disappointment. As her uncle wryly remarked, she had 'been under a great mistake through her whole life, about the most probable way of getting a husband'. When William heard the full story, concerned for his sister's welfare, he agreed that she needed protection. As Antony was away for long periods, and Dolly was alone in Exwick House, it was suggested that she give up the house in Topsham, which was far too large for her and go to live with Dolly to help with the children. Betsy reluctantly agreed and she and William returned to Topsham to begin packing.

William remained in Topsham for several days to help Betsy move into Exwick House, while the house in Shapter Street was let and the furniture was sold. There, he met a Mrs Ley, a clergyman's wife, and her young daughter Susanna, called Susan, who were moving into a small house opposite, which had also belonged to his parents. William, who was in his early thirties, was immediately attracted to Susanna who was much flattered by his attentions. As he was returning to Bristol within a few days, he sought permission from Mrs Ley to write to her. Once Betsy was settled in her new home, with promises to write and return at the end of his voyage, William travelled up to Bristol to join his ship.

Although Betsy was happy living at Exwick House, it was not long before she became aware of Antony's financial difficulties and it was a shock when both he and her uncle were declared bankrupt. Under the terms of the trust set up three years before, all the properties left to her and her brothers by their parents were sold and the proceeds used to offset her uncle's debts. Naturally enough, Betsy and William were happy to do something to help at such a difficult time and were assured that the value of their inheritance would be treated as a loan, to be repaid with interest at the earliest opportunity. In August, Antony's decision to leave Exeter with his family for Spain yet again dealt Betsy a harsh blow. Six months before she had reluctantly given up her home and her independence to live under the protection of her extended family. Now, through no fault of her own, she was completely dependent on them for support, having no alternative but to agree to go with them.

During the difficult voyage to La Corunna, Betsy, sea sick and suffering from a constant headache, kept to her cabin. Madrid in August was stifling and after Antony's departure, ill with the heat, Betsy remained in her darkened room, feeling too unwell to help her cousin. She and Dolly found it difficult to cope in such cramped conditions and she found herself confined to a small apartment with no friends and unable to speak the language. Dolly too was unwell, suffering with morning sickness, and having to cope almost single-handed with her family, she grew more irritable and bad tempered as her pregnancy progressed.

Several weeks later, the two women were barely speaking; each blaming the other for the situation. Betsy resented Dolly's attitude towards her, claiming that she was now treated like a servant and Dolly complained that Betsy was uncooperative and refusing to help with the children. Antony tried to calm matters and Betsy agreed to try to be more cooperative, but admitted that she resented living in such 'reduced circumstances', with little opportunity to meet 'agreeable people'. Dolly seemed oblivious to her position. Antony, sensitive to his cousin's plight, understood that Betsy 'was uneasy and uncomfortable in her present situation', and asked that she try to be more helpful until Dolly's confinement. Then he promised that he would look for a 'convenient way of her returning to England in the Spring'.

Knowing that she would soon be leaving Spain lifted Betsy's spirits and she became more 'attentive and desirious' to Dolly's demands. She wrote to her friends telling them that she would be back in Devon by the end of the summer. Dolly was furious when she discovered that Betsy had also made disparaging remarks about their situation and had told them that 'there has been nothing to make her comfortable, but what she [had] brought with her'. By the time Antony arrived home, the two women were barely acknowledging one another. On 25 May, Dolly gave birth to another son and as good as his word, at the end of June, Antony found his cousin a passage on a boat to Falmouth. Three weeks later, she was sent home under the care of a 'Gentleman from Birmingham'.

Betsy returned to England penniless and homeless. Now aged thirty-eight, she had almost given up hope of marriage. Her only alternative was to try to find herself a position as a housekeeper or companion. Despite an appeal from Antony, his father was adamant that he wanted nothing more to do with her. Her cousin George was much more sympathetic, aware of the sacrifice his cousins had made for his father and brother. His wife, Etty had recently died leaving him with three young children and as his sister Bell wished to return to Exeter, he offered Betsy a temporary home until her brother William returned from the West Indies.

Arriving back in Bristol a month later, William and Betsy travelled to Topsham for his marriage to Susanna (Susan) Ley. They had been writing to each other for over a year and his proposal had been accepted. A gentle, kind woman, Susan was the daughter of the Rev. Thomas Ley the rector of Doddiscombleigh in Devon. William was a well travelled thirty-three year-old and Susan some eleven years his junior, but despite the difference in their temperaments and ages, this was a love-match, for as a rector's daughter, She had no fortune of her own to boost William's modest finances. They were married in Topsham on 12 August 1790 and afterwards travelled back to Bristol with Betsy, as they too were to live with George.

George, out of consideration for his newly married cousin, offered William employment on the shorter routes to the Mediterranean so that Susan could accompany her husband on his voyages. For several years they sailed together mainly to Italy and Spain, returning to live with George between sailings. Their trips enabled Susan to meet her brothers-in-law, Abraham and Lyle. Abraham was living in Naples with his young wife Mary whilst Lyle was unmarried in Genoa. Lyle became very fond of his sister-in-law. With no family of his own, he was delighted when William and Susan's eldest son, William Henry was born in his house in Genoa on 3 July 1791, followed by their second, John Ley on 15 June 1793.[17]

With war imminent in Europe, William felt that it was too much of a risk for Susan and the children to continue sailing with him. Instead, they remained in Bristol during his absences at sea. Betsy too was still living with George and the two women became firm friends. Whether Betsy had hoped that she and her wealthy cousin would marry is unclear, but taking on a ready-made family seems to have been the last thing that she wanted, having looked after her brothers for so many years. She remained a handsome woman and not long after her arrival in Bristol, George's partner, James Richards began to call on her. Richards, like George had been recently widowed, and was fast becoming a wealthy man. When he proposed several months later, Betsy graciously accepted. At last, she would be able to live to a standard, which would ensure her acceptance into 'agreeable society'. As she had no income to provide a dowry George, proposed that Antony's outstanding debt to her be settled. Her uncle thoroughly approved of the marriage. It guaranteed Betsy's future and ensured that she would no longer be a burden on her extended family. After the wedding on 13 April 1794 at St. Augustine's church in Bristol, they moved into James's country house in the village of Abbotts Leigh, a few miles from the city centre.

With the dislocation to trade due to the war with France, by the beginning of 1795 George could no longer guarantee his cousin regular employment and William's fortunes declined. At the end of

March, he moved his family back to Topsham to live with Susan's mother, Mrs Ley and a few days later left for Falmouth to find a passage on a ship bound for Leghorn where he hoped his brother Lyle, who was still working in the Genoese office of Heath & Co, would find him some employment. On route, his ship was attacked, and William was captured and imprisoned by the French. When she heard the news Susan was distraught, expecting to never see her husband again. In June, William managed to escape and made his way to Malaga, eventually returning to Topsham at the end of July. The news of his escapade spread fast. On 29 July, George wrote to Antony that his cousin had finally 'made his escape from France and returned to his family'. On top of the relief that he had survived the ordeal, George was sympathetic for 'The poor fellow has not got an employ, but this is not an easy matter in the present state of commerce'.

William was still unemployed three months later, when a letter arrived from Lyle addressed to him 'at Mrs. Ley's, Topsham' offering financial help. During his imprisonment, Susan had corresponded regularly with her brother-in-law with all the news of the family. She had also confided in him about their mounting financial problems. She was relieved to learn that Lyle, who was trading with Granger & Banfill in Exeter had asked Banfill if he could find William a position on a ship bound for the Mediterranean as he had recently been appointed as agent for the Association of Shippers of Genoa, Leghorn and Exeter. She knew that Lyle was worried about her and the children, aware that she was completely dependent on her husband's employment for survival. As Lyle now considered himself, 'an old bachelor' and unlikely to have his own family, he wrote that both he and Abraham 'would stand forth and you may occasionally value upon us for two Hundred Pounds each to be employed in any manner' and had written to Abraham to tell him of his offer and doubted 'not of his approving'. As good as his word, William began to receive a regular allowance during his long periods of unemployment and Susan occasionally received 'small presents' from her brother-in-law to help maintain their growing family. The following year, his youngest brother Thomas, a lieutenant on *HMS Minotaur* under Admiral McBride, died of yellow fever in Jamaica leaving all his 'share of the prize money due from the *Victorieuse* and *Walshingham Packet,* and all the proceeds of his kit' in trust for his nephews William Henry and John Ley.

CHAPTER 10

ABRAHAM

Of all John's sons, Abraham was to achieve the greatest success, but his life would end in tragedy. In 1775, at the age of eighteen he was apprenticed to Henry Betts, an English merchant in Leghorn (Livorno). George Abraham's own son, another Abraham, who was in Genoa at that time, was instructed to 'put him in the hands of his master, who is one of the most considerable merchants in the place'. Two years later, his younger brother Lyle joined a merchant house in Genoa owned by the Exeter firm, Heath & Co. With Jack sailing on the *Ceres* in the Mediterranean this shrewd move not only reunited the three brothers, but enabled them to expand the Mediterranean markets for the Exeter firm.

At the end of his apprenticeship, Abraham remained in Leghorn, establishing his own agency business importing cloth and woollens from Britain and colonial produce from the Caribbean. By 1787, he was living in Naples having joined Falconnet & Co, a merchant house linked to the Rothschild Bank that had its origins in Switzerland. Falconnet, a French banker who had lived in Naples for many years, had known Abraham since his early days in Leghorn. The firm traded all over Europe acting mainly for English and Swiss merchants and manufacturers. Before long, like his cousins in England, Abraham had diversified into a number of other activities, and it was at this time that he became acquainted with Edmund and George Noble, two Englishmen who were from a prominent banking family.

In the eighteenth century, Naples was the capital of the Kingdom of the Two Sicilies, consisting of the southern half of the Italian peninsula and the island of Sicily. It had become an independent kingdom in 1754, and had been revived after Don Carlos of Bourbon (later Charles III of Spain) re-conquered it, making it a subsidiary of the Spanish crown. Four years later, Charles' younger brother, the eight-year old Ferdinand succeeded him. In 1767, Ferdinand then aged sixteen married Maria Carolina, sister of Marie Antoinette and daughter of the Empress Maria Theresa thus securing an alliance between the Bourbons and the Hapsburgs and giving Naples its own dynasty.

By the 1780s, Naples was one of the largest cities in Europe with a population of around four hundred thousand. To this must be added large numbers of foreigners, both residents and those visiting Naples on the Grand Tour. With the blue sea in a bay framed by the hills and Vesuvius, its beautiful buildings and royal palaces at Portici, Capodimonte and Caserta, and the excavations at Herculaneum and Pompeii, it was considered one of the most beautiful places in the world and for many was the climax of the Tour. Naples was an exciting city, and a magnet for English tourists because of its climate, its food, its music and the arts. They enjoyed the wildly extravagant soirees hosted by Sir William Hamilton at his ambassadorial residence in the Palazzo Sessa and in his houses among the vineyards at Portici and at Posillipo. At the frequent concerts and masquerades at the Palazzo Sessa, they were able to indulge all their passions in a foreign land. As Hamilton wrote to his nephew Charles Greville, 'The English, of whom we had a large flight this year have felt the good effects of my being on such a good footing at court, and each year one or two would decide for the rest how to enjoy 'the Arts, gaming, whoring or drinking'.[1] Music, balls and parties were an important part of Hamilton's life despite the fact that the costs of entertaining English tourists came close to bankrupting him.[2]

At the age of twenty-nine Abraham became engaged to Mary Elizabeth Douglas, the youngest daughter of Sir James Douglas, the British Consul General in Naples. More than ten years his junior, she and Abraham had to wait until Mary reached her majority before they could marry. Three years later in 1790 their marriage took place in the British embassy in Naples and, as Abraham spent much of his life travelling throughout Italy, he and Mary lived with her parents and sister Margaret in their villa at Portici 'close under Vesuvius' near the royal palace. Douglas, who had been appointed as Consul in 1780, was regarded as 'a worthy man with an agreeable wife and children', who was 'unaffectively attentive and obliging to every British gentleman in Naples'. He was a friend and distant relative of Hamilton who had been appointed as minister plenipotentiary in 1767. Following Hamilton's second marriage at age fifty-eight to the twenty-six year old Emma Hart in 1791, he and his young bride returned to this 'remote corner of the world' at a time when the Kingdom of the Two Sicillies was to become a political epicentre. His role as envoy was mainly concerned with strengthening the trading links between England and the Two Kingdoms and sending back dispatches and information on the area. Hamilton also looked after the interests of British residents, merchants as well as trying to sort out the problems encountered by English tourists and royal visitors on the Tour.

Abraham and Mary enjoyed the cosmopolitan life of Naples with its constant flow of foreign travellers. They became part of Hamilton's close circle of friends, enjoying his hospitality in the Palazzo Sessa. Abraham, who had acquired both a fortune and social standing through his marriage, used his connections to develop his business and trading interests, establishing himself as a successful merchant. This was a happy time for the Topsham family as he and his two brothers, William and Lyle, were re-united. Lyle having completed his apprenticeship had remained in Genoa whilst William, a merchant mariner with Munckley & Co of Bristol, brought his young bride Susan on a number of trips to Italy. Their first two sons, William Henry and John Ley were born in Genoa. On 13 October 1793, Abraham and Mary's happiness was complete with the birth of a daughter, who was christened Anna Maria.[3]

Naples was a city under constant threat from Vesuvius. The following June it was shaken by a 'thumping Eruption' which, with the exception of those in '79 and 1631' were the worst in its history.

Although there had been a considerable amount of strombolian activity during the last four years, the mountain had been quiet for several months. Then, as the level of the water in the wells sank and the crater was hidden by thick vapour, Neopolitans knew that an eruption was imminent. On 12 June, a massive earthquake shook the area from Puglia to Caserta. Three days later, after a second shock, 'A fountain of bright fire', spurted from the central crater, and then another from lower down. As the residents fled the city, the Hamiltons with their friends and hangers-on retired to their villa at Posillipo where they could view the events more safely. But even there 'two small balls of fire, joined together by a small link like a chain-shot...separated...and one fell in the vineyard above the house and the other in the sea'. Four days later the town of Torre del Greco was engulfed by lava, over thirty feet deep and a quarter of a mile wide, which had flowed over two hundred feet into the sea.[4] From 20 June to 6 July, after a number of minor explosions fifteen torrents of lava flowed down the mountain. It was to be another month before Vesuvius was quiet again and people could return to their homes.

During the early years of their marriage, Abraham and Mary became very close to Emma Hamilton. Thirty-seven years younger than her husband, Emma longed for a child and, living in such close proximity to them, she doted on little Anna Maria. However, their happiness was short-lived. In 1795, Sir James Douglas died, and two years later, in March 1797, Mary herself suddenly died leaving Abraham a young widower with a three-year old daughter. Although the cause of Mary's death is unknown she could well have succumbed to the yellow fever that was rife in Naples at the time, or to the after-effects of childbirth. With his wife's fortune passing to him, Abraham, was fast becoming a very wealthy man. His cousin George wryly noted that although Douglas's death had added to his cousin's fortune 'I can't say that I rejoice where it seems no heart to make a right use of it', thinking perhaps that Abraham should have made a futher contribution towards his uncle's debts.

Despite having died two years earlier, Douglas's estate had not been settled at the time of Mary's death. He had left his plantations in St.

Kitts in the West Indies to be divided equally between his three daughters, but only two survived him, Mary and her elder sister Margaret. With her mother dead, three-year-old Anna Maria became heir to her mother's share of her grandfather's estate. Although there seemed no doubt to her right, her aunt challenged her claim. There followed a protracted dispute fuelled in Naples and London by gossip over Abraham's close relationship with Emma. Knowing that it would be necessary to return to England to settle his daughter's claim, with the onset of war he was forced to postpone the trip.

The political events in France were about to reverberate throughout Italy. In April 1796, Napoleon, having made peace with Spain, launched his Italian campaign. As northern Italy fell, the British Government advised Ferdinand to remain neutral and negotiate a peace. A period of considerable unrest in Venice and Naples followed and after the Peace of Campo Formio, Napoleon aided by local Jacobins and French exiles occupied Rome, declaring it a republic five days later. An armistice was signed on 10 October 1796, under the terms of which no more than four ships of any country at war with France could use her ports. That same month Spain declared war on Britain.

There was great consternation and fear among the English residents and travellers in Italy after the evacuation of Leghorn and with the fall of Rome more tourists flocked south to enjoy the pleasures that Naples had to offer. Despite its declared neutrality, many Neopolitans were fearful that their city would be the next to fall. Two months after Mary's death, on 4 June 1797, at a dinner held at the British embassy to celebrate George III's birthday, Abraham witnessed Hamilton's announcment that the British fleet, commanded by Rear Admiral Nelson was on its way to the Eastern Mediterranean, to the heartfelt relief all of those present.

As Nelson pursued the French fleet in the Eastern Mediterranean, King Ferdinand and Queen Maria Carolina secretly began to make plans to leave the city with the court. Hamilton wrote on 8 August, 'in my humble opinion unless some unforeseen and fortunate Event should prevent it the French will pass their Christmas merrily at

Naples!' Ths time his fears were misplaced. The news of the destruction of the French fleet in the Bay of Aboukir was greeted with much rejoicing, with parades and *feux de joie* in the Court of Naples. The Queen reportedly cried for joy exclaiming 'oh brave Nelson oh God bless and protect our brave deliverer oh nelson nelson [sic] what do we not owe you oh victor saviour of itali'.[5]

Nelson's fleet arrived triumphant in Naples in September. He, sick and tired having been so long at sea, was lodged in the Palazzo Sessa with the Hamiltons, whilst they arranged a vast party to celebrate his fortieth birthday; it is likely that this was where he and Abraham first met. Despite the celebrations, Nelson disliked Naples and all things Neopolitan and was eager to leave. In a letter to Lord Vincent, written the day after his birthday, he wrote 'I trust my Lord in a week we shall be at Sea. I am unwell and the miserable conduct of this Court is not likely to cool my irritable temper. It is a country of fiddlers and poets, whores and scoundrels'[6]

Following Ferdinand's disastrous campaign to recapture Rome, on 6 December 1798, the French declared war on the Kingdom of the Two Sicilies. Before the Roman campaign, Nelson had warned that defeat would necessitate the evacuation of Naples. The city was packed with English tourists, residents and royalists who had fled south. As the French advanced through Italy, Ferdinand and Maria Carolina prepared to leave for Sicily. Amid the preparations, Nelson wrote to Hamilton on 14 December 1798:

> Sir
> As I have been informed that this Kingdom is invaded
> by a formidable French Army, I think it my duty to
> acquaint your Excellency, for the information of the
> English merchants and others residing at Naples, that
> the three English transports in this Bay have my
> directions to receive such effects of the English as they
> can stow, and that the whole squadron is ready to
> receive their persons should such an event be found

necessary for them to embark, I have the honour
to be, &c.

Nelson

N.B. – I need not say I mean valuable effects, and
not household furniture. I also beg leave to recommend that anything sent on board Ship should
be done with as little bustly, and as much secrecy
as possible.[7]

While the royal treasures were packed to keep them from falling into
French hands, Nelson stood by with the *Vanguard* ready to take the
royal party. In all, some twenty million pounds in money and jewels to
the value of sixty million pounds were smuggled on to the convoy.
Hamilton organised the evacuation of the English tourists and residents. His art treasures from the Palazzo Sessa were packed in crates
and stowed on the *Colossus*, a decision he would live to regret, as the
vessel was to founder off the Isles of Scilly with the majority of the
crates being lost at sea. On 21 December, the royal party, accompanied
by the Hamiltons, left the palace and boarded the *Vanguard* with their
courtiers and a number of prominent noble families. A further 2000
people including many royalist Neopolitans and British residents, including Abraham and little Anna Maria, were dispersed on to British
and Italian vessels under Nelson's command to sail at dawn for
Palermo.

As they waited on board for a fair wind, the weather conditions
suddenly deteriorated and it was too rough to sail. The ships lay at
anchor for two days. By then, word had spread throughout the city
that the King and Queen were on board, and hundreds of Neopolitans
rowed out to the *Vanguard* to plead with them to stay, but their pleas
fell on deaf ears. A few hours later as the wind shifted to the north the
armada set sail. The following day the wind increased to gale force and
a violent storm struck the ships. The *Vanguard* was damaged losing
her three topsails and her fore-yard and almost losing her main mast.

During the night six-year old Prince Albert became ill and died in Emma's arms. They arrived in Palermo in driving snow on Christmas night. Ferdinand went straight to his hunting lodge, while the queen, numb with sorrow at the loss of her son, moved into the Palazzina Cinese in the Coli area of the city. While some refugees found accommodation in empty villas and palazzos, others were forced to stay in lodgings in the densely populated streets or at Madame Montagne's hotel on the Marina. The Hamiltons moved into the Casa Vega in the garden of the Palazzo Cattolica on the south end of the marina, but like the Palazzina Cinese, it had been built as a summer residence and it was cold and damp and entirely unsuitable for winter occupation. Within days, they had moved into the Villa Bastioni, on the Marina Parade near the Porta Fellice. Like the Casa Vega, it was damp and 'calculated only for the summer'. Sir William, who was becoming increasingly frail and suffering from 'a fever from cold and bile', took to his bed. Abraham and little Mary (as she was always called after her mother's death), like their royal neighbours, spent a miserable time in damp lodgings during the cold January weather and whether they were living with the Hamiltons in these early days is unclear.

The refugees from Naples quickly established themselves as a tight-knit community within the city. By Easter, the weather had improved and Hamilton, who by that time had recovered from his earlier bouts of illness, had established his ambassadorial residence in the Palazzo Palagonia, a vast house a few minutes walk from the waterfront, which had been previously occupied by the Prince of Palagonia.[8] As the house was way beyond his means Nelson, Abraham and Edmund Noble with their families were invited to live there as paying guests. The Nobles too had young children and they and Mary played together, becoming firm favourites with Emma. As the Hamiltons continued to entertain lavishly and hold regular gambling parties, it must have been an advantage to have two bankers on hand to extend them credit and take their IOUs. Other residents at the Palazzo Palagonia were Emma's mother Mrs Cardogan, John and Eliza Graefer and their family as well as the ambassador's staff. Emma loved having so many children around her and grew very fond of the motherless Mary, often treating her as her own child. It was here that Emma and Nelson became lovers.

Occasional news reached Palermo about the situation in Naples. After the departure of the royal family, the Neopolitan mob embarked on a witch-hunt against the Jacobins and hundreds were massacred. In the riots that followed, prisons were stormed and prisoners released from the city's gaols. In the face of fierce resistance from the *lazzaroni* loyal to Ferdinand, the French took the city and established the Parthenopean Republic. When news of the republic reached Palermo, the Queen, vehement in her hatred of the French following the execution of her sister Marie Antoinette, sought revenge against all those who supported them. In January Cardinal Fabrizio Ruffo, who had left Naples with the Court, led a counter-revolution and against orders concluded a speedy peace allowing the French evacuation from the city. Meanwhile, Nelson had grown increasingly restless with his enforced idleness in Sicily. He disliked Palermo even more than Naples. 'Palermo is detestable, and we are all unwell and full of sorrow' he wrote, my 'situation here is not to be envied, and I hope very soon to be released from it', but was 'tied so fast by their Sicilian Majesties that I cannot move'. Furious at Ruffo's actions, Maria Carolina persuaded her husband to give Nelson supreme command of the Sicilian fleet with orders to suppress the rebellion. On 21 June, the British and Sicilian fleets under Nelson's command sailed for Naples and there followed an orgy of torture as hundreds of Jacobins and French supporters were thrown into gaol 'to lie at the King's mercy', to die in prison or on the scaffold.

* * * *

With such a sudden influx of people, Palermo grew from a small town into a cosmopolitan city as it absorbed over 3000 wealthy Neopolitans and foreigners who, despite their changed circumstances, continued to pursue the idle lifestyle that they had enjoyed in Naples. It contrasted starkly with that of the Sicilians for whom 'poverty ...seems to be the ordinary condition of the people'. Sicily, once called 'the granary of

Italy' by Cicero had a population of around 1,600,000 in 1788. Ten years later, with the general decline in agriculture, Sicily was unable to support its population without foreign aid, due mainly to the feudal system of land ownership that subjugated a peasant population, and an ineffective government dominated by a few titled families, the church and the military. Taxes, rents and feudal dues, which were collected from mainly absentee landowners, formed an important part of crown revenues.

Palermo and Messina were the two main trading centres. Messina was a beautiful town with fine buildings, which followed the curve of the shore, having a wonderful view of the Italian mainland, some three miles away. It stood at the foot of a range of mountains, partly covered with vines and olive trees. Its harbour, which had been rebuilt after the 1783 earthquake, was far superior to Palermo's and the British merchants who settled there dealt mainly in silk and citrus fruits.

In contrast, Palermo had the aura of the metropolis. The town was set in the Conca d'Oro, or Golden Shell, and had suffered little devastation in the earthquake. It was dominated by Monte Pellegrino and encircled by high mountains. The walled city with its gardens, its orange and lemon groves and vineyards, lay in a lush valley and contained remnants of former Arab, Norman and Spanish civilizations overlooking the blue Tyrrhenian Sea. The majority of the population lived in a maze of squalid houses in narrow back streets, in contrast to the palaces along the waterfront. There were also a number of smaller trading centres on the coast including Syracuse, Marsala, Catania and Licata.[9]

At the end of the eighteenth century, the only indigenous industry in Sicily was that supplying the domestic market. Even basic commodities such as bricks, nails, buttons and shoes were imported, and although the raw materials for making soap and glass were plentiful they were exported for manufacture elsewhere and re-imported as finished products. Sicily also exported small consignments of wheat, barley, beans, salted tunny fish, anchovies, cheese, wines, honey, oranges, lemons, figs, almonds and raisins to Malta and the Italian mainland. In 1778, a contemporary traveller had noted that Sicily also exported cotton, silk, hemp and flax, which were grown in abundance, but by the end of the eighteenth century, these exports had shrunk and the products were grown mainly to supply the domestic trade. The main reasons for the lack of industrialization during this period were the lack of coal or iron, internal communications or a transport system, and an uncertain water supply, as many rivers were dry for much of the year.[10]

By 1799, Abraham had become wealthy, influential and well respected amongst the British community and a confidante of the Hamiltons. The previous year, whilst he was still in Naples, there was increasing concern over the behaviour of Prince Augustus, George III's sixth son, who had spent ten years in Italy and the previous two in Naples. It was Hamilton's task to see that his royal guest kept out of trouble, but not only had the Prince secretly married, it was feared that he might convert to Catholicism. He had also run up considerable debts having 'constant dinners and suppers with bad society in his own apartment'. With no civil list and no funds to pay the Prince's debts, Hamilton 'was forced to authorize Mr. Gibbs an English merchant here, to call in a list of the Prince's debts, and he [Hamilton] as your majesty's Minister, engaged they should be paid as soon as the proper arrangements could be taken in England'.[11] Now in Palermo, the Hamiltons continued to entertain both the Neopolitan nobility and British exiles on a grand scale. As Sir William's debts increased and all other sources of credit were denied him, he began to borrow from Abraham. His difficulties had been compounded by the loss of his vases and other works of art when the *Colossus* had run aground and broken up off the Isles of Scilly in December 1798. When Hamilton had arrived in Sicily at the end of 1798, his debts were around £6,000 but by March 1800, they had risen to nearly £15,000.

On his arrival in Palermo, Abraham wasted no time in establishing a branch of Falconnet & Co, as a subsidiary of the 'Casa Madre' in Naples. Edmund and George Noble joined the firm and it was renamed Falconnet Gibbs & Co, operating for the next two years mainly in Palermo and Malta. An increasing number of British merchants, who had been forced out of Leghorn in 1796 and Naples in 1798, had established mercantile houses in Sicily.[12] They tended to be involved with the *travazzi*, the coastal trade shipping goods for the Sicilian market around the island. It was the French and other foreign merchants who dominated the *Imballi* (the exportation of previously imported goods to Malta and mainland Europe).[13] Abraham was in an ideal position to challenge this dominance, having developed trading links with Malta, England and the rest of Europe whilst resident in Naples and he immediately established a firm exporting Sicilian products and importing goods for re-export and for the local market.

He was also quick to take advantage of Sicily's most important commodity, sulphur, which had long been mined for gunpowder and medical use. Large, easily workable deposits of sulphur in open cast mines stretched over several thousand square miles of central and southern Sicily, and although the government had tried unsuccessfully to produce it on a commercial scale, the lack of internal transport and water power, made any large-scale development impossible. It was the discovery in 1797 of the Leblanc process to produce artificial soda from sulphur that provided the impetus to develop the industry and with no indigenous mercantile elite on the island it was left to foreign entrepreneurs to take the lead. Although only recently having arrived in Palermo, Abraham was able to use his established contact base outside Sicily and undercut his fellow merchants on price and profit to gain a foothold in the market. On 7 April 1799, he shipped his first consignment of sulphur to mainland Italy, quickly followed by three more. His first month's sales of sulphur totalled 8000 quintale, (800,000 kilogrammes), at 14 tari per quintale, which yielded him a profit of over 3670 onze (around £83,000 in today's money).[14] The following month he increased his price and shipped 2200 quintali at 16.5 tari per quintali, giving him a profit margin of 13.8 per cent, still less than other merchants who were making up to 15 per cent profit.[15] However, his strategy paid off and within a few months the business was established.

Most of his trade was with his existing contacts in Naples and

Leghorn but he also exported large quantities of sulphur and other commodities for a number of firms, British, French, German and Italian, both in Malta and the Italian mainland at the usual 4% commission.[16] Encouraged by the demands for everyday essentials as well as luxuries for the new residents in Palermo, he diversified into a number of different activities. Aware of the vast potential offered by the development of trade in goods and commodities that were in demand in Britain, sumac, soda ash and rags made up the bulk of his shipments from Sicily.[17] He acted as agent for a number of British merchants, including William Tough in Palermo and Bingham Richards in Naples. Tough, who had arrived in Sicily in 1792 as Consul, sold paper of all kinds and quality from his shop in the Via della Loggia, as well as trading in hemp and sulphur. Falconnet Gibbs & Co also traded with Charles Crokat and George Wood who were based in Messina, enabling the firm to take advantage of Messina's status as a 'free port' and avoid paying the duties and taxes imposed by the port of Palermo.[18]

Another factor that had inhibited the growth of trade and industry in Sicily was the lack of banking and credit facilities. Although banks existed on the island, they were not in a position to offer sophisticated services.[19] The *Tavola*, the only public bank in Palermo, was not permitted to provide loans for private use.[20] Such services as did exist were provided by Monti di Pietà (state pawnshops), Monti Frumentari (grain banks) and local money-lenders.[21] In the absence of paper money, it was left to foreign merchants to extend credit and issue their own bills of exchange to overcome the inconvenience of conducting transactions in gold or other coinage. Abraham quickly saw that immense profits that could be made by providing loans, extending credit and arranging insurance, not only to other merchants but also to the Sicilian nobility. With the capital provided by Falconnet Gibbs & Co, within a short time he had established himself as a merchant banker, and through his friendship with the Hamiltons, was able to cultivate the trust and friendship of the British and Sicilians alike.[22] As his business thrived, he imported and exported a wide variety of goods, extended credit and provided loans, arranged insurance and chartered ships to carry his cargoes between Sicily, England, Malta and America. Unlike his cousin Antony, he was meticulous at this time about keeping records to control his creditors and cash flow and for many years employed a single lawyer to draw up his sales contracts, thus ensuring that at any time he knew exactly what he was owed. However, he was not so diligent about keeping records of his purchases, and used a number of different lawyers to draw up his contracts; something he was to regret many years later.[23]

Between 1799 and 1802, the normally small underdeveloped Sicilian markets expanded rapidly with the influx of foreign capital and goods. At the same time, the large sums of money spent by foreigners increased the purchasing power of the Sicilians themselves and stimulated the economy as local entrepreneurs `quickly developed their own industries and resources to supply what had previously been unnecessary in La Citta Felice'.

It was at this time that Abraham became acquainted with Guiseppe Lenzitti whose family were local merchants. Although Lenzitti had been bankrupted in an economic slump ten years earlier, Abraham trusted him sufficiently to make him a partner in the business. Two years later, he decided to separate his banking and trading activities, and Lenzitti's eldest son Paolo joined the 'casa commerciale', the new firm called Abraham Gibbs & Co of Palermo. When Abraham returned to Naples in 1802, he appointed Paolo as his agent, responsible for all business between Palermo and mainland Italy, much of which involved smuggling goods into French dominated Europe.[24] The firm of Falconnet Gibbs & Co concentrated on banking and commerce with Britain and the United States.[25]

It was through his friendship with Abraham that Nelson had first met John Woodhouse in Naples. Originally from Liverpool, Woodhouse had settled in Marsala in 1770, with the intention of developing the barilla trade with his homeland. Impressed with the local wine, he set about creating one similar to Madeira, which had become very popular in England. Buying wine from local producers and adding alcohol to improve it for export, Woodhouse sent his first shipment of

8000 gallons to Liverpool in 1773. His wine proved popular at a time when sherry and the other Spanish and Portuguese wines were closed to the British markets and the firm of Woodhouse & Co was quickly established. This was the beginning of the development of Marsala as a wine centre. By 1787, Woodhouse had started an agrarian revolution with the development of extensive viniculture not only in Marsala, but also in the whole Trapanese area and began producing his wine on a commercial scale. The firm provided loans for local farmers to clear their fields and plant vines and modernised much of the town. As there were no roads from Marsala to Palermo, they built a new jetty and harbour to take shallow draught sailing ships to transport the wine to the capital. John Woodhouse was joined by his younger brother William it was not long before Woodhouse & Co was successfully exporting its wine to Britain and the United States through Abraham Gibbs & Co of Palermo.

A major breakthrough had come after Nelson's arrival in Naples. After tasting Woodhouse's wine Nelson wrote 'The wine is so good that any gentleman might receive it', and promptly placed an order for four thousand gallons for the British fleet that regularly sailed around the island, stopping at Palermo, Messina, Syracuse and Trapani, attempting to keep the Mediterranean sea-routes open and beat the blockade. Nelson later suggested that the Woodhouse wine should be known as 'Bronte Madeira'.[26] The last contract, agreed with Woodhouse before Nelson's departure, was for fifty thousand gallons to be shipped from Trapani to Palermo.[27] From there, Abraham Gibbs & Co arranged for it to be loaded it on to the British ships, a contract which was to be an important part of Abraham's business for some fifteen years. As the industry expanded in the Masala area, a number of other English merchants established vineyards there but despite their efforts, Woodhouse's wine remained the superior product. It is reputed that John Woodhouse was very fond of his wine and after drinking copious amounts would stagger naked through his vineyards. Abraham and 'Old John' as he was known, became firm friends, and trusted each other implicitly; all their contracts were based on a 'gentleman's agreement'.

Abraham continued to promote the Woodhouse wines above all others, and such was the trust between the two men, that his firm had the sole export contract for it.

With the end of hostilities, a triumphant Ferdinand briefly returned to Naples in the *Foudroyant* with Nelson on 1 August 1799. They were greeted by crowds of exuberant Neopolitans, who sailed out in the bay in small craft to welcome their King and Queen and the Hero of the Nile. Ferdinand did not trust their loyalty and four days later, returned to Palermo. Such was Abraham's reputation that it was then that he was appointed as banker to the court of the Two Sicilies. At Nelson's suggestion, Sir John Acton, an expatriate Englishman who was the Prime Minister and a favourite of Maria Carolina, negotiated a wartime loan from him so that the 'brave Officers and men who served the cause so well in the Roman State' could be paid.[28]

After thirty-eight years as British Ambassador and now 'nearly worn out', Hamilton was recalled to England. Weary and in failing health he had tired of Palermo, he longed to return home. Writing in his dispatch of December he described the 'general corruption at Naples and the infirmity of defects in Government.... I am sorry to say I do not yet see an intention of endeavouring to mend it. At Palermo His Majesty diverts himself much the same as He did at Naples by going from one County House to another & by shooting'.[29] Ferdinand and Maria Carolina, aware that their situation was still precarious tried to persuade him and Emma to stay and when this failed they showered them with gifts of jewellery and diamonds in the hope that it would delay their departure. Nelson was honoured with a diamond encrusted sword, the title of Duke of Bronte, and an estate of around 40,000 acres on the western slopes of Mount Etna, supposedly carrying an income of around £3000 a year which included a ducal seat, the Castello di Maniace that became known as the Castello dei Nelson.

The decision for Nelson to return to England was made for him. On 14 November, *The Times* reported that Lord Keith was to take command of the fleet in the Mediterranean and Nelson was being recalled to England. Hamilton, his departure imminent, became increasingly concerned about his outstanding accounts with both Abraham and Samuel Ragland a British merchant in Naples from whom he was also borrowing heavily. At the time of his leaving, Hamilton owed Abraham more than £5000 as well as significant amounts to other creditors. He attempted to draw funds from Coutts, his London banker, to settle his account, but because it was owed over £7,000, they refused to honour his drafts. On 9 April, his replacement, Sir Arthur Paget, arrived in Naples and two weeks later Hamilton presented his recredentials (which for practical purposes was his resignation) to the Court. After a short holiday on the *Foudroyant* with the royal party, Nelson returned to Palermo and on 4 June, Hamilton gave his last banquet in honour of George III. Before they left, Sir William and Emma showered little Mary with presents and Nelson gave her a lock of his hair. Hamilton closed his account with Falconnet Gibbs & Co, still owing his friend nearly £6000. With promises to return, they left Palermo on the *Alexander* on 10 June, to begin their journey back to England.

* * * *

With the fall of the Parthenopean republic, the Bourbons returned to Naples with the court. After Hamilton's departure, Abraham had to leave the Palazzo Palagonia and returned to Naples with Mary. There, they found things were very different. The Palazzo Sessa had been turned into a hotel and most of the embassy servants had "fallen on evil days". He wrote to Hamilton that 'Naples is totally changed. I shall regret every hour that necessity obliges me to remain'.[30] Nevertheless, by the end of 1801 he decided to stay, aware that once again Naples had become the trading epicentre in Italy.

There were a number of other opportunities for him during this period. In 1798, the French had subjugated Malta, but in September 1800, were driven out by the British who occupied the island in the name of the King of the Two Sicilies. The occupation of Malta was seen as 'promising to British mercantile interests' and of a 'solid and permanent nature'. Its strategic importance offered great opportunities because it was central to the main trading routes. Before the war, the chief export from Sicily was fish and a fishery had been established on the southern coast to supply the Maltese market. Between 1799 and 1803, Abraham and Edmund and George Noble had spent a considerable amount of time developing trading links between Palermo, Malta and the United Kingdom. With most of the ports of Europe now closed to English vessels, there was also increasing tension over impressments between Great Britain and the United States that also threatened trade in North America.

Abraham had not forgotten his old friends. With Nelson now on the *Victory* in the Mediterranean, he arranged for Emma's letters to be sent via Falconnet's office in Naples in case they were intercepted and read. He continued to correspond with the Hamiltons and, at their request, looked after their affairs in Sicily. Sir William had left many loose ends and, even after two years, was still expected to return to resolve them. Abraham and Ragland, who was still acting for Hamilton in Naples, were now owed over £8000. Ragland was maintaining the Palazzo Sessa and Hamilton's house at Posillipo, and the servants were retained in the belief that they were planning to return. Before his departure, Hamilton's friend John Graefer, the English nurseryman who had designed the gardens at Caserta and had lived in the Palazzo Palagonia in Palermo, had been appointed to look after them. Money was also owing to a number of tradesmen, including a local coach-builder, which Ragland continued to pay.[31]

Hamilton had anticipated that on his return to England he would be able to pay off his debts. Before he left Palermo, Abraham had offered him a loan to tide him over, which he had refused, believing that his arrears would soon be cleared, but for the next year, they continued to mount. By 1801, Ragland was urgently pressing him to pay the £2400 that he was owed, but to no avail. He was still paying Hamilton's servants in his house in Naples, but had not received a penny since his departure. Finally, in November Ragland received a letter from Hamilton telling him that he would not be returning and asking that the house in Posillipo be sold and his servants paid off. Hamilton had also written to Edmund Noble at Falconet Gibbs & Co, asking that he sell his furniture and other effects in Palermo. Three months later, Ragland had still received nothing and on 6 April wrote urgently to Hamilton that his old servants were now 'in very narrow Circumstances'. A number of other tradesmen, including the coachmaker and his tailor were still owed money and that he (Ragland) was still paying their bills. He begged Hamilton to let him have something on account so that he could 'pay the Coachmaker & Taylor & relieve the distress of your poor Servants'.[32]

There was a similar problem in Palermo. As Abraham was on business there, Noble wrote asking him to arrange the sale of Hamilton's furniture left in the Palazzo Palagonia. Abraham too had been convinced that his friend would be returning shortly. He wrote to Hamilton that Eliza Graefer had 'assured me she had certain intelligence of your returning shortly to Palermo and I deferred going to see Bronte [for Nelson] in hopes of having the satisfaction of accompanying you'. He was acting 'under the constant expectation of your returning shortly to Sicily, which your silence confirmed to me' and had sold some silver and lace for 236 ducats and had shipped a number of other items to England. The furniture from the Palazzo Sessa and his coach remained unsold. This was probably the one purchased for £600 just before they left Naples that was 'so heavy no tolerable offer was ever made for it'. Abraham 'having frequently had the use of it myself' offered to pay Hamilton 'the sum for it as valued at by the Coachmakers, when you left Palermo'. He also mentioned that Noble had told him of your 'pecuniary difficulties' and that he had 'entreated Mr. Ragland to suspend drawing upon you and I shall send him tomorrow, one thousand Ducats in anticipation that he may begin to pay off the most urgent debts'.[33]

Abraham asked what should be done with the cases that had been packed and sent to Malta by Emma's mother. Mrs Cardogan had instructed that he sell 'soley [sic] the old things', but he was 'less desirious of selling the 19 Cases sent to Malta at the time the French ordered all the British property to be sent off the Island which were carefully packt [sic] up by Mrs Cardogan'.[34] On 4 January, he wrote urgently to Hamilton asking him to close his account. As he had still not received any instructions about the cases, he was unwilling to open them as Mrs Cardogan 'never gave my Servant their Contents' and he asked for advice.[35] He also reported that some of Hamilton's possessions including 'four Marble Tables with a mosaic figure' had been delivered to Raglan from Malta, and 'two large Drawings of Raphael have been delivered to me by Mr Riga',[36] which he had packed up and had sent on to London. He had asked Raglan to send him a list of 'the sums claimed by several individuals' so that he could pay them on account. 'Yesterday' he went on, 'I saw your faithfull Valet de Chambre', who was still owed £600. Abraham had given him 'the value of the sum in Ducats 3333, the exchange of 431/5 being very favourable for him, against his Bill upon you of £600 Sterling in my favour at 30 days…upon his giving me your obligation which I have enclose you'.[37] Abraham never received a reply. Not long after Christmas, Hamilton was taken ill and was slow to recover his health. On 16 February, he and Emma hosted a concert in their house in 23 Piccadilly but by mid-March he had taken to his bed. Throughout his illness, Emma and Mrs Cardogan nursed him 'with unrequitted Tenderness', but on the morning of 6 April 1803, he died in Emma's arms, 'without a Sigh or a Struggle'.

For some months before Hamilton's death, Abraham had been making plans to close his Naples office, and take Mary to England to complete her education, and to resolve the long-standing dispute over her grandfather's estate. The Hamiltons had agreed that she could live with them when he returned to Italy. On 13 July 1802, he had written to them that Mary 'expects to have the happiness of seeing you soon in England. Her education occupies my mind exclusively; I must either accompany her myself to England or send her by some clever person'. Mary, who adored Emma and thought of her as a mother, was very excited at the prospect of seeing her again. 'She is extremely proud always of wearing the handsome presents made her by Lord & Lady Hamilton & Lord Nelson', Abraham wrote, and 'makes a point of telling every person that his Lordship's hair is with powder <u>exactly</u> as it was cut off his head'.

Six months later, in a letter dated 4 January, he wrote that they would 'leave Naples in the <u>Spring</u>. The education of my daughter so fully occupys [sic] my mind, that I shall not be easy until she is situated in England – she has great emulation and therefore I shall be wanting in my duty towards her in any one point. I cannot describe to you how delighted she is, as well as myself with the Idea of seeing you, My Lady, Mrs Cardogan & Lord Nelson. We have a thousand things to tell you'.[38] As he was uncertain as to the date of their departure Nelson offered to take them to England saying that 'Whenever you go to England....I will manage that you and Miss Gibbs shall go in a man-of-war'.

However, by the end of February, relations with France worsened. War seemed inevitable with Bonaparte threatening Italy over Britain's refusal to relinquish Malta to the Tsar of Russia. Abraham was forced to rethink his plans. Still in Naples, on 3 May he wrote to Sir Arthur Paget, Hamilton's successor, that the 'sudden and unexpected Turn in political affairs have totally deranged my plan of going to England, as in the event of War I shall abandon my Establishment here entirely', and return to England.[39] On 14 May, Britain declared war on France.

* * * *

Nelson's appointment as commander of the fleet in the Mediterranean had made it uncertain when he would return to Sicily to sort out his affairs at Bronte. At Hamilton's suggestion, Nelson had appointed Graefer as his steward to refurbish the Castello di Maniace and manage the estate to make it 'the happiest in Europe'. As Bronte was a gift from the King, he needed royal assent and had written to Acton asking him to mediate on his behalf. His only 'object at Bronte is to make the people happy, not by suffering them to be oppressed, [and] to enrich the country by the improvement of agriculture. For these reasons I selected Mr. Graefer, as a proper person for Governor, as his charac-ter for honesty is unimpeachable, and his abilities as an agriculturist undeniable'. Graefer was tasked with improving the land so that the peasantry were not 'more miserable than they were before the estate came into my possession' and to convert one of the farmhouses for Nelson's use when he returned to Sicily. Before he left Nelson, had taken out a loan from Abraham to fund the improvements and a further 8000 onze for his own use on his return to England. In return, he was prepared to 'give up two years' rent for 'fitting up a house and improving'.

Two years later Nelson had heard nothing from Graefer nor received the anticipated income. By April 1803, he was considerably out of pocket having had to pay all the feudal dues and taxes to the crown. Whilst touring Wales with the Hamiltons, he learned that his steward had died and, with war imminent, was worried that if the French overran Sicily, all property owned by foreign residents would be confiscated. He sent word to Abraham via the Naples office asking for news, but received no response. At that time, Abraham and Noble were in Malta and were not due back until the end of June. On his return to Naples, Abraham immediately wrote offering to go to Bronte and look into the matter, but with the renewal of hostilities, Nelson had already sailed for the Mediterranean in the *Victory* and it was several weeks later before Abraham's letter arrived in the mail. The following day, on 3 August, a very relieved Nelson gloomily replied:

> My dear Sir,
>
> I yesterday received your truly friendly letter of July 5th, with much pleasure, and I shall be truly thankful if you will have the goodness to put my Bronte estate in train, that if I cannot receive the value of it, and have done with it, that, at least, I may receive the full rental regularly; for I never will lay out another sixpence on it, but am content to pay a certain sum for the attention of some respectable person to receive the rents, and to remit them to London. As you are so good as to offer to attend to this serious concern to me, I will enter at large into the subject. I told

Graeffer [sic], on first setting out, that I would give up two years' rent for fitting up a house and improving. I paid more attention to another sovereign than my own; therefore the King of Naples' gift of Bronte to me, if it is not now settled to my advantage, and to be permanent, has cost me a fortune, and a great deal of favour which I might have enjoyed, and [much] jealousy which I should have avoided. I repine not on those accounts. I did my duty to Sicilifying my own conscience, and I am easy. It will be necessary, before you take any steps beyond enquiry, to know from Sir John Acton what has been done immediately, and that I may have it permanent. I shall never again write an order about the estate. If the estate cannot be returned, my receiving the whole value, the income nett ought to be paid to me, which the Hospital received, as delivered to me, was 6700 ounces on the average, for seven years preceding. Your kind assistance will truly oblige, my dear Sir, your very faithful humble servant.

Nelson and Bronte[40]

Nelson trusted his friend to act in his best interests and the following day he wrote to Abraham, 'Good and great must come to me if you take the business for me'.[41] He hoped that even if the estate could not yield the anticipated income, he should at the very least receive what had been paid annually to the Great Hospital at Palermo. Abraham, who was about to leave with Mary for England, agreed to delay his departure and go to Bronte if Nelson would arrange a safe passage for her. Nelson readily agreed, writing to Emma that 'Gibbs has at last fixed on sending his daughter home and I shall be glad of so good an opportunity of obliging him, as it will naturally tie him to my interest'.[42] It was arranged that while in England, Mary should go and live at Merton with Emma, who would act as her guardian and oversee her education until her father joined her.

Although Abraham had made several trips to Palermo during the preceding two years, he had never visited Bronte. He soon found that getting there was no easy matter. Bronte, on the western slopes of Mount Etna, was inaccessible by road and the last thirty miles had to be undertaken on horseback. Bands of brigands and bandits scoured the area. The estate, which had previously been owned by the *ospedale grande e nuovo* (the Grand Hospital) of Palermo, had been neglected for many years and the Castella di Maniace had been uninhabitable since the 1693 earthquake. The hospital had been relieved to relinquish responsibility for it for a guaranteed income of 5600 onze from the Treasury.[43] Bronte was one of the largest estates in Sicily consisting of around 25,000 hectares (about 40,000 acres) of which 45 per cent was arable land and the rest being woods and pasture. When Abraham eventually arrived there, he was astounded at what he found. Instead of improving an existing farmhouse for occasional occupancy, Graefer, had let his 'aesthetic sense overrule his reason' and had embarked on an orgy of extravagance at the Castella di Maniace and built a palace fit for a Duke. He also found that Graefer's widow Eliza had assumed her husband's role as steward and was continuing to receive one hundred pounds a year from Nelson.

Abraham was fond of Eliza Graefer, having known her since his early days in Naples. Initially he tried to persuade her to leave so that he could take over the management of the estate himself, but she refused to go, demanding a pension of £200 for herself and her child. Nelson was under no illusion as to Abraham's motives and wrote to Emma 'in short Gibbs wants to remove her. He is afraid of his own pocket I fancy'.[44] However, Nelson, aware that if she were removed 'it would end in her coming to me in England', agreed that she could remain there as manager.[45] After spending some weeks examining the books and leases, Abraham estimated that with careful management, within two years the estate should yield an annual income of around £2000 after the deduction of expenses. By this time, all Nelson wanted was to rid himself of Bronte. He had spent around £10,000 on improvements and so far had received nothing. His loans from Abraham remained unpaid and the interest charges continued to mount. Although he fantasised of returning there with Emma, he was well aware that he might never see Bronte again. Nelson decided it would be better to rid himself of it, but as the estate was a gift from the crown, once again he needed permission to change the existing arrangements. He asked Abraham to act as his agent and seek royal approval to sell it. If that was refused he wished to employ Abraham to manage his affairs in Sicily for him. Nelson, who had almost given up hope of ever seeing anything from the estate, pessimistically wrote to Emma on 26 September, 'I have wrote to Mr. Gibbs, again, a long history about Bronte; and I hope, if General Acton will do nothing for me, that he [Gibbs] will settle something: but, I know, whatever is settled, I shall be the loser.'[46]

In October Nelson wrote to Hugh Elliott, the younger brother of Hamilton's successor, introducing Abraham as 'lately the partner of Mr. Falconnet and always the intimate household friend of dear Sir William and Lady Hamilton, and give me leave to add my friend. I believe I am to call Mr. Gibbs a banker' and giving him power of attorney to act on his behalf.[47] With Nelson's agreement, Abraham presented two submissions for consideration by the Marquis di Tommasi, the Minister of Finance. The first was that Treasury should buy back Bronte for an agreed amount, and after the deduction of all dues and taxes, pay Nelson the capital sum. The second was that, as the Admiral was unable to return in the near future, Abraham as his agent, be granted permission to find a tenant and rent out Bronte for a four-year term. Unknown to Nelson, Abraham also presented a third submission. He asked that if the Treasury would agree to take back the estate and extend the rental term then he would act as its agent, manage the rents and leases and find a tenant who would rent Bronte directly from the treasury ' for the duration of eight or maybe 10 years'.[48]

Even if the Treasury had been in a position to buy the Dukedom, Tommasi believed that to do so would complicate the normal feudal relationship that existed with the payment of taxes and other dues. Acton also suspected Abraham's motives were purely self-interest and opposed the third submission. As a compromise, Tommasi agreed that as Nelson's agent he be allowed to manage the estate for an extended ten-year term; this would ensure that the treasury would receive the *Gabelle* and other dues for a longer fixed period. Knowing he was supposed to be neutral, Acton was anxious that Abraham should not learn of his involvement and asked that 'nothing of this must be known to Mr. Gibbs, to whom I am happy to reply, for these questions are not within my competence and must depend on the resolution of His Majesty'.[49] Two weeks later Abraham received a copy of the royal dispatch that had been sent to Nelson. It read, 'I have made known to the King, the considerations of your illustrious self on the State of Bronte, and as Your Majesty is informed about the conditions, to allow yourself [Nelson] from this time to rent the said State for 10 or more years. I will inform him under the Royal Name, so that he can arrange for the merchant Mr. Abraham Gibbs to transfer the monies to Lord Nelson for this operation'.[50] Reporting the success of his efforts to Nelson, Abraham proposed that a Sicilian nobleman and local notary, Antonio Forcella, be employed to draw up the leases and let the farms while he oversaw the financial management. With proper supervision, he believed that Bronte should yield a profit £3,200 per annum and after the deduction of local taxes, dues and administration costs, should provide Nelson with annual income of £2900. As Nelson's agent he offered to collect all rents, pay the salaries and taxes and remit the balance to his bank in London. Nelson, who at that time was on the *Victory* was delighted, wrote enthusiastically to Emma, 'you will see what interest he [Gibbs] is taking about Bronte. I begin to think, without some assistance like his, that I never should have touched a farthing. It will be 1805, before I touch the estate. Neither principal or interest of the seven thousand ounces have been paid; and, it is now eight thousand ounces debt [to Abraham].'[51]

Despite their long-standing friendship, Nelson was wary. Although he trusted Abraham, he believed all men were both corrupt and corruptible and he insisted that all their dealings be conducted on a proper legal footing. Between December 1804 and August 1805, several letters passed between them as they tried to reach agreement on the wording and terms of the contract. Even though Nelson knew he might never return to Sicily, he was determined to retain control of the administration of his ducal seat and insisted that Abraham remit him the full rent of £3200 a year from which he would pay the taxes, salaries and administration costs through his bankers in London. (see Appendix 1) After lengthy negotiations, it was agreed Abraham, as Nelson's banker would continue to oversee the improvements at Bronte, Forcella would arrange the leases and sell the produce and, because of the distance from Palermo, Eliza Graefer would continue to manage the estate. Once the arrangements were finalised Abraham was determined to follow Mary to England, but it was around this time that he first became acquainted with John Barnes, the newly appointed US Consul to the Kingdom of the Two Sicilies.

* * * *

After 1796, there had been a substantial increase in the US merchant fleet in the Mediterranean and the Baltic, supplying the European markets with American and colonial produce, especially rice, coffee and flour, which were in great demand. It was a highly speculative venture in the face of the blockades of so many ports by both the British and French. Many ships failed to reach their destinations, caught in the cross-fire of Anglo-French restrictions or captured by Barbary corsairs. This resulted in an increase in American vessels flying a neutral flag and an expansion of US consular activity in the Mediterranean. One of the first informal consulates to be established in Europe by the United States administration was in Naples where a number of local merchants were unofficially appointed as pro-consuls to try to develop trade with America, particularly on the eastern seaboard.

In 1802, Barnes was appointed as consul to the Kingdom of the Two Sicilies. Arriving in Naples the following year, he very soon became aware of Sicily's strategic importance for the development of US trade in the Mediterranean. In his first dispatch to James Madison in Washington, he reported that, with France and Britain at war, 'the commerce of the United States will now become an object of great importance in the Mediterranean, Adriatic and Levant'. With the only 'two great powers who could interrupt or crush our views being engaged in War, we should seize the Moment and expand our influence.... The British are in possession of Sicily, and the French of Naples, we should avail ourselves of their influence and power, and the imbecility of the Neopolitan Government', and 'as far as expediency will admit to obtain our objects...a Little bribery may be required...'.[52]

Within a short time, Barnes realised that the real powers in the Kingdom were the Maria Carolina and Lord Acton, whom he referred to in his dispatches as the 'Prime Minister (& in effect King)'. He planned 'to request the possibility of some commercial arrangement between the US and his Sicilian Majesty, in consequence of the rapid increase and very advantageous commerce from the US to the Sicilian States'. Barnes was alarmed to learn that the pro-consuls appointed at ports in and around the Mediterranean to promote trade with America had caused a number of problems. He had received a number of complaints from the British consulate about 'the Mal conduct of some of the American pro-consuls in Sicily, especially the Port of Palermo'. Anxious 'not only to avoid censure but to secure the approbation of my country', he wrote to Madison describing the pro-consuls as 'Creatures of Naples, who having purchased their places, it seems they wish to make the most of their own at the expense of those they ought to have protected'. He asked that he be allowed to remove 'those mercenary beings, and replace them by men of character and influence'.[53]

As consul to the Two Sicilies, much of Barnes time was spent in Naples and it was soon obvious that he needed people in Sicily with knowledge of local trading conditions to look after American interests there. With the growing importance of both Palermo and Messina to US trade, he recommended to Acton that two pro-consuls should be appointed, one in each port. Acton agreed and reported to Barnes that 'his Sicilian Majesty will with much pleasure receive any person whom the US may appoint as Minister Plenepotentiary, or as bearing proper powers, to enter into a Treaty of Commercial relations with the U.S. immediately'. Having already met Abraham, he recommended him for the post in Palermo. With his local knowledge 'of the commerce and chief commercial men of the Sicilian States; from an interest with the first bankers & principal officer of States', he considered that Abraham was the only person with sufficient influence both at Court and within the mercantile community to act as the US Envoy in Palermo.[54]

Believing that this was an opportunity not to be missed, Abraham abandoned his plans to go to England with Mary. He wrote to Nelson asking him to arrange a safe passage for her. Grateful for all the help he had received over Bronte, Nelson agreed to take her back to England himself. He told Emma that, 'I am owing very great obligations to Gibbs. His heart seems overpowered with gratitude for my sending his daughter to Gibraltar'.[55] Whether Abraham still planned to follow her when he had established his consulate is doubtful, for strong as his love was for Mary, he had always found little time for family life.

Abraham now decided to settle permanently in Palermo. For some years, he had been dividing his time between there and Naples. In June 1803, he had authorised his long-standing friend Francisco Falconnet to manage his affairs and to rent out his house in Naples before his planned trip to England.[56] Now, having put off his departure to sort out Nelson's affairs, he saw his appointment as US pro-consul as a chance to increase his wealth and influence and after Mary's departure, planned to return to Palermo.

At the end of November, Mary, who was then nine years old, excitedly bade farewell to her father and sailed from Naples to join Nelson on the *Vanguard* for her journey to England. On board, she quickly made friends with the young midshipmen who were all of her own age. In Christmas week, 1803, Nelson entertained five young guests and noted that one of them was 'not three feet high', and that 'all the Grandees dined with Campbell, and I had a midshipman's party.'[57]

CHAPTER 11

LONDON AND DULWICH

For Mary, the journey to England must have been very exciting for she had only known life in Italy. Brought up as Emma Hamilton's favourite, petted and spoilt by everyone, she was now to be separated from her beloved father and sent to live in a strange country. Despite her enthusiasm at this new adventure, at only nine years old, she was fearful at going without him even though she was thrilled at travelling with Nelson. As they sailed towards Gibraltar, news of Mary's passage preceded her. When the ship made a stop at Malaga, William, Antony's younger son, who at that time was working in the Cadiz office for his father, heard that his cousin was on board. He sent word to his family in England that, '...a Relation of ours...' is on board a ship from Palermo and she '...is either the Daughter of Mr. Lyle or Mr. Abraham Gibbs.... Mrs William Gibbs of Topsham will be very glad to hear that she is so far on her journey to England...'. It is hardly surprising that young William was unsure of his cousin's parentage, as there had been no contact between Abraham and his father for over thirty-five years.

Arriving in England some weeks later, Mary went to live with Emma Hamilton who was to act as her guardian whilst she was in London. Sir William had died the previous April, and Emma was living at Merton Place in Surrey, the house that Nelson had purchased three years before. Towards the end of January, she had given birth to her second child by Nelson, but the baby survived for only a few weeks. Despite her grief, she was delighted to see Mary again, and within a short time made the necessary arrangements for her young charge to begin her lessons. Later that year, Abraham, relieved to hear of Mary's safe arrival and grateful for the interest that Emma was taking in his daughter's welfare, sent a bolt of Palermo silk as a token of his thanks.[1]

It is not known how long she was with Emma, but after Nelson's death on 21 October, Mary appears to have left Merton and gone to her aunt Betsy's house in Abbots Leigh, where she met all her Bristol and Exeter cousins. At last Mary could enjoy a normal life with her extended family, something she had never known in Naples or Palermo. She remained at Abbots Leigh for several months; with her foreign ways and continental manners quickly becoming a great favourite with her English cousins. When Antony's younger son, William, returned to Bristol from Cadiz to work in his uncle's firm, he was soon captivated. A few weeks later, he wrote to his mother of the growing affection that he felt for his young cousin. Dolly advised her son that he should 'better try to please her, for she will make you a pretty little wife'.

Towards the end of 1807 Betsy received a letter from Abraham asking that Mary be returned to Emma's care. Having recovered from Nelson's death, Emma had offered once again to act as Mary's guardian and supervise her education with her daughter Horatia who was nearly nine. Despite the government's treatment of her in refusing to honour the codicil in Nelson's will to provide her with a pension, Emma continued to live extravagantly as if money were no object, dividing her time between Merton and her house in Clarges Street in London. While her debts mounted, she entertained friends, family and hangers-on at both houses but had been forced to move from Clarges Street to a cheaper house at 136 Bond Street. Cut off as he was from the happenings in England, Abraham, unaware of Emma's situation, had readily agreed to entrust his daughter to her care. In early 1808, a reluctant Betsy arranged for Mary to return to Emma's guardianship.

* * * *

By the beginning of 1807, Antony was living in London, determined to establish his own business and move his family there. When he told

Dolly of his plans she was very upset at the thought of leaving Devon. 'I had a letter from Mr. Gibbs that has put me sadly out of spirits', she noted in her journal. She knew that life in the metropolis would be very different from Exeter. Money was still a perennial problem but she was happier in her little cottage with her children and animals than she had been for many years. Her mother and sister had always been ready to help with loans and small gifts, which were repaid when she 'sent a pig to sell in the Market', but Eleanor had died the previous year and in May, Mrs Hucks passed away after years of declining health.[2] Now alone in Exeter, she continued to spend much of her time with Nancy and Samuel or visiting friends and relatives. Although lonely without Antony and still suffering from headaches, a glass of sherry in the evening with a sleeping pill usually did the trick.[3]

In sharp contrast, Antony loved the excitement of London spending most of his time at his compting house, clubs and coffee houses, rarely finding the time to make the journey to Exeter to see his family. At a family reunion at Exwick in the summer of 1807, he made a fleeting visit, arriving there on 4 July, but found her in the middle of haymaking. Irritated, he stayed only two days, made his excuses and returned to London. Upset at his impatience, Dolly wrote to William complaining that 'in the last 7½ years he has only been with me putting all the time together 2 years and 5 months'. The following week Vicary, and the Crawleys arrived with their children to spend the summer at Exwick and the family spent a few happy weeks together without Antony. In September, Dolly began to feel unwell and decided to visit Topsham where she 'went out in a boat & took the children & servants'. This did nothing to make her feel better, and she was shocked to find she was pregnant again at the age of forty-seven. A week before Christmas, she began to haemorrage and was so ill that her doctor sent for Antony; the following morning she miscarried. Despite her age, Dolly recovered quickly but they both knew that she must never endure another pregnancy.[4] Whether sexual relations between tham ceased from then on is unclear, but there is no evidence that Dolly ever became pregnant again.

Her constant complaints about never seeing him now that he was based in London made him more determined than ever to move his family from Devon. With his appointment as a Commissioner for the Portuguese Government, he now saw his future in the capital. Although he received a small remuneration with the post, he was worried about the costs of maintaining two homes and saw little reason for them to remain in Exeter. The following spring, he wrote to George telling him of his plans. His brother, who had supported Dolly for so many years, welcomed the news though he had no illusions that it would be easy for either of them. He hoped that, 'with respect to your long separation from Dolly – The thought of your meeting again will soften much to both of you the pain of giving which you have much and long enjoyed'.

That year Antony made his last trip to Spain. In May, William, now eighteen, spent several weeks in Tangier looking for new business while Henry remained in Cadiz. Antony was concerned that the political situation had prevented him 'from doing some considerable business in Gibraltar by the strict manner in which the prohibition of all inter-course with Spain was enforced'. His appointment as Commissioner also had its disappointments. Believing that he could sell most of the commodities sent from the peninsula, he was frustrated by his lack of resources and government restrictions requiring him to pay the import duties and taxes in advance. He complained to George telling him that he had approached Vicary to see if he could use his influence to have these restrictions lifted for him. George's reply was surprisingly unsympathetic. Although it 'is a great pity that you have not the means of advancing money for the freights & duty & charges of what you may have permission to sell', he believed that 'this would in the regular course of things be provided by any Merch^r who had goods consigned to him for Sale'. He advised Antony say nothing to the other Commissioners of 'what has passed between you and my Brother [Vicary] till you have recd from him all the information which he can give you'. It was only 'By perseverance & patience I dare say you will soon place things upon some reasonable footing with the Port^g Min^r, but in the meantime it is vexatious to have your hands tied up from making sales at a time when they might be made with some advantage'.

Now with dire financial problems, Granger & Banfill continued to press for payment. As all the trade with Spain had dried up after the embargo, Antony could not afford to pay them anything but misguidedly thought that the Exeter firm should compensate *him* for the losses he had incurred while acting on its behalf. He wrote to George for advice, and was surprised that he was opposed to the idea. Several letters passed between them and it was with some reluctance that Antony eventually dropped the notion. On 8 June George wrote, 'I am very glad my dear Anty to see that we are now agreed as to your having no claim upon your friends for an allowance on account of your losses'. Instead, he suggested that Antony write to his former partners and 'present to them in a strong point of view your losses & merely to throw out to them how differently your engagements have differed from what was supposed and intended'. He should 'ask for an abatement' and request that they consider the ongoing political situation when calculating his current losses. George was sure that Banfill would be sympathetic to his request and would grant him more time rather than 'putting the whole or great part of it in jeopardy'; He also appreciated Granger and Banfill's position. 'Putting myself in their place', he wrote 'I confess I should not like this & that way of treating the matter would not dispose me the more to any indulgence'. With no end to the hostilities in sight, he urged Antony to be satisfied with the 'profits of the Commissioner's Office', reduce his costs and try to live within his means so that he could 'set aside an allowance towards a final settlement' with the Exeter firm. He thought that he had been too enthusiastic about his appointment as commissioner and this has led 'your friends to expect that it may be the means of enabling you to make them a payment at some future time'.

George's letter plunged Antony into uncharacteristic depression, and a few days later, he gloomily wrote to Dolly of his hopes and frustrations. Despite all the setbacks over the last few years, he had still tried to look 'as much as Possible on the Fair Side of our prospects perhaps more than I ought'. Looking at his life, 'at the Whole, what is bad enough already may be made worse still. We have been living upon the Hope of better Things for twenty years', but even now have not 'yet got to the Moment of bettering our Same'. If it had not been for the losses incurred over the last year, he wrote, 'our situation would have been easy, in Comparison of what it has been' for, 'I have submitted cheerfully to so many Privations in the last twenty years in order to secure what has now been taken from me in an Hour'. Despite these problems he was confident that 'We may still however enjoy ourselves in future even the better for this Misfortune...we must take Patience....and shuffle the Cards & mix up the good with the bad'.

Dolly, who had been visiting George and Anne in Bristol, found the letter on her return to Exeter and was very worried that her husband seemed so dejected. Although she loved her little cottage, she realised that they needed to be together and suggested that he look for a home for them in London, while she made plans to move. As her plans progressed, it was agreed that rather than give up the lease on the cottage, Bell, who had been staying with George at Redland for several months would live there when it was vacated to be near Nancy at Exwick House.

By mid 1808, Spain was in turmoil. The previous November, Napoleon, having persuaded the Spanish monarch to allow French forces to enter the country, sent his army across the Bidassoa. By March, over 100,000 French soldiers led by Murat, 'as lieutenant for the Emperor' occupied its neighbour. With the abdication of the Spanish King in favour of Joseph Bonaparte, the country was in open rebellion, while Britain sided with the rebels who rose against the French in Spain and Portugal. After appealing to Britain for support, provincial 'juntas' were established in each region and Britain supplied arms and supplies, agreeing to send a British force to the Peninsula. After the siege of Cadiz, newspapers in England rejoiced at 'the spirit of patriotism of ye Spanish patriots'. Nine thousand British troops, under Sir Arthur Wellesley, headed for Lisbon and Cadiz, intent on securing the harbours to prevent the subjugation of Andalusia. They began landing unopposed on 1 August.

Meanwhile things suddenly began to improve for Antony. At the beginning of June, the Portuguese Minister finally gave permission for the Commissioners to sell some of the stock that they had been holding for over six months. Now that he was baed in London he was in an ideal position to develop personal contacts with those in banking, shipping and insurance circles in the capital, essential if he were to establish his own business. The profit made from the sale of the Portuguese property gave him the confidence to proceed with opening an office in London and one in Cadiz to re-establish his old contacts there. Cadiz was not only the most important port for imports to all parts of Spain, but was also an important entrepôt for export to South America and the Spanish colonies. After the armistice, Henry returned to Cadiz where he found that Branscombe was planning to establish his own agency business and fearful that he would lose his customers, offered Branscombe a partnership in the Spanish firm.[5]

In September, in partnership with Henry, Antony founded the banking house of Antony Gibbs & Son at 13 Sherborne Lane, Lombard Street. He owned three-quarters of the shares and Henry one quarter. On 1 October, the firm of Antony Gibbs Son and Branscombe in Cadiz opened its doors for business. Antony owned fifty percent of the shares, Branscombe one third and Henry the remainder. An identical circular was sent from both offices advertising the new businesses to all their clients. The one from Cadiz reads,

Cadiz, 14 October 1808

Sir

The late events which have taken place in Spain having restored to this country its commercial relations with England we, the undersigned, take the liberty of informing you of our intention to establish ourselves in this place, in the general commission business, under the firm of Antony Gibbs Son and Branscombe.

The security of Cadiz, and the very general demand here for British manufactures, Irish linens, Newfoundland fish etc, etc, will no doubt encourage you to renew your acquaintance with your former friends or to open a correspondence with some house established in this port; in the latter case we beg leave to offer you our best services, and we flatter ourselves that our previous residence here in the commercial line, and our general knowledge of the Spanish business will qualify us for giving satisfaction to those who may entrust the consignment of any articles to our care, and enable us to dispose of them, and procure return freights, whether of salt for the fisheries or of any produce for England upon equal term for any other house.

Mr. George Henry Gibbs and Mr. William Branscombe are now here, and Mr. Antony Gibbs remains in London, where he will be happy to receive any commands for his house at Cadiz, directed to him for the present at the office of Commissioners for Portuguese property.

We beg leave to refer you to our signatures annexed.
And remain most respectfully
Sir, Your obedient, humble servants,

ANTY. GIBBS SON & BRANSCOMBE[6]

With his offices in London and Cadiz up and running, Antony could now concentrate on his family. There were a number of things still to be resolved including his future relationship with Granger & Banfill for despite their former differences, Banfill still tried to help his brother-in-law. In August, he had written that 'he had secured in Plymouth the Consignment of a Vessel & Cargo for Sale to the House of Anty Gibbs & Son of Cadiz – The Vessell [sic] is now about to sail & her cargo consists of Newfoundland Sheet, Casimirs & Broadcloths'. Antony believed that Banfill's attitude towards him had changed with the establishment of Antony Gibbs & Son and he was anxious to negotiate a new contract between the two firms. As George noted, in Exeter 'it is certainly much to be wished that you give them some assistance in their necessities', but he warned 'it would not serve them for you to enter into any engagements by acceptances which you had not the means of answering'.

A week later, Antony travelled to Devon to help Dolly pack up the house. She was very distressed at leaving her dear friends who had loyally supported her for so many years. Two weeks later, on 22 October 1808, they bade farewell to Nancy and Samuel and with their few belongings set off by coach for London. Nancy was sad to see them go, having loyally and generously helped her brother's family for so many years. After they left, she wrote dejectedly to George that after nearly 270 years, she was 'the last of our large Family left in Devonshire'.

* * * *

On their arrival in the capital, Antony moved his family into the furnished lodgings at 34 Great Russell Street, which he had been sharing with William. Within days, a letter arrived from George who was delighted that they were together again. 'I suppose you now fancy yourself a man of great consequence strolling about with a Wife & a parcel of children at your heels', he wrote, 'this is a new experience for you & I hope I shall hear that you conduct yourself handsomely in it'. Dolly found London very different from Exeter and it was not long before she was complaining at having to live in such cramped conditions. Within a few weeks, Antony had moved his family into a larger house in Denmark Hill in Camberwell.

It was early in the New Year that he and Dolly first met their niece Mary, the daughter of his cousin, Abraham Gibbs of Palermo. Occasionally Antony had received news of Abraham's wealth and influence, but there had been no contact between the two men for over thirty-five years. Why such a rift should have developed between them is unclear, especially as they were of a similar age and had been so close as children. Whether Abraham felt betrayed by the loss of his inheritance after his uncle's bankruptcy is unclear, but in 1808, although Antony had repaid William and Betsy, his debt to Abraham was still outstanding.

Contact had been re-established by a chance mistake. The previous December, Antony learned that two ships had arrived in England from Malta with cargoes consigned the firm of A Gibbs & Co in Palermo. They were mistakenly loaded onto ships bound for England for Antony Gibbs & Son in London. One had landed in Portsmouth and the other in Plymouth, with the cargoes being eventually delivered to Antony's London office towards the end of January. Realising the mistake, he immediately wrote to his cousin to ask how he should proceed, adding 'You and I used to have long Conversations together formerly, & I very readily seize this opportunity of breaking in upon a Silence between us of more than five and thirty years'.

Once the business of the cargo had been resolved, the two men began corresponding regularly. Keen to take advantage of his cousin's gratitude, Antony offered to act as his agent in London. 'We have here a consignment of Spanish Wool, wines & Barilla,' he wrote, 'but God knows how much longer the Trade with Spain will remain open'. Anxious to impress Abraham, he added that it was 'more than a year since our government named me as one of the Commissioners of Portuguese Property, of which we receive nearly half a Million and have nearly closed these Accounts'. Both men saw the potential for new business and within a short time began trading together.

Although Mary had spent nearly two years with the Richards at Abbots Leigh, she had not met any of her London relations. Now nearly fifteen, in early 1808, she had returned to the capital to complete her education under Emma's supervision. Still pursued by her creditors, in the summer of that year Emma was forced to put Merton up for sale. The house was auctioned in June, but failed to sell and the following month she and her entourage moved to a large villa owned by her friend the Duke of Richmond. By November, with her debts now standing at nearly £8,000 with a further £10,000 in unpaid loans, Emma continued to throw lavish parties and dinners at her house in Bond Street, which was widely reported in the gossip columns. It was at this time that Mary first met Antony and Dolly.

They were very concerned at her situation, and on 23 January 1809, Antony wrote to Abraham telling him that they had met and were 'very pleased with your amiable little daughter' and asked permission for her to 'pay us a visit'. Antony also offered to help sort out the long-standing problems over Mary's inheritance from her grandfather, Sir James Douglas. Abraham, grateful that his family was taking an interest in their affairs agreed to the visit and gave Antony the authority to appoint a solicitor.

Into 1809, her late mother's sister Margaret, now the estranged wife of Lieutenant George Harris continued to challenge Mary's claim to her grandfather's estate. Before they could proceed with the case, as Abraham was in Palermo, he was required to appoint a guardian 'for the purpose of taking Miss Mary Gibbs to answer to a Seat in Chancery filed against her by Mr George Samuel Harris & his wife'. Initially Vicary suggested George as a suitable person but he declined because 'as Mr James Richards, Merchant of this place, married a sister of Mr Abm. Gibbs, & his daughter is placed under his care and is living with them, it may be better to substitute his name for mine as Guardian and Commissioner'. Abraham accepted his advice and Richards was appointed as Mary's guardian in her father's absence.

Mary's stay with Antony and Dolly was a great success. She adored Dolly whom she saw as the mother she had never had, and she and Harriet were soon inseparable. Antony wrote to his cousin that they 'received great pleasure from Mary's visit', adding that they had been very worried about Emma's influence on her. 'It was most fortunate for her', he wrote, 'that she was removed from the direction of Lady Hamilton who has lately got herself into so unfavourable a situation' and, on Antony's advice Mary returned to stay with the Richards who were now living in Ilfracombe in Devon.

Despite appearances, Antony continued to be optimistic that his business would improve, but things continued to be very difficult for him financially. Now that they were living nearer Henry Townley-Ward, Dolly now saw more of her brother-in-law.[7] Shocked at their apparent poverty, he tried to help in a number of ways, advising Antony on investments and sending small presents of fruit for the children. Dolly was embarrassed by his generousity, and in a letter to Henry dated 24 March, wrote that 'Mr Ward 'is always sending us things in the eating way'. He had also 'offered us the other day fifty pounds a year to pay part of Joseph's expenses at School', but 'we have however refused it for the present'.

Within a few months of his family moving to London, Antony abandoned any hope that they would be any happier living together. Having been apart for so many years, he quickly tired of the constraints of family life. Even though Denmark Hill was only a short distance from his compting house, he was so busy that he rarely found time to go home. With Henry in Cadiz and William working with his father, Dolly felt abandoned in a strange city. A country girl at heart she longed to move out of the capital. Lonely, depressed, and plagued by a series of minor illness she wrote to Henry complaining that 'Your dear Father is so much engaged that he very often sleeps at his Compting House, this week he has not been home at all & William only once poor fellow'. Henry had now been in Cadiz for the last six months, and despite her loneliness she managed to joke that perhaps the reason her eldest son had delayed his return to England was that he had either taken himself 'a Spanish little Wife' or had 'some attachment in Spain that we don't know of'.

Their financial situation was at last about to improve. In September, Dolly received a letter from Townley Ward, giving details of a number of small inheritances due to her from her parents, sister and brother that had been part of her marriage settlement. Some years before Antony had 'sold out the £200 three per cent reduced annuities to which he was entitled in your Right as one of the children of the late Mr & Mrs Hucks & the net money....from the sale was £137.5s.0d'. He was also entitled 'in Your Right to a further sum of £64.14s.0d' which was due to her as her brother's next-of kin. Although only small sums, having plunged the family into bankruptcy, and knowing this was rightfully Dolly's, Antony had insisted that Townley-Ward keep them 'for the benefit of your daughters'. To this 'must be added £195. 4s. 0d being the amount of my share of the stock of my late dear wife', and two further legacies totaling £950 that had been left in trust for Dolly by her mother. When invested the interest would provide her with an income for the rest of her life. Hearing of his brother's good fortune, George wrote of Antony that 'from a state of great anxiety & uncertainty he has been providentially raised to one of comparative ease & independence'. It was a great shock to Dolly when Townley-Ward died the following February. She had indeed lost a good friend.

That spring, Henry returned from Cadiz full of optimism at the potential business that could be gained by opening trade with the Spanish colonies and South America. Now with a regular income and increased financial security, Antony agreed that they should move out of London. He too loved the country believing that they would both be happier away from the metropolis. Within weeks, they found a house with a small farm on Dulwich Common that they could afford, planning to move in early summer. There they would be nearer to Vicary and Kenny at Hayes in Kent.

Towards the end of March, Antony received a letter from Betsy telling him that Abraham wanted her to send Mary back to London 'to finish her education under the best masters'. He had asked Betsy to find her a suitable finishing school in the capital. Antony immediately suggested that, once they were settled in Dulwich, Mary should live with them and he and Dolly would supervise her lessons. Even after only one visit, they had grown very fond of her and had found her a 'thoroughly sensible' girl. They wrote to Abraham for permission, and he readily agreed. Within days of them moving to Dulwich, a letter arrived from Mary telling them when she would be arriving on the coach. She was desperate to leave Ilfracombe. Life there with her elderly aunt and uncle had been very dull after the excitement of

London under Emma's guardianship. She was also thrilled that her uncle Vicary was to take an interest in her education. He was now Sir Vicary Gibbs, Lord Chief Justice and, she thought, a man almost as rich and important as her father.

Not long after they had settled into their new home an excited Mary arrived on the coach from Bristol. She brought with her a long letter from Betsy who was very concerned for her niece's welfare. 'As Mary has been very little used to Manage for herself', she wrote, 'I must beg the favor [sic] of you to advise her in <u>every thing you may</u> see necessary I will thank Mr. Antony Gibbs to supply her with any money she may want as we do not think it right to send much with her.' But 'in respect to Masters Mary will only require a few lessons of Music & Singing & perhaps Italian, for the former, a Mr Meves is strongly recommended, but of this you will be much more capable of judging being on the spot, – as the chief object of her going to London is to visit her relations, I should wish it confirmed as much as can be with propriety – she may be rather perplexed in regard to irritations from persons who are not related to her'.

Anxious to assure Betsy that they had Mary's welfare at heart, Antony replied on 2 May, 'Mrs Gibbs understands that it is your wish as well as that of Mary's Father, for her to be introduced to his relations, as far as it can be done....with proper attention to her education', he wrote. She 'has already whilst attending to her Masters here, had the opportunity of making a friendly acquaintance with two of my nieces, the Crawleys as well as with my own Daughter'. He went on, 'Mrs Gibbs cannot suppose a better opportunity of introducing her to Mr & Mrs Crawley than of taking her with us to them on our present short visit to Stowe....I shall be able to join them in the holiday, because my two Sons will remain to manage the Business'. Anxious to impress he added 'you will be glad to here [sic] that the Attorney General and Lady Gibbs are equally desirous with her other relations to recommend what is most likely to forward Mary's improvement'. Lady Gibbs 'has had the advantage of securing the best road to it with the Young Ladies of that family, who have had the most accomplished education & are still studying under the best masters'. Once she had settled in, Mary was 'to go to Lady Gibbs every week for that purpose'. Antony was clearly delighted that she had been removed from Emma Hamilton's influence, continuing, 'This was impossible you will see when Mary was so much under the direction of Lady Hamilton, who wish'd to lead her into a Course of Company that would absolutely have been disreputable'. He assured Betsy that 'she [Mary] sees no one in that line now, & is kept quietly to her studies as my own daughters. It was a fortunate thing for Mary that she went to her Aunt Richards at Bristol when she did, for tho' she would have had better Masters here, she would have suffer[d] much from the direction of Lady Hamilton, who has lately come into the disgrace you will have heard of'.

Antony knew that Betsy and her husband would be impressed that Kenny was taking a personal interest in Mary's education for she 'recognised the importance of languages and considered them as important as music and singing for good spelling is in a decent acquaintance with any language'. Despite having spent her childhood in Italy, Mary was to have Italian lessons. Having spent the last few years in England, 'she has lost, & it was impossible to prevent it without a Master for so long, a vast deal of her Italian, for which she now has an excellent Master'. Kenny felt that Mary should remain with them for at least six months during which time, 'Every attention shall be paid to her improvement which her father or you can desire'. Antony hoped that the Richards would allow her to remain with them until the end of the year, as 'I am sure that at a later age the same Studies can never be followed....with an equal degree of improvement'.

Kenny, living only a few miles from Dulwich, saw it as her duty to oversee the education of her young niece. She employed the best teachers and Mary took the majority of her lessons with Antony's daughters. Before long, she was learning 'pianoforte singing & dancing'. When not in the schoolroom, she and Harriet spent much of their time gossiping or shopping with Dolly. Her cousin William was a regular visitor as was her Topsham cousin John Ley, who was working for Thomson Hankey & Co in London. Kenny also saw it as her duty to ensure that Mary was launched into the best society if she were to find a suitable husband. A few weeks after her seventeenth birthday she made her debut at a ball in London, accompanied by Lady Gibbs and escorted by her cousin Henry. She caused quite a stir. With her family connections both in London and Palermo, her beauty and continental manners, there is little doubt that that she was an immediate success and attracted many potential suitors including her cousins Henry, William and John Ley. Antony had high hopes that one day Mary might marry young William who was particularly fond of her.

The family loved the house in Dulwich, but it was not long before Antony claimed he was finding the time spent travelling to and from his offices in Lombard Street both onerous and tiring. As one of the Commissioners for Portuguese property, he was required to live in London and within weeks he was sleeping at his compting house or in his club, rarely having time to go home to his family. By the beginning of 1811, once again he and Dolly were virtually living apart and it is probable that he was seeking solace elsewhere.[8] Often feeling guilty at his actions and knowing that she was depressed and lonely without him, he hoped that Mary would be a diversion for his family leaving him free to pursue his own interests.

Through all this, there was little progress towards resolving the long-standing dispute over Sir James Douglas' will. By the end of the year, although the solicitors acting for Mary had sought the opinion of a number of counsels, the case had yet to be heard in Chancery. She was getting very impatient, knowing that she was soon to return to the Richards. She had written to her father in November asking him what she should do, but by early January had still not received a reply. On 12 January, she contacted her uncle, James Richards asking him why there was such a delay in holding the hearing. He too was concerned, replying three weeks later that 'unless something is soon done to bring the business to a conclusion it has occurred to me whether some step may not be taken to have a hearing before the Master of the Rolls, whose judgement is very good in cases of the like kind'. He was also worried about Abraham. British troops, having been withdrawn from Sicily 'to reinforce the army in Portugal', had left it vunerable to invasion by the French. Unusually Betsy too had not heard from her brother for several months. 'In the uncertain State of Security which I consider the Island to be in I should think your Father must be much engaged in arranging his plans in case of unfavourable circumstances & too busy to write domestic Letters as your Aunt has not heard from him'. He told Mary not to worry about her father. 'Being on the spot he must of course be more capable of judging [whether an invasion was imminent] than we who are at a distance and have only news paper [sic] intelligence to form our opinions.'

He continued, 'I should hardly think he would wish to have you out until some time as he sees you may join him in some place of security, therefore both your aunt and myself hope for your company' in the near future. Mary was dismayed knowing that this would not be for a short visit. He and Betsy had decided she should return to live with them while they waited for counsel's opinion. Richards was planning to spend a few days in Bristol on business in the spring while Betsy was in Bath taking the waters for an ongoing stomach complaint, and he asked that Mary join them there and return with them to north Devon. Upset at the prospect of leaving her beloved Dolly and Harriet, she immediately wrote to her father beseeching him to let her stay in Dulwich.

Meanwhile, the delay in hearing Mary's case dragged on. At the beginning of March, Antony received a letter from Richards asking him to contact the trustees to find out why the case had not been heard. He also asked for details of the disputed inheritance, believing that as her guardian, he had a right to know the details of the case. As requested, Antony wrote to Sir Richard Neave the trustee and executor of the Douglas estate that he had been 'asked by my Friend and near relation Mr Ab. Gibbs' to enquire into the cause of the unusual delay in settling the bequest made more than 15 yrs since by Sir James Douglas to his three daughters'. Neave, a former governor of the Bank of England and a commissioner of public accounts, had an impeccable reputation. He replied that although the court had found 'on Miss Gibbs's claim to a moiety of the Estates of Sir James Douglas…[and]

establishes her right beyond doubt to an equal share in her grandfather's property', Margaret's estranged husband, Harris had put in a counter claim on his wife's behalf. Mrs Harris wished to establish whether she was 'intitled [sic] under the will of her father to two thirds of the property left by him to his three daughters or Whether [sic] that property was to be equally divided with her & her niece'. After taking advice, he informed Antony that 'it is impossible to say how many years such a suit as this may last, as it requires signatures which cannot be procured'. Antony responded that he had spoken to Mrs Harris 'who wished the suit to be dropped', and asked that details of Mary bequest to be sent to Richards.

Antony could not understand why there was such a delay in settling what appeared to be a simple matter. He wrote to George expressing his concern. He too was baffled and replied that Robert Remmett Jr, his cousin's son, had 'counselled on this business & gave an opinion' as did many other well-known solicitors, that it was quite straight-forward and there was no reason why Neave should not 'apply to the Court of Chancery to determine on the different interests of the parties under the will'.[9] To allay Antony's fears of any impropriety, George assured him that 'Neave is a model of great respectability & there appears no grounds for questioning the propriety of his conduct', but was concerned that Richards' attitude might antagonise him. 'Mr Richards', he wrote, is no more 'a Guardian for Mary Gibbs than for the purpose of carrying on the Chancery Suit& it is quite ridiculous for him to be calling for accounts from Sir Richd Neave who will consider the application as proceeding from ignorance or impertinence'. He added, 'Do you suppose any settlement could be made by Sir Richard Neave of Mary Gibb's interest in the Estate until she is of age? & does it appear by the will that in the mean time any one has the right to call on him on her behalf for accounts? In the event, Harris's counter claim was unsuccessful and Neave was directed to distribute the Douglas estate 'on the very Equivocal Terms in which the Bequests of the Will are made'. It was not until 19 September 1811 that '*Anna Maria Gibbs late of the City of Palermo in Sicily*', inherit her mother's share of her grandfather's estate which included a property in the West Indies with an estimated annual income of £200.[10] As she was still under-age, administration was granted to her uncle and guardian James Richards.

At the beginning of April, Mary reluctantly prepared to leave Dulwich. Her numerous appeals to her father to be allowed to stay with her adopted family fell on deaf ears. Betsy had insisted that as her husband was Mary's legal guardian, she should return to Ilfracombe as soon as possible. Mary was adamant that she would rather return to Italy than live with her elderly aunt and uncle. Antony too had written to his cousin asking that she remain with them, but Abraham was unmoved. Mary must go and live with his sister. Antony, astonished at his cousin's attitude, was worried at the impact it would have on her education, which in turn could affect her chances of making a good marriage. He considered that her father was acting 'in a most extraordinary way with regard to her as a parent…'.

Although reluctantly accepting Abraham's decision, Antony wrote assuring him that despite their opposition, 'Your daughter will implicitly obey your orders to follow the directions of her aunt Richards'. Whilst Mary had been under his care he wrote, she 'has very much improved in manners and accomplishments….but there is still room for improvement, and I sincerely hope she will find it where she is going, and I think you will be much pleased if she only retains what she has already acquired. She is a very good girl, is endowed with a sense beyond her years, and for the sake of improvement has contented herself in our house in a little box of a Lodging room'. He was also able to give Abraham some welcome news. The solicitor acting for Mary had discovered a further annuity of £150 bequeathed to his late wife by her father, which had been earning little interest for several years and had increased in value to £266. Antony was sure that if invested it would realise a much greater sum for Mary in the future.

On 17 May 1811, Dolly sadly recorded in her journal that 'Mary Gibbs left. We went up to Town with her'. With Mary gone, the house seemed very quiet and within a few days, Dolly went down with a bad cold. Two weeks later, a long letter arrived from Illfracombe that caused her some disquiet. Apologising for not writing sooner, Mary thanked Dolly for her many kindnesses over the last year. 'Oh my dear Mrs Gibbs', she wrote, 'my spirits were so agitated the day I left you that I did not find myself able to thank you & dear Mr Gibbs for all your kindness & attentions to me; & even now I cannot find words to express how much obliged & grateful I feel for them'. The journey to Devon had taken longer than anticipated. It took three days to reach Bath due to bad weather. There Mary met her uncle and aunt and they went on to Bristol where Betsy stopped to do some shopping. The journey to Ilfracombe had been most unpleasant. 'My Uncle was in a dreadful bad humour owing to my aunt not having been ready to set off early from Bristol on Thursday morning & her taking so many parcels as to prevent our getting into the Carriage. This disturbed him so much that he was determining my Aunt should see, & feel, his displeasure & most of the time was spent disputing & finding faults with every thing. You can easily imagine how unpleasant this was to me, being so different from what I had been used to lately'. Throughout the journey, Betsy had interrogated her about Dulwich, asking her 'so many questions that I was completely tired of answering her'. Mary believed that Betsy had written to her father 'things without foundation' which she refused to discuss with her, preferring to 'avoid the subject'. Since her arrival in Ilfracombe, she had explored the surrounding countryside and coast finding it a 'pretty place but the town is miserably built'.

Dolly was disturbed that Mary was so unhappy. A few days later, Susan brought the children to Dulwich for a few weeks before they all went to Devon for the summer. While there, it was agreed that she would invite Mary to visit them in Topsham in September for a family reunion. At the beginning of June, Antony and Dolly travelled with Susan as far as Bristol, and while she went on to Devon, they stayed at Redland for a few days. From there, they continued on to Exwick to stay with the Banfills. They also went to Topsham to visit William and Susan and the two families spent many happy times together during July and August. On their return to Exwick in September, young Henry suddenly became ill with a high fever. As he showed no sign of recovering, Antony sent for Robert Remmett, who was now an eminent physician in Plymouth. After examining his young patient, Remmett decided on the standard treatment and bled him. Henry slowly recovered and the following week was almost completely recovered when Mary arrived by coach from Ilfracombe for what was to be a short holiday.[11] They were all very concerned that she was so unhappy with the Richards and thought it a splendid idea when Susan suggested that she come to live with her and William in Topsham.

In mid-October, Antony and Dolly returned to Dulwich and for the next year their life continued very much as before. Antony spent most of his time in London, rarely sleeping or dining at his home. John Ley was a regular visitor to the house and both Dolly and Susan were silently pleased that and he and Anne seemed to be increasingly fond of one another. Now fifty-six, by 1812 the stress of so many years was beginning to take its toll on Antony's health. He had begun to suffer from severe headaches and lapses of memory. On 23 February, Dolly recorded in her journal 'Mr Gibbs had a very bad night & very poorly today'. He seemed slow to recover and three months later she noted that he was 'sleepy sick and faint'. Despite her entreaties to hand over the reins to Henry and William, he refused and argued that he needed to live nearer his office. Later that year, still worried about his health, Dolly felt she had no option but to agree to move into London and they took a house at 2 Powis Place, Great Ormond Street.

CHAPTER 12

WILLIAM AND SUSAN

At the end of 1800, William was still living in Topsham with Susan and his growing family. For some years, he had only been able to obtain short-term intermittent employment in the coastal trade and was now almost totally supported by Lyle. There had developed in him a culture of dependency and resentment, heightened by the success of his brothers and cousins. As William had so generously given all he could from his own meagre resources to his uncle at the time of his bankruptcy, now with nothing to fall back on, he was now forced to depend on his brother for financial assistance. After eleven years, Antony was still not in a position to repay the debt and as Susan had no fortune of her own, William's resentment and temper were directed at her. They were still living in the small terraced cottage opposite the large house where he had spent his childhood. It consisted of a 'messuage or tenement courtilage and gardens with appurtenances…anciently part of a field which was called the Higher Limekiln Field…. containing by estimation one hundred and twenty two feet in length & twenty two feet in breadth', situated in 'a street by the name of Lime Street, but after called Shapter Street'.[1] As their family grew, life became very cramped in the tiny house. Susan like Dolly had suffered a number of miscarriages. In 1797, she had given birth to a baby girl whom they called Frances, followed two years later by another son, named Lyle after his uncle.

By 1801, William was desperate for work once again. In April, Susan had given birth to another daughter, Mary Matilda and even with her brother-in-law's help, they were finding it hard to manage. When his cousin George offered him employment as master of his ship the *Concord*, on the Liverpool to West Indies routes, William jumped at the chance. With the decline of Bristol as a port, George had begun to transfer his operations to Liverpool and had purchased the vessel from Munckley on the latter's retirement. It was William's first voyage across the Atlantic for many years and was was to take him away from his family for several months. It seems to have been a successful venture and the following year, George proposed that they jointly purchase a Jamaicaman, which would initially sail to the Mediterranean and then on the West Indies routes. He wrote to Antony in Cadiz with the news. 'William Gibbs has at last got an enquiry. A vessel [sic]…was bought for him….she is to be employed in the Straight's trade, & is now about to proceed from Penzance for Naples with a cargo of Pilchards on freight'. If this proved profitable, it would be fitted out to sail on the transatlantic routes. Built in Bristol in 1793, the *Hope* had been used as a Barbados trader by the firm for some years.[2] William was enthusiastic and some weeks later they purchased the vessel, which was jointly financed by Gibbs Richards & Gibbs, who owned a half share, the remainder being divided equally by Gautier's Banking House in London and William, whose share was financed by the profits from his previous trip on the *Concord* and a loan from Lyle. George hoped that 'this concern will answer tolerably well, but at all events it will be better for William than going on in the idle unprofitable way he has for many years' and would also give him the opportunity of seeing his brothers.

The *Hope* was ready to sail at the end of December and on Christmas Eve William left his family for Falmouth to join his ship on its first voyage to Naples. He had heard from Abraham that he was planning to return to England with his daughter Mary, and William hoped to bring them back with him. Two months later, Susan had received no news of her husband since his departure and became very anxious. She was also very worried about her young son Lyle. A few weeks before William had sailed the child had been badly scalded. Three months later, despite constant nursing, the he could still barely stand. She grew increasingly distraught, not helped by the fact that her eldest son, William Henry, had suffered a number of convulsions and had been diagnosed with epilepsy. In February, Dolly, seeing her friend near the end of her tether, invited her to Exeter for a few days. Over the last few years, the two women had become very fond of one another, and their children were all great friends. The previous year, Susan had helped Dolly when she had suffered her stroke, and Dolly knew that she too was lonely without her husband.

Susan and the children remained in Exeter for a fortnight. Dolly was shocked at her appearance and saw that she was 'worn out by her constant attentions' upon her young son. Susan thoroughly enjoyed the rest and the two women gossiped and exchanged confidences as their children played. She confided in Dolly about her financial difficulties; young Lyle required constant medical help and since William's departure, she had received no money and could not pay her son's medical bills. In desperation, she had written to her brother-in-law in Genoa asking for help. For Susan it was a continuous struggle to support the family during her husband's absence, and she tentatively asked if Antony was in a position to settle his outstanding debt arising from the loan William had made to his uncle at the time of his bankruptcy twelve years before. Dolly, also living in considerable hardship was very sympathetic to her plight, and agreed to write to Antony immediately. After Susan's return to Topsham, as good as her word she wrote to him of her 'anxiety about her little boy and not having heard from her husband [which] makes her dreadfully nervous' and told him of her request. It was several weeks later that she heard that George had agreed and the loan was to be repaid on William's return to England.

William did not come back to Topsham as expected. As soon as he arrived back in Cork at the end of March, he planned to rejoin the *Hope* and sail to Falmouth to wait for the convoy bound for the West Indies. At the end of April news reached England of a 'calamity that befell a fleet of outward bound West India men on the coast of Portugal'. The French had attacked the convoy. At first, it was thought that William was on one of the ships and for several weeks, there were fears for his safety. Susan was beside herself, fearing that he had either been captured again or had not survived the attack. During this period, there was considerable anxiety about the 'situation of English prisoners at present in France with little prospect of release'. It later emerged that William had had a narrow escape due to his own ineptitude – he had arrived in Cork to find the convoy had already sailed. As George wrote to Antony, 'The unfortunate fleet…that sailed from Cork is the same that the much lamented William Gibbs was not in time to join – so little do we know what we should hope for or fear, rejoice in or be sorry for'. No one expected to see him for many months for his family 'had every reason to believe that he met with it off the harbour and proceeded with it'.

Instead of the long trip across the Atlantic, without contacting Susan William joined another ship in Falmouth bound for the Mediterranean in ballast to collect a cargo of pilchards. Yet again, disaster struck and the voyage ended in disaster. On his return to England in June 1803, his ship docked in London and 'all his men except the mate ran away for fear of being pressed' – a fate that befell many mariners landing in London. With no crew, he could not continue round the coast to Penzance. The news of this incident travelled fast and a few weeks later William, who had remained in London, received a letter from Lyle in Genoa who had read about the incident 'in the Public Papers'. He wrote that he and Abraham had been 'very uneasy about you for some time' and considered that William had been 'fortunate for once in your life' having survived the incident and 'must not dispair [sic] hereafter'.

After this incident, Lyle became increasingly worried for his brother's safety. The French had advanced through Italy and attacked Bologna, and it was expected that they would advance further through my 'little Blessed Island'. He advised William not to take 'any new employ during the war except in the transport or pay to the Government Services', and he should not 'regret [not] coming out again with another cargo of Pilchards however so advantageous the adventure'. Remember, he wrote, 'You are now amongst your family, make yourself easy and rejoice on being at home especially at this critical moment and defend and protect all against…an…unbounded ambitious Foe'. To help him out of his current difficulties Lyle sent a bill of exchange to London, which 'Banfill will convert immediately into cash' and told William to 'keep up your courage; never a faint Heart won a Fair Lady; remember you have two Brothers and that they both do rival in affection and readiness to come to your assistance'.

William remained in London for several months. In October, and without seeing his family he travelled to Liverpool to join the *Hope*, which was being fitted-out for its first voyage across the Atlantic. Before sailing, he sent word to her that she should enroll William Henry in Blundells School as a boarder, where Antony's son, Henry was also a pupil and where Susan's brother John was a master. Within weeks, his ship was ready and once again, William left England for a trip that would probably take the best part of a year.

Meanwhile in Topsham, Susan strove to provide a stable home for her younger children. Although she knew she would not see him for many months, now that William was guaranteed regular employment for the next few years, things would be much easier for her and the family. Lyle continued to send her a regular allowance and William was entitled to a share of the profits at the end of each voyage. As most of these were tied up in stock, George kindly agreed to give her an advance against them. Anxious to see her husband whenever possible, Susan occasionally made the long journey to Liverpool with the children between voyages, and these irregular visits were followed by pregnancies and miscarriages. In 1805, at the age of thirty-nine, she gave birth to another son, Abraham, who lived a few months, and three years later to a healthy baby, Charles. However, things were improving. The previous year, Lyle had arranged for her eldest son William Henry to join the London firm of Thomas Hankey & Son, while his younger brother John Ley took his place as a boarder at the school in Tiverton. Young Lyle, who had been scalded several years before was still a very frail child in need of constant attention, but her daughters Frances and Mary Matilda were a great comfort to her.

During William's long absences, Susan also took the opportunity of visiting her relatives in Tiverton and Abbots Leigh as often as possible. Her kind disposition made her a great favourite with Antony's sons, Henry and William who had been taught by her brother at Blundells. She and Betsy were also friends and when their young niece Mary arrived from Palermo to stay there with the Richards, the family spent many happy times together. Dolly was also a regular visitor to Topsham and the two women remained very close for many years. Susan was to miss her greatly when Antony moved his family to London.

In 1808, at the age of fifty-one, William made his last voyage for Gibbs Richards & Gibbs. His health had been deteriorating for some time and the long voyages had taken their toll. Returning to Topsham for the first time in three years, he hoped to obtain work in the coastal trade, but again could find none locally. No longer able to afford to keep John Ley at school, he wrote to John Heath asking him to find a place for him in London. Later that year John Ley followed his brother as a clerk with Thomas Hankey's firm in the capital while William Henry, having finished at Hankey's the previous year, had joined his uncle Abraham in Palermo.

The following year, William was so desperate for money that he wrote directly to Heath begging him to 'communicate to my brother Lyle....that we are all well....he has so often and affectionately expressed a wish to help me....at any time in his power, that with my not having been so fortunate as I would wish and having an expensive family that some pecuniary aid would be acceptable'. On receiving the news, Lyle immediately came to his aid and instructed Heath to send William something on account, and he continued to provide him with a regular income for many years. Other members of the family were equally concerned at his situation. Two years later, after a visit to London, Antony wrote to Abraham that 'your brother William and his family came up to Town [London] from Bristol and Topsham his being intirely [sic] out of employment now...I wish I knew of a good Bark to put in his way'.

Now completely dependent on others for support, William and

Susan spent much of their time living quietly in Topsham. It was not until 1810 that his fortunes improved. His friend William Townson, a local leather cutter, left 'a house in Topsham, with a little garden behind…with several houses adjoining….to Captain William Gibbs and his heirs, subject to a clear annuity of 4l. [£4] a year, for ever, to be paid to the Minister and Churchwardens of Topsham aforesaid….bestowed in bread to such poor ….as they should judge fit objects to receive the same'.[3] Townson appointed William as his sole executor and left fifty pounds each to Frances and Matilda upon their reaching the age of twenty-one.[4] William was now a man of property, less dependent on his relatives for financial support, and at last had some standing in the local community.

He and Susan had become very fond of their young niece Mary and were concerned to hear how unhappy she was living with his sister and brother-in-law in Ilfracombe. Torn from her beloved Dolly, Mary had become rude and rebellious and Betsy was finding it difficult to cope with her young niece. Betsy remembered her own situation at the same age, and considered it her duty to find Mary a suitable husband. However, Mary resented her aunt's interference, and the clash of characters proved too much for Betsy and when Susan wrote inviting Mary to visit them she readily agreed, relieved that her brother's family was at last taking an interest in their niece. During August, Antony's children William and Anne came to spend a short holiday in Topsham with William and Susan, before being joined by their parents, enabling the two families to spend many enjoyable times together.

Arriving in Topsham in September, Mary was taken by William and Susan to Exwick House where Antony and Dolly were staying with their family for the summer. She was thrilled to see them again, but the happy reunion was overshadowed by her unhappiness. Betsy was determined to find her a husband, but the choice in the little north Devon town was limited. After some discussion, it was suggested that Mary might be happier living with William and Susan. Not only did they have children nearer her age, but also Topsham was near Exeter, the social and political capital of Devon. Mary was thrilled at the suggestion and when she left Exwick at the end of the month, she immediately wrote to her father begging him to agree that she stay with William and Susan. Like any indulgent father, Abraham consented, and the following January, Mary moved into the little cottage in Shapter Street, opposite the family house where her father had spend his childhood.

It was not long before this sophisticated high-spirited seventeen-year-old had a number of admirers including a Robert Corrington from the nearby village of Ide. It was only six weeks later that she declared that she was in love and when Corrington proposed she accepted. Betsy thoroughly approved of the match and wrote to Abraham for his consent. The letter took several weeks to reach its destination, but William had other ideas. Since 1808, his eldest son, William Henry had been working with Mary's father in Palermo and was being trained to take over the business when Abraham retired. William was determined that the two cousins would marry. With Mary's fortune, both his own and his son's financial future would be secured. Unknown to Betsy, William wrote to Abraham telling him that he strongly opposed the match, believing that Mary was '*engaged with the idea of a love affair*' rather than marriage. Mary was furious when she learned what her uncle had done, but despite Betsy's support, Abraham took William's advice and insisted that she end the engagement. Anxious to see her again and worried that she might elope and make an unsuitable marriage Abraham insisted that she come back to Palermo. Initially Mary refused, angry at the thought of leaving England and the family she had grown to love, but she reluctantly agreed when her father promised she could return to England if she was unhappy in Sicily. Abraham asked William to accompany her and in the spring of 1812, he and Mary left for London to seek a passage for Palermo.

CHAPTER 13

PALERMO

Despite his previous intention of following Mary to England, with his appointment as US pro-consul in 1803, Abraham decided that his future lay in Palermo. Although he did not give up his association with Falconnet Gibbs & Co, within weeks of her departure he had returned to Sicily to establish the firm of Abraham Gibbs & Co of Palermo. He also renewed his association with the Lenzitti family. While resident in Sicily between 1798 and 1802, Giuseppe Lenzitti, and his son Paolo had been associates in the Palermo subsidiary of Falconnet Gibbs & Co. With the formation of the new business, both Paolo and his younger brother Gioacchino became junior partners, the latter becoming the firm's agent in Salerno.

Although he missed Mary, Abraham was now able to devote all his energies into building up his business. While he waited for his appointment as US pro-consul to be confirmed, he spent a considerable amount of time travelling between Palermo, Naples and Malta, developing trading links with the Sicilian ports. As his wealth increased, his reputation grew both at court and amongst the mercantile community. For Abraham the advantages of returning to Palermo and establishing his compting house there were considerable. The demand for British goods had grown rapidly both in Sicily and in mainland Italy, with many British merchants establishing businesses in both Messina and Palermo.

During the war, apart from Leghorn, which remained a free port, the focus of British trade in the Mediterranean was around the southern ports. Sicily, protected by the British fleet, remained independent of French domination, becoming an entrepôt for British goods in retaliation to the French blockade that prohibited any trade with ports dominated by France. Sicily was an ideal base for smuggling goods to Salerno, Calabria, Capri, Reggio or to the Adriatic ports and even to southern France.

The importance of Malta to British trade in the Mediterranean had long been recognised. In 1798, the French had occupied the island. The following year, after the Maltese uprising against their occupiers, Britain took Malta under its protection in the name of the King of the Two Sicilies. With the plague ever present at this time, a quarantine station had been built in Valetta, which was made a free port similar to Leghorn. It attracted many vessels seeking cargoes mainly of cotton, woollens and earthenware for the ports around the Mediterranean. Abraham's associates, Edmund and George Noble had settled there in 1803, and he was in an ideal position to further develop trade with the rest of Europe. As his reputation spread throughout Italy, his brother Lyle, proudly wrote from Genoa to William that throughout the war, Abraham was '…increasing rapidly once more his fortune at Palermo. He becomes daily a man of great consequence'.

Abraham also hoped that his appointment as the US pro-consul would provide a significant boost to his trade in colonial goods. As most of the ports in Europe remained closed to British vessels, his new role would enable him to expand his banking and trading activities both within the Mediterranean and beyond for vessels sailing a neutral flag. There was a growing demand for colonial products amongst the English and other foreign residents on the island as well as on the Italian mainland, mostly for coffee, rum, tobacco and rice. As the only US approved commission agent on the island, Abraham acted for American merchants, especially those on the eastern seaboard. As pro-consul, he was responsible for negotiating trade agreements, managing and coordinating American imports and organising their sale and transit to the Italian mainland. His position also put him in an enviable position for developing trade in Sicilian produce to the United States.

Another responsibility was to send regular reports to Barnes the US Consul in Naples detailing the arrivals and departures of US ships in Palermo and their cargoes. With the development of trade with Europe, American merchants needed reliable information from a source they could trust to arrange credit, advise them of the state of foreign markets, receive and dispose of cargoes, and give advice on return cargoes. Like their British counterparts, the US administration recognised the strategic importance of Europe and their policy of appointing envoys with a local knowledge around the continent gave a tremendous boost to US trade during this period.

In his half-yearly dispatches, Abraham was also required to include relevant information on the political and economic affairs in the region as well as the general gossip circulating in Palermo. On 24 September 1805, he wrote 'The scene [here] begins to be very interesting' and 'all the gunboats & Bombards were safe returned with two prizes at Syracuse on the 15 Inst with the *John Adams* [a US frigate commanded by Henry Preble] loaded with staves, & the *Constitution* is still off Tripoli with Commander Barrow and three more frigates. They [the British] have completely beaten the Turks but unfortunately have lost 6 brave officers and about 40 men'. He gloomily added, 'a Continental War is inevitable and permanent with England as long as Bonaparte continues at the head of affairs for his ambition has no bounds & Mr. Pitt has declared that England cannot disarm for that reason even in the event of peace'. Abraham also reported that there had been 'no arrivals from the United States for some time & I consider it a fortunate Circumstance for every market in the Mediterranean is overstocked with Colonial produce & any prices that I might quote you would be at random.'[1] Three months later circumstances had changed, and he wrote that we are now 'much in want of West India produce, particularly Coffee & Pimento'.

Although he had been instructed by Washington to do so, Barnes did not proceed with establishing a full consulate in the port of Palermo. He rarely visited Sicily, preferring the attractions of Naples. Abraham was frustrated at the delay because although he effectively was in post he had neither recognition nor the accompanying status. He saw the potential to his own business of developing trade with the United States and wanted a full consulate established in Palermo as soon as possible. In his September dispatch, he had asked Barnes to visit so that they could discuss the situation, but received no reply. Barnes had gone on an extended tour of Tuscany and was to be away from Naples for several months.

At the end of November, Preble the commander in chief of the US fleet in the Mediterranean, visited Palermo and it was not long before Abraham convinced him of the importance of having a full consulate in the port. Preble agreed to take up the matter with Barnes in Naples. Following his departure on 1 December, Abraham urgently wrote to Barnes telling him that 'Commander Preble arrived here two days ago & proceeds to Naples, Leghorn & Marseilles on his way to America. I believe he will sail tomorrow – His intention is to go over land from Naples to Leghorn unless the News of the Yellow fever should change his mind. entre nous'. He also warned that 'the Commodore was not pleased at your remaining so long in Tuscany for your private news as he calls it. I dare say you will make a point of having a proper explanation with him'. He added that that the Commander had agreed to take up his case for a consulate in Palermo because I already 'transact all the functions of the Office', and he 'will explain to you that I cannot be acknowledged here with the simple authority you sent me for the reasons stated'.[2]

A few weeks later Barnes was recalled to Washington in disgrace and Abraham was informed that James Madison, the Secretary of State, had agreed that full American consulates be established in the ports of Palermo and Messina and that Abraham had been appointed US Consul. On 20 March 1805, he sent a copy of Abraham's commission for the Sicilian government with a letter of confirmation. Unfortunately, they both failed to reach Palermo. Without them Abraham was unable proceed and remained unrecognised by the King, and so he appealed to Madison for a copy of the original letter. On its eventual arrival Abraham replied, 'I observe with some degree of satisfaction that the president had been pleased to name me Consul of the United States for the Port of Palermo, and superseding Mr. J Barnes…You will doubtless have heard from that Gentleman that I have for some time executed the functions of the Office.…Your said letter will now enable me to continue same more effectively until I receive my Commission, which by some accident has not reached me to this Day'. Despite Madison's letter, without his official commission, Ferdinand still refused to acknowledge him as consul. Abraham wrote urgently in July. 'The King of Two Sicilies has been pleased to acknowledge me in Virtue of your Letter, 11th May as *Consul Interim* of the United States of America at Palermo, and to grant me Permission to execute as such, the functions of the Office, with reserve however of presenting my Commission as soon as possible; until then his Royal Exchequer Cannot be granted'. He asked Madison to send him ' a Duplicate of my Commission that I may be properly acknowledged, as the Original, which has not yet reached me must certainly have miscarried'.[3] His appointment was eventually confirmed in January 1806 and the original documentation arrived in Palermo the following year.

Before he could take up his appointment he was required to provide the US Government with two $2000 bonds as security drawn against Abraham Gibbs & Co of Palermo. On 10 November, he wrote to Washington 'Here enclosed you will find one of the two Bonds of Two thousand Dollars, forwarded me, filled up and signed by my friend Mr Joachim Lenzitti and myself'. He and Lenzitti were also required to sign a solemn affidavit agreeing they were,

> 'held and firmly bound to the United States of America in the sum of two thousand dollars, money of the said United States, to the payment whereof we bind ourselves jointly, and severally, our joint and several heirs, executors, and administrators…
> …THE CONDITION of the above obligation is such, That if the above bounden Abraham Gibbs appointed Consul of the United States in certain

foreign parts, shall truly and faithfully discharge the
duties of his said office, according to law, and also
shall truly account for all monies, goods and effects,
which may come into his possession by virtue of the
laws of the United States, or if his said office, then
the above obligation to be void, otherwise to remain
in full force'[4]

Having presented his credentials, Abraham then set about establishing a consulate with a house and staff that reflected his new status.
In his first dispatch as consul he wrote to Madison, 'I have since had
the satisfaction of receiving via Malta my long delayed Commission,
which has enabled me to be properly acknowledged as Consul for the
United States of America at Palermo... .'. He went on:

'I have taken the Liberty to appoint three trusty
persons, as my Agents, in the undermentioned
Districts and ports, which I mention in order that all
faith may be given to the certificates that they may
have occasion to grant, viz:
– Mr William Woodhouse, for Marsala and Mazarra
– Mr. Ignazio Maria Polizzi, for Trapani
– Mr. Gaetano Maria Sterlini, for Girgenti
and I have likewise appointed Mr. Constantine
R Rafinesque Schmalz who has resided a long time
in America, as chancellor of this Consulate'[5]

The appointment of William Woodhouse is a further indication
of the strong connection and trust that had existed for many years between Abraham and the Woodhouse family. Since Nelson's endorsement
of Marsala wine several years previously, the firm of Abraham Gibbs &
Co had handled all the transportation and export of Woodhouse's wine.
Despite growing competition from other vineyards, in his new role as
consul, Abraham actively promoted Woodhouse wine to the American

commercial agents and masters of any US merchant vessel that docked in Palermo.

One of his tasks was to sort out any problems encountered by American sailors who landed in the port and aiding them in times of distress. This posed a number of problems. On one occasion Abraham wrote that he held $51 belonging to one 'William Smith, an American Sailor, native of Virginia, discharged at Masala last June, from the Brig *Independence of Boston*...on account of an incurable disorder of which he died One month after', and wanted to know if he should send it to his 'nearest relations'. He had also received 'several applications from Sailors on board the English men of War, now in this Station, as American Citizens', who had been impressed by the British navy into service. He was concerned that many 'could not produce Collector's protections' although some 'bear evident proof of being American born, others have our protections, which notwithstanding my Repeated Applications have not been sufficient to enable me to relieve them from their Situation.'[6] However, the British consul had informed him that even if these poor unfortunates had been able to produce the correct papers, 'they could not have been delivered up, or discharged without an order from the Court of Admiralty in England'. His accounts included a request for payment for 'all the Moneys...from the Sailors discharged at this port or in the departmt' of this Consulate, & paid for the same Account to the American Sailors for their distress in said Departt....likewise of such who have applied to me for release from the British Service'.[7]

His chief responsibility however, was to maintain the commercial relations between America and the port of Palermo and to resolve any problems that hindered the development of trade. He also dealt with complaints and sorted out any problems encountered by American merchants and mariners that had an impact on trade. One issue that occupied much of his time was the quarantining of ships arriving from the US. During the first decade of the 1800s, all US vessels arriving at Sicilian ports spent a period in quarantine to prevent the spread of plague from their cargoes and men. As British ships from the colonies had first to land their cargoes in the UK where there was no plague, they were required only to be quarantined for 21 days when they arrived in Sicily, whereas vessels sailing direct from the United States were subjected to 40 days quarantine. In his dispatch of January 1807, Abraham wrote that he had 'succeeded in having the American Navy put upon the same footing as the British in this Island, respecting quarantine….the Word of honor of the Commanding Officer, being deemed sufficient at the health offices to secure them prattick; and if coming from a Port whence a 40d is performed, the Days of their holdage are reckoned on the number assigned to Merchant Vessels. The 40^d from America is now reduced to 21 days & Vessels are allowed to land their cargoes during that time.'[8]

His appointment had a significant impact on his business. He not only performed his consular duties but as the only US approved commission agent in Palermo, he was able to take advantage of his position to increase his wealth and standing. The consular returns indicate that between 1804 and 1808, the number of American vessels arriving at Palermo increased rapidly. In 1804, only six ships had cleared the port; by 1806 the number had risen to thirty and the following year eighty vessels arrived, some having sailed directly from the United States, others stopping off on a round trip with cargoes ranging from colonial produce, sugar, coffee tobacco and rum, to iron plates, cod, silk, hats paper and marble. Virtually all cargoes arriving on American vessels were consigned to Abraham Gibbs & Co for disposal in Sicily or to other European countries.[9] Such was the level of business between Palermo and Naples, in 1808 Abraham decided to open an office in Naples to look after his dealings on mainland Italy.

In spite of the growing tension between Great Britain and the United States after the Chesapeake incident on the 22 June 1807, he remained optimistic about his future business.[10] In his dispatch in September, he noted, 'the American Carrying trade has become very considerable in our parts, owing to the Scarcity of Neutral flags in the Mediterranean…. By the Cutter arrived in Twenty two days from England, we have heard that all differences between that Country and the United States [over impressments] were likely to be accommodated, which has inclined me to allow all the American Vessels at present in this port to the Amount of ten, to proceed on their Voyages, which I had suspended for a few days, on hearing of the fatal Accident happened to the US frigate Chesapeake'.[11]

Despite Abraham's confidence, in December Congress passed the Embargo Act, which banned the departure of all ships, except foreign ships in ballast, from American ports for foreign shores. The bill was intended to put pressure on both Great Britain and France to change their policy on impressments by depriving them of American goods, which were in great demand throughout Europe. In 1807 the effects of the embargo had not yet been felt in Palermo. In his dispatch of January 1808, he wrote that 'the American Commerce was greater last year, than it ever was before in this Island & more than 80 Vessels entered the port during the same', but added 'it is to be feared it will be greatly diminished this year by the Measure adopted by the English and French Governments'.[12]

The embargo proved very unpopular in America as its merchants saw their profits plummet in the economic depression that followed. The Embargo Act was repealed by Congress in March 1809, and replaced by a policy of non-intercourse with Great Britain and France. The Non-Intercourse Act allowed US ships to trade with any other country and excluded British and French ships from all American ports. It remained in force until May 1810, with the exception of a short period in the summer of 1809, when trade with Great Britain was permitted.

During 1808, with no US vessels arriving at Palermo, Abraham's profits from the sale of colonial produce plummeted, to recover only when the trade resumed the following year. On 6 January 1810, he sent his first dispatch to Washington for two years. 'The Embargo ... in the United States has prevented the American Flag from entering this place, but since the raising of it the vessels have been very numerous as you will perceive by the enclosed statement from 1st Jan 1808 to 31st June 1809'. Even with the resumption of trade, he was worried that the American ships 'have generally bought very Sub Cargoes which unfortunately have not a very good Market owing to the immense quantity of Colonial Produce, which has come almost at the same time, & of which a great proportion landed here is still unsold'.[13]

He also reported that the seizure of American vessels was continuing. 'Tunis and Napolitan [sic] privateers have been pretty numerous last summer particularly off the Tunis Coast and the Island of Sardinia' he wrote. 'Several American vessels had been made prizes by them and either carried to Tunis or to Trieste ports;....but on the whole I think they have been extremely fortunate in escaping the Corsairs considering the great Number of them and some of them which returned almost in Sight of this port; The English have also made a few & the Sicilians Capture only two & bought them here. I however succeeded in getting Them released paying small pensions much against my obligations'. During the previous year, a large number of American sailors who had deserted British ships in Palermo appealed to the consulate for financial help. Abraham added, 'I Beg leave to receive my Expenses and the manner in which I am to reimburse the Sums Advanced to the American Seamen in Distress, they having been very numerous of late, my advance greatly exceeding the Amount of the funds I hold for the United States to that purpose'.[14]

In December 1805, with the French victory at the Battle of Austerlitz, once again Napoleon advanced into Italy, and once again Ferdinand and his queen, fled to Sicily protected by the British Navy. On 14 February, Bonaparte entered Naples installing his elder brother Joseph as King of the Two Sicilies six weeks later. Despite this, Ferdinand, protected by the British, continued to reign over Sicily, which remained independent of French domination. The British *occupation* was friendly, leading to a sharp increase in the demand for British produce as markets expanded to meet the needs of a 17,000 strong occupying force. Sicily became an entrepôt for British goods and a useful addition to Leghorn. As the French blockade of the Italian ports prevented the landing of British merchandise, the British Government retaliated and prohibited any trade with ports dominated by France. Sicily and Malta, now protected by the British Mediterranean fleet, were ideal bases from which goods transported legally or illegally, were sent to the blockaded ports markets on mainland Italy and France.

As well as being US Consul, in 1803 Abraham was appointed paymaster to the British forces and banker to the Kingdom of the Two Sicilies. As early as 1801, he had been asked to provide loans to the Sicilian nobility and government, which were underwritten by the Treasury in London. In May, Abraham had written to Paget from Naples. The 'Princess.... having demanded another 200 ounces of me, I have supplied and past [sic] a Bill upon you for the same at 49 florins 1224.49[ct] to the order of Falconnet Gibbs and Co at 60 days date, which you will have the goodness to pay; the exchange is more favourable than before'.[15] The following month Nelson had contacted Acton asking how 'the brave Officers and men who served the cause so well in the Roman State' would be paid.[16] Acton replied, 'I shall take every possible measure to obtain and satisfy the just expectation of the Officers and Ship's Companies who so bravely acted for the recovery of the Roman State' and 'I shall apply direct to Mr Gibbs for the receiving that money'.[17] This appears to have been the first time that the Sicilian government had called upon Abraham for a loan to pay for its war-time expenses and had prompted Nelson to refer to him as 'Mr Gibbs the banker'. As there was no paper money, loans to the Sicilian nobility were usually in gold and repaid by the British Government as part of their support for Ferdinand, and by 1803, all loans to the Sicilian Court were channelled through the firm of Abraham Gibbs & Co. With little available capital on the island and high interest rates, the depreciation of the pound and the fluctuating pound/onze exchange rate proved to be a major problem.[18]

With the onset of hostilities, Ferdinand, supported by British forces, returned to Sicily. This friendly *occupation* led to the establishment of a full consulate including some thirty consuls and vice-consuls, their presence made more palatable by the payment of an annual subsidy to the Sicilian Government, which enabled Ferdinand to reign over the island under British protection. The subsidy, to maintain the Sicilian army and navy, was negotiated by Sir William Drummond, the Minister Plenipotentiary at the Sicilian Court, and paid initially on an ad hoc basis to the Bourbon Government through the firm of Abraham Gibbs & Co. On 6 April 1807, Abraham negotiated Bills of Exchange in onzes for £75,000, which were paid to the Sicilian Court. However, despite his wealth, with no paper money on the island, such large sums put a great strain on his resources and on a number of occasions, he was unable to meet all the demands made on him. With the next payment of £150,000 due in May, on 30 April he wrote urgently to Drummond. 'Your Excellency is acquainted with the urgent and immediate wants of the Sicilian Government, which has rendered it necessary to assign them a credit on Messina upon the house of Messrs Brothers Grant for about Thirty Thousand Ounces. I have to request the favour of you to desire his Excellency General Fox to furnish said Gentlemen with that sum for the Term of one month should they require it or offer them secury [sic] for it, after that period I shall have it in my power to accommodate this Government with their monthly demands.'[19] Drummond had no alternative but to approve his request and wrote to Lord Hourick at the Foreign Office. 'The Copy of the Bills drawn on the Lords Commissioners of this May's Treasury which I have signed on 6th April, to the order of Mr Abraham Gibbs to the amount of £75,000 stl', as well as a number of 'Bills for £150,000 to order of said Mr Gibbs, of which sums the former is on account of the Monthly Subsidy, and the latter on account of the Arrears due to this Government, which your Lordship desired should be paid up as soon as possible,...so large a Sum would not however have been required nor paid, if the Circumstances of His Sic Maj in the perculiar [sic] exigency of the moment...had not rendered it necessary'.[20]

Between April 1807 and April 1808, the British Government authorised a total of £608,496 in ad hoc loans to the Sicilian Government, all negotiated through Abraham Gibbs & Co.[21] However, with the growing shortage of Sicilian money it was often difficult to negotiate the Bills of Exchange. On one occasion, Abraham paid 100 onze commission (at the rate of 3:1000) to buy *pezzi duri* (in Spain) to the overall value of 34,390 onze.[22] In order to 'regularise the subsidy & obtain favourable conditions for merchants and trade', on the 30 March 1808, both governments signed a treaty agreeing to an annual subsidy of £300,000, backdated to September 1805, payable at £25,000 per month. This was to be channeled through Abraham Gibbs & Co. Between 6 April 1807 and 25 October 1808 the Sicilian court was paid £828,436 in arrears and subsidy. For providing this service Abraham received a 1 per cent Commission on all transactions with an additional brokerage charge of 1/6 per cent. This was to be a profitable part of his business activity. Between March and October 1809, he paid 327 bills totaling £149,000 in subsidies and earned £2,168.1.3d in commission and brokerage.[23]

British imports increased rapidly to £211,000 in 1808, both to supply the needs of the Anglo-Sicilian force and for onward shipment, whilst Sicilian exports to Great Britain were a little more than £131,000.[24] From the scant records that exist, it is impossible to reconstruct Abraham's business activities during this period, but it appears that he became the most successful merchant in Palermo. His position as consul enabled him to develop trade with the United States and mainland Italy, and as paymaster to the British forces, he expanded his banking activities. He also provided insurance and maritime loans, and chartered ships that plied the routes from Sicily to Malta and from Sicily to America and England. He was the first merchant to export citrus fruit to the United States, sending the first shipment of Sicilian oranges and lemons there in 1807.[25]

Abraham had not forgotten his beloved Mary. Although he was still in contact with Emma Hamilton, cut off as he was from the London gossip, he was unaware of her extravagant behaviour since Nelson's death and when she offered to have Mary back to live with her again, he was thankful for her kindness and gratefully accepted. Preoccupied with his business activities in Palermo, he continued to act as Nelson's agent in Sicily but rarely visited Bronte. Antonio Forcella arranged the leases and rented out the Duchy farms to those recommended by Eliza Graefer. The profits from the rents and the sale of grain and other produce were sent to Abraham twice a year and remitted to Nelson's bank in London. After his death, the Admiral's elder brother the Reverend William and First Earl Nelson inherited Bronte but his interest in the estate was purely pecuniary. Having satisfied himself that Abraham was a man of impeccable character, he decided to retain him to manage his affairs in Sicily. In March 1806, the Earl sent him a copy of Nelson's will to register with the local authorities and a memorandum giving Abraham power of attorney to act on his behalf, which were presented to Ferdinand by Hugh Elliott, now the British Ambassador. Writing to thank the Earl in June, Abraham offered his condolences on the Admiral's death 'that great illustrious Hero, to whom I had numberless Obligations known to Lady Hamilton and his goodness to me upon every occasion'.[26] He enclosed a bill for £900 and told the Earl that he had also remitted £1057 on 6 December 1803 to the Admiral's account through Messrs Alex Davidson & Co, his bankers in London and that he would prepare and close the account on 21 October 1806. Irritated by the implied criticism in the Earl's letter that Bronte had not yielded the anticipated income for several years, Abraham wanted to set the record straight. 'Besides the above 2 sums', he wrote, 'the Estate has paid off the money borrowed for building the house Bronte, with Interest, and likewise the Ounces 8000 or about £4700 Stg, which the Late Lord Nelson borrowed at Interest, a few days before his Departure from Palermo. These large sums are paid off & I have felt hurt upon hearing on Several Occasions, that not a farthing had been forthcoming from the Bronte Estate'. Worried that he might have offended the Earl, he added, 'an offer was to the late Lord Nelson of £2800 stirling [sic] annually for the Estate which I engaged to remit <u>free of every charge</u>; this offer I think could be renewed for a certain number of years'.[27]

Despite his assurances, all was not well at Bronte. After her husband's death, Eliza Graefer had appointed an old friend, Dom Gregorio Biosa as Governor of the Duchy. Biosa, a Palermo man who was well known to Abraham, had abandoned his family in Palermo and fled to Bronte and taken shelter in Graefer's house. He had soon become a trusted friend of the widow. Described as 'an adventurer destitute of merit' and skilled at 'all manner of debaucheria imaginable', within a short time, he had seduced a young girl and returned to Palermo. Imprisoned by the Criminal Tribunal, he was only released 'by Gibbs's credit'.[28] It emerged that in collusion with Forcella and Graefer, Biosa had taken advantage of the Earl's absence, and the three had used their position at Bronte to make a fortune by renewing leases and letting farms at reduced rents to the local gentry and selling grain, produced by the Duchy, for their own profit. Whether Abraham was part of the conspiracy or closed his eyes to their activities as long as sufficient profit was generated to satisfy Nelson is unclear. Evidently he took some advantage of his position when he gave Graefer's daughter £500 from Nelson's account on her marriage to a member of the prominent Spitalieri family at Bronte and later rented the Pirato farm to them at an amount unfavourable to the Duchy.[29]

Things came to a head in 1808, when large numbers of angry Brontiese petitioned Earl Nelson in London complaining about Biosa and Graefer, referring to her as a 'rapacious' woman who actively underbid local people for leases for land and farms. They described her as an 'old cheat, to whom My Lord, You pay 100 ounces a year, settled upon her by Your generous Brother, instead of attending to Your Interests, she by means of plotting and fraud makes great profit at Your expense'.[30] They had reported 'to Gibbs so many losses and irregularities but he being engaged though partially to protect his Country-woman, listens to no other voice but that of Mrs Grefer & that of Biosa. He pleases them despite a Population of Fifteen Thousand souls who abhor them. If we complain to Gibbs, he answers us to go to Forcella. If we go to Forcella, he accuses himself by alleging that he is not the sole Attorney, but that he is dependent on Gibbs'.[31] Shocked to learn of the petition, Abraham had no alternative but to remove Graefer from her position and she was forced to return to England. Whether he took any action against Forcella and Biosa is unclear, but Abraham continued to remit the profits from the estate, averaging around £3000 each year to Nelson's bankers in London for several years.

The following February, he was surprised to receive a letter from his cousin Antony, written a month earlier. There had been no direct contact between the two cousins since Abraham had left Exeter in 1775. Although he had willingly agreed to help his uncle George Abraham at the time of their bankruptcy in 1790, nearly twenty years later his loan remained unpaid. Prompted by two cargoes from Malta that had been wrongly shipped to England, Antony's letter also told how he and Dolly had met Mary in London. Encouraged that his family was taking an interest in his daughter, Abraham readily agreed to Antony's request that she visit them.

Once the cargoes had arrived back in Malta, Abraham wrote to Antony in London, suggesting that they might do some business together. As his cousin now had offices in both London and Cadiz, Abraham felt it could be advantageous to him, not only as an alternative source of colonial products but also as a new market for Sicilian exports. Some months later he received a reply from Antony, dated 5 September, which included a list of commodities that he could supply from his London firm, and suggesting that 'the articles we should most advise as prudent now to speculate in are barilla and liquorice'. He assured Abraham that if he sent over any Sicilian cargoes 'you may always depend on our best exertions in any Business interest you may entrust to our management'. Over the next twelve months, Abraham exported a number of Sicilian commodities to Antony Gibbs & Son, but was very concerned the following year to receive a letter from his cousin telling him that in future, although he was happy to trade in 'shu-mack or brimstone', the London firm could no longer accept cargoes of barilla. 'The price has fallen so much in England and the quality of Sicilian Barilla is not as good as the Spanish which was shipped in via Gibraltar'. Over the next few months, the value of Sicilian produce shipped from Palermo to both Cadiz and London was around £2000.[32]

He also traded with a number of British merchant houses including Gibbs & Co in Genoa, Gibbs Richards & Gibbs in Bristol, and Heath & Co in London. With the drop in trade from the United States, Abraham imported sugar and rum through the Bristol firm, and exported Sicilian commodities, fruits and oils. For several years, he had been shipping colonial produce to Genoa on American vessels or those flying under his own colours, but as the war dragged on, he became increasingly despondent about the political and economic future of Europe. When news reached Sicily of Napoleon's Spanish campaign, he gloomily wrote to Heath, 'Many people flatter themselves the present revolution in Spain, will shortly bring about their former System on the Continent & that our Communication may be open again. For my part I expect no tranquility in Europe under Bonaparte's Reign'.

Despite the US policy of non-intercourse, the seizure of American commercial vessels by the British and French continued. On 1 May 1810, Congress replaced the Non-Intercourse Act with Macon's Bill No 2, giving the President the power to ban trade with any nation unless the illegal seizure of neutral ships was halted. Congress hoped that by banning trade with both Great Britain and France, the illegal seizure of neutral ships would cease, to little effect. However, it did have a dramatic effect on Abraham's business and between 1 January and 15 November 1810, no American vessels landed their cargoes in Palermo.[33]

British money continued to flow into Sicily to pay for the Anglo-Sicilian forces and the subsidies to the Court. In that year, the value of British goods purchased in Sicily was £410,000.[34] The negative balance of payments created by the flood of British goods, paid for in onze and converted at the usual rate of '11/3d per ounce', resulted in ever-increasing profits for the small number of British merchant bankers, who became the principal holders of the Sicilian currency.[35] Some, like the Woodhouses provided loans to local wine growers to plant vineyards, but the majority looked to all areas of banking and credit to invest their profits. Despite this, there was a feeling amongst them that the Sicilian government's policy restricted their ability to take advantage of the increased demands of an occupying force and of the British Mediterranean fleet in the area. Many British merchants in both Palermo and Messina believed that, despite the protection afforded by the Anglo-Sicilian force on the island and the subsidy paid to the King, the Sicilian government was aggressively hostile to them, actively encouraging trade with the United States. Its refusal to abolish the 1 per cent tax on cash transactions and payments requiring a receipt, its condoning of the illegal capture of ships with British cargoes and its insistence on a fourteen-day quarantine period for all ships coming directly from Britain which was plague-free resulted in growing tension between the two governments. As late as 1810, British contemporary visitors to Sicily observed that 'Were we to grant our planters freedom of direct intercourse with Malta, our own territory, and, ...an adopted and unalienable part of our empire' we could because of 'the vicinity of that island to Sicily,...afford to furnish the Sicilians with colonial produce, on terms at least equal to those of the Americans, even if we did not take any steps to exclude the Americans from the Mediterranean'.[36]

Before that year, despite a number of petitions from merchants for fairer trading terms, Abraham continued to take advantage of the British government's refusal to enter into a commercial treaty with Sicily. In November 1809, Joseph Mellish, the British Chargé d'Affairs had written to Lord Canning at the Foreign Office. 'I cannot but feel if my duty to take the Liberty of urging to you the expediency of some commercial arrangements with Great Britain and this Country. The Present State of Commerce here is extremely disadvantageous....to our countrymen', but to no avail.[37] With the decline in American trade, Abraham pragmatically joined the merchants of Palermo and Messina in petitioning William Bentinck, the British Minister Plenipoteniary to the Court of Sicily about the policy of the Sicilian government towards them. They asked to be granted licences to export 'any articles of the produce or manufactures of the British dominions' to 'all the ports of the Kingdom of Naples' including those on the Italian mainland, and to import British goods into Sicily.[38]

Even though Abraham had been resident in Italy since 1787, having associated with many foreign merchants and having many Sicilian friends, he retained his British citizenship and his loyalty to Great Britain. After so many years in Italy, he spoke the language fluently, and despite his position as US Consul, continued to support his fellow Englishmen. In 1810, he joined other British merchants in Palermo to form a 'Commercial Society'. The group rented a house from the Duke of Angio 'for the purpose of meeting together to consult on their general interests when necessary, to receive commercial information as a body & for other inferior objects, & ordered English Newspapers, periodicals & commercial publications to be sent regularly to them'.[39] It appears that the members of this exclusive 'club' kept very much to themselves and rarely associated with their Sicilian counterparts, except through business. The 'Commercial Society' in Palermo, unlike those in other Italian cities, which were open to all and evolved into chambers of commerce, became an exclusive club for English merchants. Modern Sicilian research into the life of Abraham Gibbs has linked the evolution of the 'Commercial Society' with the development of the massonaria – freemasonry in Palermo in the early nineteenth century.[40]

CHAPTER 14

HUMILIATION AND DESPAIR

Preoccupied as he was with his business activities, Abraham was always anxious for news of Mary in England and was delighted that she was meeting her relatives, including her young cousins. Anxious that she should complete her education, he had written to Betsy in 1807, asking that Mary return to Emma's house in London, but as the gossip over his old friend's behaviour filtered through to Sicily he feared for his daughter's reputation. It was a relief when Antony asked if she could live with them at Dulwich and reported that Vicary and Kenny had offered to supervise her education. Abraham readily agreed, delighted that his cousin the Attorney General should take an interest in his daughter's education.

During the next year, he regularly received news from both Mary and Antony. Any antagonism that he may have felt over his cousin's long-standing debt was soon forgotten. As 1811 dawned, with the withdrawal of some British troops from Sicily to help the Portugese army in the Peninsula war, fears that Murat was planning to invade the island led to delay in the mail ships arriving. In February, Abraham received a letter from the Richards, written several weeks previously, suggesting that Mary should return to live with them in Devon. In the same packet was a letter from her beseeching him to let her stay with Antony and Dolly. Despite her pleas, now that Richards was his daughter's legally appointed guardian he had little choice but to agree.

Over the next few months, he received several letters from Mary pleading with him to let her return to her beloved Dolly. Betsy wrote too, complaining that her niece had become sullen and rebellious and they were finding it difficult to cope with her. The Richards thought it was time that Mary was married and Betsy had found a young man who would make a suitable husband. A few weeks later, Abraham was disturbed to receive a letter from his daughter telling him that the young man had proposed and that she had refused. As she was so desperate to leave Ilfracombe, Abraham was finally persuaded that the best course would be for her to go to Topsham to live with William and Susan who had children of her own age. It must have stirred up many happy memories to think that she would be living in the same street as he had as a child.

Within weeks, Mary was in trouble again. This time she had fallen in love with a young man who had proposed. Betsy, who approved of the match, wrote to Abraham for his consent. At the same time another letter arrived from William, opposing the match. Worried that his daughter might elope, Abraham refused permission and demanded that she return to Sicily immediately and asked William to accompany her on the voyage. Some weeks later, a letter arrived from Mary, threatening never to return to Palermo. After an exchange of heated letters, Abraham finally agreed that if she could go back to England if she continued to be unhappy.

When Mary and William arrived in Palermo in the spring of 1812, Abraham was overjoyed at seeing her again after so many years. She had grown from a little child into a very desirable seventeen-year-old young woman who quickly settled down, helped no doubt by the presence of her cousin William Henry and the large contingent of British officers on the island. William was overwhelmed by Abraham's wealth and status. To someone who had been dependent on the charity of his family for most of his life, his brother had everything – wealth, power and influence. With little thought of Susan or his children at home in Topsham, William moved into Abraham's villa on the Mezzo Monreale, and any thoughts of returning to his family were soon forgotten.

Despite any hopes that William may have had that William Henry and Mary may marry, Abraham had other ideas for his daughter. She, no doubt encouraged by her father, enjoyed her new-found freedom and the social whirl of the British community in Palermo. There were also plenty of young officers to pay court to an attractive young woman. As a contemporary writer commented, 'the general mode of living adopted by the majority of English…is above all, the worst calculated for their own improvement….this we daily observe in Sicily where a masquerade, drinking party or faro table, appear to possess more charms than all the fascinations of intellectual pleasure.'[1] The English community kept very much to itself and 'An insuperable spirit of party is generally brought from the mother country, and soon degenerates into scandal, calumny, and envy, its usual offspring' and that 'little could be said in favour of our mode of living' in Sicily.[2]

Although delighted that Mary was with him, Abraham continued working as before and, despite his declared intention to retire, appeared in no hurry to hand over the reins to his young nephew. Appearances aside, he was becoming very worried about his finances. Macon's Bill of 1810 had failed to stop the seizure of American ships by British and French privateers and trade with the US was banned. Initially he had been positive. In his dispatch of 31 January 1811, he had reported that although no American ships had landed any colonial produce for over two years, this 'was a fortunate Circumstance & has enabled the holders of Sugar, Coffee & Rum to dispose of part of their Goods on hand & renew their privileges on the arrivals of the Levant & Industry'.[3] The year before, Sicily had braced itself as rumours mounted that Murat, who had succeeded Joseph Bonaparte as King of Naples in 1808, was planning an invasion. 'The Threat of an invasion of this Island by the…Napolitan Government', Abraham wrote, 'has also facilitated last summer the Sale of a quantity of Jamaican/American property till then unsold, as some of our Merchants, speculated on the supposition of the success of an attack, of which we apprehend nothing for the present'.[4]

In the same dispatch, he included details of the fates of a number of American merchant vessels captured by both the British and French navies. While the custom of distributing prize money amongst the crews added to the zeal of the Navy, it seems that those captured by the British and brought to Palermo fared better that those taken by the French. 'The Schooner *Friendship* recaptured from the French Privateer and Ransomed here....lays here still....should it remain much longer in the same situation I shall proceed to the Sale of the Vessel & Cargo, for the benefit of whom it may Concern.' Another ship the *Nancy*, which had been 'detained by an English Brig of War' had been brought to Palermo, 'and released'. 'This deviation in her voyage', Abraham wrote, 'will I believe prove very fortunate, I hear that all American Vessels without any distinction are sequestered on their arrival at Naples'.[5]

During this period, licences were issued to neutral ships to convey goods between Sicily and Malta and into enemy territory. American vessels were granted licences if they were under 100 tons and unarmed, but despite having a licence they were still at risk. As a British citizen, Abraham had no difficulty in obtaining vessels to sail under his own colours. On 6 January 1811, he had written to Madison with the news that 'Two Schooners from that Port & which had been Sequestered and Sold there to Messrs Seaman & Kemble. American Citizens have been detained by H Bett's Frigate, *Alicante*; one beating in this Bay was stranded, the other was carried to Naples for her Trial, the issue of which is yet unknown to me; both vessels were detained upon some Suspicions relative to their destination & to the legality of the purchase by American Citizens of America. Both were sequestered in Naples but this last objection will avail of nothing, as both Schooners were provided with British licences valid for my Vessels not bearing the French Flag'.[6]

The following year everything changed for the worst. With the onset of the Anglo-American War of 1812, no US ships landed at the port of Palermo, resulting in an immediate slump in Abraham's profits. Fortunately, an outbreak of plague in Malta the following April proved to be a godsend. Trade with Malta was banned and strict quarantine restrictions were imposed in Palermo and the other ports in Sicily on all ships from there. Although all traces of plague had disappeared by mid-1814, the Bourbon Government, persuaded by the English merchants, refused to lift the 'Free Pratique', plunging Malta into a severe depression. In his dispatch to the foreign office, Maitland the British consul in Valetta wrote, 'I am sorry to say that I apprehend their conduct has not originated more from their own feelings than from the wish of the English Merchants there & particularly a Gentleman of the name of Gibbs, to throw every obstruction in our way here'.[7] In spite of the ban on imports, Abraham continued to export goods from Palermo to Malta and in 1814, the Anglo Maltese Bank remitted just under 7500 Maltese scudi (£625) to his account for which he earned the usual four per cent commission.[8]

Meanwhile the chronic financial difficulties of the Sicilian Government mounted annually and Abraham continued to negotiate large loans in the belief that they would be repaid or under-written by the British Government. The interest charged on loans at this time was rarely less than 7% and its reserves were becoming depleted.[9] Because of the fluctuating pound/onze exchange rate, the Sicilian Government claimed that it was also owed significant amounts in arrears dating back several years. In 1804, a pound had been worth fifty-six tari (one onze equalling 11/3d). Two years later, the tari reached its lowest level and the shortage of Sicilian currency reached crisis point.[10] In 1809, 'to extinguish all claims of arrears of the Subsidy of every denomination.... in order to obviate the difficulties which have been accrued in adjusting an equitable course of Exchange between London and Palermo' the British Government increased the annual subsidy to £400,000 to be paid monthly through Abraham Gibbs & Co.[11] However, this also caused Abraham some difficulties. For some months, he had been in the habit of paying the monthly subsidy out of his own resources and, because of the delay in being reimbursed by the Treasury, was finding it increasingly difficult to meet the demands of the Sicilian Court. In October 1811, he learned that the British Government had 'purchased of Messrs Barings & Co Spanish Dollars to the amount of 176490½ Ounces & of the Value / including freight and other Charges / of £54,168.4.10d', and he considered himself perfectly secure in advancing a further £33831 to the Sicilian Court, in anticipation that he would be speedily reimbursed. In the event, the shipment was delayed and had not arrived when the next payment was due. Knowing that he had insufficient funds, in November he refused to pay the subsidy, despite repeated requests from the Court.

Following complaints to the Foreign Office, Abraham was called to account by the Treasury and asked to explain his actions. Anxious to hide the truth about his financial difficulties, and still not having been reimbursed for the October payment, he wrote to Bentinck on 24 December that as the Marquis of Circello had authorised him 'to draw on Mr Baring for the monthly subsidy of October' he had advanced the sum in full from his own resources. Having heard of the 'the Shipment of 21,000 Dollars...[he] thought it reasonable that the Subsidy would not be suspended until the circumstances had been communicated to him officially'. He had refused the 'payment of the month of Nov' as at that time it occurred to him the Subsidies might be suspended', adding that the Marquis of Circello had informed him that 'a Warrant had been past [sic] for the payment of the Subsidies to all the Months of April next'.[12] Meanwhile, Abraham was desperate for money. With the delay in receiving the arrears from the Treasury, he was now under intense pressure from a number of his creditors including a George Burgman, who had lent him 33,000 onze to pay for a cargo of corn from Malta some months before. Burgman was urgently pressing for payment and threatening to report him to Bentinck for refusing to honour his promissory note. Abraham asked Burgman for more time explaining that 'My refusing you the 33,000 depends chiefly on the Senate & Govt paying me my advances to them as Lord Bentinck is well informed of'. He added, 'If you press the Senate for the payment of the balance of the corn from Malta, they will neglect me; at all Events if you think your wants will not admit of any longer indulgence I must continue to fulfill my engagement to his Lordship'.[13]

By 1812, the Sicilian government was almost exclusively maintained by Abraham and a small number of British merchants on the island.

Although the annual subsidy had been increased to £400,000 two years before, the *Piano degli Introiti ed Esiti*, (the budget) presented to Parliament for that year, estimated a deficit of over 777,000 onze.[14] The following February a further loan of 154,000 onze at 1% interest for one month was contracted with the treasury and, unable to raise the funds in Sicily, Abraham was forced to apply to two merchant banks in Malta and Messina. Despite his hopes of being reimbursed quickly, the Sicilian Government was in no position to repay either the loan or the interest on the agreed date, and asked for a further 86,500 onze. Three months later, on 23 May 1813, Bentinck agreed to another request from the Prince of Belmonte for an additional 30,000 onze, over and above the subsidy, to pay for the Sicilian military.[15]

The demands by the Sicilian Government led to real concerns in London over its solvency. In order to persuade local merchants to continue to provide loans at the agreed interest of 1% per month, an elaborate system of compensation was agreed which proved to be very successful. The Sicilian treasury granted duty credits to individual merchants, to be used as exemptions on future customs duties. Abraham, along with Woodhouse and Ingham, agreed to advance further substantial sums of money, which were guaranteed by duty credits.[16] There were also other calls on his finances. As US consul, he had to maintain his lifestyle and entertain his British counterparts and this, as Hamilton had found many years before, proved very costly. He was also Bentinck's personal banker and was expected to extend credit to him of several hundred pounds a month for all his general household expenses and to pay his 'black Servant 163 Dollars for all [his] Demands'.[17] Fortunately, after Bentinck's departure from Sicily, Abraham was charged with selling his coach horses and was eventually reimbursed in full.[18]

Not long after Mary's return, he began making plans to embark on a new venture in marine insurance. The first 'real' Italian insurance company dealing exclusively in marine insurance had been registered in Venice in 1681, seven years before Edward Lloyd set up Lloyd's of London in 1688. By the 1740s, a number of insurance companies had sprung up in Genoa and in 1751 the 'Real Marine Insurance Company' was established in Naples. In Sicily, insurance continued to be based on individual contracts and was underdeveloped compared with the rest of Italy.[19]

With the growth of Messina as a centre of commercial activity, several small insurance companies had sprung up there in the first decade of the nineteenth century, due mainly to the pressure of English merchants in the city and the development of trade with Malta. These included the *Friendly Insurance Society* (1808), the *Anglo-Sicilian Insurance Agency* (1812) and the *New Insurance Agency* (1812), due to the presence of two agents from Lloyds of London, John Cummings and George Wood who were based in the city.[20] In Palermo, although their main interest was banking and the provision of capital, English and Maltese merchants had long recognised the importance of insurance, and like Abraham had insured their cargoes in Messina.[21] Between 1807 and 1808, a number of marine insurance companies were established in Malta, and four years later, Abraham's former partner Edmund Noble was appointed the local agent there for Lloyds of London.[22]

A system of maritime loans, '*I prestiti a cambio marittimo*' had developed in Palermo, which was a precursor of insurance contracts. While traditional forms of insurance are based on the payment of a premium, maritime loans were agreed in advance to pay the cost of transporting the goods. This type of operation was successful because the agreed premium was calculated on a percentage of the value of the insured goods; the interest rate was related to the risk and the value of the cargo. This was assessed on the length of the journey, the military and political situation, and any other potential hazards that existed at the time including such things as piracy. There were several standard exclusions including theft, smuggling, and exchanging one cargo for another. If the cargo was lost, the lender lost his money; if it arrived safely at its destination, the lender made a significant profit.

Lenders of maritime loans were usually the wealthier and more successful merchants and wealthy entrepreneurs, who gambled on the safe arrival of cargoes to their destinations. They could either end in substantial profits or heavy losses, but were indispensable for those who did not have the resources to develop their businesses.[23] Abraham was the most active insurer in this period. In December 1809, he had advanced a little over 1,206 onze at 15% to a Captain Alessandro Clumes, a merchant mariner, for a trip from Palermo to London.[24] In another contract, an English merchant, Charles Crokat, charged a Swedish merchant mariner 35% interest on a 60onze loan for a passage from Palermo to Liverpool. The interest on cargoes carried on the less risky routes from Palermo to Trapani or Malta tended to be between 14-19%.[25]

With the two Lloyds agents John Cummings and George Wood based in Messina, many of the more successful British merchants had begun to insure with Lloyds. However, in June 1813, on instructions from London, Wood and Cummings arbitrarily changed the terms of marine insurance contracts. The Commercial Society was informed that in all future policies, only the damaged part of any cargo was to be assessed and sold. Its members were so incensed that they agreed to 'resist this Mode of Sale....and...appointed a Committee to correspond direct with Lloyds'.[26] This had little effect. A few months later, Lloyds insisted 'in appointing their own agents general Surveyor'. Before then, it was the Vice Consul's responsibility to assess damaged cargoes. The merchant community in Palermo opposed this change on the grounds that a loss adjuster should be independent, whereas the new 'Agent was one of the Party interested & by the Laws of England, no man can be Judge in his own Counsel' and asked for the old system to be reinstated.[27]

In response to Lloyds refusal to change its policy, the leading merchants in Palermo decided to establish their own insurance company to meet local need. Abraham and a trusted Sicilian associate Giovanni Bottone, who had also been providing insurance and maritime loans for some years, became the driving force in the establishment on 13 December 1813 of the *Prima Compagnia di Assicurazioni di Palermo*, the '*First Insurance Agency of Palermo*, dealing exclusively with maritime insurance.[28]

The *Prima Compagnia* had a capital base of 50,000 onze, divided into 100 shares. Gibbs, Melchiorre Tamajo and the Marchese Guiseppe D'Anna were major shareholders each investing 2500 onze for five shares; the others were all members of the nobility and the wealthy mercantile elite, including owners of many of the leading merchant houses on the island as well as Messina and Malta. They were a tightly knit group; the most important merchantile class in Sicily. Of the forty-nine share-holders, only six were English, Gibbs, Crokat, Samuel Prior, William James Turner, Patterson & Brown and George Wood; the majority being Maltese merchants and bankers, local Palermitians, and a number from Portugal, Naples and France.[29]

The *Prima Compagnia's* corporate charter contained twenty articles of association. The company's capital was only to be used to fund bills of exchange and insurance policies for merchant ships sailing out of the port of Palermo and no policy could exceed a total value of 3000 onze or 10% of the current capital base. Accounts were to be produced twice yearly and profits distributed every six months. If the company incurred large losses that drained it of half of its capital base, there was a provision in the charter for the shareholders to call an extra-ordinary meeting to decide by a majority vote whether to dissolve it. Two members were appointed to act as 'deputies' empowered to negotiate policies and act on behalf of all the members and at its first meeting, Abraham and a Palermite, Giuseppe Raffo were elected as the firm's first deputies. Giovanni Bottone was appointed as insurance agent to manage the day-to-day running of the business, and Melchiorre Tamajo was appointed as banker.[30]

The shareholders soon found just how risky marine insurance could be and, in its first two years, the *Prima Compagnia* suffered a number of large claims. In September 1814, it paid out 400 onze after the *Sciabecco* was shipwrecked, carrying a large cargo of grain from Manfredonia to Palermo, and the following year, 950 onze for two hundred barrels of salt, which were lost when the *La Carmlitana*, sunk on a voyage from Palermo to Malta.[31] Another claim that year was for 2700 onze for a mixed cargo, insured for Ignazio Florio, a Sicilian entrepreneur, which was lost on a voyage from Sicily to Trieste. Shipwreck was not the only hazard. Piracy was also a major problem at this time as Sicilian and Barbary Privateers continued to prey on merchant shipping. In November, the deputies agreed to pay 460 onze, for fifty bags of cocoa, which was captured at sea by 'corsaro tripolino' while being transported from Lisbon to Palermo.[32] Despite the excessive number of large claims and the sizeable losses incurred within such a short period, at the firm's annual meeting that year, a majority of shareholders voted not to dissolve the company.[33] Ultimately, the liquidation of the *Prima Compagnia* would be due to a much more dramatic event which was to shake not only the mercantile community in Sicily, but also the banking and insurance world.

* * * *

Meanwhile, William and his son William Henry continued to live with Abraham and Mary in their villa in Palermo. Within months, it was obvious that William Henry and Mary were growing very fond of one another but when he proposed in 1814, he was to be disappointed. Mary unexpectedly refused his offer, a decision supported by her father. Perhaps Abraham, aware of his deteriotating finances wanted a more secure future for his daughter that did not include a penniless nephew and his family. As Lyle caustically commented some years later, 'What a hodge-podge it all was', with his brother and nephew living with Abraham in 'abject dependence', William Henry openly 'cohabited with Mary in her Father's house…during her childhood & yet he had the effrontery of demanding her in marriage? Which she of course distainfully declined'.

The rejected William Henry returned to the Naples office. Within months, he became a local hero. Following his attempt to reconquer Italy, Murat had moved north and declared war on Austria, while British forces, under Bentinck's command advanced on the city. Bentinck planned to take Naples from the south, while the British fleet, anchored offshore threatened to bombard it unless it surrendered. In an act of great courage, which was long remembered by the Neopolitans and British alike, William Henry, accompanied by Lord Frederick Montague, boarded *The Tremendous* and pleaded with Captain Campbell, the Commander of the squadron not to distroy the city. After some negotiation, Caroline, the Queen Regent and Murat's wife, surrendered the Neopolitan navy to the English to save her beloved Naples from destruction. Arriving back there after his defeat at the Battle of Tolentino, Murat found the city in revolt against him and on 19 May fled to France leaving Caroline under the protection of the British.[34] Over forty years later this incident was remembered by an Italian countess, who as a young English woman had been living in Naples with her mother Lady Byford, and her elder sister who later became Lady Langdale. In a letter to William Henry's brother Charles, the Countess recalled the event and hoped that it had been recorded 'in the annals of a great family – for your brother William [Henry] could never have been forgetful of that interesting episode in his life – saving the beautiful city of Naples and its numerous inhabitants from all the horrors of bombardment'.

Meanwhile in Palermo, William was dismayed at Mary's rejection of his son's proposal, having had such high hopes that the two cousins would marry. Now fifty-nine, it is unclear whether Abraham found him any employment or whether he just decided to remain there, and he appears to have abandoned his family and was now completely dependent on his brother's generosity. By the beginning of 1815, the most important thing on Abraham's mind was to get his daughter married. With her cousin now on the Italian mainland, Mary, encouraged by her father, was soon attracted to the dashing Lieutenant Colonel Charles a' Court, the third son of Sir William Pierce Ashe a'Court, whose elder brother, another William, was the minister at the Court of Naples, having replaced Bentinck. With such family connections, he was a far better match than her cousin. When he proposed a few months later Mary, flattered by his attention, happily accepted. For Charles, marriage to the pretty daughter of one of the richest men in Italy was a real catch and her dowry a great boost to his income. For his part in the marriage contract, Abraham agreed to give them £500 on their marriage and to put £30,000 in trust for Mary, which would provide an annual income of around £1500, which she would continue to receive after his death. Notice of their marriage appeared in the *Gentleman's Magazine*. It reported that on 10 May 1815 'at the house of the British Minister in Palermo, Lieut-col a'Court, Adj.-gen. to the British Forces in the Mediterranean' was married to 'Mary, only daughter of Abraham Gibbs esq.'[35] It seems that on her marriage Anna Maria Gibbs ceased to exist. Now officially recognised as Douglas's heir, she formally assumed her mother's Christian names, Mary Elizabeth Catherine. After their marriage she and Charles moved to Naples and later that summer, Abraham was delighted to learn that she was expecting a baby in the spring.

* * * *

After Napoleon's defeat in the spring of 1814, and the fall of Murat the following year, the British began withdrawing its troops from Sicily. On 24 December, Britain and the United States signed the Treaty of Ghent, signaling the end to hostilities. Within weeks, much to Abraham's relief, American vessels began arriving at Palermo with cargoes of colonial produce.[36] This enabled him to resume his trading efforts and he began to ship cargoes of Sicilian wine to his former contacts on the eastern seaboard. Despite the efforts of Benjamin Ingham, an Englishman who, in 1806, had established a *baglio* only a mile from the Woodhouse *baglio* in Masala, Abraham Gibbs & Co continued to ship the Woodhouse wine to the United States, Malta and Britain. In May 1815, Ferdinand left Palermo for Naples with his Court. The Anglo-Sicilian force was disbanded and British military continued their withdrawal from the island.

The departure of the British forces plunged Sicily into a severe economic depression. Ingham, writing to the British consul at Messina in June remarked, 'If you were to return to Palermo, you would be astonished. Never place was so much changed in so short a time. [...]

There is no trade in the shops as they sell nothing'.[37] This, combined with a number of other factors including the dislocation of trade due to the prolonged wars, and the pressures caused by the failure of the Sicilian Government to repay its wartime loans, caused Abraham severe financial difficulties. In December 1814, he wrote to Bentinck, 'The Sicilian Parliament is quite a farce, nothing good can be expected from the Barons. They have voted to pay their debts, but the ways & means of raising the money, is not a question'.[38] Within months of the restoration, the increasing government red tape and trading problems in the immediate post-war period resulted in several business failures, including some well-established firms. After the Great Powers Settlement in 1815, a number of British merchants decided to return to England but Abraham along with Woodhouse and Ingham remained. As American trade had been virtually non-existent for three years Abraham was only too well aware that unless things improved he could not meet the promised £30,000 for Mary's marriage settlement. Although earning a sizeable commission as banker to the British Government, the demands of the Sicilians had seriously depleted his reserves. In the face of his mounting financial problems, as 1816 dawned, Abraham still had high hopes of re-couping his losses. A number of American merchants arrived and were establishing businesses on the island, and he was confident both in future trade with the Americas and in the Woodhouse wine. The 1815 vintage proved to be one of the best in the vineyard's history and to celebrate Waterloo, Woodhouse set aside one *solero*, which he kept for distinguished visitors.[39]

The following January, Abraham, then aged fifty-eight, decided to make his nephew William Henry a partner of the Naples house, intending that he would take over the business when he retired. Mary's baby was due in March and Abraham was looking forward to being a grandfather. Although now on the verge of bankruptcy, he strove to maintain appearances. As banker to the Court of Naples since 1799, he had served King Ferdinand and the British Government loyally, and as US Consul, he enjoyed the status that went with such a position and continued to entertain lavishly at his consular residence. A trusted member of the banking community, he was able to obtain credit to maintain this lifestyle.

All was about to change. That same month, Abraham resumed sending dispatches to Washington on the arrival and departures of American vessels in the port of Palermo. Unknown to him, with the end of hostilities the US Government began to review its consular activity in the Mediterranean. It was several weeks before the news reached Palermo that he was to be replaced as consul. It was a cruel blow to both to his pride and his future hopes. With the island in the depths of an economic recession, without the commission from the American trade, he knew he was finished. Just as he felt things could not get worse, news reached him from Naples that on 12 March, Mary had given birth to twin girls. It had been a long and difficult labour and although she recovered from the birth, neither baby survived, both dying within forty-eight hours, having been hurredly christened Laetitia and Anna Maria.[40] Despite his own problems, uppermost in his mind at this moment was his grieving daughter. The following month, all his sources of credit dried up, and he knew he was ruined.

The spreading news of Abraham's bankruptcy shocked the business community throughout Italy and reverberated throughout the banking circles in London, America and Europe. How this could happen to a man who appeared to have such immense wealth? Benjamin Ingham, having long resented Abraham's preference for the Woodhouse wine gleefully estimated that 'Old John [Woodhouse] will lose near 10,000 onze by Gibbs failure, as scarcely anything will ever be paid'.[41] With Gibbs' compting house closed, the 'Tribunal of Commerce' confiscated his papers and records while they launched an investigation into his affairs. Rumours spread rapidly that someone had been embezzling money from the business for several years and suspicion fell on Gioacchino Lenzitti, who was arrested and imprisoned in the 'Casa di Correzione' in Palermo.[42]

Knowing it could be months before the Tribunal would be able to untangle his affairs Abraham retired with William to his house on the

Mezzo Monreale. On 5 July, he received two letters from creditors demanding immediate payment on overdue contracts. One was from his friend Guiseppe Ruffo for 400 onze, the other from Ingham for 300 onze.[43] On the face of it, these relatively small demands should not have concerned him but now they proved to be the final straw. Knowing that he had shamed his beloved Mary's, the disgrace and the humiliation proved too much for him. The following morning, after finishing a game of backgammon with William, Abraham suddenly walked out of the room and went to his office. A few minutes later, he shot himself with a single bullet. On his desk, he had left a suicide note that read:

> 'I have been too indulgent to those, who have been
> ungrateful to me – and the real state of my Affairs,
> I have not been able to discover 'till now, from the
> multiplicity thereof – I was in hopes of regaining my
> losses; I cannot pardon myself, nor do I find myself
> able to remain another moment in existence'.[44]

As news of Abraham's death spread throughout the world, no one could believe that he had taken his own life. Within three weeks, it was estimated that the financial abyss created by the tragedy was in the region of two million Spanish piasters *(pezzi duri)*, about 800,000 onze, or £450,000 (around £18 million today), of which about a quarter was owed to him by the government, although by which government, British or Sicilian is unclear.[45]

Following his uncle's death, William Henry hurried from Naples and John Ley arrived from Genoa to help sort out Abraham's affairs. John Ley had always distrusted Lenzitti. He doubted the Sicilian's motives and was suspicious when he offered to cooperate fully with any investigation and to look into Abraham's records to see if he could find anything that might shed light on his financial problems. William, shocked by his brother's death and now with no other means of financial support, had little option but to seek a passage to England

and return to his family in Topsham. The following month, William Henry went back to Naples, hoping to save the business there. Writing to his cousin Henry in London, he reported that for several months he had been 'in daily expectation of his [Abraham's] arrival here [to Naples] having faithfully promised to pay me a visit...and arrange the Capital, he promised to give me' for the new business. Despite his own efforts and help from some influential friends, he was unable to save the Naples firm and it too was liquidated to pay off the creditors in Palermo. Now unemployed, William Henry had no alternative but to accept an offer to join his uncle Lyle in Genoa where John Ley was employed.

It was to take more than a year before the true extent of Abraham's debts were known. Many of his creditors were his friends and fellow members of the *Prima Compagnia*, the Commercial Society' and the local lodge. After his death, the remaining shareholders of the *Prima Compagnia* called an extra-ordinary meeting to decide on the future of the company. Between 1813 and 1815, its losses had amounted to around 70% of its capital base and Abraham's death gave them the opportunity to cut their losses and they voted unanimously to dissolve the company.[46] It was agreed that the single shareholders, those who had invested only one 'carat', should receive preferential payout terms, as they were unable to stand the loss, whereas the larger investors could. It is not known exactly when the *Prima Compagnia* was officially dissolved, but by the end of August, all the single shareholders had received their initial capital in full and, by the end of September, the remainder had recouped a proportion of their investment.[47] In the true spirit of the *Brotherhood*, they came to an amicable agreement – an '*amichevole accordio*', on a fair and final settlement for all.

In December 1816, the notice of Abraham's death appeared in the *Gentleman's Magazine*. Making no mention of his suicide it merely read, '*Suddenly*, Mr. Gibbs, merchant of Palermo, late paymaster to the British troops. He was related to Lord Chief Justice Gibbs'. His death was a great shock to all the family in England. Although they had little contact with him for so many years, they had long admired his success and were saddened by the '...melancholy end to Poor Abraham Gibbs greatness...'. He had become so well known throughout Italy that he '...could have bought all Sicily on credit if he had wished it.... so little is known of Peoples real circumstances...'.

CHAPTER 15

SCANDAL

As the weeks went by, other details of Abraham's dealings slowly emerged, shedding light on his bankruptcy and suicide. There was also widespread gossip and speculation about whom he had referred to in his suicide note. Anxious to allay suspicion that he had anything to do with his former partner's ruin, Lenzitti issued a statement from his prison cell, which read, 'Following the tragic accident to my partner, anything that is discovered about Abraham Gibbs must be dealt with by the Supreme Magistrate of Commerce so that the correct action can be taken'.[1] The Commercial Tribunal then issued a further statement that they believed Lenzitti was in no way responsible for Gibbs' bankruptcy and had provided all the information needed to help it recover the debts.[2] He was freed immediately to work with the auditors to unravel Abraham's financial affairs. This was greeted by cynicism and disbelief by both Sicilians and foreigners alike; everyone knew the reputation of the Tribunal for corruption and bribery.

Amongst the papers found in Abraham's compting house were a number of bills and receipts indicating that Gervais Vankempen, one of the pro-Consuls attached to the British embassy in Palermo owed him large sums of money. They included a list of 22 debts totalling 26,590 onze and another 21 promissary notes for 22,489 onze, some dating back to 1812, making a total of over 49,000 onze (around £30,000). With the bills was a note written in Abraham's hand that read 'La mia rovina per la mia condiscendenza e fiducia in lui' – 'My ruin is due to my trust in him'.[3]

Vankempen and Abraham had known each other since their early days in Naples. Of Dutch origin, Vankempen had previously been an officer in the French Navy. At the start of the war, he had been living in Naples, where he had first met Gibbs. A royalist, he joined the exodus in 1798, to 'set up a store both in Palermo and Naples'. In 1803, whilst in Malta, Vankempen wrote to Nelson for a 'recommendation for some employ' and at the Admiral's suggestion was sent to Palermo where he 'could assist the Commissary'.[4] Like Abraham, he was a regular guest at the Hamiltons' soirees in the Palazzo Palagonia.

From 1805, Vankempen had been employed as the pro-Consul responsible for the payment of pensions to French and Corsican refugees. For this he received a fixed sum from the Treasury, usually paid in arrears through Abraham Gibbs & Co. On receipt of the money, he was required to sign an affidavit that he had received 'the amount of two thousand pounds Sterling, being due to the French & Corsican Emigrants for the Sum which I hold my Self Constable, & for whom the regular Vouchers & Receipts will be furnished at the usual time.'[5] Any additional sums required were drawn on Abraham Gibbs & Co. Vankempen was obliged to keep a record of all his expenditure, which was submitted at the end of each financial year and Abraham was re-imbursed when the accounts were audited. In 1805, the Treasury had found a minor discrepancy in his annual return and had refused to repay Abraham for the months of April and May of that year. Although the Treasury increased the amount allowed to Vankempen to pay for the increasing numbers of refugees, with the fluctuating exchange rate it rarely kept up with inflation. His total outgoings for 1808-9 alone amounted to over £150,000, paid through Abraham Gibbs & Co, but Abraham was not repaid until July 1810, fifteen months later.[6] Vankempen also needed money on his own account and by 1814 had borrowed a further 49000 onze from Abraham who lent him money from the subsidy, expecting to be repaid at the end of the war. However, in 1814, Vankempen died suddenly and his personal debts remained unpaid.

With the British withdrawal from Sicily and Vankempen dead,

Abraham knew that with the vouchers still unsigned the Treasury would discover his actions and refuse to reimburse him. By the beginning of 1816, with his funds now depleted and the delay by both the Sicilian and British Governments in repaying their wartime loans, he was in despair. He knew he could not honour the £30,000 bond promised to Mary on her marriage and that she would be ruined. He was unaware that in June 1816, a month before his death, that 'The Neopolitan Government had already paid the Sums which it was bound to pay....to the Treaty'.[7] It was a combination of all these factors and the shame of bankruptcy that caused Abraham Gibbs to end his life so unexpectedly on 6 July 1816.

William Henry worked with the Tribunal to try to save the Naples firm, arguing that since January it had operated as separate business and was still solvent. As the weeks went by a large number of creditors came forward hoping to salvage something from the chaos. Among thems was Mary's husband, Charles a'Court. Leaving Mary in Naples, he arrived in Palermo in September and put in a 'prefential' claim for £30,000 for his wife's dowry, which William Henry refused to consider before the other creditors were paid. Furious at his intransigence, a'Court insisted on an immediate separation from Mary until the matter was settled. The following month Mary, ill with shock at the double tragedy of losing her twins and her father, left Naples with John Ley to stay with her uncle Lyle in Genoa. William Henry wrote of her, 'Mrs Chaa'C is much to be pitied, her husband has latterly behaved in the most brutal and indelicate manner to her – I always considered it an unfortunate...match....poor girl I am at a loss to know what will become of her, the Colonel has already insisted on a separation'. John Ley too was also very worried about his cousin. 'God Knows how they [she and Charles] will continue to live for the Col. has no fortune & now her father can do nothing for him & Mary's West Indies Property on which he has always depended now brings scarcely £100 a year'.

Charles argued that his claim should be considered above all others. The fact that his elder brother, Sir William a'Court, was the British

Minister in Naples caused some disquiet among the other creditors. They suspected that Charles was taking advantage of his brother's position to influence the Sicilian court to secure a 'preference on the estate', and fearing that they would get nothing, threatened to sue Lyle in Genoa for the balance. A major scandal immediately broke and it soon became obvious that it was going to take several months, perhaps even years, to settle Abraham's affairs. During this time, Mary remained in Genoa.

The following month, William Porter, the newly appointed US consul arrived in Palermo to take up his post, to find that the Tribunal of Commerce had impounded the consulate books, which had been kept in Abraham's compting house. Because of the impact that Gibbs's bankruptcy and death was likely to have on American trade he reported to Washington that 'Having been since appointed by this Government as acting Consul, I have interfered on the part of the American Creditors, 'till such time as they can authorize their respective Agents to act for them.'[8]

While the auditors made arrangements for the sale of Abraham's furniture and other assets, the Commercial Tribunal continued to examine all aspects of his business. However, another scandal was about to erupt – this time over the management of the Duchy at Bronte.

When news reached London of Abraham's death, the Earl Nelson asked Bryant Barrett to go to Sicily to look into the running of the estate. For several years the Earl had been concerned that he had not been receiving the anticipated income from the Duchy, unaware that this was due in part to adverse exchange rates and the post-war depression. In January 1816, he had written to Abraham asking that 'his future Accounts and Papers be accompanied by an English Translation' so that he could examine them in greater detail.[9] The letter, which took six weeks to arrive, would certainly have prompted Abraham to take a closer look into the affairs at Bronte.

Arriving in Naples in January 1817, Barrett called in to see Falconnet, Abraham's former partner, who gave him an account of the happenings in Palermo and of Charles a'Court's 'preferential' claim on the Gibbs' estate. When Barrett arrived at Bronte the following month he found 'everything in delapidation but recoverable'. On examination of the accounts he soon realised that Graefer, Biosa and Forcella had been defrauding Nelson for many years and had made a fortune leasing lands and farms and profiting from the sale of grain. Biosa, knowing Barrett would immediately instigate legal proceedings against him, offered to make a full confession if he was given protection from prosecution. He claimed that he had only acted on Forcella's instructions and that he had received 'verbal Instructions from both Forcella and Gibbs to let Mrs Grefer [sic] have all she required and to do what she desired in the management of the Duchy'.[10] Forcella in turn laid all the blame on Biosa and Abraham. Barrett spent several days looking at Forcella's accounts and found that although they were 'most volumousily [sic] kept' with every payment 'vouched by a Notary' there were a number of discrepancies.[11] They indicated that between 1806 and 1816, he had sent Abraham a little over 41080 onze but only 38326 onze had been converted to sterling and remitted to Nelson's bankers in London leaving a discrepancy of 2754 onze. Forcella then claimed that he had in fact sent Abraham 44095 onzes making the difference 3015 onze. Further examination revealed that another 4098 onze, for the year 1814-15, could not been accounted for.[12] Amid speculation that Abraham had been embezzling funds from the Duchy to prop up his ailing business, the Earl was determined to recover it from Lenzitti whom he considered was now responsible for repaying his former partner's debts.[13] In February, a second scandal broke out when Barrett received a claim from a Mr. D'Angelo that Abraham, using his authority as Nelson's agent, had taken out a 3000 onze loan in the Earl's name. D'Angelo was now demanding the money back from Nelson.

At the end of March, Abraham's furniture and assets were auctioned and the following month the auditors issued an interim report. They had found his books in complete disarray and it appeared that the firm had not made a profit for several years. They showed that in 1803, Abraham had established a second trading company, completely separate from Abraham Gibbs & Co and had been speculating on his own account for many years. He had kept 'no books of his separate dealings' and, in an attempt to produce closing balances, his clerk (William Henry) had transferred monies from one account to the other. To produce an accurate figure of Abraham's debts the auditors had to transfer some 260,000 onze from his personal account to that of the firm, raising questions about William Henry's understanding of double-entry bookkeeping. It also emerged that, unknown to Lenzitti who was based in Salerno, Abraham had 'for some years back been in the habit of taking up large sums at the heavy interest of 1½ to 2% per month...to enable him to go on....to support his life....almost to the last day of his existence'. With the sale of his furniture and effects, his assets were 75910 onze or around £42,700 whereas his total losses were in the region of 220,000 onze or £124,000 (just under £5m in today's money) and these sums clearly dwarfed the amounts owed to him by Vankempen.

In June, Lenzitti, having no wish to be involved in a lengthy lawsuit or risk returning to prison, reluctantly accepted responsibility for Abraham's debts and proposed a compromise to a'Court and Barrett. He offered to pay 1600 onze to 'a'Court, a further 23 per cent of Abraham's debts to the creditors of his 'separate estate' and another 30 per cent to the creditors of Abraham Gibbs & Co 'without going to Law'. Although a'Court turned down Lenzitti's offer, Barrett advised the Earl to accept it as it might be the best he would achieve. But Nelson, bitter that he had been 'much injured by mismanagement...having been kept in complete darkness by Gibbs & others' over his affairs at Bronte, disagreed, confident he could do better.[14] In September, Lenzitti revised his proposal and offered to pay '14 per C [sic] down and another 14 pc by installments within 10 years'. This too was rejected.[15] It was then that the missing 4098 onze that Forcella claimed he had given to Abraham for 1815 suddenly turned up. The purchaser of one of Abraham's tables at the auction found a packet addressed to Nelson at the back of a drawer. He sent it to Charles a'Court who sent it on to Forcella who refused to accept it. Eventually it was given to Barrett. It seemed that Abraham had planned to send it to Nelson but it had been mislaid amongst his papers and then forgotten. This was evidence enough for Barrett that Abraham was innocent of all accusations of embezzlement and only left the 3015 onze that Forcella claimed he had given Abraham a few weeks before his death in May 1816 unaccounted for.[16]

It was when Barrett discovered that D'Angelo was the notary used by Forcella to audit his accounts, that he suspected that his claim too was a complete fabrication. Barrett distrusted Forcella, suspecting that he was using Abraham's death to divert attention from himself, and was convinced that he was 'not an honest man amongst the Servants of the Duchy'. Once he knew that Forcella and D'Angelo were linked, Barrett was certain that they were conspiring to shift the blame for their activities at Bronte to Abraham. In July, he wrote to Nelson that he believed D'Angelo's claim to 'be either a forgery or a fraud…Gibbs had no reason to take up money on Your Grace's behalf unless it could be made clear that it was actually laid out for the future benefit of the Estate'. Although Barrett had only been in Palermo a few months, he had quickly learned that 'nothing can be done in Sicily but by Bribing Judges', adding 'I expect you soon will be sued for it.…I would rather give 1000 oz to pay the Judges than 3000 to pay such a claim', but nothing could be done until D'Angelo's claim was brought before the Tribunal.[17] Biosa too was still trying to implicate Abraham in the conspiracy, insisting that he had always favoured Mrs Graefer. 'This I believe to a certain point', Barrett wrote, for 'her partner pretends that what he did in her regard was from a compliance with Gibbs inclination', but he believed that 'Gibbs was wholly ignorant of Biosa's frauds and of hers'.[18] He also expressed concern that if a'Court's 'demands for the dowry of his wife' were accepted by the auditors then the remaining creditors would get nothing, but if it was set aside then most of them would get about one third of what they were owed. Following the auditors report there was now positive proof that Abraham was insolvent 'at the time of making this contract [Mary's £30,000 marriage settlement], not only from his books but from his private records'.

As the months dragged on, Earl Nelson was becoming increasingly impatient at the lack of progress in Sicily. Despite this, Barrett was determined that the suit against Biosa, whom he considered 'a most abominable rogue & thief', should proceed as quickly as possible. By August, he had secured a full confession from him, but as both he and Forcella continued to implicate Gibbs in their conspiracy, in December the case against them both was postponed indefinitely until a further search could be made for any evidence. The following month, in a letter dated 14 January 1818, Nelson's lawyer wrote to Barrett telling him that the Earl had met Sir Willliam a'Court in London and that they had discussed the 'Gibbs affairs'. Sir William had told him that Charles, who was now on his way back to England with Mary, was so frustrated with the delays in accepting his claim 'and after various attempts had found he was likely to be involved in useless Law Suits in Sicily and consequently great expense',[19] was now resigned 'to take what he could get'. The Earl decided that Barrett 'had better do the same and accept any Composition [compensation] you can obtain to avoid the like trouble and expense'. By the time his instructions arrived in Palermo some weeks later, Barrett had died. Following her husband's death, Nelson agreed that Mrs Barrett could take over the management of the estate and he appointed Joseph di Martino as the Duchy's secretary.

Di Martino immediately set to work to try to sort out the claims and counter claims surrounding Abraham's activities. He considered that even if D'Angelo's claim for 3000 onze ever reached court Abraham, as Nelson's agent, did not have the authority to borrow money 'by way of a loan', and therefore he had no claim on the Duchy.[20] The suit against Lenzitti had also been delayed. It had emerged that to avoid 'payment of the sums he owes the Duchy', he had 'falsified his accounts in such manner that he makes himself a creditor instead of a debtor & for that reason the examination of such affair is unsettled'.[21] Lenzitti claimed that the outstanding 3015 onze had been deducted by Abraham as an additional 'Commission on receiving and remitting Rents', and for paying '100 onze a year to a clerk....for keeping the accounts in his office'. The Earl was furious, believing that all the expenses for 'attending the remittances were previously charged & deducted before anything was remitted to me'; he was determined to be repaid.[22] In September, he wrote to Di Martino that he had learned that Charles a'Court, believing that very little could 'be done by him in opposition to the general body of creditors had' undertaken to arrange all matters for himself and them' and had settled on £10,000, about twenty-four percent of his original claim. Nelson, who had recently received a letter from Lenzitti offering to 'transact any affairs for me in his line of business', was worried that if he had been involved in any agreement signed by Barrett before his death, he would be 'precluded from my claims further'.[23]

It was to take several years before Abraham's affairs were finally settled and nearly twenty years before the Earl recovered the sums embezzled by Forcella and Biosa. The fallout from their activities, amid claims and counter claims over leases and rents, dragged on indefinitely. Although nothing was ever proved against Abraham, both D'Angelo and Forcella went to their graves protesting their innocence and claiming that he had used his authority as power of attorney to appropriate 3000 onze in Earl Nelson's name to bolster his failing business and this was to cast a shadow over Mary and Charles for much of their marriage.

CHAPTER 16

LYLE

Lyle, Captain John's fifth son, was also a successful merchant in Italy. He had been apprenticed to the Genoese office of a French firm in 1778 under the care of John Heath who was employed there. Heath was the fourth son of George Abraham's old friend Benjamin Heath who had been Town Clerk of Exeter from 1752 until his death in 1766 and who was from a dissenting family of fullers and merchants with strong links with Genoa.[1] In 1764 John, then aged fifteen had been apprenticed there to Doxat & Ubert. He completed his apprenticeship in 1769, and five years later became a partner in the firm Robert Aubert & Co. Heath was 'a careful and accurate man of business'[2], eventually establishing his own firm, Heath & Co in 1789.

Genoa or to give it its full title the Most Serene Republic of Genoa, had originally come into existence in the twelfth century, becoming an important trading city second only to Venice. By the late eighteenth century, the republic was in a slow decline, and in 1768 had been forced to sell Corsica to the French. There were very few British merchants in Genoa. They preferred Leghorn (Livorno) believing the bay of Genoa unsafe in bad weather, and despite repeated requests the Genoese government refused to allow them to use Spetzia or another safe haven fearing it would reduce the city's influence in the Republic.[3] Another factor that deterred British merchants from settling there was the influence of the church and Catholic nobility who controlled all aspects of trade. Suspicious of foreigners, the church required anyone arriving in Genoa from abroad to obtain a pass from the 'foreign office', even if they were planning to stay only for a few days, and if they failed to do so, they were fined '300 corone'.[4] They regarded all non-catholics as heretics and refused to do business with them, in contrast to Leghorn (Livorno) where Protestants were accepted and had their own church and cemetery, and foreigners were welcome to establish businesses and take an active role in the city.

By the beginning of the eighteenth century, there were more than fifteen British firms in Leghorn forming a strong '*Fattoria inglese*'.[5] In Genoa, there was none. Fifty years later, there was a well-established French Hugenot community there with over twenty-four French-owned businesses and, although there were now a considerable number of agents acting for British firms, only six had offices there. The need for a British consul to promote trade with Great Britain had been recognised as early as 1616, but it was not until the beginning of the eighteenth century, the British Government agreed that its merchants could appoint one of their own to look after their interests. As there were so few English merchants in Genoa, the election of consul proved to be very much a family affair, with uncles, nephews and brothers all serving their terms. It was not long before these self appointed consuls believed themselves more important than the British ambassador. Amid accusations of corruption, they were despised by the Genoese who considered that they only acted in self-interest. By 1790, the Genoese refused to acknowledge the consuls' authority unless they had been issued with official credentials.

In the early 1770s, Heath's younger brother Charles, who had 'not much strength of character' and who had been in trouble in England was sent to Genoa to his brother John. He seems to have settled and in 1775, he joined the firm which was renamed Heath & Co six years later, with John as the senior partner. After completing his apprenticeship, Lyle also remained in Genoa, but in the early days longed to return to England. He missed his family, in particular his uncle, George Abraham and '...old aunt Gibbs' and his cousins, especially Bell with whom he seems to have entertained hopes of marriage. Many years later he wrote that '...in her younger days [she] pleased me very much and I had a particular regard for Bell....It would not be prudent to say anything more....'. Despite his intentions, as the years went by Lyle appears to have been resigned to being a confirmed bachelor, remaining in Italy which he had grown to love and called his 'little Blessed Island...'.

Lyle always longed for news of his family. He was in regular contact with Abraham who was living in Naples and was delighted when he married Mary Douglas in 1787. He was also pleased to learn, three years later that his elder brother William, who was employed by his cousin's firm, Munckley Gibbs & Richards, was to bring his new wife Susan to Genoa. Susan and Lyle quickly became firm friends, and he was overjoyed when, the following year, their first son William Henry was born at his house and baptised in the chapel in the British consulate. Susan continued to accompany William on his voyages with their young child and two years later, another son called John Ley was born in Genoa. That year, Lyle learned that Abraham too had become a father and after Anna Maria's birth the three brothers were reunited. Over the next year few years, Susan and the children spent a considerable amount of time with Lyle while William was sailing around the Mediterranean. He was devoted to his sister-in-law and young nephews, as they became the family he did not have.

By the latter half of the eighteenth century, trade between Britain and Genoa increased significantly as more and more ships began to make a stop there, en route to Algeria and Turkey or the rest of Europe. Imports included salt fish from Yarmouth and Falmouth, and large consignments of wheat from London. Genoa's chief exports had been damasks and velvets, but after the British government had banned them, its main exports were raisins and oil, pasta, cheese, playing cards and hand-made silk flowers.[6]

In 1794, John Heath offered Lyle a partnership in the firm. Although he had always planned to return to Exeter, the offer of was too good an opportunity and he decided to stay in Genoa for the forseeable future. However, with the onset of hostilities with France, things were about to change. As it became apparent that war was inevitable, Nelson, now Colonel of Marines, arrived in the summer of 1794 as commander of a Royal Navy squadron in the Gulf of Genoa. His mission was to establish a base for the British fleet from where it could harass the French on their expected campaign through Italy to Rome and Naples. Nelson was fêted throughout the city, which he thought 'most magnificent I ever beheld, superior in many respects to Naples; although it does not appear quite so fine from the sea, yet on shore it is far beyond it'.[7] Upon his arrival, he was concerned to hear from Francis Drake, the British Consul that the city was full of 'French Commissioners' who had brought with them a 'large quantity of diamonds and jewels belonging to the late King & Queen of France to mortgage to buy provisions for the French army'.[8] Although Genoa claimed neutrality, its ports were swarming with French privateers, who at night attacked and boarded neutral vessels, returning into the mole for protection in daylight. Nelson was charged with putting a stop to all trade between Genoa, France and French occupied territory. Once he had established Genoa as his base, he sent the *Agamemnon* to Leghorn for a refit before joining the British fleet off Toulon. Six months later any illusion of Genoese neutrality disappeared following the defeat of the Austrians under General de Vins and the occupation of the coast from Savona to Voltri by the French. Much to the delight of the British in Leghorn, Nelson resumed his station in the Gulf of Genoa. In the summer of 1796, Napoleon embarked on his Italian campaign and, in open contempt of the allies, advanced on Leghorn. On 27 June, Nelson evacuated the city before blockading the port.

Although he had tried to avoid offending the Genoese government, criticism against Nelson increased after the confiscation of a cargo of wheat from a Genoese vessel. In retaliation, the Genoese sequestered a number of British transport ships, including the *Queen of Naples*, which was detained for several months with a cargo of British goods valued at over £50,000. In July 1797, Lyle along with the other English merchants in the city petitioned both governments over the 'Sequestration of Several British Vessels' and the effect it would have on trade, but with little success. Referring to Nelson's actions, the British Government made it clear that in time of war nothing was more important 'to Trade and manufacturers of this Country as the establishing a Naval Superiority in the Mediterranean'. While the ports of Genoa and Leghorn were kept open, 'large quantities of British manufactures would be carried into France, & the Fish trade with Newfoundland would revive if the Burdens which War must necessarily occasion' were 'chearfully [sic] supported'.[9] As Nelson's popularity waned, he was forced to complain that he was 'very much surprised that, whenever he approaches any Town belonging to the Genoese government, they fire a shot at him'.[10] Later that year Napoleon's army occupied Genoa and created the Ligurian Republic, establishing a government there similar to that of France.

Under the protection of the British fleet, trade with Britain had increased, and Heath & Co continued to thrive. In his first year as partner, Lyle traded with his extensive network of family and contacts in Bristol, Exeter, Naples and London, earning over £1000 profit for the firm. Even after the fall of Genoa, Heath, confident that the office was now on a secure footing, returned to England in 1798 to establish a new firm in London specifically exporting colonial products there. The demand for sugar and tobacco, imported from the Spanish colonies, had risen sharply in France, Italy and Switzerland, and Heath believed that despite Britain's navigation laws, colonial produce could be supplied more cheaply from the West Indies and American plantations than if shipped directly across the Atlantic. Lyle and Charles Heath were left to run the Italian side of the business. They were confident because, despite the change of Government, the French Directory had assured the British consul that all diplomatic personnel shall 'remain under the Safe Guard by the protection of the loyalty of the Ligurian Nation'. Nor had British subjects anything to fear and they could be confident that despite the hostilities between the two countries, 'all British subjects residing in Genoa should enjoy the same Safe Guard as the Consul and might wear the English Cockade'; three months later, this was rescinded.[11]

Whilst English residents could feel safe, the same did not apply for prisoners-of-war. Lyle was worried about the treatment and safety of ten British sailors who had been taken prisoner from the transport ships that had been sequestered by the Genoese government two years before. On 17 November, 1798, he wrote to Nelson, who at that time was staying with the Hamiltons in Naples that they:

> Had the misfortune in May last to be stopped in a Carriage near Verona on their way to England by the French & carried to Mantova, from there to Milan, Genoa & Poulon, & I hear they are actually confined in the Castle at Ferrascon. My efforts to procure their liberty while in Italy availed nothing, notwithstanding my repeated solicitations and representations to the French Ministers & Commandants that these unfortunate....could not be considered as prisoners of War; not having been taken at Sea or in battle & were going home without any disguise upon the good faith of Nations: All I could do for them was to obtain (after near two months imprisonment) about eight Sols of this Currency a day for their maintenance; no provision or allowance having been granted before, except during the five days confinement in the Castle of Milan. The answer from General Brune was that in consequence of the ill-treatment of the French prisoners in England, he thought himself authorized to use reprisals.
>
> > "attendu^ le mauvais traitement qu'endurent nos freres d'armes en Angleterre, je me crois autorise' d'user de represailler".
>
> I don't know what treatment these poor men now experience, but I have made enquiry & ordered some money to be paid to them by a friend at Marseilles & I beg...to recommend them to your Lordship's consideration & protection as soon as a Cartel is opened for the exchange of Prisoners. Your Lordship's well known humane feelings &

generosity will sufficiently apologise for the liberty
I take & I shall only add that I am
> Your Lordship's
>> Most obedient humble Servant
>> Genoa 17th Nov 1798
>> Lyle Gibbs

My Partner Mr. John Heath is gone to England with
his family, but his Brother joins with me and Dr. Datt,
Capt. Wood & all our other Countrymen here in
complimenting your Lordship on his late most
glorious unprecedented & important Victory![12]

Lyle was also anxious for William's safety. With the start of the war, it was no longer prudent for Susan to sail with him on his voyages to the Mediterranean so she and the children remained in England. He wrote to her regularly and was delighted to hear that they were now living with her mother in Shapter Street in Topsham. The house is, 'I presume the one on the right hand going up for if you remember we habited for many years the one opposite'. While Susan remained in England, William continued to sail to Genoa and Leghorn for the Bristol firm and he and Lyle saw each other regularly.

He had been shocked to hear that his brother had been captured by the French on a return trip from Leghorn and was feared dead. It was some three months later that he learnt that William had escaped and returned to his family in Topsham. With the downturn in trade due to the war, Munckley Gibbs & Richards had been unable to offer him any employment and the family was now in dire financial straits. Lyle who had been importing woollen cloth through Granger & Banfill for some years, offered to use his influence with Banfill to try to find him a position on one of his ships bound for the Mediterranean. Banfill had recently been appointed agent for the Association of Shippers of Genoa, Leghorn and Exeter and Lyle was sure he would help William during such a difficult time. Despite the war with France, he advised that it would be safer sailing on the Mediterranean rather than the Atlantic routes, and it would 'give me and Abraham the chance of seeing you from time to time'. He was sure that once William had found regular employment his 'voyages hereafter would be attended with better success and prosperity'.

He was also very anxious about Susan and the children, for with no money of her own, she was completely dependent on her husband to maintain their growing family. Still unmarried, Lyle saw his own family diminishing in size. Jack had died some years before and in 1793, his twin brother George died in a horrific accident in Jamaica. His youngest brother, Thomas, who had been promoted to lieutenant in 1795, was serving under Admiral McBride on board HMS Minotaur. Hearing that Thomas's ship was moored at Falmouth, he wrote to William asking him to 'let us know if we can be of any Service to him....his pay will not go far'. When Lyle learned of the downturn in William's fortunes, he immediately offered financial help advising him not to take any employment that might endanger his life. Despite the slump in trade after the fall of Genoa, Lyle made occasional payments to him via Banfill or John Heath and frequently sent small 'gifts' to Susan to buy clothes for his young nephews, and apologetically wrote that '...till Peace be once again restored...I dare not flatter myself to be able to offer her more....'.

In the spring of 1800, Lyle too became caught up in the war. In April, the Austrian army advanced into northern Italy causing the French under General Messena to retreat into Genoa, where they found themselves besieged in the city by land and trapped by the British naval blockade at sea. Although there was little chance of rescue and French supplies were miserably low, Messena was determined to defend the city to the last man, knowing it would keep part of the Austrian army occupied while Napoleon, who had assembled a large reserve force in France was preparing to cross the Alps to attack the Austrians from the rear. The siege lasted for two months, during which time famine, fighting and typhus took the lives of over thirty thousand people, both French and Genoese. Public bakeries were closed, and horses and all the domestic animals were eaten. The inhabitants of the city resorted to collecting grass, nettles and leaves. The city fathers mowed the grass that grew on the ramparts, which was then cooked in the public squares and distributed to the sick.[13] Starved into submission, Massena was finally forced to negotiate a peace on 4 June. He agreed a surrender, which enabled the French army to leave Genoa with full honours and return to French-controlled territory. By this time, Napoleon had led the newly created 40,000 strong Army of Reserve across the Alps, narrowly defeating the Austrians at the Battle of Marengo on 14 June. After the battle, the Austrians were forced to give up their Italian conquests and retreat to northwest Italy.

Once Genoa had returned to normal, Heath & Co continued to expand. Although official trade with Britain had ceased, the contraband trade flourished. British goods were smuggled into Genoa and then through Piedmont into France. In some cases, these goods were then sent to Italy disguised as French. As the number of licences issued by the British government increased, so commodities were brought into Genoa on neutral ships for trans-shipment to French controlled Europe. The firm also saw an upturn in demand for West India produce. Sugar, tobacco and rum were imported from the Caribbean and smuggled into France and Italy through Abraham in Palermo. However, this was also a period of uncertainty for the Genoese firm. In 1803, Charles Heath became very ill, and Lyle was concerned that his partner might 'not be able to restore his place in the Counting House'. If he did not recover, John Heath might decide to close the business. Without Charles, Lyle wrote, 'we shall not continue much longer our establishment here'. For Charles, it was to be a long and lingering illness and it was several months before he was fully recovered, but his health was to be a continual cause of concern for many years.

Now forty-two, Lyle had given up all hope of marriage and children of his own, often referring to himself as 'an old bachelor'. He adored his nephews and nieces, especially little Mary in Palermo and his brother's two elder boys, William Henry and John Ley. He constantly worried about William's safety, especially after his disastrous trip to Naples in 1802 when all his men deserted ship in London, for fear of being press ganged into the navy. He cautioned him not to try run the blockade as it was no longer safe to sail in the Mediterranean. Believing that William's first duty was to his family, Lyle recommended that he look for employment on the Atlantic routes. As these voyages could often take up to a year to complete, he offered to maintain Susan and the children in his absence. Now financially secure, he told William that he and Abraham 'would stand forth and you may occasionally value upon us for two Hundred Pounds each to be employed in any manner'. Although he had not sought Abraham's agreement, he intended to write to Naples to tell him of his proposal and doubted 'not of his approving'. He was also saddened to learn that Abraham was sending Mary to England, for he knew how hard this would be for his brother who doted on his little daughter. As the date of her departure drew near, he wrote to William that 'When the awful moment comes I doubt of his [Abraham's] sufficient courage and resolution to part from an only Child...How much more happy in Similar Cases are we old Bachelors, but how much more are we to be pitied in other Circumstances of Life'.

For the next few years, Lyle remained as the junior partner in Heath & Co, continuing to maintain his brother's family from time to time. After William's retirement in 1808, he began to send them a regular allowance and offered to take his nephew, John Ley into the business when he had finished his apprenticeship in London. When Charles Heath died in 1811 after several years of ill health, Lyle took the opportunity to buy out his former partner. The firm was restyled Gibbs & Co. Despite the change of name, his long association with John Heath continued and both he and Abraham banked with Heath & Co in London.[14] Now a reputable and well-respected member of the mercantile community in Genoa, Lyle was the only English member of the local Chamber of Commerce and despite his previous intentions to return to England, he was now firmly established in Europe.

The annexation of the Ligurian Republic in 1805, when it became a *département* of France, seems to have had little effect on Lyle's business, which continued to grow. Following Napoleon's defeat in the spring of 1814, Lord William Bentinck embarked on his campaign along the Ligurian coast, taking Genoa on 18 April. A week later, supported by the population, he restored the old Republic. With a dream of a united Italy, his watchword was 'Constitution and Independence', but the republic was short-lived. At the Congress of Vienna it was decided that Genoa should become part of the Kingdom of Sardinia. Despite opposition from the local elites, which was suppressed by British troops in December, Genoa was annexed by Sardinia on 3 January 1815.

* * * *

In the spring of 1812, Lyle was delighted to hear that Mary was returning to Palermo with William. Not only would she be reunited with her father, it would also give the three brothers the opportunity to meet again after so many years apart. It was some months later that Lyle received a desperate letter from Susan asking for news of William and telling him that she had heard nothing from him since he and Mary had left Topsham and had no money to maintain her family. Lyle responded immediately, arranging for a regular allowance to be paid to her through his bankers in London. He also wrote to William to find out when he was planning to return to England and was furious to discover that his brother had used the trip as an opportunity to abandon his wife and children. Lyle loved Susan dearly and could not understand William's behaviour, but no amount of threats or persuasion had any effect. For the next four years, Lyle continued to send Susan an allowance until her husband returned to Topsham in 1816.

Lyle was stunned to learn of Abraham's bankruptcy and distressed to hear of the death of Mary's twin daughters. As he was preparing to go to Palermo the devastating news reached Genoa of his brother's suicide. Any concern for Mary was overshadowed by fear at the impact that these events would have on his own business. The Genoese firm had been trading with Abraham for many years, first in Naples and then in Palermo. With the opening of the Naples office, Lyle had high hopes of developing a considerable amount of business with his nephew William Henry and Abraham's partner Lenzitti who was based in Salerno. John Ley, who had joined the Genoese firm the year before, first heard of his uncle's bankruptcy whilst in Milan, but it was on his return to Genoa on 7 August that he learned of his tragic death. As the situation unfolded Lyle, suspicious that William Henry was acting in his own interest by trying to save the Naples office, sent John Ley to Palermo to ensure 'that his interest is not neglected & to be there on the spot to give any explanation of his accounts'.

John Ley, who had been trying to develop more business with the London firm of Antony Gibbs & Sons, wrote to his cousin Henry on 21 August to tell him of the events in Palermo. He had long distrusted Lenzitti. 'I always thought him a bad subject & that he made a Cats Paw of my Uncle Lyle here', he wrote, and 'it is said he has acquired a competent fortune...You will be happy to hear, my Dear Henry, that my Uncle Lyle has escaped without any loss in a pecuniary point of view....for if this happened a month or two later he would certainly have been compromised for several thousand pounds, for so high was my late Uncle's [Abraham] credit in this part of the world that nobody as has the means w^d have hesitated to have honoured his crd^{ts} to any amount'. William Henry, he wrote, 'has declared the House at Naples perfectly independent of that at Palermo & he has found means to satisfy all their creditors, but how far he has acted right in so doing remains to be proved'. He was opposed to 'such a doctrine for it seems clear that Abram [sic] Gibbs at Palermo & A G at Naples was one and the same person', and his uncle was 'responsible for the engagements of both Houses'. John Ley was worried that 'the Plans of separating the business if allowed will perhaps make us creditors for a few thousand pounds'. Aware of the threat to Lyle's business when the news of Abraham's suicide reached London, he assured Henry that it would have no effect on the Genoese firm, as the two were totally separate businesses. 'As the failure of the Houses at Naples & Palermo may frighten the manufacturers...I think this House may have suffered in consequence, you will tell them this is not the case'. He also asked Henry to tell George to do the same in Bristol 'as we have many valuable correspondents in that Place'.

On his arrival in Palermo, John Ley found his father had returned to England and the tribunal looking into his uncle's affairs had sequestered his house on the Mezzo Monreale. Abraham's creditors were enraged that Mary's husband, Charles a'Court had put in a preferential claim against her father's estate for the £30,000 bond that had been promised as her dowry. Angry at William Henry's attempts to save the Naples house, they also threatened to sue Lyle for the balance of Abraham's debts if he supported William Henry's actions or if the commissioners agreed to a'Court's claim. Once it was clear that the Naples office could not be saved, John Ley left Palermo for Naples leaving the other creditors arguing over their share of Abraham's assets. There, he collected Mary, who had been abandoned by her husband, to take her to Genoa, where she was to remain with Lyle while she recovered from the shock of losing her babies, her father, and the humiliation inflicted on her by her husband.[15]

Meanwhile, in Genoa the mail ship brought a letter from William who by then was back in Topsham. He wrote that he hoped to buy a farm for his retirement and asked for a financial help. Relieved that his brother was now back with his family again, Lyle generously agreed but a few days later learned the truth when the next mail brought a letter from Susan. As soon as William had arrived home, he had become as abusive and violent as ever and told her he was leaving having decided to rent a small farm in Clyst St George. Furious at William's deception, on 16 August, Lyle angrily wrote, telling him he had learned of his 'late extraordinary and extravagant behaviour to your family which you may well imagine has exercised in me the strongest feelings of displeasure and regret....which, if persisted in, will entirely alienate my affections and protection from you and compel me to adopt such decisive actions as will secure to my dear Sister [Susan] and her no less amiable and good children that domestic happiness, which if not disturbed by the ebullitions of your unfortunate temper, would be without alloy'.

Unless William's attitude changed, Lyle warned, he would 'certainly insist on a separation and take your wife and children upon my own inconsiderate [sic] care and protection'. Without his support and protection William would 'learn too late how to appreciate the advantages of having friends who have relieved you in your adversity and long as you deserved it, would never have withheld from you their assistance. I trust however that such a step will not become necessary and that hence forward you will make it your constant study to promote the comfort and happiness of your family'. In a further act of generousity, Lyle offered to pay for their youngest son Charles, then aged eight, to board at Blundell's School. It was some weeks later that he heard from Susan that William had reluctantly moved back into the family home Shapter Street.

Mary lived with Lyle for nearly two years until her husband's claim against her father's estate was agreed.[16] Only after Lyle's refusal to support his 'preferential' claim did a' Court reluctantly agree to settle for about £10,000. It was a great relief to all when Charles collected his wife in the summer of 1818 to take her to England to meet his family. As Lyle caustically commented some years later, 'It was a mere chance that Mary a'Court was not compelled as a last resort to come and live with me after her Father's death'.

Lyle's problems with nephews and nieces were ongoing. William Henry's efforts to save the Naples office were in vain. It was clear that Abraham's debts were so substantial that it too had to be liquidated. As if from a sense of duty, Lyle offered him employment in the Genoese firm, no doubt hoping that his experience and contacts in Palermo would be an asset. But if William Henry, then twenty-five, thought he was going become a partner he was mistaken. His uncle's confidence in him had been seriously undermined by his actions in Naples. Lyle was also wary of his nephew. Abraham's suicide note referred to his having been too 'indulgent to those who have been ungrateful to me', and there was a considerable amount of gossip and conjecture that someone close to Abraham had caused his downfall. William Henry may have been the toast of Naples, but in Genoa he found Lyle much less trusting. Inevitably, within a short time, the two men found the relationship unsatisfactory, and by 1819, it had become so strained that they both knew that they could not operate in the same firm. With his uncle's blessing, William Henry returned to London to start an agency business on his own account, specifically to develop trade between the Genoese firm and Antony Gibbs & Sons, but he was unable to generate sufficient business to support himself, and the following year had no option but to return to Genoa. Lyle reluctantly agreed to change the name of his firm to Gibbs & Co to reflect the contribution being made by his two nephews, but he refused to allow either William Henry or John Ley to become partners until 1825, when they had both earned £400 in commission to buy themselves into the business.[17]

* * * *

In contrast to his family problems, after the end of hostilities in Europe Lyle's firm flourished. A condition of the annexation of Genoa to Sardinia in 1815 was that a free port, with its old liberal regulations, customs and taxes was restored. This was of major importance to the British economy as Genoa supplied Piedmont and the island of Sardinia, as well as Switzerland, Parma and Lombardy and many other Italian states.[18] While much of Europe was plunged into a severe economic depression, Genoa prospered. In the first six months of 1815, sixteen British ships had arrived together with many others from elsewhere.[19] For Lyle and the other foreign merchants there, trade with the rest of Europe improved though never to its pre-war levels. Imports consisted of a wide range of colonial products from the United States and the Caribbean, fish from Newfoundland, as well as iron, steel, earthenware and woollens from Great Britain. Genoa had long been considered one of the best fish markets and Lyle's main exports were anchovies and pilchards, both to Britain and Europe, and colonial products were imported through Gibbs Bright & Co in Bristol. By 1820, Lyle and his nephews were acting as agents for a number of British and European merchant houses, and continued their efforts to develop trade with Antony Gibbs & Sons in London.

That year, fear of war swept through Europe once again. In 1814, the Treaty of Ghent had concluded the war with the United States, but it failed to resolve any of the issues for which the two countries had fought. Lyle, convinced that war was once again imminent, asked John Ley to write to Henry asking that if 'in the event of war between Great Britain and the United States of America or any act of hostility being committed by either party', he 'use secrecy' to keep their clients 'ignorant of events'. John Ley suggested that if war were declared 'profits might be made by buying up colonial produce & it is that view that my uncle is desirious of having the earliest possible intelligence'. Although John Ley did not agree that war was necessarily inevitable, he added, 'we well know the anxiety of America to get a footing in the Mediterranean & the pecuniary sacrifices she has offered. The doctrine of Ld Liverpool & the accession of Florida by the Spaniards gives the Americans full scope to pursue their ambitions'.

The following year Sardinia introduced a number of new regulations for the port, causing great concern amongst British merchants. They petitioned the Foreign Office for it was feared that as many as half of those settled in Genoa' would 'leave the place & the majority of the present British residents openly declare they will not remain unless the present system is changed'.[20] Within months, the French authorities rectified most of their grievances and Lyle decided to remain in the city that was now his home. For the next few years, trade between Genoa and Marseille increased to unprecedented levels and by 1820 there were 'upward of 2,200' vessels in the Genoese merchant fleet, with a tonnage estimated to be 'four times the amount of the Genoese navigation than at any period in the century preceding the extinction of the Republic'.[21] A Foreign Office report written in 1825 noted that Genoa's prosperity was dependent on its 'Trade & Navigation… crushed for so many years under the military scepter of France, have been regenerated under the Sardinian Government. New outlets for trade have been opened through Piedmont and Savoy, into France

Switzerland and Germany'.[22] This renewed prosperity in the immediate post-war period was not 'to be found in any other part of Italy; and the many new streets and roads, and the private & public works, which are in the course of construction offer a remarkable contrast with the dilapidated condition of most of the neighbouring Capitals'. Despite this, there remained considerable opposition to the new government amongst the nobility over the loss of sovereignty. It was recognised that 'it would be too much to expect that the Pride of Genoa republicans could in so short a time be entirely subdued…Generations must elapse before the amalgamation can be complete'.[23]

Throughout this period, Lyle supported Susan and his nieces in Topsham. By the mid 1820s, she and William had finally separated and he had moved into lodgings in a nearby seaside town. Although now a partner in the Genoese firm, William Henry continued to be at odds with his uncle and brothers. In early 1828, John Ley, then thirty-five, returned to England with twenty-one year old Charles, who had joined the firm earlier that year, to establish an agency for Gibbs & Co of Genoa in London. While there, he met the young Ellen Maria Gamble, fourteen years his junior and in they married in November. This was a true love match. Ellen, the twenty-one year old daughter of a London merchant, had no fortune of her own, but this was of no consequence to John Ley.[24] Despite his dependence on his uncle, he had high-hopes of a substantial inheritance in the future. Nine months later Ellen gave birth to their first child who sadly died on the same day.

Although preferring to have remained in London, John Ley and Ellen returned to Genoa with Charles the following year, stepping back into the business because of the worsening relationship between William Henry and his uncle. In their absence, the gap between the generations had continued to widen, so much so that things had finally come to a head. William Henry, now thirty-eight, had been a partner for nearly five years and hoped his uncle would retire to allow him and his brothers to take over the firm. Lyle, at two years short of seventy, had no such intention. In 1829, after John Ley's return, William Henry, bitter after so many years of dependency and broken

promises, decided to leave Genoa for good. An epileptic since childhood, the stress of their relationship had brought on a number of fits,
one of which was so severe that it almost killed him. After he recovered,
their relationship had deteriorated to the extent that Lyle 'couldn't bear
him as a partner but did not wish four [sic] his connection in business
to be entirely dissolved'.

By 1830, the fish market in Genoa, which only a few years before
had been considered the best in the Mediterranean, was 'by degree not
only the worst, but it is now esteemed by many Houses to be no
market at all'. Lyle, now trading through the East India Company,
believed that it was essential for the firm to have a London agent. With
John Ley back in Genoa with his new wife, rather than cast William
Henry out without a penny, Lyle offered him a contract to establish an
agency business in London. He also returned the £400 that his nephew
had paid on becoming a partner so that he had some initial capital and
arranged unlimited credit facilities for him with his bankers, Heath &
Son. William Henry thankfully returned to England determined to
prove himself. Lyle saw this as his nephew's last chance to make something of his life by breaking the cycle of dependency that pervaded his
brother's family. He was still paying Susan a quarterly allowance, and
on a number of occasions had appealed to Betsy to share the burden,
but she had always refused. After her husband's death in 1829, Betsy
had been left a wealthy woman. With no children of her own, Lyle
hoped she would take on some of the responsibility for their nieces and
nephews, but his appeals continued to fall on deaf ears.

After William's death in 1830, Susan gave up the Gibbs family house
in Topsham and moved to Tiverton with her daughters to be near her
brother. A few weeks later a letter arrived from William Henry, now
living in London, asking that her £75 quarterly allowance be increased.
Initially Lyle refused and once again wrote to Betsy, asking if she would
contribute to their sister-in-law's support. She agreed on condition that
he did not increase Susan's allowance. Lyle replied to William Henry
on 22 May, that his aunt had 'kindly consented to join her brother
in the maintenance of the Family to what extent she cannot now

22. William and Susan's little house 'on the right' in Shapter Street, Topsham, opposite the house built by his great-grandfather

23. Topsham Bridge with William Meachin's salt works on the left and the Bridge Inn on the right

24. The eruption of Vesuvius on 15th July 1794

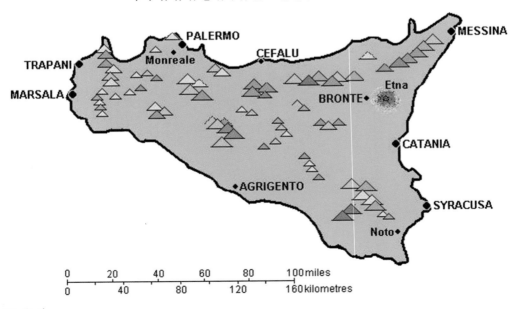

25. Sicily

26. The Marine Parade at Palermo with the Porta Felice on the right and the Casa Vega on the extreme left

27. Palazza Palagonia in Palermo where Abraham and Mary lived with Nelson and the Hamiltons. It was fully restored in 2006

28. Entrance to Palazzo Palagonia

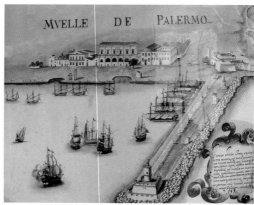

29. The chapel at the Woodhouse *baglio* in Marsala

30. The Mole at Palermo

31. The courtyard at Castella di Maniace at Bronte showing the monument erected in 1888 to commemorate Nelson. Presented to Nelson by a grateful King Ferdinand, the estate was managed by John Graefer who designed the English garden at Caserta. As Nelson's agent and banker, Abraham was charged with overseeing the improvements at Bronte

32. John Ley Gibbs

33. Colonel Charles a'Court, husband of Mary (Anna Maria) Gibbs

34. George Henry Gibbs

35. Caroline Gibbs (née Crawley)

36. William Gibbs of Tyntesfield

37. Matilda Blanche Gibbs, daughter of Sir Thomas Crawley-Boevey

38. Salvina Gibbs née Hendy painted at the time of her marriage in 1802

39. George Gibbs of Belmont painted at the time of his marriage in 1802, aged 23

40. Joanna Gibbs, George's sister who lived at Exwick House for much of her life

41. George Gibbs of Belmont, aged 71

determine what her own expenses may be', adding that she 'expressly states that the actual rate of allowance is ample sufficient and therefore cannot accede to any increase'. However, Betsy only contributed to their upkeep for a few months, and once again, the burden fell on Lyle.

When William Henry left Genoa, Lyle had given him 'unlimited command' over the £400, which was felt 'was sufficient proof of our desire in our power to uphold his character' and it was agreed that he would act exclusively for Gibbs & Co. Within months of William Henry arriving in London, news reached Genoa that he had broken the terms of his contract. Instead of acting for the Genoese firm, he 'began almost immediately by purchasing goods on his own acc^t (being precluded by our own instructions from doing so)', but made a substantial loss on his first deal by paying over the odds for a variety of commodities. Although irritated, Lyle excused him, putting his losses down to inexperience, and offered to purchase the goods from him with a 'friendly caution not to embark in such adventures again'. Despite this, within months, having found 'himself clear of his shipment, [William Henry] immediately entered on fresh investment with Parties in Mincing Lane of whom he must naturally be the Dupe'. He purchased large quantities of 'Coffees Sugars & Wax', but made a loss on everything but the wax. Once again, an exasperated Lyle supported his nephew by buying up surplus stock at a loss. William Henry had also tried to develop trade with Antony Gibbs & Sons in London and was infuriated when his uncle refused on the grounds that the firm was not 'sufficiently current' and suggested that he give the business to another house. Lyle's patience evaporated when he discovered that his nephew had kept the profits from the sale of a cargo of opium, claiming they were his commission. Such was his anger, that he stopped all lines of credit with his bankers in London. Unable to cash any cheques because he had no permanent domicile in England, William Henry quickly ran up considerable debts and got into serious financial difficulties. Angry at Lyle's actions he began to spread rumours amongst the mercantile houses in the capital that John Ley and Charles, were responsible for his situation, accusing them trying to force him out of the firm.

John Ley and Charles were furious at their brother's disloyalty. At the beginning of October, a letter arrived from Heath & Son asking for an explanation. Charles immediately replied, determined to set the record straight and giving details of a number of breaches in their contract that showed the 'gross folly & obstinacy of which he is capable'. The opium incident was the final straw; since then Lyle refused to have anything more to do with his nephew. Charles felt that William Henry was treating them with contempt and by the tone of his letters, 'you would really suppose that he was the principal and that we depended entirely on him for all the business we get'. Charles had no illusions about his elder brother, thinking he was just like their father. 'To suppose that we wished or even intended my brother's services to go unrewarded is what neither he nor you could think us capable of' he wrote, 'We did intend however that the remuneration should in great measure depend on himself...or the nature of his exertions in our favour. To give him a stipend would not in the end answer his purpose or ours tho' our principal objection to it would be the inducement it would offer to my brother to indulge his natural inclination of living easily a Gent^m [sic]. In short it would abate the stimulus for exertion by which alone a man can raise himself in the world'. Charles concluded that, 'Having grossly insulted my Uncle & of refusing to account for property entrusted to his care & honesty, until a proper atonement has been made to my uncle & the Proceeds of the opium satisfactorily accounted for, I fear nothing can be done towards a reconciliation'.

A few weeks later, a letter arrived from William Henry accusing Charles of trying to usurp his position in the firm. He demanded that a neutral person be appointed to look into the validity of his claims. Lyle, infuriated at his impudence replied 'It would be too much to suffer my peace of mind and Domestic happiness to be once more so undeserving and gratuitously disturbed and destroyed by an inconsiderate and ungrateful Nephew. I shall however confine my just resentments once more as much as possible; impressed as I am with the conviction (not understanding your own assertions that you were at the time afflicted with a relapse of your periodical disease/Paroxyisms which had nearly put an end to your existence this time 12 months), but for my humane generous and timely intervention in making a further sacrafice [sic] on your behalf. Brief, I am not to be intimidated by such gross, paltry, indecorus expressions & ungrounded recriminations ....if you do not atone in a satisfactory manner for this fresh insult offered to me and my Partner (who is ignorant of the Epithets you are so gratuitously to favour him with) and account to the Ho for what you are indebted to us, namely for the opium so friendly and generously confided to your care & <u>honesty</u>, I shall be compelled...so much against my inclination as Uncle to have recourse to other means wh^h <u>Mind</u> can only rebound to your own Shame and Dishonour – You will recollect I held the same language to you this time 12 months & after conferring with your Friends they gave you the same advice as they would now without hearing both sides of the question; judge then what would be their surprise after the perusal of your correspondence of last year coupled with what has since ensued – the idea of an Arbitration upon a matter so palpable & preposterous in which there is nothing susceptible of revoking in doubt, is ...absurd and ridiculous [sic]'.

By 1832, at the age of thirty-nine, William Henry was almost destitute. He was also a very sick man. His fits had increased in frequency and severity and he was suffering from painful arthritis. He appealed to Henry and Samuel Banfill, asking them to intercede with Lyle on his behalf, and was eventually persuaded to apologise for his behaviour; but his uncle would have none of it. Even John Ley was unsympathetic, writing to William Henry, 'your contrition coming so late as to bear the appearance of having been drawn from you by sheer necessity rather than [you] having acting improperly'. Nevertheless, he was concerned for his brother's health, and despite Lyle's opposition, offered to help him. Reluctantly Lyle agreed to give William Henry £100 a year to support him as the firm's London agent specifically to develop trade between the Genoese firm and Antony Gibbs & Sons. Knowing that this was his last chance, William Henry seems to have been successful. The London firm were so satisfied with his performance, that two years later he returned to Genoa to establish his own agency there for Antony Gibbs & Sons.

John Ley's support for his elder brother caused a serious rift between him and Lyle, so he too began to make plans to leave the firm. Whether Lyle knew of his nephew's intentions is unclear, but for several years, their relationship too had deteriorated and he continually found fault with John Ley. His opportunity came when, in the summer of 1834, Ellen found she was pregnant again and wanted the baby to be born in England. Lyle agreed they could return for an extended holiday and offered to pay all their expenses for the trip. Whether he suspected that they might never return is unclear, but he released John Ley from any debts that he owed the firm. In June, he and Ellen left Genoa with their family and travelled overland to England via Milan and Lake Como where they spent several happy weeks. They arrived in England in the autumn and their fourth child was born on 10 January. Three months later, still unable to find any employment in London, he knew he had no option but to return to Genoa. As they were preparing to leave, he heard that his mother had died on 5 May, after a long illness. He and Ellen travelled to Devon accompanied by William Henry for the funeral, and then they all went on to Ilfracombe and spent several weeks with Betsy. She was delighted to see them, but if their motives were financial, they were to be disappointed. Unknown to Lyle she offered to pay John and Ellen's expenses to return to Genoa but any hopes they may have had of an inheritance were in vain. Penniless, they arrived back in Genoa in September, but two months later, tragedy was to strike. Ellen and their eldest daughter Frances suddenly died and were buried there. Heartbroken, John Ley decided to return to England for good with his two surviving children and, after settling his affairs with Lyle, left the partnership on 31 December 1835.

Lyle was deeply distressed at the news of Susan's death, convinced that she had died 'in anguish & misery many years sooner as all her happiness & consolation consisted in believing that her Sons were contributing to my welfare & the prosperity of my Establishment; my

Sister [Betsy] would not have suffered John (like his brother Wm Henry) to enter her threshold. Indeed', he wrote to an old friend,[25] 'she had often reproved me for admitting either under my roof & more particularly for taking them in Partnership'. He was cynical about John Ley and Ellen's motives in visiting Betsy, and felt that nothing could 'account for my Sister's unnatural estrangement & alienation for me & my Nieces to the intrigues of John & Ellin [sic] during their long visit to Ilfracombe'. After Susan's death, he agreed to give Mary Matilda and Frances £200 a year to to live on and once again asked Betsy for a contribution, but once again, she refused. He was furious a few months later to learn that she had given William Henry £500 and had payed John and Ellen's expenses whilst they were in England. As a result, he became completely estranged from her. With John Ley's departure, only Charles remained in the firm. Lyle, now seventy-four, had always been very fond of his youngest nephew, treating him more like a grandson and unknown to his brothers, had made him his heir.

The late 1830s was a difficult period for foreign merchants in Genoa. The imposition of increased import duties on all British goods by Sardinia had resulted in stagnation and economic decline. This was coupled with severe cholera outbreaks in a number of Italian cities including Milan, Como, Bergamo and Brescia, resulting in the government imposing tighter quarantine laws on all imports and restricting the transportation of goods overland. By 1837, Genoa had become 'a barren city'.

Just before Christmas that year, a letter arrived from Ellen's father, John Gamble, telling him of John Ley's sudden death. After returning to England, he had settled with his two children in Manchester, but had died of cholera on 8 November. Gamble wrote that John had appointed Lyle as an executor and guardian of his children, aged four and two, now in the care of their grandmother. As Mrs Gamble was prepared to take them in and 'become a mother to the poor orphans in their helpless state', he asked if Lyle would contribute to a trust for their benefit. Lyle refused, telling Gamble that he had been giving his brother's family an allowance of between £200-£300 for over half a century. Abraham had 'promised to do half…but would not make me good a farthing'. He also declined to act as executor on the grounds of age or to take any responsibility for the children, though he later relented and made a small contribution towards their upkeep.

Now estranged from all his family except Charles, Lyle retired from the firm. He died the following year, at the age of seventy-eight, and was buried in Genoa. Although he and William Henry had been reconciled on his deathbed, he left him nothing. With the exception of two small bequests to Mary Matilda and Frances, everything went to Charles who was also his executor.

CHAPTER 17

THE ATTORNEY GENERAL

Vicary made his maiden speech in the House of Commons on 11 May 1805, but although it was well received, his style and eloquence or lack of it, did little to endear him to the members. While his ability as a lawyer was universally recognised, as a parliamentary speaker he had little success. With a 'shrill, unmusical voice' he was 'very far from being an agreeable and persuasive speaker', rarely speaking in the House, unless it was in his official capacity. An ambitious man, he despaired at ever advancing his public career finding 'party views and connections' were 'fatal to professional men hoping to succeed as a lawyer in politics'. It was alleged that he really had no place in the Commons, 'and feeling his nullity, there was no place to which he was with more reluctance dragged by the power that office gives the government of its lawyers'.[1] Although 'confident in his own legal strength, he was equally uncivil and outspoken to his clients' and 'narrow minded and impatient on the Bench'. In spite of this he was always considered a thoroughly 'conscientious judge'. Despite his failure as a speaker in the House, Vicary continued to instill terror in both his adversaries in court and those poor souls who appeared before him. As the summer recess drew near, his long-time friend and fellow judge on the western circuit, Joseph Jekyll wrote of him, 'I trust I shall get away from Bristol without any of those Scratches on the Face which Vicary's forensic Talons used to imprint for a whole Vacation on the Leaders'.[2]

His position as MP for Totnes was short-lived. Following Pitt's death

321

in January 1806, Vicary along with his colleagues resigned from his post, reluctant to serve in Grenville's so-called 'Ministry of All the talents'. He lost his Totnes seat in the election and found himself in the political wilderness. Later that year he was acting with Perceval as legal advisor to the Princess of Wales when the government launched the *Delicate Investigation* into her private life. After the commission found her innocent of all charges of adultery, Vicary was invited to a reception where the princess was presented to Queen Charlotte. The function, which was held in June on one of the hottest days of the summer, was in a crowded room and the sun 'shone with unusual ardour into the windows of the antique ball-room'. One guest was heard to remark that one of the most 'distressed beings in that heated assembly' was Vicary 'hard-featured and impatient, his wig awry, his solids yielding out all their essence; he appeared as if he had just risen, though not like Venus from the sea. Every muscle of his angular features seemed busily employed in forming hieroglyphic imprecations!... I never pitied any person more..'.[3]

With the fall of the Whig government and the return of a Tory ministry in 1807, Vicary's political fortunes changed once again for the better. He accepted a position in the Portland government and became the member for Great Bedwyn in Wiltshire, a seat previously held by Lord Ailesbury, and he was appointed attorney general. He wrote that he 'had returned [to the Bar] with perfect content, & never expected to be called from it again, but the late Events have disposed of me otherwise, & I shall be most happy if in the execution of my Office I give you no reason to Think that you have passed to [sic] partial a Judgement of me'.[4] Towards the end of the year, he was returned as the member for Cambridge, his own university, unseating the Chancellor of the Exchequer, Lord Henry Petty, much to the relief of many at the university. As one contemporary wrote, we have 'at last ridded ourselves of Lord H Petty and he was the most abnoxious man!'[5]

Vicary held the post of attorney general for five years, in both the Portland and Perceval governments. He was also highly sought-after by private clients making his legal work extremely lucrative. Before becoming attorney general, he is reputed to have earned in the region of £10,000 per annum. In office, this increased to £12,000 while the average annual income of families headed by 'persons of law' was estimated to have been around £350 between 1801-3.[6]

He was always willing to use his influence to help his family. In 1805, with the country at war with Spain, an embargo was placed on all English property there. Antony, having foreseen this had nominally transferred his existing stock to his Spanish friends to avoid confiscation, and asked his elder brother to use his influence to help him obtain a licence from the government to charter a Spanish ship to take his stranded stocks to South America. Vicary agreed and arranged for him to see the Duke of Montrose, President of the Board of Trade, who after some delay granted his request. In the event, the licence expired because of a number of delays and when Henry returned to London to try to get it extended, Vicary introduced him to the new President of the Board of Trade, Lord Auckland, who had first met his father in Madrid in 1788.

While in London, his nephew Henry lived with Vicary and Kenny at their house in Bloomsbury Square. They found him 'a most amiable young man' and he was instantly attracted to their daughter Maria. Kenny wrote to Dolly that her husband 'is as much pleased with him as I am, indeed I congratulate you on having such a son'. Vicary told Henry that he was relieved that 'you have not that disagreeable hesitation when you speak which your grandfather and father and almost all the Gibbes [sic] have so much of'. After Henry had returned to Spain, he and Maria continued to write to each other and it was not long before her parents began to worry that they were planning to form a more permanent attachment. In October 1807, Vicary was so worried that he wrote to Antony asking him to discourage the friendship. With his father so indebted to the family, Henry was unable to support himself let alone a wife, and had few prospects in the near future. Although Vicary was enjoying a lucrative income, he was not willing to support another family. Determined that Maria would find herself a more suitable husband, when she and her mother returned to their house at Hayes, Kenny insisted that she stop all correspondence with Henry.

By the beginning of 1808, this 'wearer and tearer of himself and others' was 'in sad Health – & Perceval has manumitted him from long nights in the House'. The pressure and stress of his position as attorney general was nothing to the problems he was still having with Maria. In February, his house in Hayes was burgled during the night while Maria slept there. The *Annual Register* reported that 'On Saturday morning the house of sir [sic] Vicary Gibbs, at Hayes in Kent, was robbed in the following extraordinary manner. When miss [sic] Gibbs, daughter of sir Vicary awoke in the morning she discovered that all her clothes were taken away, the quilt off the bed and everything that was portable in the room. On examining the premises, it was discovered that the robbers had, by tying some hurdles together, made a ladder, and ascending a colonnade, which goes around the house, found easy access to miss Gibbs room, and made off with the property without awakening her. A large stick was left upon the bed'.[7]

The following month Maria announced that she planned to marry a dashing major, Andrew Pilkington. It is not clear whether Vicary and Kenny approved of the match, but worn down by ill health and worry, they agreed. On 9 May 1808, a friend noted that 'Maria Gibbs this day was united with her Major'. However, he added that 'Vicary tells me that his Bowels and Stomach are totally deranged, and there is now a Character in his Countenance so much exceeding its normal Emaciation, that I never beheld out of a Coffin, and all this Wear and Tear of human Constitution has unfortunately been for the benefit of Major Pilkington'.[8] Maria's marriage did little to improve his health and four weeks later Vicary was so unwell and could 'not attend the present sittings'. He returned to Hayes to rest and recuperate, but if he thought his personal troubles were over, he was wrong. Maria's marriage was a disaster from the outset and within months, she and Pilkington had separated and she was once again living with her parents.

Despite his ill health, between 1808 and 1810 Vicary achieved notoriety for the enthusiasm he showed in implementing the Perceval government's repressive offensive against the writers and publishers of radical literature for alleged seditious libels. Fox's Libel Act of 1792 had given juries the right to judge not only the actual publication of an alleged libel but also whether it could cause a breach of the peace. The line between libellous and non-libellous writings was often blurred, and any criticism of the king, government or the church could be construed as libellous. Thus, the writers and vendors were under constant threat of prosecution.[9] Between 1808 and 1810 Vicary filed forty-two *ex officio* informations, compared with the fifteen issued by his predecessors during the previous seven years.[10] An *ex officio* information was technically a summons issued by the attorney general for alleged libel by which a defendant could be tried without a grand jury indictment. As the defendant was required to appear in court at a future date, Vicary introduced legislation authorising the arrest of persons against whom informations had been filed unless they could post bail. The required bail could be as much as £1000, and many were imprisoned for several years pending trial.[11] As twenty-five of the forty-two informations were not prosecuted, many alleged libellers spent years in prison or were ruined by their bail conditions. Among those convicted was William Cobbett, who spent two years in Newgate for an article in the *Weekly Political Register* in which he criticised the forcible suppression of a mutiny in Ely by German troops. Others included Hart and White, the printer and publisher of the *Independent Whig* and John Gale Jones the former L.C.S. leader. The latter organised a number of debates in 'The British Forum', off Covent Garden, and was committed to Newgate for a 'breach of Privilege 'involving materially the rights and liberty of the subject'.[12]

During this period, Vicary's popularity declined as he 'screwed his power more tightly' than any previous attorney general, but at times was under intense pressure from his royal masters to indict even when there was little hope of securing a guilty verdict. Such was the case in the Duke of York affair with the publication in the autumn of 1808 of allegations that Mary Anne Clarke, the Duke's mistress had used her

influence to sell military promotions. York denied any direct involvement with his former mistress's activities. In September, Hawkesbury,
then Home Secretary sent Vicary a pamphlet, entitled 'a *Plain Statement*
together with several letters relating to the Subject', including one from
James Willoughby Gordon, York's military secretary, urging him for an
opinion as to whether it was libellous. Vicary replied to Hawkesbury that
although he considered the pamphlet 'is to the last degree impudent and
offensive, yet it is so contrived that we do not feel ourselves justified in
saying it may be made the Subject of a Criminal Prosecution'.[13]

Vicary's decision so incensed York that a few days later, he received
another letter from him demanding that he 'take His Majesty's
Pleasure in order that the necessary measures be adopted for prosecut-
ing the Publishers of the Statesman…I cannot see any good reason why
my public Character or authority are to be insulted & lessened With
Impunity….I feel confident not only in the firm support of The
Government, but that a Jury of my Countrymen will give the same
Impartial protection to my insulted Honor [sic], as they would to the
Character of the meanest subject in the Empire'.[14] In the exchange
of correspondence that followed, in October Gordon sent Vicary a copy
of the *Times* which he considered contained remarks of a highly
Inflammatory and offensive nature. Although Vicary conceded that 'the
Paper to which we have referred is in point of law a Libel', there was
considerable public anger at York's behaviour and no guarantee that
a Jury would be sympathetic to his case. Now under intense pressure
from the King, he warned that 'if we were sure that a Jury would be
directed by another Consideration than the strict law of the Case in
finding their Verdict, we should think it advisable to prosecute the
Publishers of so scandalous a composition, but experience teaches us that
this is not to be depended upon….to fail in a prosecution against the
offenders on this occasion would be very Injurious to the Illustrious
Person against whom the attack is so unjustly levelled. He went on,
'We…observe that in such Cases Juries are very frequently misled by
Prejudice and Misapprehension not withstanding every attempt to
correct them….and we are deterred from advising a Prosecution'.[15]

Having consulted his royal master, Hawkesbury agreed that they were 'aware of all the difficulties which attend prosecutions of this nature at the present moment, and particularly on Subjects, on which the Publick Mind is most ...unjustly inflamed. He went on, 'I know at the same time the intention which prevails on this same subject in H.R.H^s Mind and on all those around Him, and that they will never be satisfied unless the <u>Attempt</u> is made to procure a Conviction', the same sentiments were being expressed in a 'higher quarter'.[16] The King had also asked 'Does the Atty General consider these Papers Libels in Law – if he does not, they neither can nor ought to be Prosecuted, but if he is of the opinion that they are Libels, the Prosecution should be instituted and we should take our chance of the result'.[17]

Vicary reluctantly acceded to the pressure. On 31 October he wrote to Gordon, 'I have felt myself on many late occasions of this sort placed in a very unpleasant situation. If I were to consult my own case, & nothing else, I might content myself with raging whether I thought the Papers submitted to me libellous or not...and leave it to the Government & the Party to decide whether a prosecution should or should not be initiated against the Publisher'. While he was as indignant as everyone else about the 'gross insults to York', he thought 'it would mortify me to suppose that he thought me less earnest and zealous than I ought to be in bringing the authors of them to Justice.... it is not any backwardness on my part to undertake the prosecutions, but a fair Consideration of the extrinsic circumstances which may have undue weight on the Event or Result'. Despite his misgivings he agreed to issue an information and 'will state the case as well as I can do to the Jury, & if I do not do this effectively & the Jury shall acquit....the blame must rest with them and not with me'. He also pointed out that in court 'Topics may be introduced upon which the public mind is in a high state of irritation, where prejudices, however unjust to be publicly entertained' which 'appear to me to put the success of such a prosecution in a state of hazard'.[18]

The scandal around York suddenly erupted the following January, when Gwyllym Lloyd Wardle, MP for Okehampton introduced a motion in the House accusing Clarke of using her influence with York to acquire military commissions and promotions. Perceval, expecting York to be cleared, appointed a select committee to look into Wardle's claims. In February, Clarke appeared before the committee and despite the crown lawyers' attempts to discredit her, successfully fended off their questions, much to the amusement of the opposition and the press. As Perceval wrote to George III, '[H]er [sic] whole carriage was so impudent, not to say audacious…that any member of the house could not fail to see that she did not deserve any credit'.[19] Much to the delight of the opposition and the press, many of whom had suffered from his repressive zeal, Vicary appeared bemused by her adroit handling of his questions and 'incensed' his university for his 'very illiberal examination' of her. Even his long-time friend, Joseph Jeykll, wrote that he 'disgusts the House as a Cross Examiner'.[20] Although York was acquitted, such was the public outcry at his sexual indiscretions, that he was forced to resign as commander-in-chief of the army on 25 May 1809.

As well as his successes, Vicary also lost a number of high-profile libel cases including that of the brothers John and Leigh Hunt for an article on flogging in the army taken from the *Stanford News* and published in the *Examiner* in February 1811. The acquittal of the brothers, who were defended by his arch-rival, Henry Brougham (later Lord Brougham), was a victory for free speech. Brougham based his eloquent defence on the question as to 'whether an Englishman still enjoys the privilege of freely discussing public matters'. Despite losing these cases, Vicary continued to 'bring the law of seditious libel into disrepute by the virulence of his prosecutions'. Not satisfied with 'hauling journalists, printers and editors before the Courts' he would also 'pursue old ladies who had inherited a few shares in some newspapers'.[21]

He supported Canning's bid to become Prime Minister but on Perceval's appointment in October 1809, Vicary joined his government and backed the disastrous Scheldt expedition against the United Provinces between 30 July and 10 December of that year. This was the last of a series of British military operation in Flanders, which cost the government £8million and resulted in the death of just under 4000 soldiers from malaria.[22] Despite criticism, on 23 January 1810, the opposition was soundly defeated in the debate on the expedition and the government's handling of the war, but it was only narrowly defeated three days later by 195 votes to 186 when the opposition demanded an enquiry into the Walcheren affair. Perceval's ministry continued to be beset with problems. The following week the government was defeated in three divisions on the composition of the Finance Committee, and following the publication of the Walcheren enquiry only narrowly survived four divisions on 31 March.

Although he voted with the government on the Scheldt expedition, much to Perceval's embarrassment Vicary opposed the forcible arrest of (Sir) Francis Burdett the following month. Burdett, who had been elected MP for the radical seat of Westminster in 1807, was one of the few members of the House of Commons who supported parliamentary reform and had become one of the leaders of the opposition to the Liverpool government. In April 1810, Burdett denounced the imprisonment of John Gale Jones as illegal and supported 'the rights of the people and the press' to watch and report on the proceedings of the House of Commons. His speech was published in Cobbett's *Weekly Political Register* and an outraged parliament committed him to the Tower for an alleged breach of Parliamentary privilege. Burdett refused to surrender and barricaded himself in his house in Piccadilly. Later Lord Cochrane arrived at his house in a hackney coach with a barrel of gunpowder ready to defend him.[23] Eventually Burdett was forced to surrender and was sent to the Tower amid widespread rioting in his support. He was released in June after Parliament had gone into its summer recess, much to the delight of his radical constituents.

After the Walcheren affair, Vicary voted with the government for the next two years and was generally regarded as a Perceval man. Although a bitter enemy of reform, he supported Curwen's Bill in June 1809, but voted against it a few weeks after Burdett's imprisonment.[24] Later that year while the country was celebrating George III's golden jubilee, there was growing concern that the King was showing the first signs of the return of his insanity and Vicary advised Perceval on the enactment of the Regency Bill, that severely restricted the Regent's powers. The new Bill, which had been agreed in Cabinet was presented to the Prince of Wales in December, and eventually passed on 4 February 1811. The following month Vicary was censored in parliament for the rise in the number of *ex officio* informations since he had become attorney general, many of which were still awaiting trial. Stung by the criticism, he responded in the debate, arguing that with over 200 publications in London alone, the number of prosecutions was not excessive. It is possible that, after the high profile acquittals of John and Leigh Hunt and Perry and Lambert, the government had lost much of its enthusiasm for libel prosecutions.

After Perceval's assassination in the lobby of the House of Commons in May 1812, Vicary suddenly decided to withdraw from political life and 'descended from his position as attorney-general to that of a puisine judge in the common pleas'.[25] Whether his resignation was due to ill health or the shock of Perceval's death is unclear, although many of his colleagues believed that 'his nerves suddenly and entirely failed him' after Bellingham's trial. Like many of his friends, Jeykll thought that, 'Upon the whole Gibbs has done wisely, he was worn down with Fatigue, and if his friends ever return to office he is still on the Cards for Mansfield's seat' as Chief Justice of the Common Pleas.[26] Despite the cynicism surrounding Vicary's resignation, his new position suited him. 'In the civil business he is prompt, decisive and clear; on the crown side, very patient and careful. His temper is perfectly as it ought to be, having no longer any of that personal conflict which at the bar kept him always nettled and sore'.[27]

His move to the bench resulted in a considerable reduction in both his status and income as he exchanged his fee-based earnings of around £10,000 for a judge's salary of £2500. The following year his fortunes improved. In June, Chief Justice Mansfield's health deteriorated so much so that he looked 'more dead than alive'. On his death in 1814, Vicary was his natural successor. In November he was appointed chief baron of the exchequer and took his seat on 8 November, his sixty-second birthday. He and his family moved back to London for the parliamentary session, but at the end of January it was reported that 'The new Chief baron has been robbed at his Villa [in Hayes] of Linen & to ye Tune of 300£; this his third Burglary'.[28]

Despite his own ill health and the change in his fortunes, Vicary continued to use his influence to help his extended family. When Abraham's daughter, Mary was sent to London to finish her education, he and Kenny welcomed her into their home, employed the best teachers for her, and launched her into London society. A few months after his resignation as attorney general, his sister Mary Crawley asked if he could arrange for her eldest son Charles to obtain a commission in the army. Having no sons of his own, Vicary was very fond of all his nephews and willingly supported her application. Charles joined Gordon's regiment, fighting with Wellesley in Spain. All seemed well, until just before Christmas when the family received word that Charles had been seriously ill for several months. On 14 December, Vicary wrote to Gordon thanking him for 'his kindness and attention to Charles in his present and suffering state & for the full Communication you sent me of his condition'. He asked if his nephew could return to England, 'until he is sufficiently recovered to take the field again', adding, 'I have no doubt that Lord Wellington would permit it'.[29]

As news of Wellington's victory reached England, Vicary learned that the Exwick firm, run by his brother-in-law Samuel Banfill was in serious financial difficulties. His partner Edmund Granger wished to retire and withdraw his capital from the business and although Banfill had found a new partner, with the decline of the woollen industry, he was unable to raise sufficient funds to buy Granger out. The irony of the situation would not have escaped Vicary. Thirty years before he had purchased Exwick House for £3000, which had been transferred to the firm in 1787. Now if the business ceased trading, it would revert to his ownership, but if it went into liquidation, he would lose the entire estate. Vicary was also aware that Antony still owed Granger around £5500 from his original loan thirty years before, and therefore had no alternative but offer Banfill a loan to keep the firm afloat, on condition that both the house, factory and the mill were transferred back to his ownership. In a contract dated 24 October 1816, he agreed 'to advance and transfer for the joint accommodation of....Samuel Banfill and George Shute [Banfill's new partner], Four thousand and Four Hundred navy [sic] five per cent annuities upon having the retransfer of the like sum of stock and the payment in the meantime of sums of money equal to and in him of the dividends thereof', on condition that the partners agreed to 'bargain sell and demise' the freehold of the premises to him, until the loan was repaid.[30] His daughter Maria was childless and still separated from her husband, and as he had no heir of his own, he decided to settle part of his estate in favour of his many nephews and nieces. As the Banfills were also childless, Vicary decided that that on his death the Exeter firm would go to the sons of his sister Mary Crawley. It was agreed that when his nephew Charles returned from Spain, he and his brother George Abraham would join the business with a view to running it when Banfill retired.

In December, Vicary was stunned to hear of Antony's death. He knew that he had been complaining of feeling unwell for some months and had been suffering lapses of memory, but the suddenness of his death was a great shock. In a long letter to George he wrote,

'Our only consolation under this most grievous affliction is that he expired without any corporal sufferg, that everything was done which the greatest skill, applys at the earliest moment cou'd suggest or execute. His whole life was a constant preparation for that awful account to which he is now call'd, with the exception of what proceeded from the giddiness & levity of youth, & which was immediately corrected by his entrance into a more sober course of life... I know no man whose conduct was more exemplary – & the steadiness of his temper, his simple and unoffending manners, his charitable constructions of the acts of others, the warmth & openness of his heart, his charity to the extent of his means, his universal

benevolence, the candor & purity of his mind in
which no bad passion ever found a place, his patience
& submission unto misfortunes, & the steady perseverance with which he constantly follow'd what he
thought to be right, his strict exercise of every duty,
religious, civil, domestic which belongs to a man &
a Christian - these virtues will I humbly trust thro'
the merits of our Blessed Redeemer have sent him to
his reward'.

After Antony's death, Vicary decided to retire. Aware that his
income would now be significantly reduced, he tried to lessen the
financial burden on his family of maintaining his relatives. Having
secured the Exeter firm on his Crawley nephews, he lacked confidence
in Henry and William's ability to run Antony Gibbs & Sons, and
was worried that if it ran into financial difficulties, the responsibility
of maintaining them would fall on him. After George's death in 1818,
he suggested that the Bristol and London firms merge to form one
family business. Not surprisingly, his nephew George was in favour,
but both Henry and William rejected it the idea, afraid they would lose
control to the Bristol firm. Although irritated at their attitude Vicary
had no choice but to accept their decision. He continued to provide
a small pension for Bell, who was now living at Exwick House with the
Banfills and supported his youngest sister Kitty, who had long been
estranged from the family for a number of years. It was a great relief
both for him and Kenny when, at the age of forty-nine, she married
a Mr. Bellett Boroughs of Taunton.

CHAPTER 18

BRISTOL

During the long years of conflict over American Independence, abolitionism was overshadowed by war. The African trade was suspended and large numbers of Bristol ships were laid up in the ensuing economic crisis. Slave voyages failed to yield expected profits for a number of years and in the financial crisis of 1793, many Bristol merchants were ruined.[31] Three years later, of a fleet of one hundred Jamaica merchantmen convoyed by the navy, only seven belonged to Bristol merchants. By the end of the century, Bristol had not only been overtaken by Liverpool as a slaving port but had also fallen behind in terms of sugar imports. While some blamed the city's decline on abolition, in reality it had more to do with the limited size of its harbour and the failure of the city to modernise its port facilities. The exceptionally high tidal ranges and fast currents of the River Avon made it difficult for vessels to navigate the seven miles of twisting river from the Bristol Channel to the quay at the centre of the city. Larger vessels found it impossible to negotiate the bends in the river and were often tide-bound or stranded on the mud.

Improvements to the harbour were urgently required. As early as 1765 a number of schemes had been put forward to improve the docks by damming the River Avon to keep 'ships afloat at all times in the Harbour of Bristol' and for building a floating harbour.[32] Liverpool not only provided cheaper and better port facilities and had lower wages, but its ships sailed directly across the Atlantic to the north of Ireland; avoiding enemy privateers in the English Channel. In Bristol, the

Society of Merchant Venturers controlled the charges for anchorage, pilotage and moorage in the Channel as well as the right for merchants to use the quays. The majority of merchants, including George and his friend Richard Bright were also Merchant Venturers, and therefore had no incentive to reduce the charges.

At the onset of the French Revolutionary Wars in 1793, Munckley decided to retire from the firm, although he continued to take an active interest in the business, which was now run by George and his partner James Richards. Out of respect for their friend, they left the name of the firm unchanged, and it continued operating as Munckley Gibbs & Richards until Munckley's death. At the same time, George brought in his son, George Jr, then aged fourteen, to train in all aspects of the business. Despite the decline in profits caused by the long years of conflict, the firm survived the economic crisis in the early seventeen-ninetees, and with the end of the American Wars came the resumption of trade with the Caribbean without the need for convoys. Jamaica remained the chief source for sugar imports and the demand for both coffee and sugar remained bouyant in the early seventeen-ninetees. But peace was short-lived. In 1793, the French invaded Flanders and Britain was at war with France. This had a serious impact on trade with the Mediterranean, due to the closure of many trading routes. Convoys were again a necessity with vessels having to sail to Falmouth or Cork to wait for a convoy to the Mediterranean, but the French occupation of Holland the following year, and Napoleon's Italian campaign of 1796-7 saw the closure of these markets. As Britain anxiously waited for news that Spain was to enter the conflict as France's ally, George wrote to Antony, 'I fear that the apprehension of a war with Spain (which however I hope is without foundation) will be an obstacle in the way of taking up ships for that country'.

In November 1794, George's father died at the age of seventy-six. At the time of his death, the family's debts were still in the region of £20,000 and the burden of maintaining his mother and sisters had mainly fallen on him and Vicary. They were also supporting Antony's family, but with the decline in the West India trade, the balance of the financial responsibility shifted to Vicary. George's need was for an injection of capital to consolidate his business. This came the following July with his marriage to Anne Alleyne, the heiress daughter of Thomas Alleyne, a West India merchant and long-time acquaintance. The Alleynes, who had extensive plantations in Barbados, had returned to Bristol and were living in the leafy suburb of Clifton, which had become a favourite with retired families from the British Caribbean. As well as having a substantial dowry, Anne was also well connected. Her cousin was one of his friends, Alleyne Fitzherbert, who was later to become Baron St. Helens.[33] On their marriage, Susan who had been living with George while her husband was away at sea returned, to Topsham with her children.

Meanwhile Antony, who had been unable to return to Spain after his accident began to work with Munckley Gibbs & Richards. Following his tour of the northern cities in April 1794 to generate future business, he secured a number of contracts to supply Mediterranean produce through the Bristol firm. Despite the downturn in the trade, with Antony acting as its agent in Spain, the firm saw an increase in profits during these difficult times. Initially all seemed well as imports of Spanish produce increased to meet the growing demand. In July, George received a draft for £1000 from Antony with instructions that it be used to repay his debts to his mother and sisters rather than Vicary. Although he agreed in principle with this proposal, George was aware that his elder brother was hoping to be reimbursed, but thought that he might be persuaded to 'postpone his claim for the expenses of the family subsequent to my father's misfortunes' for the foreseeable future.

As the war dragged on, any plans for the abolition of the slave trade in the British Empire were abandoned. While Wilberforce continued to gain support in the Commons, planters and traders hoped they were saved for the duration of the conflict. Europe slipped into another economic slump with prices rising sharply. Through unavoidable delays as ships waited for a convoy, perishable cargoes were in danger of arriving too late and having to be destroyed. In November, Pomar sent a large consignment of raisins to Bristol for the Christmas markets, but they arrived two days after Christmas, and the customer refused to take them. George offered to store the fruit and try to dispose of it. Four weeks later, it remained unsold, and he was forced to sell the raisins at a loss. Knowing how vulnerable Antony's position was, he was also very concerned at the effect the embargo on British shipping would have on his brother's business, and he advised him to begin looking for other opportunities, which initially might appear less profitable but would be more beneficial in the long-term.

In February 1796, a letter arrived from Nancy, telling him that Banfill had proposed marriage. The news surprised George because Banfill was 'not the sort of man that I thought would have suited Nancy's taste or inclination'. Despite his misgivings about his 'perculiarities', he acknowledged that Banfill had 'a good heart and good intentions…and was worth as much as £4000'. As Nancy had no income of her own, she was hesitant about giving up her independence and asked her brother to 'come down to Exeter & by an inspection of his books, satisfy myself of the reality of the acct [sic] he has given of his circumstances'. George felt compromised, having known Banfill since their childhood and he refused his sister's request, thinking that to agree would seem 'like a distrust of his [Banfill's] integrity'. He was delighted to hear the following month of their marriage in Exeter Cathedral, and he and Anne sent their good wishes.

In June, as rumours increased that war with Spain was imminent, Antony was forced to return to England. After a whistle-stop tour of his clients, he stayed in Bristol for a few days before going on to Exeter. British merchants were finding it increasingly difficult to operate in Spain, so George suggested he look for something 'more beneficial' in neutral Portugal. There had long been an established British merchant community in both Lisbon and Oporto, and his brother had many contacts in the region. Before Antony returned to the Iberian Peninsula, George wrote to him, 'I see the complexion of the times does not shake your resolution for proceeding….to Lisbon – God grant that the cloud that hangs over this country may disperse. The present is a most awful critical period for us all'. He and Anne were worried about Dolly and he promised that 'whatever Dolly wants …I shall readily supply her with'.

Two weeks later, George and Anne travelled to Exeter with their children, Joanna and George Jr, to stay with the Banfills at Exwick for a short holiday. They visited Dolly and invited her to spend a few days with them at Dawlish, on the south Devon coast. While there, George became aware of some tension between her and Nancy that surprised him, as he knew the two women were great friends. Banfill confided in him that since their marriage, the wool trade had collapsed and the Exeter firm was finding it difficult to survive in such difficult times. They were aware that Antony had settled his mother's loan while Nancy's still remained unpaid. George was sympathetic to their troubles and on his return to Bristol, wrote urgently to Antony that 'The Spanish war must be felt very severely at Exeter & you do well to take measures for satisfying your debt there….I thank God there is not the same reason for any anxiety about mine'. Although the sugar industry was now in a period of long-term recession, it continued to sustain his business. The Bristol firm's trade was not dependent on the export trade with Europe, and he was thankful that his own 'particular business has not been affected as yet in any unfavourable measure by the unhappiness of the time'.

In October, a letter arrived from Antony with the news that he and Pomar were optimistic that they could beat the embargo on Spanish goods by smuggling them into Portugal for shipment to England. George thought this an excellent idea, suggesting that they should be channelled through Munckley Gibbs & Richards and we 'will readily take charge of it & do the best we can with it'. In December, the first shipment of Spanish fruit arrived in Bristol via Lisbon As usual, the consignment was of a very high quality and George had no difficulty selling it. As there was now a shortage of Mediterranean fruit in the city, he wrote, another 'cargo or 2 [sic] would sell very well here'.

Antony told George that he had learned from Vicary that the British

Government had given permission for some Spanish cargoes to be shipped to England in American vessels to prevent them being sequestered. George was more cautious. As there was no way of knowing 'how far the Government could continue to grant the same indulgence', he advised that Spanish produce should be sent via the Bristol firm in the usual way. It was not long before he began to have second thoughts about the legality of importing smuggled Spanish produce into England whilst the two countries were at war. Concerned for his reputation and anxious that nothing could be traced through his books, he asked Antony to record all such consignments through his Lisbon account to ensure that 'we know nothing of Mr. Pomar in the consignment of fruit if you ship to our address'. Despite the continued downturn in trade in colonial produce, 1796 proved to be a good year for Munckley Gibbs & Richards and George felt 'great satisfaction that the profits for last year give an addition to my stock of £500 or £600'.

Despite his repeated warnings about the need for caution, George continued to be frustrated by Antony's unrealistic expectations towards business. His brother still owed substantial sums to his family and friends, and with the death of their father was now responsible for their combined debts. George and Vicary continued to maintain their mother and sisters and occasionally sent Dolly small 'presents' of cash. While sympathetic to his brother's predicament, George knew that it was essential for him to remain focused. 'How far in the present instance you see a temptation sufficient to justify your departing from it is for you to judge', he wrote, ' You are not being called on for any advance on acct of the concern unless, in this case, the general objection to you introducing yourself in any adventures or speculations... .'.

Throughout this period, he continued to oversee Antony's finances and administer his debts. The two men could not have been more different. George was naturally conservative, having been well grounded in all aspects of commerce at the Exeter Academy. He had married two wealthy women and had used his extensive network of family and contacts to further his commercial interests, particularly in the West Indies. His temperament was disposed towards caution and prudence, whereas Antony had a 'sanguine speculative disposition' with an inclination towards undue risk-taking. Aware of these *defects* in his younger brother's character, George acted as his mentor, and guided him in his business affairs for many years.

Despite this, he was often exasperated by Antony's careless attitude towards keeping accounts, believing that this was one of the main reasons for his failure ten years before. By the end of the eighteenth century, double-entry bookkeeping was widely practiced and George considered it was essential to the success of any business. He wanted Antony to ensure that his affairs were always 'in a state of forwardness which is necessary to making a right estimate of your situation for it does not require a sanguine temper to deceive oneself in this respect'. He thought that in his business dealings, his brother 'had not reckoned on a war with Spain' before agreeing payment terms with his customers. On a number of occasions, he was forced to remind him that confused accounts and any delay in paying his bills could result in another business failure.

* * * *

In 1796, the French armies moved south into Italy and occupied Leghorn. Napoleon's Italian campaign, together with the withdrawal of the British fleet from the Mediterranean and the blockade of the Italian ports, cut off those markets. Although a numner of Bristol merchants attempted to run the blockade, trade with Italy was virtually suspended. West-country merchants had previously used neutral entrepôts during periods of war, and George could not understand why they no longer did so. When Spain entered the war on the side of France, the invasion of Portugal seemed inevitable. It was relief to hear the following January, that Antony was to close his office in Lisbon and return to England, but any hopes that George or Vicary may have had that he would be in a position to pay off his debts or maintain his family were soon dashed. Wartime inflation resulted in an adverse exchange rate causing him to lose a considerable amount in repatriation. Sympathetic to his plight, George generously offered Antony extended credit on the Munckley Gibbs & Richards account until the problem was resolved. He sent him £100 and told him not to hesitate to ask for more for 'I trust I need not say a word to convince you, my dear Anty [sic], how cheerfully I shall continue to supply your wants'. For, he wrote, 'these are times when we who can get money ought to assist our friends…and I can well afford [to] out of the profits of the company'.

While the country waited for news of the peace between France and Portugal, the general decline in both trade and industry in Bristol was masked by the patriotic fervour gripping the nation as news of the victories reached England. Naval successes were wildly celebrated, contrasting with the increasing unpopularity of the Corporation due to its brutal suppression of the riots against the increase in toll bridge charges in 1793. The Corporation was so disliked that it had difficulty filling the Chamber. The following year George was elected as a Councillor but was fined for refusing to take his seat.[34]

With no sign of peace, George continued to be worried at the 'state of commerce…in some places…with the decline in manufacturing' in the south west of England, while in the north it was buoyant. In December 1797, he gloomily asked Antony 'do you suppose that there are any manufactures in this county that have been encreasing [sic] during the war?' Unlike merchants in other parts of the West Country, Bristol was relatively unaffected by the decline as its commerce did not depend on exports. Although the Africa trade was virtually suspended, Bristol had a well-developed import trade in colonial produce and its merchants were able to withstand the financial pressures brought on by a war in Europe. Munckley Gibbs & Richards continued to make a profit from sugar imports, but George was quite naturally concerned for Banfill. He knew that many Exeter merchants, dependent on woollen exports were crippled by heavy losses with the closure of their chief markets in Europe, having been slow to switch to neutral ports during wartime.

Despite concerns about the combined effects of war and a prolonged abolitionist campaign might have on his business, life went on as normal for George and his family. He and Anne continued to entertain their friends, often visiting the Richards at Abbots Leigh and the Brights at Ham Green, and going to the theatre. That summer, while they spent some weeks in Bath taking the waters, Joanna, who had suffered from a number of ailments during her childhood, went to stay with her aunt at Exwick House. While there, she became ill and it was feared that she had succumbed to consumption. She remained in Exwick, to be nursed by Nancy for several weeks.

In early February 1797, the unsuccessful invasion of Pembrokeshire and the planned strike on Bristol increased patriotic fervour in the city. The attack was to 'produce total ruin of the town, the port, the docks, and the vessels and to strike terror and amazement into the very heart of the capital of England'.[35] The Bristol Regiment of Voluntary Infantry was quickly formed to defend the city and guard prisoners of war and £31,300 was raised to pay for the force. With the threat of invasion imminent, George Jr was appointed lieutenant in the Voluntary Infantry.[36] His father, fearful for the family's safety, decided that Anne should move to the country and wanted Joanna to return immediately to Bristol, but she was still too unwell. Antony had written urgently, asking him to arrange for his mother to go to Stowe, but George was opposed the idea because of her age and failing health. As volunteers massed in College Green on 2 March before marching to fight the enemy, merchants provided wagons and carts to convey their baggage. Thousands gathered to see them leave for the Pill, where they would board ships bound for Tenby. Just as they reached the outskirts of the city, news reached them that the Pembrokeshire landing was a false alarm.[37]

With the threat of invasion over, George and Anne returned to their house in Bristol and life continued very much as before. Still anxious about Joanna's health, in early summer they took the coach to Exwick to see her, but she was still too unwell to go back with them. Whilst there they spent a few days with Dolly, and George visited the school that his nephews Henry and William attended to check on both the curriculum and their progress. They hurredly returned to Bristol at the end of August amid reports that the Spanish and French fleets were massing at Brest. Once again, the country held its breath fearing invasion, as the British fleet under Lord Keith gathered at Torbay. The following month, when the danger had passed, George and Anne, accompanied by her younger sister, embarked on a tour of the south coast, visiting Weymouth and Sidmouth, before returning to Exwick to continue their holiday.

As news of Nelson's victory of the Nile on 1 August 1798 reached Bristol in October, the population shared in the national celebrations. A fund was started to support the families of those killed or injured in the fleet. While naval victories provided a welcome opportunity for festivities, and Bristolians enjoyed the excitement of the colour and ceremony of the increasing number of military occasions, these were offset by rising prices, hunger and business failures. The winter of 1788-79 was particularly harsh. Throughout Europe, severe frosts and heavy snow disrupted transport. Food prices rose sharply. The British blockade of the Dutch ports and the Anglo-Russian invasion of north Holland resulted in severe financial difficulties for Dutch merchants, causing a number of bankruptcies. Fortunately, the fluctuations in the exchange rates had little effect on the Bristol firm, but George was worried that the problems in Holland would have an adverse in London, which in turn might affect Antony's efforts. He wrote to him in November that, 'our house is not otherwise affected by them [the exchange rates] as they have operated to lower the price of Sugar, in this respect we are not likely to feel any loss beyond a little diminution of our commission'. It was not long before he was once again frustrated by his brother's approach to business. Although Antony wrote to George nearly every day asking for guidance, he rarely took any advice. Responding to the news that that he had obtained a large order by undercutting his competitors, George replied impatiently, 'you do not say whether you are selling the goods at a profit. The exchange is sadly against you & your friends in the present state [of affairs]' and he cautioned 'I doubt not that you do well to make your remittances in Dollars'.

After Christmas, he received an urgent letter from Nancy asking him to come to Exeter. His mother's health had deteriorated rapidly and it was thought she would not recover. Although frail, she eventually rallied. While there, he was relieved to see that Joanna's health had improved and it was agreed that if this continued, she would return to Bristol in the spring. However, this was not to be. Three months later, she had a sudden relapse and began coughing up blood. Anxious that the air in the city was too polluted for her condition, he took a house in the fashionable suburb Redland not far from the Richards at Abbots Leigh. It was there that Dolly's younger brother, Joseph Hucks, called to see them on his way back to Devonshire to stay with his mother. They were shocked at his appearance, especially in view of Joanna's condition. Hucks who was also suffering from advanced consumption, rested in Bristol for several days to regain his strength before going on to Exeter.

In July 1800, George was pleased to hear that Antony was planning to take his family with him when he returned to Lisbon in the autumn. He and Anne had been increasingly concerned about Dolly's mental state for some time; when he was away, she was very lonely and depressed and often complained of severe headaches. In September, the mail coach brought a letter with the distressing news that Dolly had collapsed and the doctors had diagnosed a 'severe stroke'. A shocked George replied by return, 'Your dear Wife will be supported under the heavy affliction that she is suffering' and that 'when she has a little recovered from this severe stroke, will mend, to which nothing may be more likely than in the climate to which she is going to remove'. Dolly's slow recovery forced Antony to put off his departure to Lisbon for several months. The following spring, he decided that she should remain in Exeter and once again, George readily agreed to look after her and the children in his brother's absence.

A few weeks after Antony's departure, a letter arrived from Dolly urgently asking for money. Both William and Anne had been unwell and she was unable to pay her doctor's bills. George sent her £20 by return for her immediate needs. At the beginning of June, he and Anne hurried to Exeter when they heard that she was in danger of going into premature labour. They were so shocked at her appearance that they decided to remain there until the danger had passed. On his return to Bristol, George wrote to Antony suggesting he return as soon as possible, but despite his promises to be home for the birth, he did not arrive until 31 August, three weeks after her confinement.

The following July, Samuel Munckley died at the age of seventy-seven. Throughout his life he had remained true to his Presbyterian beliefs, and was laid to rest in the burial ground at the Lewins Mead meeting in Brunswick Square 'in a vault under [the] west side of [the] Speaking House'.[38] He left an estate of over £36,000 (around £1.5 million in today's money), the bulk of it going to his nieces and nephews, the children of his half-brother Sir John Duntze. He also made a number of smaller bequests including £1200 to George as 'a token of my Esteem for him'; Joanna and George Jr each received £600. Nor had Munckley forgotten the other members of the Gibbs family. George's mother Anne was his cousin and he had long admired the courage in which she had borne their misfortune. He left her £100, and her other children, including Vicary his "respected Relation and ffriend" £50 each.[39]

After Munckley's death, George set about reorganising the business. He and Richards sought to bring the next generation into the firm. George Jr, now twenty-two, had finished his apprenticeship and had recently become engaged. The £600 legacy from Munckley was timely but he needed an income before he could marry. George began making the necessary arrangements for him to become a partner. As Richards had no children, his nephew, Samuel (Thomas's son), who had been working in the firm for some years, was also offered a partnership. It was decided to change the name of the firm to Gibbs Richards & Gibbs to reflect the new arrangements. As his plans progressed, George wrote that, 'Everything is arranged respecting the partnership of Gibbs Richards & Gibbs, and on terms very tolerably liberal for George' although 'his income is not likely to be more than moderate for some time'. The following year, twenty-three year old George Jr married Salvina Hendy, the daughter of Henry and Henrietta Hendy, wealthy Barbadan merchants.

* * * *

Reduced trade in the woollen industry in the southwest resulted in the further decline in Bristol's importance as Liverpool expanded and by 1800, it had been overtaken by its northern rival. As well as offering cheaper port facilities, with its proximity to the northern coalfields and the growing cotton industry many merchants found it more cost-effective to use Liverpool, prompting them to transfer their operations to the northern port and transport goods to Bristol. In March, the *Bristol Felix Farley Journal* reported that 'Several cargoes of West Indian and American produce have been recently imported into this city from Liverpool'.[40] For forty years, the Corporation and the Society of Merchant Venturers had considered a number of dock improvement schemes but they were unwilling to make the necessary investment. In 1802, William Jessop put forward a plan to divert the rivers Avon and Frome into a floating harbour covering around 70 acres. It was estimated that the cost of the scheme would be in the region of £300,000. The Members of the Society recognised that something needed to be done if Bristol was to maintain a share of the Atlantic trade. Under pressure from Richard Bright who had been collecting details of winds and tides and comparative information and calculations on the rates charged at both Bristol and Liverpool, the Society supported the Corporation and in February approved Jessop's plan.[41]

A committee of twenty-seven, with equal representation from the Corporation, Merchant Venturers and subscribers was formed to look at ways of raising the money and to push a Dock Bill through Parliament. It was agreed that £250,000 was to be raised by public subscription and the remaining £50,000 was to be borrowed on 'the credit of Rates & Duties ...on Houses, Shipping and Goods of Foreign Import'.[42] There was such confidence in the scheme that the shares in the new venture, valued at £100 each were quickly taken up by members of the Corporation and leading merchants and manufacturers in the city, with George and James Richards each investing £1000 in the project.

The following year an Act for improving the Port and Harbour was passed in the face of spirited opposition at its second reading. The main reservations from those opposing the scheme were that the 'Expense of the Undertaking had been greatly under-rated and that the benefits were not commensurate with the 'magnitude' of the undertaking'. Such was the level of concern that a condition of the Act was that subscribers should 'receive no more than 4 per Cent for the first six years, and 8 per Cent afterwards.[43] The Act provided for the formation of the Bristol Docks Company to manage the construction and the administration of the work, with similar representation to the committee that had led to its formation. The following year work began.

Despite his commitment to the harbour improvements, George had been considering transferring some of his business to Liverpool because of the high costs of operating out of Bristol, but had hesitated because of the difficulties of operating from the distant northern port. In 1801, he decided to test the market by purchasing the *Concord* from Munckley's estate to sail on the Liverpool-West Indies routes and employed his cousin William as its master. William had been underemployed for many years and George hoped this would give him some temporary respite from his financial troubles. The *Concord* left Liverpool just before Christmas and such was the success of the venture that two years later George purchased the *Hope*, a Jamaicaman which had originally been built in Bristol in 1793 for Munckley Gibbs & Richards. The vessel needed an extensive refit before it was ready to sail the Atlantic and he offered William the chance of investing in this new venture and to captain the ship to the West Indies. As a shareholder he would be entitled to a percentage of the profits, thus providing him with an income to support his family.

The following year the refit completed, the *Hope* set off from Liverpool on her maiden voyage to the West Indies captained by William Gibbs. Between 1802 and 1805, while the improvements to the docks in Bristol were underway, the vessel made four voyages to the Caribbean, each taking the best part of a year. Aware of Susan's financial difficulties, George kindly gave her small advances on her husband's share of the profits so that she could maintain her family in his absence. He was very fond of Susan. She had become much loved within the family especially for her kindness and fortitude in the face of what appeared to be a difficult marriage. While William was at sea, she and her children were regular visitors at his house in Long Ashton and at the Richards in Abbots Leigh. The Bristol firm employed William until his retirement in 1808, when he returned to Topsham. Their investment had been a great success and George considered that his family's long-standing debt to his cousin was finally repaid.

For the next few years, Gibbs Richards & Gibbs continued to operate from Bristol, albeit on a much smaller scale. Although still heavily committed to the harbour and docks improvement scheme, by 1805 George had opened a permanent office in Liverpool and was transferring more and more of his business there. That year, after a brief peace, England and Spain were at war again and when he learned that Antony was closing his Spanish office and moving his operations to Lisbon, he offered him a partnership in the Liverpool firm. Although disappointed when Antony refused, later that year George took in William Thompson and established the firm of Gibbs Thompson & Co in Liverpool. When Parliament passed the Abolition of the Slave Trade Act in 1807, banning British subjects from conducting the trade and making it illegal to carry slaves on British ships, the firm was well established, importing sugar into Liverpool, and it continued to profit from increasing demands for colonial produce.[44]

In April, amidst accusations of fraud and mismanagement it emerged that, without informing the Corporation or the shareholders, the directors of the Bristol Dock Company had presented a second bill to Parliament, which was already in its second reading. Since the commencement of the project, another act had been passed requiring that all shareholders pay a further £35 per share at 4 per cent for the first six years and then six per cent thereafter to raise the required sum. Initially it was thought the new bill was to enable the company to raise the additional £50,000 for the work on the basin, but it emerged that as there were now so few ships entering the docks in Bristol, the Directors were unable to raise sufficient funds from the port dues and had applied to increase local taxes. Because of rising costs, instead of the original £50,000 they estimated that £100,000 was required to complete the work. The new bill proposed changes to the provisions of the original act, giving the Dock Company the power to raise extra taxes on houses in the city and on all goods arriving at the port, not just on imports but also on goods from the coastal trade. It would also give it the power 'to perpetuate the Rate even should the works fail in their execution', which in effect repealed the provisions of the original act.

Public confidence in the scheme evaporated and there was fury at the actions of the Directors. At a meeting of 'a number of wealthy merchants and traders' on 26 March 1807, the Bristol Dock Bill Committee was formed consisting 'of men of fortune with a long connection in trade and as such have the interests of the Port and the City of Bristol at heart'.[45] On the committee were many local wealthy entrepreneurs, including George, George Jr, John Harford, Sir Henry Prothero and Charles Saunders. At its first meeting, George Jr was appointed Chairman. The committee was empowered to consult with the directors of the Dock Company and to 'meet them on the fair ground of computing the value of the new Improvements' of the bill. It called on the mayor of Bristol to determine the propriety of either opposing or supporting the current bill in Parliament.[46]

There followed a hectic couple of months as the committee organised a number of petitions from the Corporation, merchants, shipowners and ratepayers opposing the bill. Such was the furore that the Directors agreed to drop the clauses relating to the increases in tax and port dues until a compromise was reached. On 20 April, a hand-bill was distributed throughout the city by a jubilant Bristol Dock Bill Committee and signed by it chairman, George Jr, congratulating his 'Fellow Citizens on the Success already obtained in the temporary abandonment of the Coasting Rates'. It urged them 'not to relax their

Opposition to the Present Bill until the Directors shall have given a sufficient Pledge to abandon altogether these obnoxious Rates and shall agree to other fair and reasonable Amendments of the said Bill'.[47]

This presented the shareholders of the Dock Company with a dilemma. Many, like George and Richard Bright, were both shareholders and members of the Society of Merchant Venturers or of the Corporation, leading to a conflict of interest. While recognising that they needed to keep harbour dues low to compete with their northern rival, they also needed to recoup their investment as quickly as possible. However, like his father, George Jr was a pragmatist and was anxious to avoid an impasse. He knew that if the floating harbour was not completed, no one would realise a profit on their investment. In April he wrote to Bright, suggesting that the Committee might accept a compromise if the Directors of the Dock Company would agree to the proposal that 'New Rates to the amount of £50,000 – Those on foreign trade as proposed by the present bill & the remainder by additional rates on coasters & houses – on these rates to be final'. This was conditional on them completing the works specified in the original bill. In spite of this ultimatum, the Directors were adamant that they only needed £100,000 to complete the works. Despite their assurances, when the improvements to the dock basin were completed in 1809 the total cost was £600,000, twice the original estimate. By this time, many saw the increased charges imposed by the Docks Company as the final nail in the coffin for the port and the majority of firms connected with the West India trade, including Gibbs Richards & Gibbs, had stopped using the docks altogether, having transferred their operations to Liverpool.

As the work on the floating harbour neared completion, George, then in his mid-fifties, began to think of retiring. That year his partner James Richards retired and he and Betsy moved to Ilfracombe in Devon. The firm was renamed George Gibbs & Son.[48] After six years of marriage, George Jr and Salvina remained childless and any hopes his father may have had of them founding a dynasty diminished as each year passed. Salvina been diagnosed with consumption not long after their marriage and her health had caused the family considerable concern for some years. By the beginning of 1808, the disease had taken such a grip that 'The pain on her chest in some degree mitigated the severity of her cough'. After a trip to Bath in the early summer, she arrived home in August in such a weak condition that leeches were applied in an attempt to relieve her distress. George had hoped that his nephew William, who had been working in the Bristol office since the beginning of 1806, would remain in the firm and eventually become a partner, but his plans were thwarted when later that year, the French overran Portugal and Antony returned to England to open an office in London. In October, William left to join his father. The following month, Salvina was taken to London to see her doctor but the journey proved too much for her. On 15 November, at the age of twenty-nine she died there. George Jr who had accompanied her was devastated by his loss and made the necessary arrangements to bring her body back to Bristol, where she was buried some days later.

For the next few years, George's role in the firm declined as George Jr took over its day-to-day operation. After Salvina's death, and with no heir of his own, George suggested that Richard Bright's youngest son Robert join the firm.[49] Robert had graduated at Glasgow University and had initially planned to join Antony Gibbs & Son. George and Bright agreed that after 'two years of satisfactory experience of him" and on condition that he learned Spanish, Robert would become a partner at no cost to himself or his father. In 1814, Bright joined the Bristol firm and two years later, was sent to the Spanish offices of Antony Gibbs & Son to learn the language and become familiar with trade and banking. By this time George Gibbs & Son were acting as shippers for Antony Gibbs & Son, and it was essential to have someone at Bristol who was fluent in Spanish.

A widower at the young age of thirty, George Jr threw himself into his work, knowing that his father was still hoping to retire. Five years later, he announced that he was to marry his cousin Harriet, Antony's eldest daughter. The two cousins had always been close as children, and after Salvina's death, had begun corresponding regularly. They were married at Cheltenham on 8 March 1814, and made their home in his father's house at Redland. Whatever hopes George may have had that his son and new daughter-in-law would produce an heir were not to be. They too remained childless and so he devoted himself to training his young protégé, Robert Bright. With the company's future now secure, at the age of sixty-two George was persuaded to retire and for the next few years, he and Anne spent much of their time visiting friends and relatives in Exeter, London and Stowe.

CHAPTER 19

THE END OF AN ERA

After the move to Powis Place, life continued very much as usual for Antony and Dolly. Although the venture to Peru with *La Hermosa Mexicana* had not been as profitable as first anticipated, its success on the outward voyage gave the family some temporary financial relief. In 1813, William was taken into the partnership and the firm was renamed Antony Gibbs & Sons. While he remained in London with his father, the Cadiz office prospered under Henry's supervision. Cadiz remained the main port for the export of goods to the Spanish colonies as well as for imports into Andalusia and other parts of Spain. Henry was quick to see the potential of Gibraltar as a base to develop the entrepôt trade and appointed John Lee Casson as the firm's agent there to expand the business.[1] By 1814, Antony had virtually handed over the reins to his sons and Henry returned to England to run the London office while William went to Cadiz. That year the firm made over £6,000 in commission, almost double that of the previous year, but with the end of hostilities across Europe, both England and Spain were plunged into severe depression. As social unrest spread across the country the following year, profits dropped to £1700, although in 1816 they picked up slightly to £2500.

In 1814, they were delighted when Harriet announced that she was to marry her first cousin George Jr. Harriet was twenty-eight and without a dowry, and her parents had long given up hope that she would ever marry; so it came as a real surprise to learn that she and George had been writing to each other for many months. In March, the family travelled to Cheltenham for the wedding, staying at Stowe with the Crawleys.

Later that year, at the age of fifty-eight, Antony was taken ill. For some months, he had complained of feeling unwell and his doctors thought that he was suffering the after-effects from his accident in Spain twenty years before, notably the loss of his short-term memory. As his conditioned worsened, he was forced to give up working and he and Dolly continued to live quietly at Powis Place, occasionally visiting George and Harriet at Redland and the Banfills at Exwick. Surprisingly, he and Dolly seemed more contented than they had been for many years. But in the summer of 1815, Antony's condition deteriorated suddenly. Dolly was so worried that on 13 July she wrote to Harriet, 'Your father is too unwell to think about my own complaints, he has not been comfortable for many days but yesterday his tracts were very bad & all night he was in a fever, ...his breathing too is very difficult.'.

When he had recovered sufficiently to travel, he and Dolly went to Redland for an extended visit, remaining there for several weeks. In mid-November, Antony decided to return to London. Leaving Dolly in Bristol, Harriet accompanied him to Powis Place. Two weeks later, at 10.30pm on 5 December, not long after he had gone to bed he suffered a massive stroke. Harriet, grief stricken, wrote urgently to her husband asking him to break the news to her mother. 'My dearest Father', she wrote, 'is exceedingly ill. I hardly have the courage to tell you that he was attacked last night after he got into bed with an apoplectic fit, which has deprived him of the use of one half of his body. His speech is difficult but he is perfectly in his senses tho' he does not yet know the state that he is in. I must leave it to you my Dear George to prepare my mother for this trial'. The doctors were called and Antony was 'bled and blistered', but to no avail. He died on 10 December 1815. Five days later, on a cold December day, he was buried at Hayes.

William, who had been in Cadiz for several months, knew nothing of his father's death. Henry, knowing he must write to tell him the news was concerned at how he would react. To prepare him for the worst, he sent two letters to the Cadiz office, one addressed to William

Branscombe the other to William. In the first, he told Branscombe of his father's death, but asked him not to tell his brother, as he wanted to break the news gently. In the second, Henry only told William that Antony had suffered a stroke. It is pitiful 'to see our poor Father reduced to a state of helplessness', he wrote, 'the Physicians are decidedly of the opinion that this is only a part of his original accident in Spain, & that the only wonder is that he has been spared to us so long. 25 years we have enjoyed the blessing of him amongst us since his accident & have abundant reasons to be thankful...'.

Knowing that William would want to return to England, immediately after the funeral Henry wrote to tell him of Antony's death. The relationship between his father and brother had sometimes been very strained. William had always resented being removed from school at such an early age, and made to go into the family business instead of having the freedom to pursue his chosen profession. Aware that he would now be filled with remorse and that he had had little contact with his parents for many months, Henry was anxious to spare him any guilt and tried to reassure him of their father's motivation. 'His anxiety & assertions in business', he wrote, 'proceeded solely from his great love for his wife and children, & the honourable wish he always had at heart of discharging the debts of his youth....I believe his only fault was a quickness of temper, which was then only for a short time overcame his judgement, & had its origin no doubt in the shock he suffered from his fall in Spain'.

Some months after Antony's death, Harriet invited her mother and sister to Redland for an extended visit. Anxious to leave London, Dolly gratefully accepted. There, she became unwell and she and Anne were forced to remain there for the next fifteen months. William, still in Cadiz, planned to return to England in 1817 for Henry's marriage to their cousin Caroline Crawley, but changed his plans at the last minute, deciding to stay in Spain. Dolly, believing that her health was failing and worried that she might not see her younger son again, petulantly wrote to Henry. 'William again putting off his departure is a great disappointment. I have all my life been so used to such changes that

I ought to feel it less than I do, but a day is of more consequence to me now than a year was in former times, for the best that can be said of my health is that it is in a very precarious state:...though I have been...through many a severe attack I feel that both mind and body have undergone a great change and I have not the strength I used to have in any respect. I am however doing all I am advised to do in the hope of receiving benefit'. It was to be several months before she had recovered sufficiently to return with Anne to Powis Place.

Not long after her return, Dolly learned from Harriet that her father-in-law was seriously ill. For some time George had been complaining of feeling under the weather but his doctors could find nothing obviously wrong. Throughout his life, George had always appeared to be in good health and the 'life of the party'. After Christmas, his condition had deteriorated; he was losing weight and complained of feeling tired. By April, it was obvious that he was critically ill. He and Anne travelled to Bath to see if the waters would improve his strength, but to no avail. In June, his health worsened and they were forced to return to Redland. Now close to death the family gathered at his bedside, and Anne sent word to Vicary and Dolly that they should come at once.

Arriving in Bristol at the end of July, Dolly was shocked at his appearance. On 3 August she noted in her journal, 'My dear brother asked Dr. Barland to tell him the state he was in. Poor Mrs Gibbs, she is only to be pitied; our dear brother is in an unenviable state'. With his family around him, George died on 16 August 1818 aged sixty-five. That day Dolly wrote in her journal, 'At 2o'c this morning our dear brother breathed his last, and we have lost a most dear and valued friend. Oh may my end be like this!'2 He was buried five days later in the Chapelry of Redland. George had always been a kind, generous man, aware of his own good fortune, and well loved by all the family. Throughout Dolly's marriage, he had been a stalwart friend, having supported her and Antony through many difficult years. Henry, who was in Cadiz, heard the news of his uncle's death from William, who wrote, '...His brotherly love and kindness towards our dearest father during the whole course of his life and his generous and affectionate behaviour towards us will never be obliterated from my memory...'. George's fortune was estimated to be in the region of £33,000. In his will, he bequeathed £1000 to Anne to provide for her future needs; he left his compting house in Bristol to his son George, and the rest of the estate to be divided between him and Joanna.

After George's funeral, Dolly returned to Powis Place, but ill health continued to plague her. She was suffering from severe gout and rheumatism and in September gladly accepted an invitation from Nancy to go to Exwick House for an extended stay. George and Harriet were there, visiting Joanna who now lived with the Banfills. They took Dolly to Sidmouth for a short holiday by the sea, but on their return, she was in so much pain that the now very elderly Robert Remmett was summoned from Plymouth. In November, Dolly's condition continued to deteriorate and Harriet was so worried that she and George insisted that she return with them to Redland until she recovered her strength. Gratefully Dolly wrote, 'How gratifying it is to be sure that both he & Harriet are equally anxious for me to remain with them'. The following March she and Anne returned to Powis Place where Henry and Caroline were now living. In July, after the birth of their second child, another Henry, Dolly and Anne went for a short holiday to Brighton to take the sea air. On their return Dolly decided to leave Powis Place for good and accepted her daughter's invitation to live with her and George at Redland.

By 1817, Vicary too was becoming increasing frail. Ill health had dogged him for years and he had been absent from the western circuit for several months. That year, his condition suddenly worsened and in December, he approached the Lord Chancellor and offered to resign, 'but for reasons too flattering to me, he would not then hear of it'. In the autumn, although he was 'gradually recovering to a certain degree ... from a very serious illness' he had 'struggled for a year with a Disorder which rendered me incapable of executing the Duties of my Office, without more aid from my brother Judges than it was reasonable to ask from them'. In October 1818, he wrote to Lord Liverpool that 'I feel that this [recovery] is now improbable, & that I shall never again be able to encounter the common fatigues of the Profession without extreme danger'. On the advice of his physicians, he asked Liverpool to 'humbly to pray His Royal Highness, the Prince Regent, that I may be permitted to retire from it, a request which I make with reluctance, but am driven to it by a sense of propriety of Duty'. He was sure that in 'My present state, of which I have apprized [sic] His Lordship, will I am sure convince him that it is now become necessary.[3] Liverpool replied by return, expressing his regret at Vicary's decision, but as it 'appears to have been taken by the advice of your Physicians, I have nothing else to say upon it but to express the high Sense which I feel with the Profession and the World of yr [sic] valuable Services'. He added, 'and if I may be allowed to add the satisfaction it has been to me and in any way instrumental in bringing them forward in Solutions where they cd [sic] be justly appreciated'.[4]

Now too frail to make the arduous journey to Devon for the summer, Vicary was always anxious for news from Exwick, and continued to correspond regularly with Nancy and Bell. In December 1819, he was shocked to hear from Nancy that the Exeter firm was on the verge of bankruptcy. As he and Kenny had only recently returned to their house in Russell Square, he delayed replying until after Christmas. Still in a state of shock, on 11 January, he wrote to Bell asking her to pass on his apologies to Nancy 'since the state of affairs at Exwick was communicated to me by Mrs Banfill…but I knew not what to say. He continued, 'my breast bleeds of the affliction of my sister [Nancy] though I cannot as yet know the extent of her calamity, but I fear that it is extreme'. However, before Vicary could reply to Nancy his health suddenly deteriorated and, four weeks later on 8 February 1820 he died at his home in Russell Square, with his cousin Robert Remmett in attendance and his family at his bedside. He was buried near Antony in the family vault at St. Mary the Virgin in Hayes.

Two weeks later, Dolly who had been living at Redland for the last two years, died on 24 February. She too was buried at Hayes next to Antony not far from Vicary's grave. The bulk of her estate, valued at £7,900 was left in trust for her youngest daughter Anne, with a number of small bequests to other members of the family. Strangely, she also left £380 towards the education of a 'Thomas Michael Gilman of Hastings in the County of Sussex, an infant of …five years or thereabouts'.[5] This was reputed to be an orphan child adopted by Antony and herself, but included with Dolly's will was a note for her children that perhaps sheds more light on the child's true identity. It read, 'For your Father's sake and mine you will I hope all interest yourselves about him. The taking him might not be prudent but remember it was the soul of charity and kindness that prompted the deed and most anxious I have ever been that the blessed intention should succeed. I wish if possible to have him kept from very low people. By his own industry he must get bread. God grant he may be in all his actions governed by the principles of religion and honesty I have endeavoured to instill in his mind.'[6] It would appear that even in death Dolly, who had supported and stood by her husband for over thirty-one years of marriage, continued to take care his indiscretions.

* * * *

After William's departure to Palermo with Mary in 1812, Susan remained in Topsham with their younger children, Frances, Mary Matilda, Lyle and Charles, assuming that her husband would return within a few months. William had other plans; on arrival in Palermo, he was overwhelmed by his Abraham's position and status. Now in his mid-fifties, he loved the warm Sicilian climate, but more importantly, he quickly adapted to his brother's affluent lifestyle. With no thought for his wife and children, he quickly settled into Abraham's house in Palermo. After so many years apart, and with such a difference in their ages, William and Susan had found it increasingly difficult to live together. With their continual financial difficulties and the dependence on others, any love they had for each other had long disappeared. Whether they had separated by mutual consent, or whether Abraham found him some employment in Palermo is unclear but from 1812, William appears to have abdicated all responsibility for his family, providing them with no financial support for the next four years. Even when their young son Lyle died aged only fifteen, he refused to return to her. It was only Abraham's tragic death in 1816 that forced him to go back to Topsham.

After the freedom he had enjoyed in Palermo, life in Topsham was monotonous and dull and William found it impossible to settle down with his wife and daughters. For Susan too, his return made life intolerable. With the exception of the first few years of their marriage, they had rarely lived under the same roof. Although they tried to do so now, their differences remained unresolved but divorce was out of the question. Unknown to Susan, William began making plans to leave her again. He hoped to take a lease on a farm just outside Topsham on the road to Clyst St George. He wrote to Lyle asking for a loan, but refrained from mentioning his real intentions. Initially Lyle agreed to his request, but when he learned of William's plans, he angrily refused, threatening to cut him off without a penny. Afraid of losing his livelihood, William abandoned his plans, knowing better than to alienate Lyle or threaten his sons' futures for, after Abraham's death, William Henry had joined John Ley in the Genoese firm and Lyle was paying for young Charles to board at Blundells School. It appears that William took Lyle's threat seriously enough and had no alternative but to settle down with his family, somewhat surprisingly becoming a pillar of the local community.

He had always taken his duties as William Townson's executor very seriously. It was only after his return to Topsham that he learned that the Townson legacy, that had put a number of properties in trust for the benefit of the poor, was void under the Mortmain Act 1736, which applied to gifts for all charitable uses.[7] Now that he was no longer bound by the conditions of Townson's will, William set about converting the 'three messuages and lofts', into 'five dwelling-houses and lofts and cellars, two of which ..were situate in the High-street of Topsham, and the other dwelling houses and lofts and cellar near the lane called Passage Lane to maximise the income from them'.[8] Still wishing to comply with his friend's bequest, in a deed dated 4 July 1822, and enrolled in the court of chancery in September of that year, William set up a trust granting the churchwardens and overseers of the parish 'a yearly rent charge of 4£ so that they should yearly forever, at Christmas, lay out the same rent charge, in the purchase of bread', and distribute it 'among such poor persons….as they at their discretion should think proper'. The charity was known as the *Gift of Townson and Gibbs*.[9] Now a man of property, William was able to keep the excess profits from the rents and his finances improved for the first time in his life. Whether he managed to curb his violence towards Susan is unclear and at times his conduct 'was such as to endanger the continuance of Lyle's generosity'.

In the end, William and Susan could barely suppress their mutual loathing. Two years later, when he was in his early sixties, they formally separated and he moved into lodgings leaving her with their daughters Frances and Mary Matilda in the little house in Shapter Street. Such was the relief that Susan and the girls felt at his departure that it compensated them for their complete dependence on Lyle for support. As good as his word, he took them under his protection and continued to maintain them for the next eleven years. William died in 1831. The *Trewman's Exeter Flying Post* reported that 'On Saturday [February 19th] at his lodgings in Budleigh Salterton, Mr William Gibbs, late of Topsham, aged 75' had died.[10] He was buried in Topsham.

After his death, Susan decided to give up the house in Topsham and move with her daughters to Tiverton to be near her brother Rev^d. John Ley. She rarely saw her sons who were now all employed by her brother-in-law in Genoa. The sale of the house in Shapter Street ended five generations of the residence of the Gibbs family in Topsham. Now completely supported by Lyle she was distressed to learn two years later, that both William Henry and John Ley had left the Genoese firm and returned to England. Knowing how much Lyle had done for her family, she believed that they should have been more grateful to their uncle. Susan continued to live with her daughters until her death in 1834. She bequeathed her estate, valued at £200 to her daughters Frances and Mary Matilda and left 'for her life… a small Leasehold Estate in the parish of Doddiscombleigh' to her sister Frances Davis.[11] Now alone in Devon, Frances and Mary Matilda remained in Tiverton, almost totally supported by their uncle. Some years later, Lyle calculated that he had been giving his brother's family between £250-£300 a year for some fifty years, as well as employing William's three sons, William Henry, John Ley, and Charles.

Betsy continued to live in Ilfracombe with her husband until his death in 1829. By that time it was reported, 'she was as deaf as a post and uses a trumpet'. Richards' fortune was estimated to be in the region of £30,000 and he left Betsy wealthy woman.[12] He bequeathed her £2000 and all his 'ffurniture and plate' plus £600 a year 'for the rest of her natural life'. After a number of legacies including £2000 to 'George Gibbs the Younger', and his nephews and nieces, the children of his late brother Thomas, the rest of his fortune went to his brother Samuel, a sugar refiner in Bristol.

After her husband's death, despite repeated requests from Lyle, Betsy refused to contribute to the support of her nieces and nephews. Both William Henry and John Ley had also hoped that she might be persuaded to change her will in their favour but to no avail. Although she did not always see eye to eye with Lyle, Betsy was no fool and thought that her nephews were too like their father. Despite this, she had some sympathy for William Henry. He now suffered from severe arthritis and his epilepsy had worsened since his return to England and she knew he bitterly resented his financial dependence on his uncle. She agreed to put £500 in trust for him with Antony Gibbs & Sons on condition that on his death it was to go to his sisters, Frances and Mary Matilda. When John Ley and Ellen brought their children to Ilfracombe for the summer in 1836, Betsy was delighted to see them but refused to give them a regular allowance. Instead, knowing it would irritate her brother she paid their expenses back to Genoa. Whatever Lyle may have thought, Betsy was not fooled by either of her nephews and was well aware that her fortune had come from her husband's family. She continued to live in Ilfracombe, dying there in 1840, and her 'ffurniture and plate and other chattels' went to her husband's nephews and nieces according to his wishes, with nothing for her brother's children.

In 1810, Edmund Granger wished to retire from the Exwick firm of Granger & Banfill. He contacted Antony to ask if he were in a position to repay his long-outstanding debt, still standing at over £3500, but again Antony claimed that he had insufficient funds. However, he assured Granger that once his latest venture to sell Spanish stock to South America had been completed he would do so. This persuaded Granger to change his plans and he and Banfill decided to look to the future of the business. With no children of his own, Banfill wished to leave his share to his nephews Charles and George Abraham Crawley, the sons of his sister-in-law, Mary. Charles, aged twenty, had been in the army with Wellington in Spain, but had been forced to return to England after a serious illness and had joined the firm. It was agreed that young George Abraham, then aged fifteen, would also join the business with a view to the brothers taking it over within the next few years. As there were still another six years to run on the lease for the mill, in November, Banfill and Granger surrendered the existing lease and a new ninety-nine year lease was re-assigned to Banfill, Charles Crawley and Henry Ley, a nephew of Susan Gibbs.

Despite the impact that the prolonged war with France was having on businesses in Exeter, the city was in a buoyant mood, convinced of ultimate victory. The bullion crisis of 1810 had resulted in a number of banking failures in the city.[14] Over the last few years, Barings and a number of the larger banks had moved their operations to London leaving the smaller banks vulnerable to local business failures. That year, Granger and Banfill, along with other prosperous men of property, assembled in the Guildhall to declare their confidence 'in the strict honour and undeniable credit and respectability' of the local banks. Banfill, an ardent pamphleteer, entered the controversy, publishing a pamphlet entitled '*A Letter to Dennis Giddy Esq MP*' in answer to Giddy's pamphlet a '*Plain Statement on the Bullion Question*'.

Three years later, with no sign of a peace, Granger once again expressed a wish to retire and withdraw his capital from the firm. Despite Banfill's appeals to wait until the end of the war, this time Granger was determined, his patience worn thin. He felt very bitter towards Antony whose debts remained unpaid after twenty-four years despite him apparently having a flourishing business in London. He had asked him that his loan should be repaid on a number of occasions but the Gibbs family was unsympathetic to his request. I have 'seen enough of both these worthy gentlemen' wrote George Jr. to his wife Harriet 'to have a very poor opinion of both of them and whatever they may both suffer on this occasion, I shall consider as well merited punishment for their unjustifiable conduct to your dear father in former times'. They appeared to have forgotten that it was only through Granger and Samuel Banfill's generosity that Antony had been able to continue trading after his bankruptcy.

This made things very difficult for Banfill for although the firm still traded in the Iberian Peninsula through the Cadiz office of Antony Gibbs & Son, the principal market for his cloth remained London's East India Company. What remained of Devon's once thriving woollen industry had moved north to Bradford and a number of other Yorkshire towns and it was only through Banfill's good management that the business had survived for so long, having diversified and now concentrating on producing cashmere and shawls for the luxury overseas markets. Initially Banfill found it difficult to raise sufficient funds to buy Granger's share, but eventually obtained a loan from Bowring's Bank. By the end of September 1813, their partnership was dissolved and Granger 'had been paid or taken security for the payment of his share & interest in the sd Co-partnership'.[14] Banfill's plan to leave the business to Charles and George Abraham Crawley was thwarted when neither of his nephews would join the firm. With manufacturing in decline, Exeter's economic prospects looked bleak and when their uncle George offered them positions in the Liverpool office of George Gibbs & Son, they jumped at the chance. Disappointed, Banfill looked for a new partner and three months later signed a new twelve-year agreement with George Shute, a clothier from the nearby town of Crediton. The firm was renamed Banfill Shute & Co and when Shute's son Stephen, joined the business, its future seemed secured.

In 1814, the war was over. The end of hostilities was hailed as the 'permanent return of Peace and Plenty', with celebrations all over the city. In May, the *Trewman's Exeter Flying Post* reported that Banfill Shute & Co had entertained their employees 'on the occasion of peace'.

> 'On Friday night last Samuel Banfill Esq., of Exwick-house gave a dinner to the residents of Exwick in the employ of Banfill Shute & Co. About two hundred sat down in one of the rooms of the manufactory to celebrate the return of Peace on old English fare; and after disposing of two hogsheads of Exwick cyder in toast to their King and Country, to the heroes by sea and land who have fought for us, and to the government by whose counsels our efforts in just cause have been brought to this happy issue; they adjourned in the evening to a rising spot of the tenter-ground where an effigy of Bonaparte sunk amidst the flames of an immense bonfire surrounded by fireworks. Mr. Banfill gave the following toast :- "health to all – long to enjoy the blessings of a lasting peace – and may we never forget that our title to this blessing is the watchword of the immortal Nelson: *God and our Country expect that we should every Man do our duty*'.[15]

The following month, their differences forgotten, Banfill and Granger both marched in the procession in the annual pageant along with members of the Chamber and other civic dignitaries. The theme of the 1814 pageant was the story of a lost world, namely the woollen industry. Also marching in the procession were tradesmen and artisans from all sections of manufacturing and agriculture.[16] Despite this lavish display of pride in its past, the mills, once the main source of employment were closing one by one and the majority of the population of Exeter was living below the poverty line. During the peace celebrations, some 8000 'poor persons', the majority of whom were classified as the 'deserving poor', were provided with a hot meal.[17]

Within months of peace being declared, England was in the depths of an economic depression. As prices escalated, so did the numbers applying for relief. Poor rates rose and there was great pressure in the city to increase wages. Any expectations that Banfill may have had that with peace his business would improve were soon dashed as exports to Europe continued to decline. The following year saw serious cash flow problems for the firm. Granger, who still owned a stake of the mill, wanted to be paid out for his share of the value of the site, but Banfill could not afford to and the banks refused him any more credit. Once again, out of affection for his sister, Vicary came to the rescue. He agreed to lend Banfill £4000 at five per cent interest to pay Granger out, on condition that the partners agreed to 'bargain sell and demise' the freehold of the premises to him, until the loan was repaid. Banfill and Shute had no alternative but to agree and all the estate, including Exwick House and the mill, with the exception of a small strip of land known as the Nursery or Little Orchard, which Granger had assigned to him for his own use in 1813, was transferred to Vicary's ownership.[18]

His brother-in-law's intervention gave Banfill the breathing space he needed to ride the depression. Whether Nancy knew the true extent of her husband's financial difficulties is unclear, but she and Samuel continued to entertain the local gentry as lavishly as before. That year, the Company of Weavers Fullers and Shearman relaxed its apprenticeship rules, and Banfill was appointed as Warden of the Society, an honour that he had sought for many years. He and Nancy maintained appearances, subscribing to a number of local causes including the Devon and Exeter Hospital and the Devon and Exeter Institution, founded in 1813 for the promotion of science, literature and the arts. They also provided their niece Joanna with a permanent home. Following her father's death in 1818, Joanna had left Bristol for good, coming to live at Exwick House. She had suffered from a crippling illness for many years, but she loved Exwick, having spent so much time there.

Banfill was a well-respected member of the mercantile community in Exeter. In 1817, he joined the national debate following the Select Committee's report on the Poor Laws, responding to a pamphlet written by Sir T D Acland, Bart. MP. in a letter, entitled '*On the Means of Improving the Condition of the Labouring Classes*'. While he agreed in principle with the Select Committee's report, Banfill argued that the main reason for the increase in poor relief expenditure was that inflationary war-time prices had far out-stripped wages.[19] Despite his own financial situation, he advocated a system of poor relief that would deter 'every applicant from an inducement to seek parochial relief as a substitute for labor', and proposed the formation of 'Central Boards' in each area so that poor relief would be regulated by those 'acquainted with the resources of the districts in which they act'. Provision would be made for the deserving poor so that payment to 'the sick, impotent and aged, may be beneficially made from a parish rate'. Poor houses and workhouses would become 'places of retreat...where potatoes, milk, soups will be most wholesome, as well as the cheapest diet'.[20] In all Banfill wrote three pamphlets on the subject, putting forward his ideas to reduce the rapidly rising poor rates and between 1818 and 1828 conducted an experiment amongst his own workers in the parish of St Thomas the Apostle on the 'better relief and employment of the poor', which was published in 1828.[21]

Yet, while he was debating the problems of the labouring poor, their friends and family had no idea that the firm was heading for collapse. By 1819, Banfill and Shute were finally forced to admit that they were bankrupt. Just before Christmas, Nancy wrote to Vicary to tell him of their situation and that they were unable to pay the interest on the loan. When Vicary had lent the firm £4400 four years earlier, it had been agreed that he would receive 5% interest plus dividends. Although Banfill had repaid a part of it, a considerable amount remained owing. Now they had no choice but to put the firm into liquidation. However, Vicary was too ill to respond to her letter. As the news spread, the family was shocked. On 2 February, Banfill wrote to his nephew Henry. 'It is as you observe a very painful measure to give up a concern which was, as it was, my child, but circumstances do occur when parental separation is expedient; & in this instance the prospect of being permanently relieved from the dreadful anxiety of the last three or four years I regard as the greatest possible alleviation of the sacrifices & of property & of means'.

It must have been the hardest letter Banfill had ever written. Nancy added her own poignant message thanking her nephew for his 'very kind attention to us in our present unfortunate situation'. In what was perhaps a veiled reference to her brother Antony, she continued 'the only alleviating circumstance....is that he has not brought it upon himself – I need not tell you that the Determination of giving up the Establishment has not been made without a most severe struggle on Mr B's part – and when one considers that he has been...slaving nearly forty years of his life in the concern – one cannot wonder at the poignancy of his present feelings'.

Before the family could decide how to help them, it suffered a double blow. On 8 February 1820, Vicary died and two weeks later, Dolly, who had been unwell for several months suddenly took a turn for the worst and on 24 February, she too passed away. After a brief period of mourning, Vicary's executors, his nephews George (of Bristol) and George Abraham Crawley applied officially to Banfill & Shute for 'the money he should have been entitled to receive for the dividends and annual produce of the sd £4400'. George and his cousin William, who had returned to England from Cadiz for Dolly's funeral, came to Exeter and stayed at Exwick House for several weeks. William loved Devon and was very fond of his uncle and aunt who had played a major role in his childhood during his father's long absences abroad. Both he and George were appalled to find the Exeter firm in such financial difficulties and their uncle and aunt living in such reduced circumstances. George wrote to Harriet that Banfill must have hidden the true situation of the business from Nancy or she would '...not have gone on year after year entertaining the country gentry'. Having often criticised them for their apparent meanness, he added, 'we must acquit them both of a fault we used to consider belonged to them, that of stinginess'. William too was shocked and wrote to Henry that, 'Poor uncle Banfil's [sic] misfortune. I am truly sorry for it. He has sometimes behaved improperly, but I cannot forget that he is the husband of an Aunt who is justly dear to us & that to me at least whilst a boy & ever since he has always behaved with great kindness'. He was aghast when he discovered that Nancy was still owed the £158 and Banfill the £284 which they had generously loaned their father over thirty years before. Despite their own worries, neither had liked to ask that the debts be settled in case the family became aware of their straitened circumstances.

Henry and William came to an agreement with Vicary's executors that on payment of £525 still owing as dividends and interest on the loan, the executors would 'exonerate and discharge the premises from the same sum of £4400. They paid the £442 owing to their uncle and aunt to the executors and Banfill's partner George Shute paid the balance. As Vicary owned the premises, it was agreed that the firm would be closed down and sold. It was advertised in the *Sherborne Mercury* on 20 March 1820 but was not sold.[22] Five months later, it was advertised for sale in *Trewman's Exeter Flying Post* of 1 September 1820 but again it remained unsold. On Banfill's retirement, Shute took over the lease and continued trading as George Shute & Sons. The firm struggled on but within two years all production had virtually ceased. By 1822, the Exeter woollen industry had completely collapsed and cloth manufacturers were 'of small extent, chiefly coarse cloths and employing 300-400 hands...'[23]. Despite this, in his *Magna Britannica*, published in 1822, Lyson describes Banfill as 'an eminent mercantile man, now residing in the neighbourhood of Exeter' and notes that 'There was till lately a considerable manufactury of cashmere and shawls at Exwick'.[24] By 1824, George Shute had died and the mill was advertised for sale again but remained unsold. His son Stephen, who had been working in the business for some years, joined Gibbs Son & Bright in Bristol.[25] In all, the mill was put up for sale four times. As part of it was was still occupied by a firm of lace manufacturers whose lease was due to expire in December 1829,

Vicary's executors decided to wait until then and try to sell it with Exwick House.

After her husband's death, Kenny agreed that the Banfills could continue to live at Exwick House with Joanna for as long as they wished. William remained with them for several months before returning to Cadiz. He felt at home in Exwick, and had 'lost none of his affection for this part of the world'. He was also very fond of Joanna and it upset him to see her so ill. She never returned to Bristol. Three years later, at the age of forty-six, she died after what was described as 'a final period of distressing illness'. After her death, Nancy and Samuel continued to live quietly at the Exwick House on a small pension provided by the family. Five years later, in 1828, Nancy too died at the age of seventy and was buried in the churchyard at Exwick. After her death, Bell moved in to look after her brother-in-law, but the arrangement was short-lived. Within two years, she too was finding it increasingly difficult to manage such a large house. Now nearly seventy, Bell accepted an invitation from her nephew George to go to live near him and Harriet at Redland. With Kenny's agreement, Vicary's executors decided that now was the time to sell both Exwick House and the mill. After much persuasion, Banfill reluctantly agreed to move but only when the family agreed that he would be provided with a home.

Exwick House and the manufacturing plant were put up for auction on 7 May 1830. The auction catalogue described the house as a mansion 'with every requisite for a Family of the first respectability' and with seventeen acres of gardens, was sold as a separate freehold estate. The Fulling Mill and Factory, which were held by Banfill, a James Townsend, and George Crawley on a one thousand-year lease, was divided into eleven lots. Robert Maunder, a local clothier, purchased the mills, counting houses weaving shops and workers cottages for £1100. Samuel Banfill purchased Lot 11, which consisted of two cottages and a plot of land known as Little Orchard, for his own use.[26]

Within days, Banfill had moved his possessions into one of the cottages, known as the Hermitage, which was short distance from Exwick House. At age sixty-six, he remained in good health and his niece, Jane

Mardon, came to live with him as his housekeeper. Once settled, he contacted his nephews to discuss erecting a memorial plaque 'within Exwick pew under the Cleve monument' to record his and Anne's 40-year occupation of Exwick House. The Gibbs family was strongly opposed to the idea (possibly because they did not want a permanent reminder of Antony's failure there), and Banfill reluctantly abandoned the plan.

Despite his reduced circumstances, he continued to be an active and influential member of the local community, retaining an interest in poor law reform. After the enactment of the Poor Law Amendment Act in 1834 and the formation of the St Thomas Union, he was elected as one of the Guardians for the St. Thomas District. Two years later, he was appointed Chairman of the Committee of Governors of the Devon and Exeter Hospital. Banfill continued to live in the Hermitage on a small pension provided by the Gibbs family, cared for by his niece, until his death in 1842 at the age of seventy-eight.

At some time between 1832 and 1873, Exwick House was demolished. Part of the house was incorporated into the Lamb Inn, which is situated on the road that runs through the village, nearly opposite the church. It was described in the sale as 'Another Out-House for Coach House or Stabling, 18 feet by 18 feet, Beer Cellars &c'.[27] The gardens were incorporated into the grounds of the present vicarage (not to be confused with the present Exwick House, which is behind the mill, on the opposite side of the road). All that remains of the original Exwick House and the old Lamb Inn (now the Village Inn) is a cob wall bounding what is now St. Andrew's Road.

The mill and factory continued to operate as a cloth factory for some years under the name of Messrs Maunder, Exeter and Exwick, albeit on a much smaller scale.[28] It was then converted into a flour mill and operated as such until 1893, when it became a steam laundry and was still in use in the 1920s. In the 1980s, it was demolished and replaced by a small estate of houses.

CHAPTER 20

CHANGING FORTUNES

Only after their father's death did Henry and William discover the true extent of his debts and were shocked to find that very little had been repaid in the last twenty-five years. Despite all Antony's efforts, between 1790 and 1816 only some £826 had been repaid against the loans to his cousins Robert Remmett; Betsy, William and Abraham Gibbs; and his brother-in-law, Charles Crawley. Over and above what he needed to maintain his family, virtually the entire commission earned over the last twenty-six years had been used to offset his outstanding account with the Exeter firm. A balance of around £18,000 was still owed.[1]

For Henry and William these were debts of honour, which they were determined to repay. Their father's bankruptcy had had a significant impact on their lives. Throughout his self-imposed exile in Spain, they were constantly aware of their dependency on their relations, making them even more determined to rebuild the family's dignity and reputation. In 1816, William wrote to Henry, 'before I came abroad with you in Dec 1812, I made a verbal promise to my father to consider his debts as my own in case he should not have it in his power to discharge them.... You will easily conceive that the promise was perfectly voluntary on my part'. Henry was of the same mind, and after some discussion it was agreed that they create 'a fund & keep it on deposit in Antony Gibbs & Sons from which debts could be paid as & when the firm could afford to release the capital'. The account was called the DS account (Duedas Sagradas or Sacred Debts). Despite their intentions, there was some doubt that they would ever achieve their aim and it was not until 1819 that they made the first contribution of £1000 into the account. Dolly, delighted that at last they were 'engaged in a great act of piety & meant in the beginning to discharge their father's debt', contributed £200 to the fund.

During this time they were in regular contact with their cousins William Henry and John Ley. The four boys had been great friends as children in Exeter and Topsham. With William Henry in Palermo and John Ley in Genoa, they had been trying to promote business between the three firms, but this came to abrupt halt with their uncle Abraham's bankruptcy and subsequent suicide in Palermo in 1816. Abraham's success and reputation amongst the financial establishment had been something they had long admired, leaving the family in England bewildered at how it could have happened. Henry was also very concerned for his cousin Mary, especially after receiving a letter from William Henry telling him that Charles had abandoned her and she was now with Lyle in Genoa.

While William remained in Cadiz developing trade between Spain and South America, Henry, now the senior partner, managed the London office of Antony Gibbs & Sons. In 1810, Henry had become a member of Lloyds and from that time, underwriting became an important part of the business.[2] Despite his obvious ability, within a few months of his father's death, there was concern in the family that at times he exhibited similar traits to his father. His uncles, Vicary and George were worried about his commitment and thought that the London firm should be merged with and managed by George Gibbs & Son of Bristol. His cousin George Jr, who had been advising them since Antony's death, believed that they would always need his advice and support if they were to survive and was concerned that Henry was too like his father. 'In spite of my prudential caution' he told him, 'you will pursue your old habits of pushing hope & expectation as far and perhaps further that you ought in reason to do'. Despite pressure from all sides, Henry and William resisted the suggestion that the two firms merge. In 1817, Henry married his first cousin Caroline, the fourth daughter of his aunt and uncle Mary and Charles Crawley. Within a year their first child was born. Although he had a wide range of other interests, Henry remained committed to the firm. An enthusiastic champion of Brunel, he became heavily involved with the development of the railways, first as a promoter on the London committee and then as a director from 1835 until his death in 1842.

The London house continued to expand, albeit slowly, for the next three years. In 1818, they made Casson a partner and opened Gibbs Casson & Co in Gibralter. Between 1819 and 1821, the brothers contributed equally to the *DS* fund, some £2230 being paid out. Even so, in 1823, with interest still mounting, their grandfather's debts were still in the region of £9000 and their father's at £7,000.[3] In 1820, their cousin Charles Crawley Jr, who had been working at the Liverpool office of Gibbs Thompson & Co, joined the London firm as a junior partner and over the next few years, branches were opened in Lima (1822), Guyaquil and Arequipa (1823), and Valparaiso (1826), but contributions to the 'fund' remained few- and far between.[4] With the opening of the offices in Peru, the firm continued to develop trade in the former Spanish colonies in South America. Most of their income was made importing guano on a very small scale into London, but there was little demand for it and much ended up being thrown into the Thames. For some years, the firm suffered considerable losses and neither Henry nor William could afford to make any further payments to the *DS* account. By 1826, Henry's family was increasing in size at regular intervals, making it difficult for him to match his brother's contributions. William, who was still unmarried, agreed that he could withdraw his share until he was in a position to make good. For the next few years, only William contributed to the fund, resulting in a significant reduction in the available capital. It was in the early 1830s, that the firm had begun to prosper becoming the leading 'London trading house on the Pacific coast' but despite this, no further repayments were made to the DS account until 1838.

It was in 1841 that the fortunes of the Gibbs family changed forever. That year, after a convoluted search through his mother's lineage, Henry inherited the Hucks estates of Clifton Hampden in Oxfordshire and the following year unexpectedly inherited a further 1500 acres in Hertfordshire, the whole estate being worth £6000 a year.[5] The inheritance enabled him to finally discharge *Las Duedas Sagradas* incurred by their father some fifty years before and twenty-five years after his death. The bond between the brothers had always been strong and, believing that the fortunes of one belonged to the family, Henry immediately decided to share his inheritance for it 'is not mine but one which Dame Fortune has been pleased to shower upon our family'. Both he and William believed that it was their common determination to repay their father's debts that had brought them together. Henry thought that this brotherly spirit should be passed to the next generation 'convinced as I am that strong family affection when chastened and cemented by religion is one of the best preservatives against the temptation of the world and a happy means of confirming us in our hopes of a better life. Sadly, he had little time to enjoy his inheritance. Later that year he and Caroline travelled to Italy for a short holiday. After arriving in Venice, Henry, whose health had always been somewhat indifferent, suddenly became ill with a fever. He died a few days later on 21 August 1842, aged fifty-seven. His body was brought back to England to be buried at Clifton Hampden. He and Caroline had been married for twenty-five years and had fourteen children. At the time of his death, Henry was Lord of the Manors of Burston in Hertfordshire, North Moreton in Berkshire and Clifton Hamden in Oxfordshire.[6] His eldest son Henry Hucks Gibbs succeeded him.[7]

Meanwhile William, who had returned to England in 1820 for his mother's funeral, went back to Cadiz the following year. There he met and fell in love with the young Doña Francisca de la Peña. Within weeks, they were engaged but the match was not to be as both families disapproved on religious grounds. The engagement was ended and a heartbroken William came back to England. The following year he went to Spain with his sisters Anne and Harriet and his brother-in-law George for a short visit before returning to London where he lived in Henry's house at 11 Bedford Square. Burying himself in his work, he seemed a confirmed batchelor but in 1839, at the age of forty-nine, he married another Crawley cousin, Matilda Blanche Crawley-Boevey, the twenty-two year-old daughter of Sir Thomas Crawley-Boevey, Charles Crawley's elder brother. He and Matilda were married for thirty-six years and had seven children and eighteen grandchildren.

After Henry's sudden death, William became prior (as the senior partner was known) in Antony Gibbs & Sons. The following year his nephew, Henry Hucks joined the business. Until 1842, the firm had been a relatively modest concern trading mainly with Spain and its Latin American colonies. The importance of nitrate as a fertiliser was becoming widely recognised in Europe, and guano, nitrate rich bird droppings, was to change the face of British agriculture. As the demand for it increased, William learned that one of his agents in South America, in what he described as 'an act of insanity', had signed an exclusive guano-trading contract with the Peruvian government. The gamble paid off and was to transform the fortunes of Antony Gibbs & Sons from the first shipment in 1842. The following year William published a pamphlet promoting the value of guano called, *Guano: Its Analysis and Effects Illustrated by the Latest Experiments*, which included many tributes enthusing about its effectiveness as a fertiliser. The pamphlet also included a letter from the firm:

> Sir,
> Being largely engaged, as Agents to the Peruvian and Bolivian Governments, in the recent introduction into Europe, from the west coast of South America, of the manure GUANO, we beg leave to lay before you the following particulars and experiments, which we trust will prove interesting and useful to you. Of the genuine article, imported by ourselves, we have deposits on sale both here and in the hands of our friends Messrs. GIBBS, BRIGHT, AND Co., of Liverpool and Bristol, deliverable from the Import Warehouses.'[8]

As the demand rose, the firm purchased guano for $15 dollars a ton and sold it for around $50 dollars a ton in Europe and North America, with around 100,000 tons a year imported into Britain.[9] From 1842 to 1861, it enjoyed a lucrative monopoly of the trade that peaked between 1850 and 1856 when it disposed of 214,707 tons of guano in Britain alone. William saw the profits rise from £17,156 in 1848 to £125,562 ten years later, the year he retired from active involvement in the firm having reaped the rewards and diversified into a number of other areas including trading in copper, tin, silver and wool.[10] As the family triumphed in their success Henry Hucks wrote to his cousin George in Bristol, 'As Louis XIV said, for us now "il n'y plus de Pyrenees, ni d'Alpes non plus", France, Spain, Italy and Belguim are united in a vast monarchy of Guano'. A humorous jingle echoed throughout the city at this time 'The house of Gibbs that made their dibs by selling turds of foreign birds'. It was also during this period that the foundations were laid for the firm to make the transition into one of the City's most prestigious merchant banks.

In 1843, the profits enabled William to purchase Tyntes Place as a country house for his growing family. It was a Regency gothic house with a small estate outside Bristol, bordering on Belmont House, the home of his sister Harriet and brother-in-law, George. He also owned a house near Hyde Park, and when in London would regularly walk to the docks cane in hand, to inspect the huge piles of guano outside his warehouses. In 1858, he retired from Antony Gibbs & Sons, handing over the reins, not to his own son but to his nephew Henry Hucks, but retained an interest in the business, having left £1 million pounds of capital in the firm at 5%.[11] In 1863, as profits continued to soar, William, then in his late sixties, employed John Norton to rebuild Tyntesfield (as the house became called) into a romantic gothic extravangaza in the style of the town hall in Prague and the cathedral of San Marco. He also employed Arthur Blomfield to design a large chapel in the style of Sainte-Chapelle. The cost of the rebuilding was in the region of £70,000 – less than one year's average profit of Antony Gibbs & Sons.[12]

William was a man of deep religious beliefs, motivated by a social conscience, no doubt influenced by his wife and his Crawley cousins. He was a Tractarian and one of the greatest philanthropists of his age and was involved in the building and restoration of nineteen churches including Keble College, the epicentre of the Oxford movement, and the restoration of Bristol and Exeter Cathedrals. He built almshouses and schools and even though his wife Matilda was strictly teetotal, she built a public house for the workers on the estate. When he died in 1875, at the age of eighty-five, William left the ownership of Antony Gibbs & Sons to his nephew Henry Hucks Gibbs who became prior. So as not to drain the business of all its capital, the £1 million pounds that had been left in the firm on his retirement was lent to his nephew for a further twenty years.

His cousin George also lived into his eighties. Following his father's death in 1818, George had become head of the Bristol firm with Robert Bright as his junior partner. The company was restyled Gibbs, Bright, & Co of Liverpool and Bristol and continued to expand. Despite the difference in their ages, George and Robert were great friends as well as business partners. George continued to support Robert's father Richard, who had been like an uncle to him for most of his life. Richard, whose partners in his plantations in Jamaica and in the West India trade had died, retired in 1818 to care for his wife and transferred many of his interests in the Caribbean to both his son and to Gibbs Bright & Co.

Throughout the 1820s, as its profits in colonial produce declined, the West India interest in Bristol continued to resist abolition. 1831 was a particularly bad year. The reform crisis resulted in riots in the city whilst economic depression led to a number of business failures. Despite widespread opposition, Lord Grey's Whig ministry pushed through the Reform Act of 1832 that extended the electoral franchise and the 1833 Emancipation Act, which proposed that all slaves be emancipated the following year. The bill offered emancipation with £20 million compensation for planters and owners for the loss of their human 'property' who were to be freed on 1 August 1834; their slaves were to receive nothing. It was the compensation that gave George and his fellow merchants 'a tolerable escape from a financial situation in which dissatisfaction at returns on investment was accompanied by fear of total loss'.[13] He was paid £800 compensation for the 61 slaves that he owned in Barbados, and an additional £1138 for another 63 that he and Robert jointly owned in Jamaica. Richard Bright, although no longer active in the plantation trade, received £12,000 for 640 slaves and Robert a further £7274 for the 300 slaves on their plantations in Jamaica. This however, was only a fraction of the compensation paid to other Bristol families. In contrast, the Baillie family received £110,000 for some 3000 slaves and £102,000 was paid to T & J Daniel for 3,400 slaves in British Guiana, Nevis and Monserrat.[14]

With their compensation, West India merchants looked to other areas for investment.[15] Both George and Robert Bright purchased shares in the Bristol Dock and Canal company and in the Great West Cotton Company, a factory established to challenge the dominance of the northern cities. They each invested £3000 in this new venture and Bright became one of its directors.[16] They also invested in the Clifton Bridge project, for George, like his cousin Henry in London, was an enthusiastic Brunelian. He saw the railways as a 'gentlemanly investment', 'preferring to replace slaves by sleepers' by 'linking them to London and not the plantations....'.[17] As the railway network between London and the north progressed, there was a fear that Bristol might find itself at a commercial disadvantage unless an interregional line from Bristol to London was built. A number of bills had been introduced into Parliament in 1831, but any plans to build a line from Bristol to the capital were interrupted by the riots in October, which discouraged investors and promoters alike.[18]

The question of a line to London was re-opened in 1832 by four enthusiastic Bristoleans. By the end of the year, they had succeeded in convincing the mercantile elite of the city that the idea was worth investigating. George was appointed by the Merchant Venturers onto a committee, which held its first meeting on 21 January 1833 to look at the feasibility of connecting London and Bristol, and to secure support for the project. He and Bright worked closely with Henry who had already formed a committee in London. The first joint meeting of the two committees was held on 22 August 1833 at the London offices of Antony Gibbs & Sons at 47 Lime Street. Brunel referred to them as 'rather an old women's set, a regular jobbing committee. Must hope for somebody to give them a little life and sense'.[19] At the meeting, the infant project was officially called *The Great Western Railway*.[20] After completing a detailed survey, Brunel, who had been appointed engineer, explained his proposals at the first public meeting of the Bristol Railway Committee in July. The line would be 116 miles long with the total cost in the region of £2.5 million. Following the publication of the *Prospectus* at the end of August, the committees set about persuading investors to take up the £100 shares in the project. The members of the Bristol Committee each made a substantial investment with George investing £7000 and Bright £15,900 in the project. By September, the Corporation and the Society of Merchant Venturers had each taken 100 shares (£10,000), but they had difficulty in raising the full amount. The Bill was presented to Parliament in early 1834, and went to the Committee stage on 16 April. It was thrown out by the Lords on 25 July, but was re-submitted with fresh proposals the following year. Royal Assent was finally given to the Great Western Railway Bill on 31 August 1835. In the original Act of Incorporation, both George and Bright became promoters and later directors of the Bristol Committee of the Great Western Railway (GWR) Board while Henry was their counterpart in London.

In October 1835, Brunel persuaded the directors of the GWR to let him build a steamship to cross the Atlantic from Bristol to New York, and the Great Western Steamship Company was formed. By 1838, the *SS Great Western* was ready to make its first voyage. It was the largest steamship ever to be built, with a wooden hull measuring 212 feet long and with a 35-foot beam. The Liverpool office of Gibbs Bright & Co became one of the loading agents for the first steam-powered crossing of the Atlantic. The *SS Great Western* steamed out of Bristol on 8 April 1838, arriving in New York fifteen days later, making 60 crossings over the next eight years.

The notice advertising the crossing read:

STEAM TO NEW YORK
THE GREAT WESTERN
of 1340 tons Register and 450 Horse Power
strongly built, coppered & copper fastened with engines of the
very best construction by Maudsley Sons & Field and
expressly adopted for the Bristol – New York Station
Lieut. James Hosken, R.N. Commander
will sail direct from Bristol on 7th April, 1838 at 2 p.m.
The rate of Cabin Passage is 35 guineas to be paid on application
for State Rooms
To G.W.R. London
Gibbs, Bright & Co Liverpool
Hamilton Brothers & Co, Glasgow
Robert Hall, Cork

The Bristol and Liverpool firm of Gibbs Bright & Co further expanded and continued to act as agents for the sale of West Indian produce. In 1824, Robert's brother Samuel joined the company, becoming a partner of the Liverpool firm. He had previously been employed by Gibbs Bright & Co in the West Indies with Stephen Shute whose father had been a partner in the Exeter firm, Banfill Shute & Co.[21] For several years Richard Bright had been transferring his assets to Gibbs Son & Bright. On his own death in 1835, he bequeathed the Meylersfield, Beeston Spring and Garredu plantations in Jamaica to 'his respected friend George Gibbs' and to his four sons Robert, Samuel, Henry, and Benjamin. Four years later George, then aged sixty, decided to retire, but he wished to retain an interest in the company. Instead of withdrawing his capital, on his retirement he entered into a new seven-year contract with Robert and Samuel Bright and Stephen Shute to further develop the plantation trade. They invested £9000 between them with the shares being divided so that Gibbs and Shute each owned three twenty-fourths, Robert ten twenty-fourths and

Samuel the remaining eight twenty-fourths. The partnership deed stated that George was not 'obliged personally to attend the Business farther [sic] than he shall think proper'. The links between the Gibbs and Bright families were further strengthened through the marriage of John Lomax Gibbs, Henry's youngest son to Robert's daughter, Isobel.

After George's retirement, Bright continued as managing partner. The firm flourished, with offices in Bristol, Liverpool and London, developing shipping lines to supply their markets in Australia. In 1850, to complement their fleet, they purchased the *SS Great Britain*. Designed by Brunel and built in Bristol in 1843, the 3,500-ton iron clad the *Great Britain* was a revolutionary vessel. She made her maiden voyage across the Atlantic from Liverpool to New York in 1845, but the following year was badly damaged after running aground in Dundrum Bay near Belfast. The purchase of the ship in 1850 enabled Gibbs Bright & Co to take advantage of the upsurge in emigration caused by the Australian gold rush. After a major refit, it became an emigrant carrier on the Australia run capable of transporting 750 passengers in three classes. The *SS Great Britain* first sailed for Australia on 21 August 1852, completing the round trip in 120-days, a time that was very competitive in the mid-nineteenth century. The following year, Reginald Bright, Robert's seventh and youngest son, who had sailed on the first voyage, opened an office in Melbourne, known as Bright Bros. His elder brother Charles and cousin Samuel later joined the firm, which was to become the Australian arm of Gibbs Bright & Co. Over the next twenty-four years, the vessel made thirty-two voyages and carried 16,000 emigrants to Australia, before being laid up in 1876 awaiting sale. In 1882, it was purchased by Antony Gibbs & Sons, and converted to carry coal and wheat from San Francisco and later nitrate between Chile and Europe.[22]

George remained a shareholder in the firm, taking an active interest in it until 1862. He and Harriet continued to live at Belmont House until his death in April the following year at the age of eighty-four when he was buried at Wraxall in Somerset. Harriet died two years later. As they had no children, he left Belmont House to Antony's youngest son,

Joseph and his wife Emily, who lived there until 1870 when it was sold to William who 'reunited' it into one estate at Tyntesfield.

On George's death, his £60,000 capital in the firm was paid out to his estate. Six years later, in 1869, Robert Bright died and his share of the business was distributed amongst his sons. With the *SS Great Britain* now laid up, the firm saw its profits in decline. By 1880, sugar beet had replaced cane as the main source of sugar in Europe, and trade with the West Indies had become increasingly unprofitable. On 2 July 1880, the *London Gazette* published a notice that 'the partnership of Gibbs Bright & Co, Liverpool & Bristol, Bright Bros. & Co., in Melbourne, Sidney & Brisbane & Dunedin in New Zealand, has expired by the effluxion of time, but that the business will be continued, in all its branches by Tyndall Bright, Charles Edward Bright, and Reginald Bright'.[23] The following year, Gibbs Bright & Co of Liverpool and Bristol, including its plantations in the Caribbean, was absorbed into Antony Gibbs & Co, along with Bright Brothers in Melbourne, Sidney, Brisbane and Dunedin. The firm that had been originally started in the early eighteenth century by Michael Adkins, the largest sugar merchant in Bristol, and had operated continuously in the sugar trade for more than one hundred and fifty years, finally ceased trading in 1887.[24]

* * * *

After her father's suicide, Mary remained with Lyle in Genoa while Charles tried to settle the matter of her dowry. Nearly two years later, with the matter still not resolved, they were reconciled and in the autumn of 1818, they travelled to England. On her arrival in London, Mary called to see Dolly and met several members of the family before going on to Heytesbury, the home of Charles's elder brother Sir William Ashe áCourt, arriving there in the spring of 1819. By this time, she was six months pregnant. The previous year Charles had been created a Knight of the Guelphic order and there was some concern in his family over the legality of his marriage and the legitimacy of their offspring, especially if the child was a son. This was not helped by their long separation and that Mary had assumed her mother's name on her marriage. Although she and Charles had been married in Palermo 'with all the formality which circumstances permitted', they were advised that they should be remarried 'to remove every shade of doubt…from any constitution of the law of England of the validity'. On 7 July 1819, Mary Elizabeth Catherine Gibbs remarried Charles Ashe a'Court by special licence in the little church at Heytesbury 'for greater security'. Three months later, she gave birth to a son, whom they called Charles Henry Wyndham. A daughter Maria Elizabeth followed him three years later.[25]

In March 1820, Charles was elected as the second Member of Parliament for Heytesbury but his political life only lasted six months when he lost his seat in August. He and Mary continued to live there until 1832, when his brother, now Lord Heytesbury returned to England.[26] They then moved to Southampton where Charles was appointed as an Assistant Poor Law Commissioner at £700 a year to oversee the implementation of the 1832 Poor Law Reform Act and manage the building of the Andover Workhouse, which was opened in March 1836. His mission complete, he left this position in the autumn and he and Mary continued to live in Southampton until 1842 when they moved to Amington Hall in Warwickshire which belonged to another brother, Admiral a'Court Repington. On the Admiral's death in 1855, Charles succeeded to Amington Hall taking the name of Repington. However, for Mary there was no escape from the scandal surrounding her father. In 1845, with her husband now dead, the Marchese Forcella was determined to clear his name of the charge that he had fabricated his claim that Abraham had embezzled 3000 onze from the Bronte estate to prop up his failing business. Convinced of Abraham's guilt, she appealed to the 'Gran Court dei Palermo' [sic] to re-open the case and re-examine the evidence in an attempt to prove his innocence. The enquiry took many months to complete and it must have been a relief for Mary when it concluded that there was no case to answer. Although Abraham had the motive, opportunity and authority to act as D'Angelo and Forcella both claimed, after so many years there was no evidence that he had embezzled funds from Earl

Nelson, and the case against him was not proven; and neither was Forcella's innocence.

Throughout this time Mary had no contact with her English cousins despite the happy times she had spent with them as a child. Whether this was from choice on both sides is unclear. In 1848, after the publication of the report, Harriet, anxious to heal the breach, wrote to her explaining that they had found it difficult to re-establish their friendship because the family felt so strongly at the scandal surrounding her father and the way Charles had treated her over her dowry. Mary's reply was polite and to the point. 'It was very kind & friendly on your part, my dear Harriet to tell me the <u>truth</u> & to explain <u>why</u> you and all your dear belongings had kept…out of my way, and had apparently given up all interest in me, whom you loved formerly & who, be assured, has not forgotten the many kindnesses received from your branch of the family'. She went on to reveal the anxiety she had felt about the gossip over her father's death and her husband's 'preference' on the estate, referring to it as the 'misapprehension in 1816'. 'If you had known my husband', she wrote, 'you would never have credited them'. She told Harriet that she had become a keen 'gardener & the Admiral does all the planting'. In fact, Mary was being modest. She had become an accomplished gardener and a well-respected amateur botanist, having had a genus of plant, *Acourtia*, named after her.

Charles died in 1861, the same year as her son-in-law, Sidney Herbert, who had recently been created Baron Herbert of Lea. Mary, then in her late sixties, went to live with her son and his family in Chelsea. Four years later, at the age of seventy-two, she and her daughter Elizabeth Herbert made the long journey to Italy, visiting Rome and Naples. From there, they went on to Palermo. For Mary this must have been a poignant visit, not only reliving the happy memories of her childhood, but also the sad memories of the deaths of her father and twin daughters. On her return to England the following year she continued to live in Chelsea until 1878, when she died at the age of eighty-four.

After Lyle's death, his nephew Charles and his partner Camillo Serra continued to run Gibbs & Co, Genoa. In 1852, Charles married Stuarta, the eldest daughter of Timothy Yeats Brown, the British consul in Genoa. They had one daughter born in February 1857. In December of that year, Charles died suddenly and was buried in Genoa. He left his share of the firm to Stuarta, who with Serra and her brother Frederick, carried on the business for the next three years, at which time both she and Serra retired.[27] In 1861, Stuarta married Emilio Brioshi of Milan and she died there in 1873.

William Henry continued to act for Antony Gibbs & Sons in Genoa for some years, but as his health deteriorated, once again he was dependent on his family for support. After John Ley's death in the winter of 1837, his only source of income was the interest from the £500 deposited by Betsy with Antony Gibbs & Sons. He had been on very friendly terms with his cousins since childhood and Henry wrote of him, 'Experience and misfortune have taught him the value of money....I know indeed very few men who are more grateful for kindness...or who in his very reduced circumstances would have conducted themselves in so praiseworthy and contented a manner as he has done for some years past'.

Some months later, though still penniless William Henry's health slowly improved. Now a wealthy man, Charles felt sorry for his elder brother and decided to give him £600 from his own inheritance. Finding the Italian climate better for his arthritis, William Henry returned to Genoa to act as agent for Antony Gibbs & Sons and Gibbs & Co once more. He remained there for the next few years, making occasional trips to England, usually staying with his cousin William at Tyntesfield. In 1846, William Henry retired and returned to Topsham but within a short time began complaining about the climate. Like his father, he too found it damp and monotonous there after so many years in Italy. Some months later, he moved into one of the 'Claypitt' cottages on the Pytte estate in Clyst St George, and Charles continued to pay him a small allowance.[28] William Henry's life had been dogged by misfortune and ill health and he like his father resented the culture of dependency that surrounded his family. He continued to live there until his death in 1848 and was buried in the churchyard at Clyst St. George. In his will, written ten years earlier, while acknowledging the 'many obligations to my cousins George Henry and William Gibbs …in London', he appointed Lyle and his brother Charles as his executors. After John Ley's death, William Henry had been shocked by his uncle's refusal to support his dead brother's children. As his estate consisted only of the money that Betsy had invested for him, he left £50 each to Charles and his sisters, Frances and Mary Matilda 'much regretting that the sum to each is so small'. He hoped they would understand that 'I am duty bound to leave the rest to my dead brother's children….such having been the wish of my dear kind aunt Richards in making me a present of the said £500.'[29] In 1851 when the Genoese firm merged with Antony Gibbs & Sons, the accounts showed that in total the Topsham family had received over £22,622 (£904,880 at today's value) from Gibbs & Co of Genoa.

With William Henry's death, the Gibbs family connection with Pytte and Clyst St. George was severed until 1858 when William (of Tyntesfield) purchased the advowson of the parish for £2500. Two years later, he paid £400 for the five acres of the area known as 'Clay Pitt' that included several cottages, outbuildings, orchards and meadow.[30] Both he and his nephew, Henry Hucks had long vied to be the one to regain their 'lost inheritance' in Clyst St. George and restore the family's honour. On 9 July 1872 at an auction held at the Globe Hotel in Topsham, he purchased a further 123 acres including 'the Messuages Tenems and lands namely Clay Pitt House & premises, gardens & home orchards and also part of Court Farm and Brook Farm for £2055.[31] After William's death, both the living and the estate passed to his son and grandson, George Abraham Gibbs of Tyntesfield whose younger brother Antony took up residence at Pytte in 1899.[32] Thus one hundred and ten years after the loss of the estate, it was once more in the possession of the Gibbs family. In 1910, the house was enlarged and remained in their ownership until 1952, when it was sold to a developer and converted into five dwellings.

APPENDIX I

Schedule of loans from friends and family to George Abraham Gibbs and Antony Gibbs

Name	Place	LOANS in 1789 incl. interest — GAG	ANT	REPAID 1790-1815	1818	1819	1821	Balance	Repaid 1821-40	
Mary Jope	Topsham	164 1 9				10 1 9	154 0 0	0 0 0		
Rev. Stephen Weston	London	82 8 10				5 8 10	77 0 0	0 0 0		
Thomas Gibbs	Topsham	19 0 6				1 0 6	18 0 0	0 0 0		
Abraham Gibbs	Palermo	268 14 6		251 14 6				17 0 0	17 0 0	Settled by A Gibbs & Son
Rev. C Crawley	Northants.	839 15 0		285 15 0		554 0 0		0 0 0		Settled by A Gibbs & Son
R Remmett MD	Plymouth	394 15 4		133 15 4		261 0 0		0 0 0		Settled by A Gibbs & Son
Anne(Nancy)										
Banff nee Gibbs	Exwick	158 10 10				9 10 10	149 0 0	0 0 0		Settled by A Gibbs & Son
Sibella (Bel) Gibbs	Exeter	158 10 10				3 10 10	155 0 0	0 0 0		Settled by A Gibbs & Son
Edward Addicott	Exeter	1080 9 3				67 7 9		1013 1 6		
William Pitfield	Exeter	321 16 9			160 18 5	10 18 5	149	19 11		
Edmund Granger	Exeter		5961 7 1			408 9 0		5452 18 1	3150 0 0	
Granger & Banfill	Exeter		1472 1 2				1472	1 2 264		
Rev. Thomas Morgan (uncle)	Cornwal	98 16 1	766 18 11			54 7 1		811 7 11	811 7 11	
Mrs Hull	Exmouth	1636 3 0				102 3 0	1534	0 0 0	900 0 0	
Mrs Elizabeth Tucker	Exeter	733 5 1				45 5 1	344 0 0	344 0 0		
General Simcoe	Woodford Lodge		1952 6 10				122 6 10	1830 0 0	1000 0 0	Settled by A Gibbs & Son
Richard Collins	Exeter		930 13 10			50	13 10	880 0 0		
John J Short	Exeter		400 11 6			25	11 6	0 0 0	375	Payment to widow
George Waymouth	Exeter		296 15 1	155 1 3		8 13 1	202	133 0 9	133 0 9	
Grace Treats	Exeter	202 19 11						19 11 8000		
		6159 7 8	11680 14 5	826 6 1	160 18 5	1541 16 2	1095 12 2	14215 9 3	14275 8 8	

William Gibbs   repaid 1803

Betsy Gibbs   repaid 1795

Source: D.R.O. 4508 M/F78

APPENDIX II

My Dear Gibbs,

I rest assured that in all business respecting Bronte I feel confident that you will act in the letting of Bronte to you and Zorcelli [Forcella] in the same manner as if you were letting it for me to an entire stranger, but in business we must perfectly strictly understand each other, for I know that the Lawyers will (if we do not settle everything) find difficultys.

There, I will endeavor to make myself understood, then you will be able to draw up something clearer than your postcript.

In your letter of Decr. 24th you offer to remit to my bankers the net sum of 3200£ sterling from which must be deducted about 300 £ for fees still dependent upon the estate and salaries to people who must represent your Lordship so that we engage to pay your Lordship the neat sum of 2900 £ Stg. Annually. In that case Mrs Graefer may be removed. I refer you to my answer to this letter that you shall pay me 3200 £ a year and that I will pay what salaries are just (confining myself to the sum you mention) of abt 300 £. I should of course concluded that I should have the credit of paying all the salaries wanted for the care of the estate out of the 300 £ and that at least I should have 2900 £ neat in my pocket, in short Govt. Campeiaris, College c &c included in the 300 £ but as I was to have a list of salaries I should be the proper judge of what was just, and if it could be done I am sure the thing would take the Public burdens from me and I should have the rent net.

You have not told me what has been done with the Stock &c &c on the farm not whether the tenant is to keep the premises in repair, not what it let for although I agree that if you take the farm, let that be for what it will, it is to be included in the original sum of 3200 £ as you first offered, the stock I think you mentioned in one of your letters would be sold for my benefit. You will see the necessity of everything being mentioned in the first lease as it will be the pattern for future ones when I have no friend Gibbs to look up to for justice. Nothing in short which man can think of must be left unsaid in the lease respecting the farm, House, Rents, Salaries, Taxes that is the permanent ones such as the College &c. Now your last letter leaves me quite adrift. You agree to pay me 3200 £ and pay his Lordships free of every duty, charges and fees belonging to the Estate which they take upon themselves to discharge (that amounts yearly to ounces 962) these expenses however are to be paid by the Renters in the name of Lord Nelson that his Lordship may be respected, considered and acknowledged as the Sole proprietor of the Bronte Estate consequently all acts of whatever nature must be in the same manner appear in his Lordship's name, His Lordship having to pay solely the salary of the Governor to be appointed upon the Estate to take charge of his concerns.

Now I am at a loss what Governor, what concerns have I, if I let all to you, is the administration of….,am I to pay for the state of the Govt. to keep Camperis &c &c what would I give for ten minutes of conversation to beat it into my noddle, Graefer was my Governor factotum and everything after his death some person was appointed by Sir John Acton as Governor who paid him what was his salary the Campieres have 20 £ I think each year, are the rentors to pay them that is out of the original sum of 3200 £ is that meant in the 2800 £. I am afraid I cannot make myself understood, but in as few words as possible,

I mean you should give me 3200 £ a year in quarterly payments and that I should pay the salaries, fees &c Govt. to take care of my Bronte Campieres &c &c. If you send me a list of the demands for salaries fees &c &c &c mentioning every name and sum then if they are improper I can withhold remove &c &c. and if I choose to give the poor of Bronte, or any particular gratuity for services to my estate I can order it and all other things to be paid by my Rentors Abram Gibbs Esq and Chev [Chevalier] Zorchelli [Forcella], as I said before this first lease and schedule attached must contain every possible contingency as a pattern for future ones.

I have tired you I daresay as much as myself but when I recollect that the Great Hospital in Palermo in the paper delivered to me, which Graefer had, that the gross amount was abt. 7,000 ounces and the net I think for seven years 6,400 ounces, that I spent more than 10,000 £ sterling upon it and that my neat income will be under 2,800 £ for if the salary is to be taken out of it will be less as two ounces are more than one pound, it is enough to make me look about me and to think a little. I expect that Sir John Acton will if it can be done with propriety take these salaries off the Estate with the fees &c &c. I well know His Excellencies kind regard for my interest and that it was the good King's intention to give me a fine rental.

I am ever My Dear Gibbs most faithfully

Your obliged friend,

NELSON & BRONTE[1]

NOTES

The main sources used in the writing of this book are the records of Antony Gibbs & Sons in the Guildhall Library, principally MSS11021/1-30, 11023, 11024/1-2, 11036/1, 11062, 11069, 11079, 19862/1, 19863, 19888.

Introduction

1   Above the fireplace in the great hall at Fenton is the Gibbs family crest with 'An Arme in Armor Sable, garnished Or, holding on the Gauntlet a Battle axe Sable, a Cross bottony at the end Or'. See J A Gibbs, p. xvii My thanks to Nicholas Gibbs for this information

2   My thanks to Anne Webster of Venton Manor for the information about Fenton and the Gibbs family.

3   After 1620, Fenton was sold to a John Glanville, probably Sir John Glanville who was the Recorder of Plymouth in 1614, MP for Plymouth and Speaker of the House of Commons in 1640. Fenton was purchased by John Baring in 1742.

4   White's *Devonshire Directory* (1850). The name Clyst is thought to signify a sluggish river. The river Clyst rises at Clyst William and passes through Clyst St. Lawrence, Clyst Hydon, Cliston (Broad or Borard Clyst), Clyst Honiton, Clyst Moys (Poltimore), Clyst St. Michael (Sowton or Clyst Fomizon), Bishop's Clyst (Clyst Sackville or de Siccaville), Clyst St. Mary and finally Clyst St. George, before it joins the river Exe below Topsham.

5   Rev. H. T. Ellacombe, MA, FSA, the *History and Antiquities of The Parish of Clyst S. George*, Exeter, 1865, p. 36. By 1865, all the pavement stones had either been broken or obliterated, but the names and dates were preserved on memorial tiles on the floor of the nave.

6   There are a number of other references to the Gibbs family in the Clyst St. George parish records during this period.

Chapter 1, George and Abraham

MS 11021/1

1   Ibid, p. 2, note 3, George Gibbs's younger brother John moved to Exeter, and is described as a Grocer (his will in Worthy, Charles, *Devonshire Wills*, p150)

2   Ibid.

3   The Clyst St. Mary parish records show that George Gibbs owned Ashmore Manor when he died in 1723.

4   Ellacombe, op cit., p.35

5   Lewis, *Topographical Dictionary of England* (1844)

6   John Leyland, *The Itinerary of John Leland the Antiquary* (Oxford 1710-1712), Vol. 3, pp. 55

7   E. A. G. Clark, *The Ports of the Exe Estuary 1660-1860*, University of Exeter, 1968. pp. 52-53

8   DRO, Petition of William Northmore (Glyde and Sandford), 1693

9   *Extract from the Calendar of State Papers, Domestic Series, 1654*, pp. 247 and 248. The petition read, 'Our town and parish of 1,000 souls is the port of Exeter, and yet we have only 20 marks a year for the maintenance of a minister. This was assigned by the Dean and Chapter of Exeter to a reading priest, by the canons sometimes preaching themselves, and payable by William Brewton, who has all the tithes, value 140 pounds a year. The town has many poor who live on the monthly rate, and has been much impoverished by the late wars, the inhabitants living by sea affairs and too poor to raise a minister's livelihood'.

10 Robin Stanes, ed., *The Compton Census for the Diocese of Exeter, 1676*, Part II in *The Devon Historian*, No. 10, pp 4-5 and R D Woodall, *Echoes of an Old Chapel*, typewritten sheet.

11 By the early eighteenth century, there were a number of limekilns both north and south of Lime Street and in the area now known as the Strand.

12 Lime Street was renamed Shapter Street and then Lower Shapter Street after John Shapter who died in 1725 and who owned land and property there.

13 Clarke, op cit. p. 52

14 PRO, E 134/9 and 10 Hil, 20

15 DRO, 352/PF9

16 Neremiah was thought to be a descendent of General Monke. His wife Mary was the granddaughter of John Baker, who had inherited Claypitt and Court Place from his uncle, William Gibbs in 1639

17 D&EI, Exeter Marriage Licences

18 PRO, c/1/1737/31

19 The house was built in 1708 in what is now known as Shapter Street

20 PRO, c/1/1737/31 op. cit.

21 Worthy, op. cit., pp. 42-43

22 D Lysons, *Magna Britannica, Devon*, Vol. 11, 1822

23 In 1722, Old Kiddecott was owned by Arnold Bielfield

24 D&EI, Exeter Marriage Licences. On 21/10/1719, the following caveat was published. 'Let noe licence be granted to Mistress Sarah Lyle of Topsham to marry with Mr Robert Ewins [sic] of the same place until Mrs Martha Wade, widow of Topsham aforesaid, be first called who has entered this caveat'

25 Robert Lyle, the son of a prosperous merchant mariner, made at least one trip to Holland as master of the *Providence* in 1690. A widower, in 1693, he married Mary Down, the daughter of Nicholas Downe, another wealthy merchant mariner, who owned the *Sarah Elizabeth* and later of the *Henry*.

26 There is no evidence that George Abraham inherited any lands in Crediton.

27 Ibid

28 Worthy, op. cit., p. 99

29 PRO, C/11/1814/8, *Wilcox v Pease*

30 Worthy, op. cit., p. 138

Chapter 2, George Abraham
MS 11021/1

1 A Cameron, *Thomas Glass MD, Physician of Georgian Exeter*, 1996, Devon Books, pp. 22-23
   Following the publication of a pamphlet by Peters entitled '*Observations on the state of the dispute between a physician and an apothecary, concerning a prescription of Sydenham....etc*'.. Parr spoke of him with respect and affection, noting that 'Mr Peters, as Apothecary at Topsham deserved to have been known in a more extensive sphere. He was a good classical Scholar, an experienced practical Chemist, and a correct, comprehensive Philosopher. He drew with accuracy and elegance, his conversation was lively, and his Humour facetious. It gives me pleasure to records these traits of a man, to whom I was greatly indebted; whose merit and good Humour enlivened many of my boyish Hours; whose Friendship and assistance were of essential service, at another Period'.

2 DRO., Z19/21/38/2. His son Nicholas Peters Jr was appointed to take his place and the following year and entry reads 'Pd myself (NP) a years salary for taking care of the poor in Physick and Surgery, £10'

3 Report of the Commissioners for Inquiring Concerning Charities, Co. of Devon, pp. 530-535

4 It is not known where George Abraham was educated. It may well have been at the Exeter Grammar School, where he sent his own sons. Carlisle's Grammar Schools lists other pupils as being John Heath, the judge, Dr H Downham and General Simcoe

5 These are part of the Thomas Glass collection in the Exeter Cathedral Library.

6 DRO, DD 70210, Clyst St. George Deeds. The estate is described as consisting of Pytt (formerly Claypitt) Leach's close, Orchard close, Bothays, and a messuage called Court, making around 100 acres in total.

7 Ibid., In all the documents dealing with the ownership of Pytte, Anne is sometimes spelt without an *e*. Throughout the book I have spelt it as Anne
8 She was baptised at the Mint Chapel in Exeter on 4 November 1722
9 On the death of her brothers, Anne later inherited a fortune of around £10,000.
10 Cameron, op. cit., p. 23
11 The Glass family also had links with Topsham. Thomas Glass's father, Michael
   (1685-1732), dyer in Tiverton and his mother was Elizabeth Hanford the
   daughter of a local tanner. Following his wife's death, Michael Glass married
   Mary Hodges in 1737. She was the daughter of Sir Nicholas Hodges and Mary
   Buttall, who had inherited the Sugar House in Topsham from a relative, Samual
   Buttall, a West Indies sugar merchant.
12 DRO, DD 70210, op. cit.
13 The Chapel is so called because it was situated in Mint Lane, Exeter
14 RG4/Piece 336/Folio 8., *Register of Births and Baptisms at the Mint Presbyterian
   Meeting in Exeter, Devon from 1719 to 1810.*
15 Cardogan, William, *An Essay upon Nursing and the Management of Children
   from their Birth to Three years of Age, By a Physician,* London: J Roberts, 1748
16 EFP, June 29, 1787 and Sept 12, 1797
17 Newton, Robert, *Eighteenth Century Exeter,* University of Exeter, 1984, p.71
18 Clarke, op.cit., p.116
19 John Ewings had been master of the *Mary* of Topsham and part owner of the
   Amsterdam. He also owned a share of the *Seafarer.* His son Daniel was master
   of the *John and Lucia* (named after his parents) a frigate that was trading with
   Rotterdam in 1738. Between 1751-1755, he owned the *Mermade* [sic], which
   carried cargoes of woollens to Amsterdam.
20 DRO, DD 70209., op. cit.
21 Clarke, op. cit., p.117
22 DRO, Z19/38/9, Admiralty Court Records, Letters of Marque declaration 20
   December 1780 and 2 January 1781, transcribed by H Tapley-Soper, 1928.
23 My thanks to Dr Denis Gibbs for providing the information about Remmett's
   career.
24 Gibbs, J A, op. cit. pp. 17-18
25 Ibid
26 In 1812, Remmett became a Plymouth alderman, and ten years later was listed
   in Pigot's Directory as living in Eastwell Street in Plymouth. He died on 25
   May 1823, aged 73, and was buried in the north aisle of St Andrew's Church
   near both his wives.
27 EFP, 10 November 1775

28 J Delpratt Harris, MD, *The Royal Devon and Exeter Hospital,* Exeter 1922, p. 57

29 Russell, P. M. G., *History of Exeter Hospital, 1170-1948,* p. 84

30 In the 2nd edition published in 1791, were sonnets to Mr. Pitfield, Mr Patch, Mr Jackson, Lieut-Col. Simcoe. Hugh Downham also wrote some lines to Vicary Gibbs, which were taken from 'a paper in Lady Pilkington's possession'.

31 J Delpratt Harris, op. cit., p. 57

32 DRO, 1260 F/HM2, p. 305

33 EFP, 2 October, 1788

Chapter 3, Humiliation and Ruin

MSS 11021/3, 11021/4

1 Dolly's grandfather, Joseph Hucks was the younger brother of William Hucks, MP for Wallingford, and a well-known 18th century brewer, who established one of the earliest London breweries on the banks of the Thames, east of the Tower of London. He was also brewer to George I. His son Robert of Aldenham House in Hertfordshire succeeded him on his death in 1740. Robert was MP for Abingdon, and had purchased the village of Clifton Hampden in 1726. Dolly's issue became heir to the Hucks family, and it was through her that Henry Hucks Gibbs inherited the estates in Hertfordshire and Oxfordshire.

2 Henry Townley-Ward, a solicitor from Ingatestone in Essex, was the son of the Reverend Henry Ward.

3 DRO, DD 70209, op. cit., 24/25 December 1788

4 DRO, 4508M/F77, papers of Edmund Granger

5 Ibid

6 He died on 3 March 1790.

7 PRO. Leaflet, *Bankrupts and Insolvent Debtors: 1710-1869.* Until 1841, the legal status of a bankrupt was confined to traders owing more than £100. Debtors who were not traders did not qualify to become bankrupt, remained as insolvent debtors, responsible for their debts, and subject to common law proceedings and indefinite imprisonment.

8 EFP, July 7th 1789, 3c

9 DRO, 2065M/T2/9

10 DRO, T2/9/6/4/b

11 NEJ, 17 September 1789

12 ibid, 2nd November 1789

13 EFP, 12 November 1794

14 Ellacombe, op. cit., p. 37. The window was destroyed when the church was bombed in 1940

Chapter 4, Vicary

MSS11021/1, 11021/3, 11021/5

1 RG4/Piece 336/Folio 9. *Register of Births and Baptisms at the Mint Presbyterian Meeting in Exeter, Devon from 1719 to 1810*. Vicary was baptised by William West on 12 November 1751

2 Creasy's *Eminent Etonians* (1850)

3 Townsend, W. C., *The Lives of twelve eminent judges*, 1 (1846)

4 Ibid

5 Foss, *Judges of England, 1790-1820*, published 1848-62, p.228

6 Ibid

7 DRO, DD 70210, op. cit.

8 The *Exeter Flying Post*, recorded that Vicary was 'one of the four stewards at the anniversary meeting of the Exeter Grammar School Society on 21 September 1797'

9 DRO, 4508M/F77, op. cit

10 The trustees were his old friends James Mansfield and Sir Peter Burrell (later the Rt. Hon. Peter Baron Gwyder of Caernavon) of the Middle Temple

11 CLB, *1790 Census of Inhabitants*. The census of Hayes lists Vicary and Kenny as living at Hayes Common with their daughter, with three female and three male servants

12 DD 70210, op. cit.

13 Woolmer's Exeter and Plymouth Gazette, Friday 11 August, 1793, p. 4, c,d.

14 John Latimer, *The Annals of Bristol in the Eighteenth Century*, Printed by the Author, 1893, pp.505-6

15 Martin Daunton, Dictionary of National Biogaphy, p. 43

16 John Horne, the son of a wealthy poulterer, was born in 1736. Educated at Eton and Cambridge he went on to become a lawyer and was ordained a priest. An advocate of parliamentary reform, Tooke became friends with William Tooke and in 1782 adopted his surname. After the publication of Paine's *Rights of Man* in 1791, Horne Tooke worked closely with Thomas Hardy and the Corresponding Society.

17 H Brougham, *Historical sketches of statesmen who flourished in the time of George III*, (1839), pp. 130-131

18 Matthew Spong, *The Percy Anecdotes: Anecdotes of The Bar*, Sidney, 2000

19 Foss, op. cit., p. 289

20 *The Erskines of Buchan and Cardross*, www.electricscotland.com/webclans/families/erskines_buchan.htm,

21 BL, Add 34453, ff. 184, *Lord Aukland Papers*, Gibbs to Aukland, 22 February 1795

22 Alleyne Fitzherbert was a relative of George's second wife Anne Alleyne. His christian name came from his maternal grandmother Judith, the daughter of Thomas Alleyne of Barbados. He was created Baron St. Helens in 1791.

23 R G Thorne, (ed), *The House of Commons*, vol. IV, p. 17

24 ibid, p. 17, and note 3

Chapter 5, George

MSS 11021/1, 11021/2, 11021/3

1 The Academy was based in a house in Paris Street in Exeter that had been provided by William Mackworth Praed, the father of the poet Winthrop Mackworth Praed.

2 H McLachlan, English education under the Test Acts, 1931, pp. 230-2

3 Elizabeth Munckley, Samuel's mother, was the daughter of James Hawker of Luppit in Devon

4 Gibbs, p14, note 2. In a letter, written in 1776 by Geo. Gibbs to Samual Munckley, he mentions that the firm of Farr & Co also owned a dock at Bristol at which a ship was being built.

5 BRO, 04353(5), Bristol Apprentice Books.

6 BRO, BCC/D/MG/208

7 BRO, 04359 (10), Bristol Burgess Books

8 Madge Dresser, *Slavery Obscured*, Continuum, 2001, p.105

9 With her marriage to Duntze, Nicholas knew that his mother was well provided for. Despite his gratitude to his stepfather, he left bequeathed ten guineas each to his mother, stepfather and two half brothers; the rest of his estate went to Samuel. His will reads, '...The reason why I have left my half brothers so little is that their father is in a fair way to amasse a large fortune....', whereas '...my only whole brother the son of my Father who by the narrowness of his paternal fortune stands more in need of it'. In C. H. Cave's, *A History of Banking in Bristol from 1750-1899*, published privately in 1789, it states that by the 1780s, Duntze Jr., had become an Exeter woollen merchant like his father had diversified into banking. He became a partner in The Exeter Bank, the oldest bank in Exeter, which later became Duntze Sanders Hamilton & Co. Created a baronet in 1774, Duntze Jr. moved to London and established the London bank of Halliday Duntze Praed & Co.

10 Dresser, op. cit., p.104

11 I. V. Hall, '*Whitson Court Sugar House*', Bristol, 1665-1824', *Transactions of the Bristol and Glos. Archaeological Society*, 65 (1944), pp. 1-97

Notes

12 SMV, West India Club Minutes, 1782

13 David Richardson, *The Bristol Slave Traders, A Collective Portrait*, Bristol Record Society Publication. Pp 16-17. Shows that many of the 32 principal slave agents in the eighteenth century, had been apprenticed to leading Bristol merchant families, and had achieved high office in the Society of Merchant Venturers.

14 BRO, MU2(6 a-v)

15 Morgan states in a recent study of firms involved in the sugar trade, that those whose name included '& Co' were usually 'ad hoc slaving groups, in which several individuals combined to cope with the high risks and potential profits from black cargoes'

16 BRO, 39461, Unitarian Records

17 Richards, op.cit, p. 16-17, Between 1726 and 1745, Richard Farr Sr. managed 37 voyages and between 1747 and 1772, his son had managed 20

18 These plantations were to pass to the Gibbs family in the mid-nineteenth century

19 Pamela Bright, *Dr Richard Bright (1789-1858)*, Bodley Head, p.5

20 Morgan, op. cit, p. 191

21 Pip Jones & Rita Youseph, *The Black Population of Bristol in the Eighteenth Century*, Bristol Branch of the Historical Association, 1970

22 It is likely that the Richards brothers were distantly related to the Gibbs family by marriage. Mary Rowe, George's great aunt had married a James Richards at Shobrooke in the early eighteenth century.

23 K. Morgan, *The Letters of William Miles, a Bristol Indian merchant, to John Tharp, a Jamaican Sugar Planter, 1770-1789*, calendared with an introduction in Patrick McGrath, ed., *A Bristol Miscellany*. (B.R.S. publications, vol. XXXVII, pp. 92-98

24 Morgan , op. cit, pp. 37-38

25 BRO, 37169/3

26 Dresser, op.cit., p. 108

27 Sombart and Max Weber in Harrington, p. 68

28 Clarkson, op.cit, I, 297

29 Peter Marshall, *The Anti Slave Trade Movement in Bristol*, Bristol Branch of the Historical Association, 1975

30 SMV, Book of Petitions, 1765-1850, 1792.

31 SMV, Africa Box, 5, 13th April 1789

32 BRO, Common Council Proceedings, 1783-1790., ff. 285, 289-290

33 W Mathews, *The New History, survey and description of the city and suburbs of Bristol, or Complete Guide and Bristol Directory for the Year 1793-4'*, pp. 38-9

34 Dresser, op cit, p. 164

35 Richardson, op. cit.,

36 SMV, New West India Society, Minutes and Proceedings, January 28th 1782.

Chapter 6, Antony

MSS 11021/1, 11021/2, 11021/3

1 Clark, E. G. A., The Ports of the Exe Estuary 1660-1860, University of Exeter, p. 116

2 EFP, May 14th 1882 *1782*

3 In 1778, Mrs Hucks reportedly reproached Dolly for 'over heating' herself contrary to Baker's instructions by 'playing at ball'.

4 Rose Heath, the wife of George Abraham's friend John Heath wrote after Abraham's death, 'I hear he was soon to have been married to a very pleasing and agreeable woman.

5 Clarke, op. cit., p18, note 3. Letter from S Tremlett of Exeter to J Baring, 11 December 1788 (Add. MSS. 38223, f.295: B.M.)

6 Very little is known about Banfill's origins although he may have been the son of a Samuel and Anne Banfill who had lived in Topsham in the early decades of the eighteenth century at the same time as George Abraham. Samuel and Anne had a son, also called Samuel who was baptised in Topsham in 1739, and it is likely that they were old family friends of the Gibbs. The links between the Banfill family and the Gibbs continued for many years. Banfill's nephew, William Mardon was later apprenticed to Antony Gibbs and another nephew Samuel Banfill Mardon, was later to become a partner in Gibbs Crawley & Co in South America in 1825.

7 Granger was the son of the Reverend Edmund Granger, rector of Sowton and Prebendary of Exeter. A Tory, he was an unsuccessful parliamentary candidate in the July 1802 election.

8 John Baring senior died in 1748 and his widow carried on the Larkbear business until her death in 1766. He had three grandsons, John, Francis and Charles. John and Francis had left Exeter to establish a wool-importing firm in London, connected to the Exeter business, leaving Charles to develop the Exeter firm. After his mother's death in 1755, John returned to Exeter and purchased Mount Radford House, leaving Francis to look after the London firm. With the purchase of Mount Radford, John acquired the necessary social status to join the landed gentry and to stand in the 1776 election. Instead of standing for one of the traditional parties, he chose to do so as an independent, declaring, 'I cannot suppose 'that a great commercial city would be unwilling to have a Man of Business for one of its Representatives'. He was

elected and represented Exeter until 1802.

9   Jenkins, op cit., p. 434
10   William Kennaway, father of Sir John Kennaway (1758-1836), 1st Bart
11   DRO, 4508M/B3a, Papers of Edmund Granger, Cash Book & Ledger
12   DRO, 2065M/T2/9, Details obtained from the auction catalogue
13   ibid
14   It was always known as Lower Mill
15   DRO, 4058M/B2, Cash Book
16   EFP, 12 January 1787
17   Ibid, March 13th 1787, 3b
18   Granger's sister had married James Yonge of Puslinch, whose younger brother married Catharina Crawley, the daughter of Sir Thomas Crawley Boevey, the elder brother of Antony's brother-in-law, Charles Crawley,
19   DRO, 4508M/F77, Papers of Edmund Granger
20   Ibid.
21   DRO, 2065M/T2/4
22   DRO, 2065M/T2/9
23   DRO, T2/9/6/4/8
24   Ibid.
25   EFP, 7 July 1789, 3c
26   DRO, 2065M/T2/4, op. cit.

Chapter 7, Exwick and Madrid
MSS 11021/3, 11021/4, 19862/1 pt 3

1   DRO, 4508M/F78, Papers of Edmund Granger
2   Ibid
3   Ibid
4   ibid
5   DRO, 2065M/T2/4
6   Antony Merry was Secretary to the Madrid Legation for some years, before becoming Ambassador in Paris in 1802, Washington 1803, Denmark 1807 and Sweden 1808. He became a great friend to both Antony and Dolly and amongst the in the letters in the Guildhall, it is mentioned that on one occasion he sent his carriage to collect Dolly for a dinner at his house and on another he escorted her to the Royal Palace.
7   The following year he was created Lord St Helens for his part in the negotiations.
8   Laudanum is an opium mixture used as a narcotic painkiller
9   Extract from Sir John Head's diary in MS 11021/4, 1 February 1793,

10 Ibid, 29 September, 1793

11 Lewis, John, William and Jediadiah Stephens originated from Devon and lived at Madford House in Exeter. They were friends of Antony and Dolly. Lewis and John were merchants in Lisbon, and in 1798, Lewis established a glass-making factory in Marinha. John Stephens died in Lisbon in 1803. The *Portuguese Almanack de Lembrancas Luso Brasilio*, 1896, notes that in 1826, his son J J Stephens gave his glass factory to the Portuguese nation.

Chapter 8, Exwick and the Iberian Peninsula
MSS 11021/3, 11021/4, 11021/5, 11021/6, 11021/7, 11021/8

1 DRO 2065M/T2/9

2 Clark, op. cit., p. 118

3 The Kennaways, one of the most prosperous of Devon's woollen cloth merchants whom Antony had long admired, suffered crippling losses with the closure of the Italian and Spanish markets in 1793. That year, their Italian debts alone were £52,393. They continued to ship cloth to London, albeit on a much reduced scale, and concentrated on importing wine from Spain. See *Clark, Ports of the Exe*, 118-1123 and DRO. Wharfinger's Journals, 1790.

4 EFP, 18 January, 1796

5 Jenkins, op cit, p. 432

6 DRO, DD 70210, op. cit. states that on 3 April 1797, the whole Pytte estate was sold to Edward Cotsford for £3600. It consisted of '4 Messuages 4 Barns 4 Stables 4 Gardens 7 Orchards 100 acres of land 50 acres meadows 50 acres of Pasture 10 acres of Woods & 10 acres of ffurze & heath with the appurtenances in the parish of Clist St George'.

7 Ibid, p.120

8 Lyson, op. cit. p. 196

9 Clarke, op cit. pp. 99-100

10 Newton, op.cit, p. 105

11 DRO, DQS 1/11, Books of Session Orders, 1792-1802

12 These journal entries are from the '*Private Journal of Dorothea Gibbs*' in the possession of Lord Aldenham.

13 Cowley, Cottage was situated on the Exeter-Crediton road almost opposite the lodge of Cowley Place. It was then renamed The Manor. It was said to have been a cell of the priory of St. Nicholas of Exeter. During restoration early in the last century, two fine stone mantlepieces were exposed. In 1868, William, Antony's second son, built the Chapel of Ease of St Antony at Cowley in memory of his parents. See N.3, *Antony and Dorothea*, p.145

14 EFP, 6 May 1802
15 Newton, op. cit., p. 108
16 Ibid, p. 109
17 EFP, 11 August 1803
18 Hoskins. W G, Exeter Militia List 1804, Devon & Cornwall Record Society
19 Robert Remmett's second wife had died on 3 August 1794
20 Gibbs, op cit. p. 157
21 DRO, 4508 M/F84, Articles of Co-partnership, 7th May 1804
22 Alexander Jenkins, *The History and Description of the City of Exeter*, Exeter, 1806, Chap VI, St Thomas, p. 437

Chapter 9, The Topsham Family

1 The two families remained close and twenty years later, on 26th March 1776, Robert Remmett married his first cousin, Elizabeth (Nelly).
2 DRO, DD 538
3 DRO, D.D. 532
4 DRO, Z/9/21/38/4, *Notes by the late Nicholas Brand about the year 1833*, transcribed by F W L Ross 1905
5 PRO, PROB 11/1047, Elizabeth was unmarried at the time of her grandfather's death in 1749. Having already settled a considerable sum on Elizabeth's sister Margaret and brother William, he appointed her his sole executrice. He bequeathed his estate to his second wife Martha, and on her death, it passed to Elizabeth. Her sister Catherine had married Thomas Roper and had died giving birth to a daughter, another Elizabeth.
6 It was the custom during the mid-eighteenth century for the first son to carry his mother's surname as a middle name.
7 DRO, DD.100274. The plot was leased to Richard Granger, a Topsham victualler and was extended, eventually becoming a public house now known as the Bridge Inn.
8 PRO, PROB 11/1055
9 In 1776 Nicholas Peters Jr, the grandson of Nicholas Peters and Mary Gibbs, married Ann Sanford the heiress daughter of William Sanford.
10 Abraham and Tryphaena's daughter Elizabeth had married into the Pett family of Liskeard. It is likely that Joan Pett was her daughter and therefore George Abraham's cousin.
11 Clarke, op. cit., pp. 161- 163
12 DRO, D.D. 48723.
13 Ibid

14 Ibid

15 In 1786 he was a party to a deed with his brothers and sister

16 Family Search Internet Genealogy Service of the Church of Jesus Christ of the
    Latter-day Saints

Chapter 10, Abraham

MSS 11021/2, 11021/3, 11021/4

1   David Constantine, *Fields of Fire, A Life of Sir William Hamilton*, p. 12-13

2   Ibid, p. 84, The Palazzo Sessa is reached from the present-day Piazza dei
    Martiri from the Vico S. Maria a Capella Vecchia. The Palazzo Sessa was built
    on ground belonging to Santa Maria a Cappella Vechia, and was sold to the
    Marchese Giuseppe Sessa in 1741. Hamilton rented twelve rooms on the first
    and second floors for Hamilton for 800 ducats (£150) a year. Today the
    building houses the Jewish Synagogue.

3   PRO, IR26/283, 118. It has always been thought that she had been
    christened Mary Elizabeth Catherine after her mother, but the administration
    records in the National Archives at Kew, dated 19 September 1811 indicates
    that her name was Anna Maria. It appears that she adopted the name Mary
    Elizabeth Catherine after her marriage.

4   Constantine, op. cit., pp. 194-5. Torre dei Greco, which is situated 7 kms from
    the crater, had been destroyed several times after the Pompei eruption in 79 and
    in 1794 when the lava flow reached the sea. The present town was built on the
    lava after 1794.

5   Ibid, p. 217

6   Jack Russell, *Nelson and the Hamiltons*, p. 43

7   Sir Harris Nicholas, *The Dispatches and Letters of Vice-Admiral Lord Viscount
    Nelson*, Vol 3, p. 200

8   The Palazzo Palagonia is situated just off the Via Alloro near the Porta Felice
    and the Mole in the old city of Palermo. It was not the Palazzo Palagonia built
    in 1797 by the Prince of Palagonia as a country residence and situated to the
    east of the city on the road to Monreale in the area now know as Bagheria.

9   Raleigh Trevelyan, *Princes under the Volcano*, Milan, Rizzoli, pp. 4-5

10 Dennis Mack Smith, *Modern Sicily after 1713*, Chapter 41, Industry

11 Aspinal, Arthur, ed. *The later correspondence of George III*, Vol 3, 1727,
    E Livingstone to the King, 1 May 1798, p. 55

12 Michela D'Angela, *Mercanti inglesi in Sicilia 1806-1815*, Milan 1988, pp. 11-14

13 Rosario Lentini, *British Merchants and Goods in Palermo 1797-1816*, p. 3. Paper
    presented at the Conference entitled Relaunching Maritime Trade, organised

by the University of Messina and held in Taormina in May 2006

14 In 1810, an onze was worth 11/3d

15 Rosario Lentini, *Note su un operatore commerceriale in Sicilia: Abraham Gibbs (1799-1802, in 'Nuovi quaderni del Meridione'*, m56, anno XIV, pp. 386-394. I am extremely grateful to Rosario Lentini for giving me copies of all his research papers into Gibbs's business activities and for his suggestions and advice.

16 Lentini, *Note su un operatore.........*, ibid, p. 390.

17 Rosario Lentini, *The British in Sicily and their influence on the island's economy, in The history of the Whitakers*, Sellerio editore Palermo, p. 16. Sumac dust was obtained by grinding the tannin-rich leaves and was used in the tanning process. Soda ash was produced by burning certain plants (salsole and riscolo), grew in abundance on the island, and rags were the essential material for the manufacture of paper.

18 Rosario Lentini, *Financial Activities of English Merchant-Bankers in Western Sicily between 18th and 19th Centuries*, Paper presented at the Fourth International Congress of Maritime History, Corfu, June 2004, p.1

19 The Tavola, the only public bank in Palermo was established in 1551

20 Lentini, *Financial Activities of English Merchant bankers... .'*, op. cit. p. 3 and note 11. V Cusumanio, Storia dei banchi della Sicilia, Palermo 1974, p. 419

21 Lentini, *The British in Sicily and their influence on the island's economy*, in Raleigh Trevelyan, *The History of the Whitakers*, English version by Peter Dawson, 1993 Enzo Sellerio Palermo, p. 17

22 Ibid, p. 14

23 Ibid

24 Rosario Lentini, *I Whitaker e il Capitale Inglesettra l'Ottocento e il Novecento in Sicilia*, Atti del seminario svoltosi a Trapani, nell'Aula Magna della Libera Universita del Mediterraneo, nei giorni 29-30 novembre e 1 dicembre 1990, con l'adesione della Societa Siciliana per la Storia Patria, dell'Accademia di Scienze, Lettre Arti di Palermo, della Fondazione Culturale Whitaker di Palermo, dell'Associazione Marsalese per la Storia Patria, p. 95

25 ASP, Archivio della Ducea Nelson, b. 330, Bryant Barrett to Earl Nelson, 25 July 1817

26 Trevelyan, Raleigh, *The History of the Whitakers*, Sellerio Editore Palermo, p. 5. The name 'Bronte Madeira' stuck and all white masala became known as this or Sicily Madeira in the trade.

27 A contemporary traveller in Sicily, writing in 1824, states that the road from Palermo towards Messina went about thirty miles, as far as Alcamo. From then on, there was a "pretty good" mule path on the west coast, and from there,

a similar path to Marsala. (Travels through Sicily and the Lipari Islands in the month of December, 1824, by a Naval Officer [London, 1827], pp. 50, 70)

28 General Sir John Acton, the heir to a Shropshire baronetcy, had arrived in Naples in 1777. Although English by birth, he had been born in Besançon of a French mother. Having lived in Europe for most of his life, he served in the French navy and then the Tuscan and was sent to Naples by the Grand Duke of Tuscany, 'to give advice & assistance towards the putting His Sicn Majestys Marine upon a respectable footing'. Alfred Morrison, *The Hamilton and Nelson Papers*, vol I, f.246

29 BL., Add 41197, ff96-7

30 Ibid

31 Constantine, op. cit., pp. 259-260

32 BL., Add MS 41200, ff 217-18

33 Ibid, ff222

34 Ibid, ff221

35 Ibid, ff227

36 Ibid

37 Ibid

39 BL, Add. 41197-41200, ff221

39 BL., Add 48412, ff 175

40 Nicholas, V, op cit., pp. 160-161

42 Ibid, Nelson to Emma, 18 October 1803, p. 253

43 Lucy Riall, *Nelson versus Bronte: Land, Litigation and Local Politics in Sicily, 1799-1860*, European History Quarterly, Vol. 29, No 1, January 1999, p. 40 and n. 7

44 Nicholas, VI, Nelson to Emma, 1 August 1804, p. 95

45 Ibid, Nelson to Emma, 14 March 1804, p. 440

46 Ibid, Nelson to Elliott, 19 October 1803, p. 256

47 ASN, A Tommasi, INV I, No 62, f6 VIII, No 23

48 Ibid

49 ASN, A Tommasi, INV I, No 67, f 6 VIII, No 25, Acton to Gibbs, 26 October, 1803 'Ho fatto presente al Re le considerrazioni di K S M[msullo] Stato di Bronte, ed esson dosi S.M.uniformata circa alla convenienza, di doversi permettere in questo momento l'affitto dello Stato per dieci anni o piu se occorresse, glie lo partecipo nel Real Nom, perche possa andar i concerto col Negoziante Sig[n] Abram Gibbs Incombensato da Mi Lord Nelson per questa operazione.

50 Quoted in J A Gibbs

51　NARA, *Dispatches from United States Consuls in Palermo.* Barnes to James Madison, Secretary of State, June 27th 1803

52　Ibid

53　Ibid

54　Gibbs, op. cit., p. 16

55　Lentini, *Note su un Operatore... .'*, op cit., p. 391, n. 16 ANDP, Distrettuale di Palermo, atti del notaio Francesco Maria Albertini, reg. 32919, c. 260 r.e.v., 30-6-1803. The document reads '...il sig. Don Abramo Gibbs, pubblico negoziante degente in questa....ha constituito, fatto, creato e solennemente ordinato e ordina in suo vero, certo, legittimo ed indubitato procuratore, attore, fattore, il sig. Dom Fancesco Falconnet di Napoli....a porter in nome e parte di detto constituente e per esso in detta città di Naplol affittare e sopraffittare a qualunque person che volesse condurre e prendere a piggione la casa ove abitava detto sig. Gibbs, sita e posta in detta città di Napoli... .'

56　Carola Oman's *Nelson*, Hodder and Stoughton, London 1948, pp. 543-544

Chapter 11, London and Dulwich
MSS 11021/7, 11021/9, 11021/10, 19863,

1　Fiona Fraser, *Beloved Emma – The Life of Emma, Lady Hamilton*, pp. 307-310

2　Mrs Hucks was buried in the little church of St. John in the Wilderness, outside Exmouth where her son Joseph had been buried a few years before.

3　Private Journal of Dorothea Gibbs, 16/17 December 1806

4　Ibid,

5　In 1805, while Antony was in Lisbon, Branscombe had returned to Devon. He went back to Cadiz after the armistice with the intention of establishing his own business there

6　Maude, Wilfred, *Antony Gibbs & Sons, Merchant Bankers, 1808-1958*, p. 20

7　Dolly's sister, Eleanor died without issue in December 1800, a few months after her brother Joseph

8　Journal, op. cit., 1808-1811

9　The Robert Remmett referred to in this letter was the son of his brother-in-law Robert Remmett, the physician from Plymouth

10　PRO, IR 26/383, 19 September 1811.

11　Journal, op. cit, 23 September 1811

Chapter 12, William and Susan
MS 11021/6, MS 11021/7, MS11021/10, MS 19862

1　TOPMS, Shapter Street is now called Higher Shapter Street.

2 Graham Farr, *Records of Bristol Ships, 1800-1838*, Bristol Record Society publications Vol.XV, p 236
3 PRO, PROB 11/1514
4 Ibid

Chapter 13, Palermo
1 NARA, *Dispatches*, op. cit. Gibbs to Barnes, 24 September, 1804
2 Ibid. 13 December 1804
3 Ibid, date
4 Ibid, Gibbs to Madison, July 1805
5 Ibid, the standard contract signed by Gibbs's successor, dated 1 June 1816
6 Ibid, Gibbs to Madison, 10 November 1806
7 Ibid
8 Ibid, Gibbs to Madison, 20 January 1807. By the beginning of 1807, the British navy had impressed over 6,000 American sailors.
9 Ibid
10 Ibid
11 On 22 June 1807, an English warship, the *Leopard*, opened fire on an American frigate, the *Chesapeake*, off Virginia. Several American sailors were killed or wounded, and four men were seized (impressed).
12 NARA, *Dispatches*, op cit, 24 September 1807
13 Ibid, 6 January 1810
14 Ibid.
15 Nicolas, op. cit., Vol 1V, September 1799 to December 1801, London, p250
16 Ibid, note 8
17 Lentini, *Financial Activities of English Merchant Bankers... .*, op. cit. p. 3, note 37.
18 BL, Add 48412, ff 75
19 ibid, ff 139
20 PRO, FO 165/1, Drummond to Lord Hourick, 2 May 1807
21 PRO, AO 1/11/23
22 Lentini, *Financial Activities of English Merchant Bankers... .*, op. cit., p.9 and note 41
23 PRO, AO 1/11/23, op cit.
24 Lentini, op. cit. p. 9 and note 42
25 NRA, *Dispatches*
26 ASP, *Archivio Nelson*, b. 580, Various Correspondence, Gibbs to Earl Nelson, 7 June 1806

27 Ibid

28 Ibid, b. 581, Memorial from Bronte to Earl Nelson, 11 March 1812

29 Riall, op cit., p. 51

30 ASP, op. cit., Memorial from Bronte, No. 101

31 Ibid.

32 About £80,000 at today's values

33 NARA, Dispatches, op. cit., 31 July 1811, Gibbs to Munroe

34 Blow-Williams, op cit., p. 367 and n, 2 & 3

35 Lentini, op. cit. p. 9

36 Galt, op cit., pp. 133-4

37 PRO, FO165/1 Folio 32-48, Mellish to Canning, 6 November 1809

38 UN, PwJd 5640/2/1

39 UN, PwJd5640/3, November 10th 1812

40 Lentini, op. cit., pp. 9-10

Chapter 14, Humiliation and Despair

MSS11021/11, 11021/12, 11021/13, 11021/23, 19888

1 Edward Blaquiere, *Letters from the Mediterranean, containing a civil and political account of Sicily, Tripoli, Tunis and Malta, with biographical sketches, anecdotes and observations… ..*, Colburn, 1813, Letter X, p. 275

2 Ibid

3 NARA, *Dispatches…*, op. cit, 31 January 1811

4 Ibid

5 Ibid

6 Ibid

7 PRO, CO 158/26, 8 March 1815, Maitland to Bunbury

8 BV, *Anglo Maltese Bank Archives*, Register of Bills Tendered and Approved, 1812-1815. Gibbs name appears in four transaction dated January 18, 1814. The amount is calculated at 1 Scudi = 1/8d. My thanks to Victor Tortelli, Curator of the Bank of Valetta for this information.

9 Lentini, *Financial Activities of English Merchant Bankers… .*', op. cit. p. 9 and note 43

10 ibid

11 PRO, FO352/60B

12 Ibid

13 UN, PwJd 917

14 Lentini, *Financial Activities of English Merchant Bankers… ..,,* op. cit. pp. 9-10 and note 44

15 Ibid, p. 10 and note 45

16 Ibid, p. 10 and note 49

17 UN, PwJd 2649

18 ibid, 2640-2645

19 Rosario Lentini, *Alle origini del capitalismo finanziario: la nascita della 'prima compagnia di assicurazioni di Palermo'*, in I Whitaker e il capitale Inglese tra l'Ottocento e il Novecento in Sicilia, Libera Universita del Mediterraneo, 1990 p. 88

20 Lentini, *Alle origini del capitalismo…* . op. cit., p. 88

21 ASM, Notary G. Micale, 1482, 11 December 1801. That year Abraham had insured a large cargo of biscuits, being transported from Palermo to Malta was for 2000 onze (£400). Quoted in Michela D'Angelo, *Mercanti Iinglesi a Malta 1800-1825*, Franco Angeli, Milan, 1990, Note 8, p. 89

22 BV, Archives of the Banco Espirito Santo, op. cit.

23 Ibid, pp. 84-87

24 Lentini, *Financial Activities of English Merchant-Bankers… .*, p. 7 and note 32

25 Ibid

26 PRO, FO 70/60 25 June 1813, Fagan to William Hamilton Esq.,

27 PRO, FO70/66, 16 December, 1814, Fagan to Castlereagh

28 Ibid

29 Rosario Lentini, *Dal Commercio Alla Finanza: I Negozianti-Banchieri Inglese nella Sicilia Occidentale tra XVIII e XIX Secolo*, University Mediterranea, 1 December 2004, note 59, cfr ASP, Notaio Francesco Maria Albertini, vol. 32983. Palermo, 11 December 1813, cc. 51r-58r,
    The British shareholders were Gibbs, Rogers Brothers & Co., William John Turner and Samuel Prior, Patterson & Brown, George Wood and Charles Crokat.

30 Lentini, *Alle origini del calitalismo…*, op. cit ., p. 91

31 Ibid, p. 92

32 NARA, *Dispatches*, op. cit.,

33 Lentini, *Alles origini del capitalismo…*, Ibid, p. 93

34 C. Northcote Parkinson, *Edward Pellew*, London, 1934, Chap. XII – Algiers, notes that Captain Campbell, who commanded the squadron before the city, granted Caroline protection under the British flag and agreed to take her to France. Lord Exmouth arriving in Naples the following evening annulled the agreement, refusing to allow her to leave.

35 *Gentleman's Magazine*, 1815, pt II, p. 82

36 NARA, *Dispatches*, op. cit. 10 March 1816

37 Trevelyan, op. cit., p. 5

38 UN, PwJd 2649 op. cit.

39 Trevelyan, *Princes under the volcano.*, op. cit., p. 22

40 My thanks to Polly Holmes a'Court for this information. Laetitia was named after Charles's mother and Anna Maria after herself. Now that she was officially known as Mary, it is not clear whether she had formerly assumed her mother's names of Mary Elizabeth Catherine before 1816, but she certainly had by her marriage.

41 Trevelyn, op., cit, p. 26.

42 Lentini, *Alle origini del capitalismo...*, op. cit., p. 96

43 Ibid

44 Ibid., p. 96 and note 86

45 Lentini, *Financial Activities of English Merchant Bankers... .*, op. cit., p. 8

46 Ibid

47 Lentini, *Alle origini del capitalismo... .,.*, op. cit, p. 97

48 *Gentleman's Magazine*, no. 86, Pt. 2, Dec 1816, p. 571

Chapter 15, Scandal

1 Lentini, *Alle origini del capitalismo... .,.*, op. cit, p 96, The original statement reads: 'Per il noto accidente accaduto nella persona del fu mio socio signor Abramo Gibbs tutti gli interessi trovandosi occupati dal Supremo Magistrato del Commercio, così bisognerà far capo dallo stesso per li provvedimenti opportuni'.

2 Ibid., p. 97, The original reads: 'il signor Don Gioacchino Lenzitti non ebbe veruna colpa nel disgaziato fallimento della sua ragione che anzi si è onestamente verso di noi condotto, con aver date tutti il lumi necessarj alla recuperazione del patrimonio, alla esigenza de'crediti e tutt'altro che è occorso'.

3 Ibid, p. 97

4 Nicholas, *The Dispatches and Letters... .*, op. cit., Nelson to Sir Alexander John Ball, Bart, 12 August 1803

5 PRO FO 30/7/1, p. 47, 11 October 1811

6 PRO, AO 1/11/24

7 PRO, FO/70/76, 9 June 1816, Snape Douglas to Vicount Castlereagh

8 NARA, *Dispatches*, October 1816.

9 ASP, *Archivio Nelson*, op. cit., b.581, A. Correspondence, 1807-1818

10 Ibid, b.330, *List of Persons being or having been in some way connected with the Duke of Bronte or the Affairs of the Duchy with observations relating to them.* 1812-1842

11 Ibid

12 Ibid., b 245

13 b 330. pt II., *Volume de Contralle di Gabelle de anno 1812-1818 dello Stato di Bronte*, Barret to Nelson, 23 March 1817 and 25 July 1817

14 *List of Persons... .*, op. cit, 26 July 1718

15 ASP, b. 583, 16 September 1817, Barrett to Hutchinson

16 *List of Persons... .*, op. cit. 25 July 1817

17 Ibid

18 Ibid., 26 July 1817, Barrett to Nelson

19 ASP, b581. *Correspondence Thovez – di Martino, A. 1818-1822.*, Hutchinson to Barrett, 14 January 1818

20 Ibid., 2 March 1818, Martino to Nelson

21 Ibid

22 Ibid, 11 September, Nelson to di Martino

23 Ibid

Chapter 16, Lyle

MSS 11021/4, 11021/7, 11021/13, 11021/14, 19888

1   Benjamine Heath was the son of a successful Exeter merchant who had made a considerable fortune. He matriculated from Oxford around the time of his father's death, planning to become a barrister. On inheriting £30,000, he gave up the idea of law, and instead left England on a Grand Tour. In Europe, he met and married Rose Mary Michelet, the daughter of a Swiss merchant and they returned to live in Exeter. They had five sons and four daughters. The eldest son Benjamine became the headmaster of Harrow school and entered the church; the second, George, became the headmaster of Eton; the third William, joined the navy, eventually becoming a Rear Admiral; John and his younger brother Charles became merchants.

2   Sir William Drake, *Heathiania: Notes Geneological and Bibliographical of the Family of Heath, Especially of the Descendents of Benjamine Heath of Exeter.*, London 1881 p. 21

3   Eduardo Grendi, *Gli Inglesi a Genova (Secoli XVII-XVIII), in Quadermi Storici*, n.115 (2004), pp. 240-249

4   Ibid

5   English community, but literally translated as English Farm or Factory

6   Grendi, op. cit, p. 263

7   Nicolas, op. cit., I, 491, 492

8   PRO, FO 28/12, Drake to Grenville, 20 November 1794

9   PRO, FO 28/19, *Letters & Papers Advices, Intelligences Correspondences & Communications.* 9 July 1797

10 Quoted in Oman, p. 158

11 FO 28/19, op. cit, 5 January 1799

12 Add, 34908 f.150

13 Baron de Marbot, *Memoirs of General Baron de Marbot,* Vol 2, chap.11, pp. 1-6

14 The Heath family retained their Italian connections. John Heath's son, John Benjamin, who was a director of the Bank of England for fifty years, was the Italian Consul-General in London, and was created Baron Heath by the Italian Government.

15 Despite an extensive search in Palermo, no trace has been found of Abraham's grave.

16 In a letter to Harriet Gibbs written in 1848, Mary refers to rumours over this 'preference' on her father's estate. See p.385

17 See reference in Antony Gibbs & Son ledgers and Gibbs & Co letter book

18 Blow-Williams, op. cit.

20 PRO, FO 168/2, Hill to Foreign Office, 14 March 1817

21 PRO, F.O. 168/6, Dispatches, H S Fox, 1 July 1825

22 ibid

23 Ibid

24 John Richard Gamble, a merchant of Finsbury Park, London

25 It is likely that John Furse was the Exeter merchant mariner who made a number of trips from Exeter to Genoa in the 1790s, and later became a partner in the London firm of Heath & Son & Furse, established by John Heath.

Chapter 17, The Attorney General

MSS 11021/1, 11021/3, 11021/5, 11021/13

1   Henry Brougham, Baron Brougham and Vaux, *Sketches of statesmen of the time of George III,* vol 1, 223

2   DoRO, D/BOH/c4, Bond mss., Jekyll to Bond, 13 July 1804

3   *Personal Sketches of Sir Johan Barrington,* Chapter XXXIV, in Chapters of Irish History, Internet.

4   BL, Add 49173, f276, Spencer Perceval Papers, Gibbs to Auckland, 1 April 1807

5   LL&RRO DE718/D/4, *Martin Manuscripts; Deeds and Papers of the Martin Family,* 9 May 1807, T Sowerby (Queens College) to Rev. R Martin

6   Melikan, op.cit, pp. 44-46

7   *Annual Register,* 1808, p. 48

8   DoRO, Bond mss, op. cit.., Jeykll to Bond, 9 May 1808

9   Philip Harling, *The Law of Libel and the Limits of Repression, 1790-1832*, The Historical Journal, 44, 1 (2001), p. 111

10 ibid, Table 1, p. 109

11 ibid, p. 113

12 Cobbett's *Parliamentary Debates*, Vol. 14, 1809, p. 298

13 BL, Add 49476, ff 72-77, Gibbs to Hawkesbury, 21 September 1808

14 Ibid, ff 76, York to Hawkesbury, 20 Sept. 1808

15 Ibid, ff. 78, 13 Oct. 1808

16 BL, Add 38321, *Lord Liverpool Papers*, Liverpool to Gibbs, 28 Oct. 1808

17 Ibid

18 BL, Add 49474, *Willoughby Gordon Papers*, ff50, Gibbs to Gordon, 31 Oct. 1808

19 Arthur Aspinal, ed *The later correspondence of George III*, Perceval to George III, 2 Feb. 1809, vol. V, p. 187

20 Do.R.O., Bond mss, op cit., Jekyll to Bond, 15 February 1809

21 G T Garrett, *Lord Brougham*, Macmillan, 1935, p. 46

22 Around 40,000 soldiers crossed the North Sea to attack the French-controlled base at Antwerp. They seized Walcheren, a swampy fever-ridden island at the mouth of the river Scheldt, South Beveland island. Within a month, malaria struck and there were over 8,000 cases amongst the British troops. Medical provision was completely inadequate. The expedition was called off in early September and of the 12,000 soldiers that stayed on Walcheren, in October only 5500 remained fit for duty. The expedition cost the British government almost £8 million, and of the 4067 men that died, only 106 had died in combat.

23 E. P. Thompson, *The Making of the English Working Class*, Penguin Books, (1963), p. 511

24 Curwen's Act was passed in June 1809 to prevent the sale of parliamentary seats, which resulted in the reduction of seats, which the government manipulated for its own supporters.

25 Brougham, i. 133

26 Do.R.O., Bond Mss, Jekyll to Bond, 1 June 1812

27 Horner mss, f321

28 Ibid., 25 Jan 1814

29 Add, 49506, f.77, *Gordon Papers*, Gibbs to Gordon, 14 Dec. 1812

30 D.R.O, 4508M/F78

Chapter 18, Bristol

MSS 11021/4, 11021/5, 11021/6, 11021/10

1 Kenneth Morgan, *James Morgan and the Bristol slave trade*, Historical Research, vol. 76, no. 193 (May 2003)

2 BRO, 11168/1/a/i-ii, 1766-67

3 Alleyne Fitzherbert, later Baron St. Helens, had been appointed as British Ambassador in Madrid where he was on very friendly terms with Antony.

4 FFJ, Bristol, 1794. In September 1796, the FFJ reported that Richard Bright and Evan Baillie were each fined £400 for refusing the office of mayor.

5 Cited in Stephen Poole, *Popular Politics in Bristol*, p. 246

6 FFJ, Bristol, 18 February 1797

7 John Penny, *A military history of Bristol during the Revolutionary War 1793-1892*, pp. 4-5

8 BRO, 39461/R/2(a), Lewin's Mead Chapel burial register.

9 PRO, Prob, 11/1363

10 FFBJ, 29th March 1800

11 Ibid, 1168(37)a

12 Ibid

13 Although a number of other nations bowed to British pressure to follow suit, the Atlantic trade continued, as the abolition of the slave trade did not abolish slavery.

14 BRO, 11168/54/b

15 Ibid

16 BRO, 11168(14)j

17 Richards continued to be a shareholder and sleeping partner, and took an active interest in the business until his death in 1829.

18 The Bright family had continued to be deeply involved in all aspects of city life. Richard was a member of the Corporation from 1783 to 1835, and his brother was a Bristol M.P.

Chapter 19, The end of an era

MSS 11021/13, 11021/14, 11021/15, 19888

1 Maude, op. cit., p. 20

2 *Dorothea Gibbs Journal*, op. cit.,

3 BL, Add 38574, ff 74, op. cit., Gibbs to Liverpool, 17 October 1818

4 Ibid, ff. 76, Liverpool to Gibbs, 17 October 1818

5 PRO, Prob 11/1626

6 Gibbs, op. cit., pp 366-7 and note, Henry complied with his mother's request and Thomas Gilman attended Christ's School

7   The Mortmain Act 1736 declared void any devise of land (or property) to charity and instead vested the land in the testators heir-at-law or next of kin. Until recent times, most charities were trusts and were not incorporated. While the Mortmain Act, 1736, used the same name as earlier legislation, it was substantially different in that it applied to gifts for all charitable uses irrespective of whether the recipient was incorporated or not. See Blake Bromley, *The Historical Origins of the Definition of Religion in Charitable Law.* See www.blakebromley.com pp. 1-2

8   *Report of the Public Charities of the County of Devon, Topsham,* p. 165

9   Ibid

10 EFP, February 14th 1831, p2. col. 4

11 DRO, 1078/IRW/G/203

12 PRO, PROB 11/1760

13 DRO, 2065M/L2/5, 13th November 1810

14 DRO, 2065M/T2/4

15 EFP, 11 May 1814, p4, b,c.

16 Ibid, 29 June 1814, P4, b.

17 Newton, op.cit, pp. 112-113

18 DRO, 4508M/F78

19 D&EI, *A Second Letter to Sir T D Acland, Bart. M.P. on the Means of Improving the Condition of The Labouring Classes and Reducing parochial Assessments by Adapting the Poor Laws to the Present State of Society,* Exeter, 1818

20 ibid.

21 D&E., the three pamplets and the report are: 1817, *A letter to Sir T D Acland, Bart, MP., containing hints for improving the condition of the labouring classes of the community and reducing parochial assessments by adapting the Poor Laws to the present state of Society,* Exeter, T Flindell, 18171818, *A second letter to Sir T D Acland, Bart, MP on the means of reducing the condition of the labouring classes and reducing parochial assessments by adapting the Poor laws to the present state of society,* T Flindell for Longman, 18181828, *A third letter to Sir T D Acland Bart, MP (with the first and second letters originally printed in 1817 & 1818) on the means of improving the condition of the labouring classes and reducing parochial assessments; the report of an attempt made in 1818 to bring into action such of those means as were applicable to the parish of St Thomas the Apostle, and of the results during a trial of ten years,* Exeter W C Pollard, 18281828, *Report of an attempt made in the parish of St Thomas the Apostle since the year 1818, for the better relief and employment of the poor: and of its results during a trial of ten years.* Exeter, W C Pollard, 1828

22 The details of the sale list the mill as being a three-storey building with six acres of land. On the ground floor was the gearing from the water wheel, which powered four shearing frames, each working 4 pairs of shears, a brushing and napping machine, a calendar and cylinder and two breakers. On the second and third floors were thirteen scribbling and carding machines, five billies, eight jennies and one breaker. There were a number of outbuildings housing another twenty jennies, a building containing two blue vats heated by five flues, two large copper furnaces heated by steam, two wool vats and a drying loft. My thanks to David Cornforth for this information.

23 ibid.

24 Lysons, *Magna Britannia*, Devon Vol., part II, 196,

25 He was later employed as a West India Merchant and partner in the plantations owned by Gibbs Bright & Co. from 1827 in the plantations owned by the firm. He returned to England in 1839, and was employed by the Liverpool office until his death in 1848.

26 DRO, op.cit.

27 Ibid

28 Moore, *History of Devon*, op. cit.

Chapter 20, Changing Fortunes

MSS 11021/13, 11021/14, 11021/15, 11021/16, 11021/18, 11024/2, 11024/3, 11036/1, 11069, 11079, 19888

1 DRO, 4508M/F78

2 Wilfred Maude, *Antony Gibbs & Sons Limited, Merchant Bankers, 1808-1958*, pp. 22-23

3 DRO, 4508M/F78, op cit.

4 Maude, op. cit., p. 23

5 Martin Daunton, *Oxford Dictionary of Bibliography*, pp, 41-44

6 George Henry Gibbs lived at Aldenham House in Hertfordshire and had a house at 11 Bedford Square in the capital. He left money towards the restoration of the church at Clifton Hampden.

7 Henry Hucks Gibbs was a historian and prolific writer of works on currency and bi-metallism. He was Director of the Bank of England (1875-7), the High Sheriff of Herts (1884), created Baron Aldenham (1890) and MP for the City of London (1891-2).

8 Miller, op. cit, p. 33

9 Information on guano obtained from the internet

10 Daunton, op. cit., p. 42

11 Ibid

12 Tyntesfield is now owned by the National Trust

13 Peter Marshall, *Bristol and the Abolition of Slavery, The Politics of Emancipation*, Bristol Branch of the Historical Association, 1975, p. 27

14 Parliamentary and Sessional Papers, vol XLVIII, pp 1-600

15 Marshall, op. cit., p. 27

16 BRO, 12142(10), a & b.

17 Marshall, op. cit., p. 27

18 Geoffrey Channon, *Bristol and the promotion of The Great Western Railway, 1835*. Bristol Branch of the Historical Association pamphlet, p. 27

19 Adrian Vaughan, *Isambard Kingdom Brunel, Engineering Knight-Errant*, p. 49

20 Ibid

21 Shute had joined the Liverpool firm as early as 1827, after the closure of the factory at Exwick, and was a partner from 1839 to 1848.

22 In 1876, the *SS Great Britain* was damaged off Cape Horn and remained there until 1970 when she was repaired and returned to Bristol.

23 *London Gazette*, 2 July 1880, p. 3792

24 Michael Adkins had left his business to his nephew John Curtis, who on his death agreed that the business be divided between his executors, one of whom was Samuel Munckley and William Miles. Munckley took George Gibbs into the firm in 1767, and was in partnership with him and James Richards from 1789 until 1802. After Munckley's death, George took his son into the firm, which was renamed Gibbs, Richards & Gibbs between 1802 and 1808. After Richards's retirement the firm became George Gibbs & Son, and from 1818 until 1839, Gibbs Son & Bright.

25 [Maria] Elizabeth a' Court-Repington was born in Heytesbury on 21 July 1822. She married Sidney Herbert, 1st Baron Herbert on 12 August 1846. Sidney was the second son of George Augustus Herbert, 11th Earl of Pembroke. He was one of the most promising young politicians of his time, and was made Secretary of War during the Crimean Campaign. Sidney died in 1861 at the age of fifty, shortly after being created Baron Herbert of Lea, leaving Elizabeth a young widow with four sons and three daughters. Elizabeth too was an enthusiastic Peelite, an author and ardent helper of Florence Nightingale. While in Palermo with her mother in 1866, she was converted to Catholicism and became a zealous supporter of all Catholic charities. As an author, she produced a large number of books, partly original and partly translations, including *Impressions of Spain* (1866), *Cradle Lands* (1867), and *Wives and Mothers of Olden Time* (1871). She also wrote a number of short stories, some autobiographical,

and translated the lives of several saints from the French originals. She died in London on 8 August 1911, at the age of 89.

26 Lord Heytesbury was the British Ambassador at St. Petersburg (1828-32) and Lord Lieutenant of Ireland (1844-6)

27 Four years later, in 1864, the name of the firm was changed to Granet Brown & Co and it continued to operate until 1910, when it became Kirby & Le Mesurier.

28 The Tithe map indicates that the cottage was previously occupied by a distant kinsman, Richard Gibbs. These cottages were on the site of the present Addlepool Farm

29 Will of William Henry Gibbs in MS 11024/3

30 DRO, 1926/W/E6/2, Deeds and documents relating to the sale of part of William Waldron's estate.

31 Ibid.

32 Antony Hubert Gibbs was a director of the Exeter branch of the Union of London & Smiths bank, which took over a firm, which had been formed by the merger of two of the oldest banks in Exeter, the City Bank (Milford Snow & Co) and The Exeter Bank (Sanders & Co).

APPENDIX I

DRO 4508 M/F7/8. Schedule of loans and repayments to George Abraham and Antony Gibbs.

APPENDIX II

1 Letter from Lord Nelson to Abraham Gibbs, 26 August 1804, reproduced in J A Gibbs, *Antony and Dorothea... .'* , pp. 262-263

BIBLIOGRAPHY

ABBREVIATIONS

ASM   Archivio di Stato di Messina
ASN   Archivio di Stato di Napoli
ASP   Archivio di Stato di Palermo
BL   British Library
BPLLSA   Bromley Public Libraries, Local Studies & Archives
BRO.   Bristol Record Office
BV   Bank of Valetta
D&EI   Devon & Exeter Institution
DRO   Devon Record Office
DoRO   Dorset Record Office
GL   Guildhall Library
LL&RRO   Leicestershire, Leicester and Rutland Record Office
NARA   National Archives Records Administration
PRO   Public Record Office
UN   University of Nottingham Manuscripts Department
WCSL   West Country Studies Library

PRIMARY SOURCES

Archivio di Stato di Messina
   G Michale, 1482

Archivio di Stato di Napoli
   Archivio Tommasi, B, Viii inc. 73 & 75

Archivio di Stato di Palermo
   Archivio Nelson, B, 101, 580, 581, 583

Banco di Spiritu Santo, Malta (Bank of Valetta)
   Anglo-Maltese Bank, Register of Bills Tendered and Approved, 1812-1815

Bristol Record Office
   Bright Papers
   Bristol Burgess Books
   Munckley Papers

420

Bibliography

Records of Great West Cotton Company
Records of Lewins Mead (Presbyterian/Unitarian) Congregation

British Library
Additional MSS, principally:
307050, 34457, 34908, 42776, 41197-41200, 48412

Central Library, Bromley
1790 Census of Inhabitants
617/1, Folio 111,415,701 798
617/3, Folio 13

Devon Record Office
Buller Papers
Granger Papers
DQS I/11 Book of Session Orders, 1792-1802
Topsham Records, 1st – 8th series (transcripts and contemporary accounts)
352M/PF9&10, D7/1294/596
Wharfinger Journals
Z19/38/9, Admiralty Court Records, Letters of Marque Declarations,
transcribed by H Tapley-Soper, 1928

Dorset Record Office
Bond Papers, D/BOH/C1-30, L1,2

Guildhall Library
Records of Antony Gibbs & Sons, principally:
MS 11021/1-30, 11023, 11024/1, 11024/2, 11024/2, 11036/1, 11062,
11069, 11079, 19862, 19888,

Leicestershire, Leicester and Rutland Record Office
DE718/D/4, Martin Manuscripts; Deeds and papers of the Martin Family

National Archives and Records Administration
Microfilm Publications T420, 'Despatches from
U.S. Consuls in Palermo, Italy, 1803-1906'

Private Papers
> Private Journal of Dorothea Gibbs

Public Record Office
> ADM35/1055,1057, 36/1055,11815,11818
> AO 1/11/23
> B.T. 1/101,
> C/1/1737/31, C/11/1814/8, CO158/26,
> C107/9, James Rogers Papers
> E 134/9 and 10 Hil, 20
> FO165/1, 168/2, 168/6
> FO70/44, 70/60, 70/66, 70/76,
> FO28, FO28/12, FO 28/19,
> FO30/7/1,
> FO352/60B,
> PROB 11/1055, 11/1514, 11/1760, 11/1053, 11/1363, 11/1626

Society of Merchant Venturers of the City of Bristol Archives
> African Trade
>> Letters; bundles C-G: 1730-79
>> Papers of the West India Association
>> Proceedings, Misc. Papers, 1813-26 and 1825-30
>> Book of Petitions

Topsham Museum
> Misc Topsham deeds

University of Nottingham, Department of Manuscripts and Special Collections
> Papers of Sir William Bentinck, PWJd 6164, 2944/1, 6224/1&2,
> 5640/1/2/3, 2156

PRIMARY PRINTED SOURCES
Newspapers
> Trewman's Exeter Flying Post, from December 1770
> Woolmer's Exeter and Plymouth Gazette, 1792-3, 1798-1800, 1809-
> The New Exeter Journal, 1789
> Flindell's Western Luminary, 1813-1826, 1828-
> Felix Farley's Journal Bristol 1796-1800

Bibliography

Periodicals and Magazines
Lloyds Shipping Registers
The Annual Register, 1800-1820
The Gentleman's Magazine 1816

CONTEMPORARY WORKS

Banfill, Samuel, *A Second letter to Sir T. D. Acland, Bart. M.P. on the means of Improving the Condition of The Labouring Classes and reducing parochial Assessments by Adapting the Poor Laws to the present State of Society*, Exeter, 1818

Baron de Marbot, *Memoirs of General Baron de Marbot*, Vol 2

Brice, T., *The History and Description of the City of Exeter*, Exeter, 1802,

Brougham, H., *Historical sketches of statesmen who flourished in the time of George III*, (3 vols, London, 1855)

Cardogan, William, *An Essay upon Nursing and the Management of Children from their Birth to Three years of Age, By a Physician*, London: J Roberts, 1748

Cobbett's *Parliamentary Debates*, Vols 10 - 14

Defoe, D., *A Tour thro' the whole Island*. (With additions and improvements by Samuel Richardson) London, 1742

Drake, Sir William, *Heathiania: Notes Geneological and Bibliographical of the Family of Heath, Especially of the Descendents of Benjamine Heath of Exeter.* London 1881

Dymond, R., *Exeter and Devonshire, 1714-1837*, (reprint of newspaper articles)

Ellacombe, Rev. H. T., MA., F.S.A., *The History and Antiquities of The Parish of Clyst St. George*, Exeter, 1865

Fiennes, Celia, *The Journeys of Celia Fiennes* (ed. C Morris, London 1947)

Jenkins, Alexander, *The History and Description of the City of Exeter*, Exeter, 1806 and 1841

Latimer, John, *History of the Society of Merchant Venturers of the City of Bristol*, Bristol, 1903
The Annals of Bristol in the Eighteenth Century, Bristol, 1893

Lewis, *Topographical Dictionary of England*, 1844

Leyland, John, *The Itinerary of John Leyland the Antiquary*, Oxford, Vol. 3, 1710-1711

Lysons, D., *Magna Britannica*, Devon, Vol. 11, 1822

Morrison, Alfred, (ed), *The Hamilton and Nelson Papers*, 1893

Nicholas, Sir Harris, *The Dispatches and Letters of Vice-Admiral Lord Viscount Nelson*, 1849

Paget, Sir Augustus, *The Paget Papers*, 2 vols, London, 1896

White's *Devonshire Directory*, 1850

SECONDARY SOURCES

Aspinal, Arthur, ed. *The later correspondence of George III*, 5 vols. Cambridge

Bromley, Blake, *The Historical Origins of the Definition of Religion in Charitable Law.*

Blaquiere, Edward, *Letters from the Mediterranean, containing a civil and political account of Sicily, Tripoli, Tunis and Malta, with biographical sketches, anecdotes and observations... .*', Colburn, 1813

Blow Williams, Judith, *British Commercial Policy & Trade Expansion, 1750-1850*, Oxford Clarendon Press, 1972

Bright, Pamela, *Dr. Richard Bright (1789-1858)*, Bodley Head

Cameron, Alick, *Thomas Glass MD, Physician of Georgian Exeter*, Devon Books, 1996,

Cave, C.H., *A History of Banking in Bristol from 1750-1899*, privately published in 1899

Channon, Geoffrey, *Bristol and the promotion of the Great Western Railway, 1835*, Pamphlet, Bristol Branch of The Historical Association

Clark, E. A. G., *Three Exeter Pioneers in the Italian Trade in The New Maritime History of Devon, Vol 1, From Early Times to the Late Eighteenth Century*, Conway Maritime Press, 1992
The Ports of the Exe Estuary 1660-1860, A Study in Historical Geography, University of Exeter, 1960

Constantine, David, *Fields of Fire: A Life of Sir William Hamilton*, London, Phoenix Press, 2001

Delpratt Harris, J, MD, *The Royal Devon and Exeter Hospital*, Exeter, 1922

Dresser, Madge, *Slavery Obscured, The Social History of the Slave trade in an English Provincial Port*, London, Continuum, 2001

Farr, Grahame, *Records of Bristol Ships, 1800-1838*, Bristol Record Society, Vol. XV, Bristol 1950

Fraser, Flora, *Beloved Emma*, London, Weidenfeld & Nicholson, 1986

Garrett, J. T., *Lord Brougham*, London, Macmillan, 1935

Gibbs, J. A., *The History of Antony and Dorothea Gibbs and of their contemporary relatives, including the History of the origin & Early Years of the House of Antony Gibbs and Sons*, London, 1922

Grendi, Eduardo, *Gli Inglesi a Genova (Secoli XVII-XVIII)*, in Quadermi Storici, n.115 (2004)

Hall, I.V., *Whitson Court Sugar House, Bristol*, in Transactions of the Bristol and Glos. Archaeological Society, 65, 1994

Harling, Philip, *The Law of Libel and the Limits of Repression, 1790-1832*, The Historical Journal, 44 (2001), pp 107-134, Cambridge University Press

Hamer, Philip, M, (ed) *The Papers of Henry Laurens*, South Carolina Historical Society, 1968

Bibliography

Hamilton, Gerald & Stewart, Desmond, *Emma in Blue, A Romance of Friendship*, London, 1957

Hibbert, Christopher, *Nelson, A Personal History*, Penguin Books, 1994

Hoskins, W.G., *Exeter Militia List 1804*, Devon & Cornwall Record Society, New Series

Jones, Pip & Youseph Rita, *The Black Population of Bristol in the Eighteenth Century*, Bristol Branch of the Historical Association pamplet, 1970

Lentini, Rosario, *Note su un operatore commerceriale in Sicilia: Abraham Gibbs (1799-1802)*, in 'Nuovi quaderni del meridione' , m56, anno XIV
I Whitaker e il Capitale Inglesettra l'Ottocento e il Novecento in Sicilia, presented at a seminar in Trapani for the Libera Universita del Mediterraneo, 29th November to 1 December 1990, as part of della Societa Siciliana per la Storia Patria, dell'Accademia di Scienze, Lettre Arti di Palermo, della Fondazione Culturale Whitaker
The British in Sicily and their influence on the island's economy, in Raleigh Trevelyan, *The History of the Whitakers*, English version by Peter Dawson, Enzo Sellerio Palermo, 1993
Constantin Samuel Rafinesque Schamlz negoziante e naturalista a Palermo (1805-1815)
Financial Activities of English Merchant Bankers in Western Sicily between the 18th and 19th Centuries. Paper presented at the Fourth International Congress of Maritime History, Corfu, June 2004
Alle origini del capitalismo finanziario: la nascita della 'prima compagnia di assicurazioni di Palermo', in I Whitaker e il capitale Inglese tra l'Ottocento e il Novecento in Sicilia, Libera Universita del Mediterraneo, 1990

Mack Smith, Dennis, *Modern Sicily after 1713*, London, Chatto & Windus, 1968

Maude, Wilfred, *Antony Gibbs & Sons, Merchant Bankers, 1808-1958*, London 1958

Marshall, Peter, *Bristol and the Abolition of Slavery, The Politics of Emancipation*, Pamphlet, Bristol Branch of The Historical Association, Bristol, 1975
Bristol and the abolition of slavery, Bristol, 1975

Mathews, W., *The New History, survey and description of the city and suburbs of Bristol, or Complete Guide and Bristol Directory for the year 1793-4*

Maxwell, Kenneth, *The Atlantic in the eighteenth century: A southern perspective on the need to return to the "Big Picture"*, Transactions of the Royal Historical Society, 6th Series, III, 1993

McGrath, Patrick, *John Whitson and the merchant community of Bristol*, Bristol Branch of the Historical Association, 1970

The Merchant Venturers of Bristol, Bristol Society of Merchant Venturers, 1975
    Merchants and Merchandise in the Seventeenth Century, Bristol Record Society,
    1955
Melikan, R. A., *Mr Attorney General and the Politicians*, The Historical Journal,
    40. 1, (1997), Cambridge University Press
Miller, James, *Fertile Fortune, The Story of Tyntesfield*, The National Trust, 2003
Minchinton, W.E., *The trade of Bristol in the 18th century*, Bristol Records
    Society, Vol. 20, 1957
    The port of Bristol in the 18th century, Bristol, 1962
Morgan, K., *The Economic Development of Bristol, 1780-1850*, in M Dresser &
    P Ollerenshaw (ed), *The Making of Modern Bristol*, Bristol, 1996
    Bristol and the Atlantic Trade in the Eighteenth Century, English Historical
    Review, CVII, 1992
    Bristol West India Merchants in the Eighteenth Century, Transactions of the
    Royal Historical Society, 6th Series, III, 1993
    Shipping Patterns and the Atlantic Trade of Bristol, 1749-1770, William and
    Mary Quarterly
    James Morgan and the Bristol slave trade, Historical Research, vol. 76, no. 193
    (May 2003)
Newton, Robert, *Eighteenth Century Exeter*, University of Exeter, 1984
Oman, Carola, *Nelson*, London, 1947
O'Shaughnessy, Andrew J., *The Formation of a Commercial Lobby: The West India
    Interest, British Colonial Policy and the American Revolution*, The Historical
    Journal, 40, 1 (1997), Cambridge University Press
Penny, John, *Is the Economic History of the Bristol Region between 1780 and 1850
    a Story of Relative Decline?* in The Economic History of the Bristol Region,
    Bath Spa University College, 1997
    A military history of Bristol during the Revolutionary War 1793-1892,
    Fishponds Local History Society
Pockock, Tom, *Horatio Nelson*, Pimlico, 1987
Riall, Lucy, *Nelson versus Bronte: Land, Litigation and Local Politics in Sicily,
    1799-1860*, European History Quarterly, Vol. 29, No 1, January 1999
Richardson, David, *Bristol, Africa and the Eighteenth Century Slave Trade to
    America*, Bristol Record Society, Vols. 1-4, Bristol
    The Bristol Slave Traders: A Collective Portrait, Bristol Branch of the Historical
    Association, pamplet 60, Bristol, 1985
Rosselli, John, *Lord William Bentinck and the British Occupation of Sicily:
    1811-1814*, Cambridge, 1956

Bibliography

Russell, Jack, *Nelson and the Hamiltons*, London, Antony Blond, 1969

Russell, P.M. J., *The History of Exeter Hospital, 1170-1948*, Exeter Postgraduate Medical Centre, Exeter, 1976

Spong, Matthew, *The Percy Anecdotes: Anecdotes of The Bar*, Sidney, 2000

Stanes, Robin, ed. *The Compton Census for the Diocese of Exeter, 1676*, Pt. II in The Devon Historian, No. 10

Thompson, E. P., *The Making of the English Working Class*, Penguin Books, 1963,

Trevelyan, Raleigh, *Princes under the Volcano*, London, Macmillan, 1972

Vaughan, Adrian, *Isambard Kingdom Brunel, Engineering Knight-Errant*, John Murray, London, 1991

White, Colin, ed. Nelson, *The New Letters*, National Maritime Museums, 2005

Williams, Kate, *England's Mistress: The Infamous Life of Emma Hamilton*, Hutchinson, London, 2006

Woodall, R.D., *Echoes of an Old Chapel*, typewritten sheet in Topsham Museum

Worthy, Charles, *Devonshire Wills*

INTERNET SOURCES

http://college.hmco.com/history for general information on the Napoleonic War and the Chesapeake-Leopard Incident, Embargo Act, Macon's Bill No 2, and the Non-Intercourse Act

Holmes a'Court family website

Register of Births and Baptisms at the Mint Presbyterian Meeting in Exeter, Devon from 1719 to 1810.

INDEX

Index